Along the Archival Grain

Along the Archival Grain

EPISTEMIC ANXIETIES AND COLONIAL COMMON SENSE

Ann Laura Stoler

PRINCETON UNIVERSITY PRESS

PRINCETON AND OXFORD

Published by Princeton University Press, 41 William Street, Princeton, New Jersey 08540
In the United Kingdom: Princeton University Press, 6 Oxford Street, Woodstock,
Oxfordshire OX20 1TW

LIBRARY OF CONGRESS CATALOGING-IN-PUBLICATION DATA

Stoler, Ann Laura.
  Along the archival grain : epistemic anxieties and colonial common sense / Ann Laura
Stoler.
      p. cm.
  Includes bibliographical references and index.
  ISBN 978-0-691-01578-1 (cl.) ISBN 978-0-691-01577-4 (pb.)
  1. Indonesia—Politics and government—19th century.   2. Indonesia—Social policy—
19th century.   3. Archives—Indonesia—History.   4. Colonial administrators—Indonesia.
5. Colonial administrators—Netherlands.   I. Title.
  DS643.S787 2009
  959.8'022—dc22   2008023414

British Library Cataloging-in-Publication Data is available

This book has been composed in Sabon
Printed on acid-free paper. ∞
press.princeton.edu

Printed in the United States of America

10 9 8 7 6 5 4 3 2 1

TO LARRY

CONTENTS

ILLUSTRATIONS

APPRECIATIONS

THE TERM "ACKNOWLEDGMENT" has always struck me as a misnomer that carries with it more an obligatory recognition of debt than the valued recognition that appreciation implies. How to convey the gratitude that comes from those savored friendships, nourished by trust and care, that in turn enable bolder forays and more engaged critique?

I thank first of all those who became such dear friends as we collectively built the Doctoral Program in Anthropology and History at the University of Michigan during the luminous years I was there and who graced me with their attentive readings of parts of this book: Frederick Cooper, Fernando Coronil, Valentine Daniel, Nicholas Dirks, Nancy Hunt, Webb Keane, Brinkley Messick, Sherry Ortner, and Julie Skurski. I especially thank Val, Webb, and Nick, who shared in my first forays into this venture and then were there to read and think with me again nearly twenty years later—at its finish if not its end.

Students with whom I have been honored to work shaped the content and form of this book in successive waves. Beginning in 1995, when I gave my first graduate seminar on Ethnography in the Archives, the students who thought with me about archives (there, and everywhere in classes on sentiment, on empire, on memory, on race) animate these pages with insights that went beyond my own. I especially thank Javier Alicea-Morillo, Laura Bear, John Collins, Grace Davie, Laurent Dubois, Paul Eiss, Ilana Feldman, Jennifer Gaynor, Anjan Ghosh, Andrew Goss, Kate Jellema, Laura Kunreuther, Veve Lele, Ken Maclean, Delphine Mauger, Carole McGranahan, Penelope Papailias, David Pedersen, Stephen Pierce, Anuparna Rao, Natalie Rothman, Eric Stein, Karen Strassler, Greta Uehling, and Sarah Womack, each of whom captured what I call "the pulse of the archive" in their own unique and innovative ways.

The years in which this book took form coincided with the heady rush of another intellectual venture of which I was privileged to be a part: the program in Comparative Studies in Societal Transformation, a dynamic constellation of faculty from the departments of Sociology, Anthropology, History, Comparative Literature, and Political Science who reveled in reaching beyond their disciplines to engage one another's work and the different understandings of social critique and history that each brought to it. From the collective exhilaration of those late-night seminars, I owe most to those who helped me think about form and content, history and power, affect and archives. Julia Adams, Charlie Bright, Jane Burbank,

Julie Ellison, Juan Cole, Nancy Florida, Ray Grew, Linda Gregerson, Liisa Malkki, Bruce Mannheim, Rudolph Mrazek, Marty Pernick, Adela Pinch, Peggy Somers, Ron Suny, George Steinmetz, and Katherine Verdery all leave traces here beyond any specific things they read or said. Geoff Eley encouraged my first effort to present my new thinking on colonial states of sentiment in 1991. Bill Sewell encouraged me to do more.

I thank the Lewis Henry Morgan selection committee at the University of Rochester for inviting me to give the 1996 lectures where I first delivered this work in its emergent form. I owe special thanks to friends in the Netherlands: Peter Boomgaard, who steered me to sites and sources to which I would not otherwise have gone; to Mrs. F. van Anrooij and Mr. G. H. A. de Graaf, archivists at the Algemeen Rijksarchief who navigated me through archival movements I could not have made without their guidance; Rob van Drie at the Central Bureau of Genealogy, who welcomed my work, and Dieuwke Valck-Lucassen, who spent days with me at the bureau photocopying letters and working through her family's genealogies; Benjamin White and Ratna Saptari, who so warmly housed me in Scheveningen and shared my delight as I read each letter and realized that my daily route to the archives took me directly past Frans Carl Valck's house in The Hague.

Other friends and family mark these pages with wisdom and sensibilities they so graciously shared: Lisa Albert, Arjun Appadurai, Scott Atran, Bernard de Bonnerive, Carol Breckenridge, Leonoor Broeder, Barbara Cain, Peggy Choy, Jean and John Comaroff, Victoria Ebin, Chantal and Michel Février, Oz Frankel, Douglas Holmes, Henk Maier, Marjorie Levinson, Nancy Lutkehaus, Hazel Markus, Adeline Medalia, Martine Perney, Paul Rabinow, Henk Schulte Nordholt, Karen Seeley, Dan Sperber, Will and Linda Stoler, and Gary Wilder. With their acute vision and serenity, Ed West and Kate West's friendship carried me through the book's finish. I owe special thanks to the Center for Advanced Study in Palo Alto, California, for providing me with an environment that pushed the book forward; to Dominick LaCapra, for inviting me to participate as a seminar leader at the School of Criticism and Theory in summer 2007; and to colleagues and students in Ithaca, who shared my excitement as final revisions took unanticipated forms. Earlier versions of these chapters were given at the New York Academy of Sciences, University of Alberta, Barnard College, Boston University, University of British Columbia, Cambridge University, University of Chicago, University of Colorado, Columbia University, the KITLV, London School of Economics, Melbourne University, Michigan State University, New York University, Oxford University, University of Pennsylvania, University of Washington, and as keynote addresses at Cornell University and the Australian Historical Association in Adelaide. I thank those audiences for their engagements and hope that I have adequately addressed their queries here. I thank Trude Stevenson, Kim Schoen, Maria Speller, Geke de Vries, Henrike Florubosch, and Arthur Verhoogt for transcribing and translating Dutch documents that I did not have time to do myself, and some of which I would have struggled to decipher. Andrew Goss kindly helped me track various persons through the colonial civil service and their itineraries through the archives.

My colleagues and students at The New School for Social Research not only made the return home to New York a delight; they have nourished my sense of an intellectual home. I owe very special thanks to the philosopher Jay Bernstein, a childhood sweetheart whom I had not seen for thirty years until we were to meet again under the sign of Adorno and Foucault. He is a cherished reader and interlocutor, who dazzles me with his insights and who continues to teach me about epistemology. I owe deepest thanks to my dear colleague Richard Bernstein who, with such perspicuous critique and care, read every page. Larry Hirschfeld, Claudio Lomnitz, Adriana Petryna, Hugh Raffles, Janet Roitman, Vyjayanthi Rao, and Hylton White have all made these last four years in the New School's Department of Anthropology a transformed and transformative place. Charles Whitcroft's proficient calm and finesse makes our department work.

Teaching at the New School over the last four years has allowed me to reconfigure this book in ways I had only broached in early renditions: students in my seminars on the History of Sentiment, The Politics of Truth, and Anthropology as a History of the Present have asked some of the hardest questions, which I still wrestle to address. I thank two students with whom I thought these pages when I first returned to the manuscript in New York: David Bond and the late Imogen Bunting, whom I so sorely miss. Tjitske Holtrop meticulously checked the Dutch in the midst of classes; Emily Sogn deftly gathered the book together in its proper form. It is she who has crafted the index that attends to watermarks and grains. I thank Heleen Vieveen at the Iconography Bureau in The Hague for so readily making the Valcks's portraits available to me, and Ingeborg Eggink at the Koninklijk Instituut voor de Tropen for helping me to locate images.

Finally, I thank Mary Murrell, former anthropology editor at Princeton, who first signed on the book more than a decade ago, and Fred Appel for so seamlessly bringing it to closure. Bruno and Tessa make my world afresh with love and life-force everyday. My dearest historian niece, Gwenn, reminds me for whom I write. Without Larry, there would be no book.

21 December 2007
New York City

Along the Archival Grain

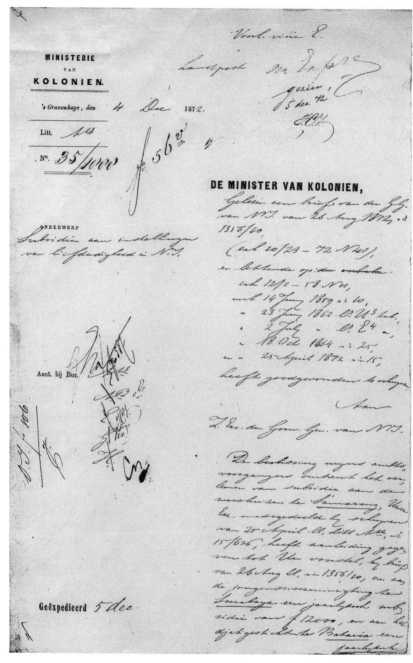

Figure 1. A typical first page of a "*verbaal*," a document generated from the office of the Minister of Colonies (*Ministerie van Koloniën*) in the Hague that might be a decree, a demand for information, a decision, or comment on colonial issues. It notes the document to which it is a response and previous documents that have been consulted (listed on the right), some included as "*exhibitum*" and used as "evidence" for decisions and pronouncements in colonial policy.

CHAPTER ONE

Prologue in Two Parts

> Ethnology is especially interested in what is *not written*. [It
> deals with what is] *different* from everything that men usually
> dream of engraving in stone or committing to paper.
> —Claude Lévi-Strauss, *Structural Anthropology*, 1958

> The primary function of writing . . . is to facilitate the
> enslavement of other human beings.
> —Claude Lévi-Strauss, *Tristes Tropiques*, 1955

PART 1: WRITING AND ITS IMPERIAL MUTATIONS

THIS BOOK is about the force of writing and the feel of documents, about
lettered governance and written traces colonial lives. It is about commitments to paper, and the political and personal work that such inscriptions perform. Not least, it is about colonial archives as sites of the expectant and conjured—about dreams of comforting futures and
forebodings of future failures. It is a book that asks what we might learn
about the nature of imperial rule and the dispositions it engendered from
the writerly forms through which it was managed, how attentions were
trained and selectively cast. In short, it is a book precisely about that
which Lévi-Strauss says anthropology is not.

Colonial administrations were prolific producers of social categories.
This book deals with these categories and their enumeration, but its focus
is less on taxonomy than on the unsure and hesitant sorts of documentation and sensibilities that gathered around them. It starts from the observation that producing rules of classification was an unruly and piecemeal
venture at best. Nor is there much that is hegemonic about how those taxonomies worked on the ground. Grids of intelligibility were fashioned
from uncertain knowledge; disquiet and anxieties registered the uncommon sense of events and things; epistemic uncertainties repeatedly unset-
tled the imperial conceit that all was in order, because papers classified
people, because directives were properly acknowledged, and because
colonial civil servants were schooled to assure that records were prepared,
circulated, securely stored, and sometimes rendered to ash.

In these chapters Dutch colonial archival documents serve less as stories
for a colonial history than as active, generative substances with histories,
as documents with itineraries of their own. What was written in prescribed

form and in the archive's margins, what was written oblique to official prescriptions and on the ragged edges of protocol produced the administrative apparatus as it opened to a space that extended beyond it. Contrapuntal intrusions emanated from outside the corridors of governance but they also erupted—and were centrally located—within that sequestered space. Against the sober formulaics of officialese, these archives register the febrile movements of persons off balance—of thoughts and feelings in and out of place. In tone and temper they convey the rough interior ridges of governance and disruptions to the deceptive clarity of its mandates.

If anthropology is "different" from that which is engraved in brick and mortar, as Lévi-Strauss insisted, this book embraces ethno-graphy of another kind. Fearful colonial visions and their attendant policies were engraved in consequential excess on paper and chiseled "in stone." Their material force appeared in elaborate "coolie ordinances" repeatedly rewritten to fix the degrees of unfreedom that would keep Sumatra's plantation workers coerced and confined. Often it manifested in thousands of pages of intricate plans to establish fitting places to park colonial embarrassments—like mixed blood orphans. Material force was engraved in phantasmic scenarios of potential revolt that called for militias readied with arms.

Kilometers of administrative archives called up massive buildings to house them. Government offices, filled with directors, assistant directors, scribes, and clerks, were made necessary by the proliferation of documents that passed, step by meticulous step, through the official ranks. Accumulations of paper and edifices of stone were both monuments to the asserted know-how of rule, artifacts of bureaucratic labor duly performed, artifices of a colonial state declared to be in efficient operation.

Colonial commissions, incessant reportage in the absence of evidence, and secret missives contained political content in their archival form. Blueprints to reshape what people felt, what language elders should speak to their young, and how they should live in their homes evince visions of social design often inadequate to those tasks. Governing agents reeled uncomfortably between attention to the minutiae of domestic arrangements and generic social kinds, between probabilities and positivistic evidence, between what could be known about the past and what could be predicted for the future, between abstract principles and a keen awareness that what mattered as much to a managed colony was attentiveness to what people did in their everyday lives. In all of these concerns the middling and elite echelons of government stumbled in the face of sentiments that were as hard to assess among their own ranks as among the colonized. Affections and attachments—familial and otherwise—were often impervious to the meddling priorities of a supposedly "rational" and reasoned state. Efforts to redirect those sentiments—or cancel them out—

revealed "epistemological worries" (to use Lorraine Daston and Peter Galison's term) about what they could know and how they could know it.[1] From efforts to mold affective states and monitor the parameters of racial ontologies, we can read their confused assessments of what kinds of knowledge they needed, what they needed to know—and what they often knew they did not.

As such, documents in these colonial archives were not dead matter once the moment of their making had passed. What was "left" was not "left behind" or obsolete. In the Netherlands Indies, these colonial archives were an arsenal of sorts that were reactivated to suit new governing strategies. Documents honed in the pursuit of prior issues could be requisitioned to write new histories, could be reclassified for new initiatives, could be renewed to fortify security measures against what were perceived as new assaults on imperial sovereignty and its moralizing claims. In this sense Lévi-Strauss's conjunction of writing and exploitation quintessentially captures an imperial project and a colonial situation.[2] But as the last decade of colonial scholarship so rightly insists, pursuits of exploitation and enlightenment are not mutually exclusive but deeply entangled projects.

Yet in attending to that which is "not written," there is something of Lévi-Strauss's vision of anthropology in what follows. By this I do not mean that it plumbs for the "hidden message" or those subliminal texts that couch "the real" below the surface and between the written lines. Rather it seeks to identify the pliable coordinates of what constituted colonial common sense in a changing imperial order in which social reform, questions of rights and representation, and liberal impulses and more explicit racisms played an increasing role. As imperial orders changed, so did common sense. Here I attempt to distinguish between what was "unwritten" because it could go without saying and "everyone knew it," what was unwritten because it could not yet be articulated, and what was unwritten because it could not be said. Similarly, in attention to "imperial dispositions"—what it took to live a colonial life, to live in and off empire and was reflective of its practices—Lévi-Strauss's adherence to the unwritten joins with the written to become piercingly relevant again.

But perhaps the unwritten looms largest in the making of colonial ontologies themselves. "Ontology," as I use the term here, does not refer to

---

[1] Lorraine Daston and Peter Galison, *Objectivity* (New York: Zone, 2007), 35.

[2] The fuller quote reads: "When writing makes its debut, it seems to favor exploitation rather than the enlightenment of mankind. . . . If my hypothesis is correct, the primary function of writing, as a mode of communication, is to facilitate the enslavement of other human beings" (Claude Lévi-Strauss, "On Writing," in *Tristes Tropiques* [New York: Atheneum, 1964], 292).

the disciplined pursuits of analytic philosophy about the real ontological status of things in the world. Rather, I understand ontology as that which is about the *ascribed* being or essence of things, the categories of things that are thought to exist or can exist in any specific domain, and the specific attributes assigned to them. Ontologies, as Ian Hacking writes, refer to "what comes into existence with the historical dynamics of naming."[3] Pursuing an "historical ontology," then, demands something that philosophical study of ontology tout court might pursue but more often does not: identification of *mutating* assignments of essence and its predicates in specific time and place.[4] On the face of it, the notion of essence implies stability and fixity, the enduring properties of people and things. But if there is anything we can learn from the colonial ontologies of racial kinds, it is that such "essences" were protean, not fixed, subject to reformulation again and again.

The claim that there are "essences" that distinguish social kinds is very different from positing that these essences are unchanging and stable in time. In the Indies, colonial agents constantly sought new ways to secure the qualities of social kinds—most clearly when assigned attributes fell short of differentiating the gradations of exclusions and exemptions that new colonial administrations sought to make. Such reassessments called into question the epistemic habits on which they were based. As I argue throughout this book, these were not passive inhabitings but achieved, anticipatory states. Those epistemic practices were not just recorded in the colonial archive, but developed and worked through the genres of documentation that civil servants were required to make.

As such, these archives are not simply accounts of actions or records of what people thought happened. They are records of uncertainty and doubt in how people imagined they could and might make the rubrics of rule correspond to a changing imperial world. Not least they record anxious efforts to "catch up" with what was emergent and "becoming" in new colonial situations. Ontologies are both productive and responsive, expectant and late. Thus when questions of poor relief for impoverished whites come increasingly to the fore in the second half of the nineteenth century—in debates that anticipated many twentieth-century questions about race in metropolitan state welfare politics about the deserving and undeserving poor—designations of kinds of people that were once deemed

---

[3] Ian Hacking, *Historical Ontology* (Cambridge, Mass.: Harvard University Press, 2002), 26.

[4] On attention to these ontological mutations with respect to race and the plasticity with which they get reassigned, see my "Racial Histories and their Regimes of Truth," *Political Power and Social Theory* 11 (1997): 183–255. With respect to scientific objects, see Lorraine Daston, who writes of "an ontology in motion" in *Biographies of Scientific Objects* (Chicago: University of Chicago Press, 2000), 14.

adequate were no more. Ethnographic sensibilities have particular purchase in this quixotic space of premonition, probability, and speculation.

Many of the "events" on which I focus here are really not "events" at all. Sometimes, as in chapter 4, I refer to them as "non-events" since they are records of things that never happened. Similarly, often those events to which I attend are not those that figure as central in the colonial and postcolonial historiography of the Netherlands Indies. In fact, many of them would be considered to have little consequence. The European Pauperism Commissions discussed in chapters 4 and 5 have rarely been accorded an historiographic entry;[5] the May 1848 demonstration of creole Europeans and "Indos," the subject of chapter 3, receives only occasional and passing reference by students of Dutch colonial history.[6] Similarly, in studies of the Dutch colonial policy, the artisanal schools and agricultural colonies for mixed blood children, described in chapter 4, leave barely a historiographic trace.

The history of the Indo-European population, those of "mixed" parentage (usually European fathers and native mothers) both in the Netherlands Indies and Holland after Indonesian independence, has garnered far more attention.[7] Still what was, in early twentieth-century colonial circles,

---

[5] For an important exception, see Ulbe Bosma, *Karel Zaalberg: journalist en strijder voor de Indo* (Leiden: KITLV, 1997).

[6] Dutch historians of Holland's history of political dissension and social criticism treat it very differently—according it a full, if marginal, chapter.

[7] Reference to specific works on the subject are scattered throughout these chapters but for quick reference to this extensive literature, see Paul W. van der Veur, *The Eurasians of Indonesia: a political-historical bibliography* (Ithaca: Modern Indonesia Project, 1971). Numerous novels and plays were published about "the Indo" from the late colonial period. Only some of them are cited here. Memoirs published in Dutch have had a resurgence. As Tessel Pollman and Ingrid Harms note, "Indo," a word that could not be used even five years ago (except by Indos themselves), as of 1987 was again common, even a badge of honor. See Tessel Pollman and Ingrid Harms, *In Nederland door omstandigheden* (Den Haag: Novib, 1987), 9. Among publications by Indos who have reclaimed the name and this history for themselves, see, for example, Paul van der Put, *Het boek der Indo's: Kroniek* (Rotterdam: Indonet, 1997), and Frank Neijndorff, *Nederlands-Indië: Een familiegeheim* (Den Haag: Nederlandse Document Reproductie, 2001). My discussion does not go beyond the early twentieth century. For an overview of the history of the Indo political movement in the Indies, see J. Th. Petrus Blumberger, *De Indo-Europeesche beweging in Nederlandsch-Indië* (Haarlem: Willink, 1939), and Takahashi Shiraishi's discussion of the "Indo-Javanese-Chinese" consortium of persons who animated early popular radicalism in *An Age in Motion: Popular Radicalism in Java, 1912–11926* (Ithaca: Cornell University Press, 1990). See also the essays in Wim Willems, *Indische Nederlanders in de ogen van de wetenschap* (Leiden: Centrum voor Onderzoek van Maatschappelijke Tegenstellingen, 1990); idem, *Bronnen van kennis over Indische Nederlanders* (Leiden: Centrum voor Onderzoek van Maatschappelijke Tegenstellingen, 1991); and idem, *Sporen van een Indisch verleden, 1600–1942* (Leiden: Centrum voor Onderzoek van Maatschappelijke Tegenstellingen, 1992). Among the most compelling histories of Indo politics are biographies of key figures, such as Bosma's study, cited above.

referred to as "the Indo problem"—galvanizing contrary sentiments ranging from contempt and compassion to pity, fear, and disdain—is often shorn of attention to the burgeoning archive of administrative energy that, for nearly a century, was mobilized around it.

Certain moments of "the Indo problem" have been given more attention than others: that of the late 1890s and 1900s appears as a prelude of sorts to the nationalist movement; that of the 1930s, when the fascist-like *Vaderlandsche* Club took up their cause and demand for settler land rights in Dutch-controlled New Guinea;[8] and again, following independence, in the 1950s when many Indo-Europeans were ousted from Indonesia or fled for refuge to southern California, Australia, and South Africa, and, perhaps most uncomfortably, to Holland.

But that ambiguous nineteenth-century nomenclature of the *Inlandsche kinderen*—a term that could designate mixed bloods, Indies born Dutch, and poor whites that figures so centrally in this book—is barely recalled.[9] This is not because colonial officials did not write about them. On the contrary, kings and governor generals, regional officers, and social engineers of all sorts were obsessed with their welfare, their homes, morals, speech, rearing, and resentments—and, most importantly, their vengeful and potentially subversive inclinations. The fact that they led no revolts and produced no martyrs to their cause had little bearing on the high-pitched fears that eddied around them. As we shall see in the chapters that follow, intense debates about what was conceived as the repressed rage of *Inlandsche kinderen* point elsewhere: to what Doris Sommer in another context calls the "foundational fictions" of colonial rule.[10]

Consternations among those who governed were reactions to quiet and sustained assaults on the warped logic of "European" supremacy. Challenges took unexpected forms that showed imperial principles were not, and could not be, consistent with themselves. *Inlandsche kinderen* embodied and exposed hypocrisies that stretched beyond the native population— that only some Europeans had rights, that rights and race were not always aligned, and that awareness of those inconsistencies were evident to, and expressed among, empire's practitioners themselves.

---

[8] See P.J. Drooglever's important study of this strange and failed alliance in *De Vaderlandse Club, 1929–1942* (Franeker: Wever, 1980).

[9] Paul van der Veur's dissertation is a notable exception. See his "Introduction to a Socio-Political Study of the Eurasians of Indonesia" (Ann Arbor: UMI, 1955). The term "*Inlandsche kinderen*" is spelled and capitalized variously throughout these documents (sometimes as "*inlandse kinderen*," sometimes capitalized, other times not.. I follow the convention of the specific documents to which I am referring. By 1918 "*inlandsche kinderen*" refers simply to children in the native population.

[10] Doris Sommer, *Foundational Fictions: The National Romances of Latin America* (Berkeley: University of California Press, 1991).

A Colonial Incision

In the late nineteenth century the Netherlands Indies included more than forty million people classed as *Inlander* (native), hundreds of thousands "Foreign Orientals," and tens of thousands classified as "European" (the latter exploding to over three hundred thousand by the 1930s). With such proportions, one could imagine that debates over the relatively few *Inlandsche kinderen* were no more than distractions and deferrals from more pressing concerns. But "minor" histories should not be mistaken for trivial ones. Nor are they iconic, mere microcosms of events played out elsewhere on a larger central stage. Minor history, as I use it here, marks a differential political temper and a critical space.[11] It attends to structures of feeling and force that in "major" history might be otherwise displaced.[12] This is not to suggest that administrative anxieties about the *Inlandsche kinderen* tell the real story of empire. Nor is it to suggest that the concerns voiced here somehow mattered more than the elaborate legal, economic, military, and political infrastructure designed to subdue, coerce, and control those designated as the native population. It is rather to identify a symptomatic space in the craft of governance, a diacritic of sorts that accents the epistemic habits in motion and the wary, conditional tense of their anticipatory and often violent register.

For here was a category that neither color nor race could readily or reliably delimit or contain. Everyone knew about the "so-called *Inlandsche kinderen*," but few agreed on who and how many they were. Nor did naming alone, as Hacking argues, call upon and secure a common set of attributes. If knowledge is made not for understanding but "for cutting," as

[11] I think here of Foucault's description of what constitutes a statement/event as that which

emerges in its *historical irruption*; what we try to examine is *the incision* that it makes, the irreducible—and very often tiny—emergence. However banal it maybe, however unimportant its consequences may appear to be, *however quickly it may be forgotten after its appearance*, however little heard or badly deciphered we may suppose it to be, a statement is always an event that neither the language nor the meaning can quite exhaust. It is certainly a strange event . . . *it is linked to the gesture of writing*. . . . [I]t opens up to itself a residual existence . . . *in the materiality of manuscripts, books, or any other form of recording*; like every event, it is unique, yet subject to repetition, transformation, and reactivation.

(*The Archaeology of Knowledge* [New York: Pantheon, 1972], 28)

[12] My treatment of "minor history" here has some alliance with Deleuze and Guattari's notion of "minor literature," but not in all ways. In their characterization, minor literature is always political, imbued with a "collective value" and a language "affected by a high coefficient of deterritorialization." See Gilles Deleuze and Felix Guattari, *Kafka: Toward a Minor Literature* (Minneapolis: University of Minnesota Press, 1986), 16–17.

Foucault charged, then here is knowledge that has participated in its own self-mutilation, a history that cuts long and deep.[13] It carves incisions into the flesh of race, slices through the legal armature of white privilege, slashes through the history of public welfare, and, not least, cleaves into the conceit that more knowledge secures a more durable empire.

Lévi-Strauss once (in)famously wrote that history is a fine departure point in "any quest for intelligibility" as long as one "gets out of it."[14] But quick exit is more dangerous and more compromised than his bon mot suggests. In the case of empire it is really not an option. What I call "watermarks in colonial history" are indelibly inscribed in past and present. The visibility of watermarks depends on angle and light. Watermarks are embossed on the surface and in the grain. As I use the term here, they denote signatures of a history that neither can be scraped off nor removed without destroying the paper. Watermarks cannot be erased. Governments devised watermarks as protections against counterfeit currency and falsified documents that claimed state provenance. In 1848, development of the "shaded watermark" provided "tonal depth" by rendering areas "in relief."

In this book each chapter is a watermark of sorts, shaded to provide tonal depth and temperament, to render imperial governance and its dispositions in bolder relief. Watermarking techniques were fashioned for the privileged, with tools that engraved their rights and bore their stamp. Those that emboss these pages were tools of the privileged but engraved with impressions that were sometimes used to other ends. Unlike watermarks that protect against counterfeit versions, these chapters take up another sense of counterfeit that does the opposite. From the same thirteenth-century moment in the social etymology of "counterfeit" emerges a contrary sense—one that partakes of a critical stance. It is not the false or imitative that carries the weight of meaning but that derived from "*con-trafactio*"—the "setting in opposition or contrast." It is this play on the oppositional that these watermarks embrace. The only "counterfeits" they stamp against are those that argue that there are no watermarks and there was no stamp, simply because light has been cast with darker shadows in other, more commanding directions.

PART 2: ARCHIVAL HABITS IN THE NETHERLANDS INDIES

Transparency is not what archival collections are known for and the Dutch colonial archives in which this book plunges are no exception. This is not

---

[13] Michel Foucault, "Nietzsche, Genealogy, History," in *The Foucault Reader*, ed. Paul Rabinow (New York: Pantheon, 1984), 88.

[14] Claude Lévi-Strauss, *The Savage Mind* (Chicago: University of Chicago Press, 1966), 262.

because they are not "accessible" in the sense that their many collections are still classified or closed, or that the archivists are unhelpful, or that hard-to-procure permission is required to enter. Nor is it because the reading room is cramped with long lines of too many eager dissertators (as in the French colonial holdings in Aix-en-Provence) or because the documents are in disrepair or computers and pens are forbidden, or because the collections are difficult to find or in places hard to reach. Fiches can be ordered by mail. Microfilms are made. By all of these measures, the Dutch colonial archival collections housed at the public Algemeen Rijksarchief right next to the central train station in The Hague—with its spacious, air-conditioned hall and multiple computer terminals—is among the most accessible, ultramodern depositories.

But the question of "accessibility" to the workings of the Dutch colonial administration in the nineteenth-century Indies is a real one that eludes the contemporary inventory numbers by which documents are requested and searched. Inaccessibility has more to do with the principles that organized colonial governance and the "common sense" that underwrote what were deemed political issues and how those issues traveled by paper through the bureaucratic pathways of the colonial administration. Not least, "access" rests on knowledge of the history of colonial Indonesia, on changing perceptions of danger as much as the structures of command.

Given that strikingly few scholars of colonial Indonesia actually describe their methods of archival labor or the administrative forms that shaped the circuits of reportage, accountability, and decision making that in turn produced densities of documents, their frequency, as well as procedures of cross-referencing and culling. If Dutch historians of colonial Indonesia can assume common knowledge about how the principal collection of state-generated documents about the Netherlands Indies at the Algemeen Rijksarchief are organized, foreign scholars cannot do the same.

Because the archives of the Ministry of Colonies (MK) are organized *chronologically* and not by topic, there is no easy entry by theme. Indices provide some access by subject, but only to a limited degree. It is rather specific names and dates that matter. Knowing what one is after is not always enough. More important is a reckoning with how colonial sense and reason conjoined social kinds with the political order of colonial things. But even then, as I argue throughout this book, that "common sense" was subject to revision and actively changed. Navigating the archives is to map the multiple imaginaries that made breastfeeding benign at one moment and politically charged at another; that made nurseries a tense racial question; that elevated something to the status of an "event"; that animated public concern or clandestine scrutiny, turning it into what the French call an "*affaire*." In short, an interest in European paupers or abandoned mixed blood children gets you nowhere, unless you know how they mattered to whom, when, and why they did so. This does not mean that one is wholly bound by concerns of state. The documents generated and the mandated reports produced surfeits over and again that exceeded the demands of proof and causation. Some contradicted the questions asked, others stretched for relevance. Still others pushed against the required call for useful information.

In the spirit of achieving some small modicum of clarity in an often muddled and confusing archival world—of which, after some twenty-five years, I know, and work admittedly with, only a fraction—it seems worth describing at least some of the vectors of official assemblages I encountered and the sometimes unexpected documents that were gathered around them.

The bulk of the archival documents cited in this book comes from the Algemeen Rijksarchief (now the Nationaal Archief) at Prins Willem-Alexanderhof in The Hague. This repository is the largest in the Netherlands, with ninety-three kilometers of documents in their holdings. Established in 1802 as the Rijksarchief and opened to the public in 1918, colonial matters make up only a part of a vast collection of maps, family archives; private papers of personages of national importance, archives of government bodies (like the States-General), and religious organizations. It houses the extensive collection of the Dutch East Indies Company (*Vereenigde Oost-Indische Compagnie*; VOC) that exercised sovereignty on the Dutch state's behalf from the beginning of the seventeenth century when the official monopoly on all Dutch trade in a broad region began, until the company went bankrupt in 1799.

For the period with which this book is concerned, roughly the 1830s to 1930s, the principal collection of matters dealing with the Netherlands Indies are found in the repository of the Ministry of Colonies (MK) set up by royal decree in 1814 and that continued through 1959. Communications between Java and the Netherlands before 1845 made their long journey around the Cape of Good Hope and took months to arrive. It was not until 1845 that a shorter so called "*landmail*" (sometimes called "*landpost*") through Egypt made consultation between the ministers of colonies and the governors-general—and more direct control over the latter by the former—more feasible.[15]

In 1869 when the Suez Canal opened, the routing of mail between Java and the Netherlands was faster still, producing a steady stream of correspondence between their offices. By official decree of 28 May 1869, the

---

[15] For the rich flow of "semiofficial" and private letters that passed between Minister of Colonies J.C. Baud (1840–1848) and Governor-General J.J. Rochussen, see the three volumes of *De semi-officiële en particuliere briefwisseling tussen J.C. Baud en J. J. Rochussen, 1845–1851* (Assen: Van Gorcum, 1983).

Governor-General was required to report "on all important events, proceedings, proposals and other issues separately, sending where necessary transcripts of the relevant supporting documents."[16] This produced a very particular kind of administrative document, designated as a mail report (*mailrapport*; MR) and expedited to The Hague apart from the regular post.

The *mailrapporten* were generated by the Governor-General in Batavia. Each was made up of a folded double sheet of foolscap paper on which was provided a summary statement of the issue at hand. Bundled within it were supporting documents. The summary report, then, was from the Governor-General, but what the *mailrapporten* contained could be documents from many sources: those within and outside the government apparatus—information solicited from middling "social engineers" in health, education, and industry with comments on a regional or local matter. By administrative design, these gathered documents constituted the evidentiary packages for decisions to be made. Such accumulations of conflicting assessments, extraneous detail, anecdote, and local know-how are flash points of something else: of epistemic habits called into question, of certain knowledge in the face of uncertain conditions, of bold and equivocal interpretations of the everyday.

Mailrapporten were classified as "*geheim*" (secret, usually marked with an *X*) or remained unmarked. Since the Minister of Colonies archives were only open to the public in 1918, at the tail end of the period discussed in these chapters, the question of "secret" was never about public access. *Geheim* marked rather the care taken to limit circulation of such documents *within* the colonial administration itself and, as I note in chapter 2, many matters were not "secret" at all. The designation "secret" was an administrative label. Appended documents might be marked "*vertrouwelijk*" (confidential) by a lower-level official as a warning and assessment, less often as an official category.

The more important rubric in the Dutch colonial archives is the "*verbaal*" (Vb). A *verbaal* was generated from the office of the Minister of Colonies, a message that might be a decree, a demand for information, a decision or comment on a *mailrapport* of the Governor-General or of someone else. Because the *verbaal* contained the Minister's message, also on double foolscap paper, and the materials he consulted or deemed relevant to write the message or make a decision, mail reports and their appended documentation often were included in *verbalen*. *Verbalen* were organized chronologically by the date they were sent. But the reports and letters therein could span an extended period of time. The first page is

---

[16] The full text is available online at http://wwwmoranmicropublications.nl/Mailrapporten .html.

key: the Minister's text opens with reference to the Governor-General's previous communication to which the *verbaal* was a response. Secondly, it provides a listing of earlier documents seen as relevant or called upon. This system of flagging not only creates paper trails; it provides a trace through time, an administrative genealogy of precedence, an implicit regime of relevance that might be ignored or pursued. For example, a *verbaal* of 4 December 1872 (listed as V 4 December 72, no.35/1888) notes that the Minister has read the Governor-General's letter of 26 August 1872 and has "taken notice of" other documents, some which might be included as items of relevance "*exhibitum.*" This particular *verbaal* references six other documents dating from 1858 to 1872.

Verbalen from the 1870s had printed on the title page "subject." Thus the 4 December 1872 *verbaal* is titled "subsidies to charitable institutions in the Indies." But this only partially reflects what the *verbaal* was about; not charities in any general sense, but exclusively those orphanages in the urban centers of Semarang, Batavia, and Surabaya where most of the European population lived and where most of their destitute descendants and abandoned mixed blood offspring ended up. An appended letter of the Resident of Batavia writes of the increasing number of impoverished Europeans with no means of support; another from the Director of Education provides detailed lists of the cost and materials—number of towels and pillows, cotton undershirts and pants—allocated for each interned child. This is not among the most interesting of *verbalen* for the subjects I treat here, but it does indicate the range of particulars of the everyday that could make their way into documents passed between the highest echelons of the colonial administration.

In the case of the unpublished commission on needy Europeans in the Indies, treated in chapter 5, the report of the commission was sent to the Governor-General in piecemeal fashion as parts were completed. The Minister of Colonies in turn might gather all or some of those documents together in his response. Between 1872 when the commission on needy Europeans was inaugurated and 1874 when the final report was sent (and a decision was made not to make it public) a thick set of *verbalen* (especially those of V 25 April 1872, No.15/626, and 28 March 1874, no.47/506) were produced. Under the subject heading "Government care for the upbringing and education on behalf of the European population of the Netherlands Indies." (*"Staatszorg van opvoeding en onderwijs ten behoeve van den Europeesche bevolking van N.I."*) the *verbaal* of 28 March 1874 referenced twenty-four other documents, providing at once a genealogy of prior discussions and decisions and a selective citational map.

Subject headings of such *verbalen* could both conceal and reveal what they contained and what constituted the political rationalities that produced them. For example, reference to "upbringing" (*opvoeding*) as well

as "education"(*onderwijs*) in the subject title for the unpublished commission signaled a new urgency (though not a new phenomenon) in addressing child-rearing practices as a potential threat to the state. Political
dangers resided in the domestic milieus in which "mixed blood" children
lived and the misguided affections those environments provided. In this
context "upbringing" turned attention less to the provision of artisan
schools for adolescents (as had been the case in preceding decades) than
to the need for earlier intervention with the very young, with their bodily
"physical development" and their habits "of heart." The reference to the
"European population" raises an issue at the center of this book, for most
of those children discussed in these reports were not legally acknowledged as European, could not speak Dutch, and were living outside the
European quarters.

Such "official" circuits of communication between the Minister of
Colonies and the Governor-General were crisscrossed with voices that
were never contained by official pronouncements alone. In the case of the
May 1848 demonstration, the subject of chapter 3, the number of detailed reports is staggering: they named names; recounted multiple and
fractured versions of what transpired; and contested one another's understanding of who was involved, how subversive they were, evincing phantasmic speculations on why they were so. Here, in 1848, the included
documents reached low and deep onto the streets of Batavia and far to the
outskirts of the city where soldiers were ready with arms. There are those
between the *Assistent Resident* of Batavia and its Resident, the Resident
and the Governor-General, the Governor-General and the Minister of
Colonies, and the Minister of Colonies and the Netherlands' King. But
many other forms of communication swept across Batavia over that month:
petitions, letters, and announcements that placed the threat of European
treason, communist influence, Indo-European revolt, revolution in Europe,
and state concerns over the political potential of outraged "parental feelings" at the heart of administrative fears and on virtually every page.

Published correspondence between Governor-General Rochussen and
Minister of Colonies Baud, collected in their "semiofficial" and private
letters, provides another window onto their joint contempt and unfettered
disdain for the *Inlandsche kinderen*—idioms of a "common sense" that
would continue to permeate a politics of "sympathy" more overtly expressed in later years.

One of the most critical documents about the May 1848 demonstration
and the kind of event it was has rarely been called upon by the few scholars who have sought to write about the gathering. This is no surprise because the document only shows up in the *verbaal* of the Minister of
Colonies a full nine years later. Referenced in a brief essay on Van
Hoëvell written twenty years ago, neither the author nor others have

drawn on this investigative inquisition by the Resident of Batavia. Transcribed interviews in both Dutch and Malay evince scores of people who participated in the demonstration, were hailed to join, or heard about its planning on the preceding days.[17] Thus even when we do know the dates and actors, documents slip from time and place. Sometimes it is only when they are called upon to legitimate or situate new predicaments in the lineage of older ones that we have "access" to them.

"The" colonial archives occupy a space that transcends officially designated archival collections. *Mailrapporten* and *verbalen* occupy only part of the force field in which documents were produced. Over the last twenty-five years I have drawn on pamphlets, books, newspapers, statutes, letters at the KITLV (Koninlijk Instituut voor Taal-, Land-, and Volkenkunde), the KIT (Koninlijk Instituut voor de Tropen), the Koninklijke Biblotheek, Leiden University library, missionary collections in Oegstgeest, the Ministry of Defense (MD), Central Bureau of Genealogy (CBG), and, less frequently, those at the National Archives in Jakarta (NA), most of which were requested and sent to me via the Nationaal Archief in The Hague. Describing this archival space is not an attempt to define its outer limits, all that it includes and excludes and all that I have left out. My interest is not in the finite boundaries of the official state archives but in their surplus production, what defines their interior ridges and porous seams, what closures are transgressed by unanticipated exposition and writerly forms.

Political summaries, published colonial statistics, and contemporary articles in newspapers and journals in the Indies and in the Netherlands responded to the official record, as chapter 4 on colonial commissions attests. Journalists and literati were active during the late nineteenth and early twentieth centuries, and they boldly critiqued the autocratic nature of the colonial administration, as well. Excellent studies have been done of many of them.[18] I draw more fully on articles in the press and elsewhere where they butted up against the common sense of the colonial administration to show just how uncommon that sense was. But sometimes

---

[17] See Herman Stapelkamp, "De Rol van Van Hoëvell in de Bataviase mei-beweging van 1848," *Jambatan* 4 (3): 11–20n38. Stapelkamp references the document as MK 571, resolution openbaar archief 8 Jan 1857, dossier no. 14. I thank Benjamin White for procuring this document for me and Ms. F. van Anrooij of the Algemeen Rijksarchief for making it available.

[18] See, for example, Gerard Termorshuizen, *Journalisten en heethoofden: een geschiedenis van de Indisch-Nederlandse dagbladpers, 11744–1905* (Leiden: KITLV, 2001); Ulbe Bosma, *Karel Zaalberg: journalist en strijder voor de Indo* (Leiden: KITLV, 1997); Paul van der Velde, *Een Indische liefde: P. J. Veth, 1814–1895* (Leiden: Balans, 2000); Ahmat B. Adam, *The Vernacular Press and the Emergence of the Modern Indonesian Consciousness (1855–1913)* (Ithaca: SEAP, 1995); and, for a later period, W. *Walraven, Eendagsvliegen: Journalistieke getuigenissen uit kranten en tijdschriften* (Amsterdam: G.A. van Oorschot, 1971).

I draw on newspapers simply to show how widely state "secrets" were shared.

Sometimes the borders that define the "official" and the "non-official" are hard to trace. Government civil servants wrote newspaper articles based on material culled from official records to which the public was not supposed to have access. Leaks soaked through and across confidential missives, private letters, and the sequestered archival page. Stylistically there is overlap, as well. When Frans Carl Valck, years after dismissal from his post, wrote a letter to his son-in-law to inform him of the Minister of Foreign Affairs's wish to speak with him, he writes "*geheim*" in bold letters at the top of the page, as though reliving his involvement in colonial affairs from which he has been so long banished. But this leakage between the protocols of office and the private world of Valck had more poignant and painful manifestations still, which will be explored in chapter 6, as for instance when this father and civil servant would inadvertently slip, signing letters to his ten-year-old daughter not "Papa" but "Valck."

The breadth of the archive that spans Frans Carl Valck's life and work, discussed in chapters 5 and 6, thus takes us elsewhere, through the tiers of colonial governance in other ways. It was the *Binnenlandsch Bestuur* (BB), a distinct and powerful governing structure that ran the administrative corps of the Indies and consolidated its formal and rigid hierarchy of civil service jobs in the mid-nineteenth century, that was to seal Valck's fate. When Valck was upbraided for his performance, it was the influential director of the *Binnenlandsch Bestuur* who scathingly made the case.

Many of the documents I work with here are those the *Binnenlandsch Bestuur* generated and sent on to the Governor-General, who in turn conveyed them to the Minister of Colonies. The *Raad van Indië*, the elite advisory board to the Governor-General, often emerges with a premier role in making decisions that the Governor-General on his own could or would not. Events in Deli also take us into the relationships between the Dutch military corps and the civil service through correspondence that underscores how divergent were their assessments of danger and how poor and haphazard their communications were.

The story of Frans Carl Valck's failed career produces another extended colonial archive of its own. Relations of family and friends among the richest sugar barons and highest-placed administrators show through in moments of crisis, in requests for exceptional treatment, on vacations, and in the deadening calm of forced retirement. In short, the reach is beyond the Algemeen Rijksarchief's secure walls to linger in its opacities, to muddy its reflection, to refract away from its shadow, and sometimes to shatter what has been so fittingly referred to as colonialism's "house of glass."

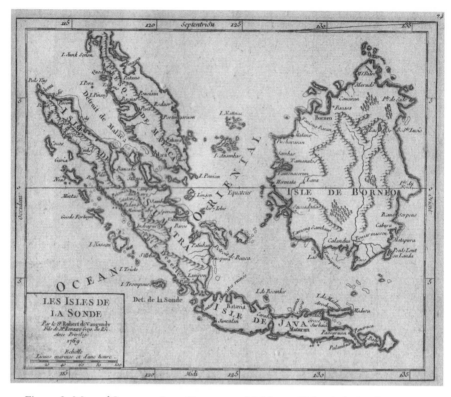

Figure 2. Map of Sumatra, Java, Borneo, and Malacca "Isles de la Sonde." Robert de Vaugondy, 1769, before Deli was "opened" for the European plantation industry in the 1860s. *Source*: private collection of A. Stoler.

CHAPTER TWO

The Pulse of the Archive

> But it seems you do not realize, Meneer Pangemanann, that your report is not for the general public. Only a very few people in the Indies and in the world have read and studied it. . . . You will never know, and indeed do not need to know, who else has read it. Your work of scholarship, as you like to call it, will *never receive the honor of being kept in the State archives.* Once being read, it will become dust and smoke, in the safekeeping of the devils of darkness.
>
> —Pramoedya Ananta Toer, *House of Glass*

IT IS 1912. Pramoedya Ananta Toer's novel, *House of Glass*, begins in the chill of the Dutch East Indies' state archives and in the heat of colonial Java's emergent Indonesian nationalist movement.[1] Dutch authorities call on Jacques Pangemanann, a Eurasian former police officer, newly appointed native commissioner to the elite Indies intelligence service, to defuse the movement's spread. His mission is to read the classified state archives, and spy, report on, and then destroy Minke, the movement's leader. But this complicity undoes Pangemanann and ravages his soul. He hears voices, develops a verbal tick and high blood pressure, becomes estranged from his family and falls into alcoholic despair. His descent from colonial officer to "bandit," and ultimately to archive-bound "terrorist," is rapid.[2] By the book's end he will have destroyed his own hero, Minke, and himself.

When the novel opens, Pangemanann has just completed his meticulous report, assessing the strength of the nascent anticolonial movement and the commitments of its alleged instigators, the mostly Muslim-educated elite on Java. Those few architects and agents of empire with privileged

---

[1] Pramoedya Ananta Toer, *House of Glass* (New York: William Morrow, 1992). In this edition Max Lane translates *"para iblis dalam kegelapan"* as "devils of the night." Henk Meier has encouraged me to translate it (in the epigraph) rather as "devils of darkness" to underscore the richer connotations that darkness affords. I have also altered Lane's translation of the first part of this sentence to accord more closely with the Indonesian text. See Pramoedya Ananta Toer, *Rumah Kaca* (Kuala Lumpur: Wira Karya, 1988), 24.

[2] Ibid., 31.

access eagerly read it. Leaders of the sugar industry syndicate laud his work. But his words will never enter the "nearly ten miles of closely packed papers" that make up the sanctified space of the government archive.[3] He may enter the inner sanctum but leave no trace: as spy he can have no presence, as an "Indo" (a "mixed blood") of tainted native, if elevated, origin, he can only have a muffled voice. Too lowly to be acknowledged, his "findings" are too sensitive to be preserved. As his European superior bluntly informs him, "he need not know" who has read it: "[It] will never receive the honor of being kept in the State archives." Burned as soon as it is read, it is reduced to "dust and smoke"—an archive that is to remain in darkness.

House of Glass is the name Pangemanann gives to his report but "house of glass" references a more fundamentally disquieting space in the colonial imaginary—at once the fragile security of the Dutch police state and the false security of Europeans living nestled in it. The quest for affective knowledge—that which moves people to feel and act—was the coveted pursuit of state intelligence yet beyond its grasp. Framed by the deceptions of archival access, *House of Glass* begins with the state archive only to veer far from it, for Pangemanann hides his most precious document in the safety of his house. In Pramoedya Ananta Toer's vision, disappeared documents and distorted reports are the archive's paltry truths. The building that houses the state's records is a "mausoleum" with palatial columns and thick stone walls. It does more than chill and still the air. It keeps out both the tropical heat, and the resilient motion of a resistant social world that is Java.

House of Glass reads at once as a condemnation of colonial rule and a fierce parable of the contemporary seductions of power in what was Suharto-ruled, postcolonial Indonesia. For Pramoedya, whose banned stories were transmitted orally while he was in prison for fourteen years, it is not surprising how sharply his assault is aimed—at the erudite, educated ignorance that Java's Dutch officialdom cultivated and that the colonial archives produced and contained.[4] Pramoedya Ananta Toer mocks those officials (and scholars) who hold tight to their paper documents, who imagine they can know the Indies without setting foot outside the archive and their carefully tended inscriptions in it.

One of his targets is clear: those who study to become "colonial expert[s] by going in and out of these buildings," those who believe that

---

[3] Ibid., 63.

[4] See John David Morley, "Warped by Empire" *New York Times Book Review* (9 June 1996), and Christopher GoGwitt, "Pramoedya's Fiction and History: An Interview with Indonesian Novelist Pramoedya Ananta Toer," *Yale Journal of Criticism* 9 (1) 1996: 147–64.

"documents are more reliable . . . than the mouths of their authors."[5] If the "taste of the archive" is in the heady rush of discovery, in the sensations and desires the archives stir, for Pramoedya the colonial archives are the bitter aftertaste of empire, the morsels left for us, their voracious contemporary readers.[6] Regimes of official documentation in his account are inert remnants, iconic roadmaps to regimes of domination that warp the integrity of the best of men. Such closed-circuited regimes of impoverished testimony produce their experts who in turn produce them.

This site of safekeeping, a pyre of empire, is one plausible way to describe the deadening weight of colonial archives. But it is not the one I have in mind. Pramoedya's caricature is a pointillist still life, that captures the rigidities and distortions of a colonial optic. In his novel the archive has barely a living pulse.[7] For Pramoedya official paper stands in relief from the vibrant political culture of a Java that high and low officials labored to grasp but could barely comprehend.

Yet colonial state archives are sites of perturbations of other kinds—less monuments to the absence or ubiquity of knowledge than its piecemeal partiality, less documents to the force of reasoned judgment than to both the spasmodic and sustained currents of anxious labor that paper trails could not contain. Nietzsche warns that "the legislation of language" establishes truth.[8] But here that legislated lexicon produces a surfeit that spills over and smudges the archive's policed edges. In these Dutch colonial archives, what could, should, and need not be done or said colludes and collides on the ragged ridges of racial categories, and in the constricted political space of a never-stable, Dutch-inflected "colonial situation."

For Pramoedya the tremors of colonial rule are outside the archives. In the present volume I pursue how deeply epistemic anxieties stir affective tremors within them. The pulse of the archive and the forms of governance that it belies are in the finished reports and in the process of their

---

[5] Toer, 69.

[6] See Arlette Farge, *Le Gout de l'Archive* (Paris: Seuil, 1989) for a richly tender treatment of the relationship between the sensation of the historian's reading of archives and the material texture of such collections. See Carolyn Steedman, *Dust: The Archive and Cultural History* (New Brunswick: Rutgers University Press, 2002) on the reader's longings to animate these silent relics. My search for the "pulse" cannot but share in that, as well.

[7] What the archive does hold, for Pramoedya, are only bundled traces of colonialism's ghostly victims, born a century earlier, who leave behind "the filth in colonial life [on the archive's] clean white sheets." Toer, 46. On this spectral quality "of contaminating marks on the colonial archive's pristine sheets," see Pheng Cheah, *Spectral Nationality: Passages of Freedom from Kant to Postcolonial Literatures of Liberation* (New York: Columbia, 2003), esp. 309–47, 310.

[8] Friedrich Nietzsche, "On Truth and Lies in a Nonmoral Sense" [1874], in *Philosophy and Truth: Selections from Nietzsche's Notebooks of the Early 1870's*, ed. and trans. Daniel Breazale (Atlantic Highlands, N.J.: Humanities, 1979), 79–91.

making, in the fine crafts of cribbing and culling on which colonial bureaucracies so relied. In the interstices of sanctioned formulae these Netherlands Indies archives of the late nineteenth and early twentieth centuries
mark the distance between recognized and disqualified knowledge, between intelligible accounts and those deemed inappropriate for exchange.
Not least, here is what Michel de Certeau might include as a space of "displaced histories," contrary and subjacent—but not necessarily subaltern—
that hover in the archive's long shadows.[9] Sometimes these are emergent
and awkward, sometimes suspended and unfulfilled narratives within the
archive's dominant mode. And sometimes there are stammers, what I
would call "disabled histories," a few brief words in Malay, seized from a
"native informant," not given the due of a narrative at all.

This book is about such a colonial order of things as seen through the
record of archival productions. I ask what insights into the social imaginaries of colonial rule might be gained from attending not only to colonialism's archival content, but to the principles and practices of governance lodged in particular archival forms. By "archival form" I allude to
several things: prose style, repetitive refrain, the arts of persuasion, affective strains that shape "rational" response, categories of confidentiality
and classification, and not least, genres of documentation. The book's focus
is on archiving-as-process rather than archives-as-things. Most importantly, it looks to archives as condensed sites of epistemological and political anxiety rather than as skewed and biased sources. These colonial
archives were both transparencies on which power relations were inscribed and intricate technologies of rule in themselves.

Those on which I draw here are of the official archives of the Dutch colonial state, missives and reports that passed up and down the bureaucratic
ladder, or stayed secreted within its privileged echelons. But the archive's
sweep is not confined to these domains alone. Filling that archive are those
people loosely tied to the Indies' administrative apparatus but not salaried
by it. These were doctors, clergymen, private school teachers and orphanage directors whose local knowledge and expertise on specific populations and practices were intermittently sought, those who took these

---

[9] De Certeau uses the term "displaced history" as a history "recounting both the proximity of the past and the foreignness of your private life, or the present as a metaphor for a
somewhere else." I use "displaced history" to convey something closer to the relationship
Foucault articulates between erudite and disqualified knowledge, where the latter is preserved if not emergent within the former. On "displaced history," see Michel de Certeau,
"The Theater of the Quidproquo: Alexandre Dumas," in *Heterologies: Discourses on the
Other*, trans. Brian Massumi (Minneapolis: University of Minnesota Press, 1986), 150–55,
151; on erudite and disqualified knowledge, see Foucault, "Two Lectures," in *Culture,
Power, History: A Reader in Contemporary Social Theory*, ed. Nicholas Dirks, Geoff Eley,
and Sherry Ortner (Princeton: Princeton University Press, 1994), 200–221.

occasions to rehearse common sense or share their views on what it meant to be Dutch, on what they thought of concubinage across racial lines, or on what they imagined were the attributes of "mixed blood" children and the nature of their moral character.

Along with the surefooted views on policies by which we have come to identify colonial enterprises are the remnants of writerly practices of a very different kind: those that chronicle failed projects, delusional imaginings, equivocal explanations of unanticipated outbursts of distrust directed toward a state apparatus on which European comforts would so precariously depend. Relegated to archival asides are lowly civil servants gone bankrupt in efforts to pay for their sons' requisite schooling in Holland. European women go mad in throwaway sentences. In abbreviated asides impoverished widows of lowly Dutch officials send their servants to beg from their neighbors for food and funds on their behalf. These are archives peopled with Dutch administrators, as well as German and French planters scrambling to figure out whether their plantation holdings might be attacked by a few workers bent on revenge against an abusive planter—or by phantasmic "hoards" of Islamic insurgents armed to storm their guarded gates. Within the constricted ontologies of rule, understandings of outrage often escaped the reasoned state.

Because imagining what *might be* was as important as knowing what was, these archives of the visionary and expectant should rivet our attention upon their erratic movement back and forth in verbal tense: the conditional could powerfully reshape an immediate response as it recursively rewrote the present and refigured events that had long passed.[10] The portent-laden future of revolt and betrayal is always on the imminent and dangerous horizon. When colonial social reformers conceived scrupulously planned utopias made of small-scale farmers drawn from the mixed blood orphanages, their minute descriptions of those children's inclinations mirrored visions of what they conceived adults to be and what they feared improperly schooled children might become. Such projections, in turn, made more real the visceral fear of the resentments such subjects in the making were thought to harbor. Plans to school the young for state loyalty and humble aspirations underscored their lack of both. Resplendent in the feared, the unrealized, and the ill-conceived, such visions invite, what I call in chapter 4, a strategy of "developing historical negatives" to track a microspace of the everyday through what might become and could never be. I take these to be "blueprints of distress" that trace

---

[10] For a related but different sense of the future orientation and possibilities written into archival production by "intentional communities," see Arjun Appadurai, "Archive and Aspiration," in *Information Is Alive*, ed. Joke Brouwer and Arjen Mulder (Rotterdam: V2/NAI, 2003), 14–25.

out agitations of a peculiar kind—not events but the "negative prints" of what stirred official anxiety to which colonial agents responded with infeasible policies for implausible arrangements that could neither be carried out nor sustained. If historians "tell of things that have been," and poets "of things as might be," as Paul Ricoeur's parsing of the Aristotelian distinction insists, this ethnographic history of these colonial imaginaries seeps across the futuristic and the actual to capture something of both.[11]

Here I treat these colonial archives both as a corpus of writing and as a force field that animates political energies and expertise, that pulls on some "social facts" and converts them into qualified knowledge, that attends to some ways of knowing while repelling and refusing others.[12] Such a field has centripetal and centrifugal force. In no small part it inscribes the authority of the colonial state and the analytic energies mobilized to make its assertions. But it also registers other reverberations, crosscurrent frictions, attractions, and aversions that worked within and against those assertions of imperial rights to property, persons, and profits that colonial regimes claimed as their own.

This Roland Barthes might have called a "storeyed" archival field in both senses of the term: *layered* and *crafted* from practical and unevenly sedimented deceptions and dispositions that accumulated as acceptable or discarded knowledge.[13] The Pangemananns, whose reports were destroyed as soon as they were read, leave only a faint trace. Rather, these chapters pause at the hands and habits of those charged with the writing, recording, sorting, and proliferation of documents, in the unremarkable forms in which writerly practices appeared; in the tone and tenor of a reprimand, a dismissal, or praise, in floridly clear or illegible signatures at the bottom of a neatly copied page. Sometimes persons become visible in the entitled scrawls of an angry query across a report, or remain invisible in the faceless, careful handwriting of "copy machines" (as Eurasian clerks were disparagingly called)—subjects whose racially marked positions conferred no place for, nor right to, a signature at all.

---

[11] See Paul Ricoeur's discussion of Aristotle's distinction between poets and historians in *Time and Narrative*, Vol. 1 (Chicago: University of Chicago Press, 1984), esp. 40–41.

[12] On Walter Benjamin and Theodor Adorno's uses of the term (*Kraftfeld*), see Martin Jay, *Force fields: Between Intellectual History and Cultural Critique* (New York: Routledge, 1993), 1–3. See also Richard Bernstein, *The New Constellation* (Cambridge, Mass.: The MIT Press, 1993), 9.

[13] See Roland Barthes's discussion of Tzvetan Todorov's distinction in narrative between the "unfolding of a story" and "its construction in storeys" of horizontal movement in *Image-Music-Text*, trans. Stephen Heath (New York: Hill and Wang, 1977), 87.

ARCHIVAL CONVENTIONS

> When the archive . . . seems easily to give access to what one ex-
> pects of it, the work is all the more demanding. One has to pa-
> tiently give up one's natural "sympathy" for it and consider it an
> adversary to fight, a piece of knowledge that isn't to annex but
> disrupt. It is not simply a matter of undoing something whose
> meaning is too easy to find; to be able to know it, you have to un-
> learn and not think you know it from a first reading.
>
> —Arlette Farge, *Le Gout de l'Archive*

Farge's warning to proceed with caution, to allow oneself to falter in the
face of the archive's repetitions, formulae, and obviousness is one I take
to heart. The official documents of colonial archives like those of the
Netherlands Indies are so weighted with fixed formats, empty phrases,
and racial clichés that one is easily blinded by their flattened prose and
numbing dullness. Our readings are blunted by what often has been parsed
as the seemingly panoptic glare of a vacuous, stylized official gaze. But in
these archives the panoptic is a frail conceit. Administrative overviews
index conventional forms of assumed mastery less than comprehensive
knowledge. Such overviews—of regions, problems, or target populations—
were rendered from cribbed and cluttered, spare and hurried reports of the
disorder of things, written in the studied ineloquence of bureaucratese.
Sometimes they were impressionistic and distant, elsewhere animated by intimate fear less than intimate knowledge of what multiple colonial civil
servants thought they saw, what was reported by an unnamed underling,
or what they claimed others had said.

Wedged within those folds of truth-claims emerges something else:
uncensored turns of phrase, loud asides in the imperative tense, hesitant
asides in sotto voce. These register confused assessments, parenthetic
doubts about what might count as evidence, the records of eyewitnesses
with dubious credentials, dismissed rumors laced with pertinent truths,
contradictory testimonies called upon and quickly discarded. These too
were assessments that implicitly weighed the stature and sensibility of
their authors, and the distance that separated their words from the received scenarios of colonial common sense. In chapter 6, I refer to these
as elements that make up a "hierarchy of credibility," scales of trust that
measured what forms of witness, words and deeds, could be taken as reliably relevant.

But these hierarchies too are sometimes inverted. In the brutal immediacy of a murder, in the panic of an impeding attack, in the anxious rush
to fulfill a superior's demand for information (and for proof of one's

vigilance), in the concerted effort to ward off disaster, words could slip from their safe moorings to reappear unauthorized, inappropriate, and unrehearsed. These are not *outside* the archival field. Nor are they outside the grids of intelligibility in which those documents are lodged, but rather the subjacent coordinates of, and counterpoints within, them. Such confusions and "asides" work in and around prevailing narratives as they push on the archive's storied edges.

Derrida's evocative image of the archive as a site of "house arrest," one that "gathers together signs," suggests no entry for the wayward, no access to intruders.[14] But the paper trails left by European colonial projects could never be sealed that tight; not in the Indies, where magazines, pamphlets, journals, and dailies both pilfered from the official record and were made an evidentiary part of it. Here an image of *house-breaking* might better be joined with house arrest to more vividly capture what those in command feared (as much as native insurgence)—that their houses of glass might be shattered by "inside" jobs: by civil servants improperly schooled in what not to see or say, as was Assistent-Resident of Deli, Frans Carl Valck, who is center stage in chapters 6 and 7; by recalcitrant Indo-Europeans who refused to answer a state commission on their domestic and sexual affairs, as shall be seen in chapter 5; and by the unseemly action of the colony's most respected city fathers, European high officials described in chapter 3 who, in protesting government policy, circulated documents and directives meant only for their rarified readings and well-trained ears.

This is the ethnographic space of the colonial archives, where truthclaims compete, impervious or fragile, crushed by the weight of convention or resilient in the immediate threat of the everyday; where trust is put to the test and credibility wavers. Here I linger over unspoken orders of rubric and reference that did more than define plausible evidence. Specific if not unique to the shape of these colonial archives is a racialized common sense about people and places—about Javanese coolies and Acehnese insurgents, about the sensibilities of the *Indische* population, Indies-born and bred Dutch versus imported, transient, and *echte* Europeans. Such implicit common sense figured centrally when reporting *preceded* inquiry, when evidence was spare—or absent.

Conventions suggest consensus but it is not clear what colonial practitioners actually shared. District reports were built upon changing beliefs about what mattered to state security and what sorts of people were deemed a present or possible threat. Consensus was also shaped by how skillfully or poorly seasoned bureaucrats and fledgling practitioners could

---

[14] Derrida, *Archive Fever: A Freudian Impression* (Chicago: University of Chicago Press, 1995), 2.

apprehend the tacit changing rules of decorum and protocol, what rhetorical devices were deemed persuasive and currently active in the game.

Conventions also suggest familiarity and durability. I take them instead as moving targets and, sometimes, so did those in office themselves. Irony and humor are not lacking, mockery targets those who are too literal or not literal enough. Misinterpretations of directives were subject to ridicule when reports were sent that got things "wrong." Stock phrases took on different political import depending on where they were placed. Contexts of relevance rapidly changed. References to the need for European nurseries might seem unremarkable in lengthy reports on education but offer striking openings to political thinking when colonial administrators obsessed over them in classified documents elsewhere: in a commission on European pauperism, in recommendations to quell creole discontent, in debates over mixed bloods "too proud" to learn manual labor. As I have argued elsewhere, this was not "information out of place."[15] In these contexts, such conjoinings of the banal and political mark implicit anxieties about subject-formation, about the psychic space of empire, about what went without saying, about the common sense that made these reasoned pairings.

The Seductions of State Secrets

> Institutions create shadowed places in which nothing can be seen and no questions asked. They make other areas show in finely discriminated detail, which is closely scrutinized and ordered. History emerges in an unintended shape as a result of practices directed to immediate, practical ends. To watch these practices establish selective principles that highlight some kinds of events and obscure others is to inspect the social order operating on individual minds.
>
> —Mary Douglas, *How Institutions Think*

Archivists are the first to note that to understand an archive, one needs to understand the institutions that it served. "State secrets" are one of those key conventions of concealment that produce the "shadowed places" to

---

[15] See Ann Laura Stoler, "A Sentimental Education: Children on the Colonial Divide," in Stoler, *Carnal Knowledge and Imperial Power* (Berkeley: University of California Press, 2002), 112–39, and idem, *Race and the Education of Desire* (Durham: Duke University Press, 1995), 137–64. See also Paul Starr, "Social Categories and Claims in the Liberal State," in *How Classification Works: Nelson Goodman among the Social Sciences*, ed. Mary Douglas and David Hull (Edinburgh: Edinburgh University Press, 1992), 154–79.

which Douglas refers: such shadows are cast by persons with cryptic titles; bureaus with nondescript names; pieces of paper that become "lost," inaccessible, "miscatalogued," and thus are rendered unusable and irrelevant. Shadowed places are what states create, emblematic conventions of the archival form. States do more than traffic in the production of secrets and their selective dissemination. State sovereignty resides in the power to designate arbitrary social facts of the world as matters of security and concerns of state. Once so assigned, these social facts—Indo children breastfed by native servants (who were sometimes their mothers) poor whites who went by non-Christian names, Indos "disguised" in the dress of native traders, language-use at home—are dislodged from their contexts, flung into the orbit of a political world that is often not their own. These otherwise innocuous practices become iconic indices of a colonial world perceived as being at risk, signs of alert that accrue political deliberations, that sanction the rushing in of more evidence, that confirm causal connections that warrant more secreted documentation.

Max Weber claimed that the "official secret" was a "specific invention of bureaucracy," its "fanatically defended" prize possession.[16] In the Netherlands Indies documents marked with an X as "secret," "very secret," or "highly confidential" were elevated to sacred status, to be guarded and then later revealed. As in the European Pauperism Commission of 1901, the stature of its recommendations derived in part from an earlier secreted commission that it exposed. And as with Pangemanann, both honored and shamed by the secrets to which he was privy, to gather information was not necessarily to know who would read it, or the narratives that it would fortify before being set afire, shredded, or stored away.

State secrets excite expectations, not least among students of empire. For we often covet that which the state conceals, regarding its secrets as accurate measures of its most nefarious intents: unmasking its magic and deceptive opacities is our calling. But we also know that codes of concealment are the fetishes of the state itself.[17] Within colonial bureaucracies,

---

[16] Max Weber, "Bureaucracy," in *Essays in Sociology*, trans. and ed. H. H. Gerth and C. Wright Mills (New York: Oxford University Press, 1946), 233–34.

[17] Philip Abrams held that "the state is . . . a triumph of concealment. It conceals the real history and relations of subjection behind an a-historical mask of legitimating illusion; contrives to deny the existence of connections and conflicts which would if recognized be incompatible with claimed autonomy and integration of the state. The real official secret . . . is the secret of the non-existence of the state." Abrams, I think, gets it right and wrong. There is no "a-historical mask" but rather an elaborate apparatus geared to the task of historical reproduction. Nor was the colonial state nonexistent if we understand it rather as an *imperial* one that stretched across multiple locations—in the Indies and the Netherlands—and multiple sites and technologies of command. See Philip Abrams, "Notes on the Difficulty of Studying the State" [1977], *Journal of Historical Sociology* 1 (1) (March 1988): 58–89, 77.

such secrets sometimes have strange biographies. Secrets may earmark privileged knowledge, or, as with commissions of inquiry, create the categories they purport only to describe. In the Indies colonial archives, they do some of both. Classified documents served as a signal to direct attention and cued for one's repeated return to what knowledge should be valued and what their readers should know. They also called up and upon technologies of intelligence: secret police, fingerprinting, coded scripts, and men like Pangemanann, whose names were expunged from documents. Secret documents could have as their source native paid informants who were *vertrouwensmannen* (trustworthy men, who one took into one's confidence); Eurasians who were charged—as was Pangemannan—to interpret native signs of discontent and distress; and, not least, purveyors of culture and psychology, anthropologists and others deemed Java experts.

Secrets do more than limit access. They promise confidences and confidence in limited circulation about something others do not and should not know. Items about clandestine police maneuvers, military preparations, and deliberations about an impending revolt are what we expect to be marked as *geheim*, with an X. But sometimes promises of access to the unknown were bizarre fictions at best. Confidential documents both secret and secrete what becomes elevated to "vital" information. Throughout the official archives of the Dutch colonial state are documents earmarked for confidentiality that were not secrets at all.

If one could argue that the presence of European beggars and homeless Dutchmen in the streets of Batavia in the 1870s were "secrets" to those in the Netherlands, they certainly were not to European post office clerks, Javanese construction workers, or Chinese storekeepers who lived on the sprawling low-lying peripheries inhabited by the impoverished of Java's urban centers.[18] Similarly, was a letter written in 1848 by a Dutch lawyer to the Resident of Batavia a "highly secret" document because he signed it—"I remain like our King, a liberal Dutchman"—when to be "*vrijzinnig*" (liberal and modern) in the colonies bordered on a subversive act?[19] Or was it because it was "unseemly" for a high official to so brazenly declare his similarity to the modern King and refrain from deference? Or was it because he boldly declared his intent to participate in the colonies in a European demonstration?

Both instances suggest that what were secret in such documents were not the their specific subject matters but their timing and the interpretive

---

[18] AR, Geheim No. 1144/2284. Department of Justice to the Governor-General, Batavia, 29 April 1873.

[19] C. Ardesche to Resident van Rees, KV, no. 317, 1848, Zeer Geheim, Exh. E, 19 March 1848.

uncertainties about an appropriate government response that gathered around them. Similarly, classified missives on European beggars were less about what to do with the destitute than measures of disagreement and disquiet about how to racially classify those who fell into such straits. Reports on vagabond whites were "secret" in 1874 and not twenty-five years later when the public Pauper Commission appeared because officials could not agree on whether there were thirty-nine white paupers living among natives in the urban slums of Batavia, or thousands.[20]

Documents were sometimes marked *geheim* because of the magnitude of a problem, at other times because officials could not agree on a shared sense of what the problems were. Rather than secreted truths about the state, they point to sites of unease, anticipatory warnings of emergent movement among subject populations (what Raymond Williams might even include as "structures of feeling"), of resentments that may not yet have had a name.[21] As Frederick Barth once observed, secrets do more than sanctify—they invoke deeper secrets of their own.[22]

Not least they invite disclosure. Critique emerges in the interstices of what goes without saying and what should not be said: sometimes documents referred to those who parodied commonsense conventions. As we shall see, the "dirty secrets" of Sumatra's planters were in classified missives not because the planters' abuses of their laboring populations were not known, but precisely because they were not to be acknowledged and aired by an "inept" civil servant like Frans Carl Valck.

COLONIAL COMMISSIONS

If it is obvious that colonial archives are products of state machines, it is only now that we are seeing them, in their own right, as technologies that reproduced those states themselves.[23] Andrew Ashforth has strongly stated

---

[20] AR, KV 28 March 1874, no. 47x, No. 1144/2284. Director of Justice D. de Pauly to the Governor-General.

[21] Statistical information in the eighteenth century was considered a source of state power and therefore *not* published. Public access to state statistics was a nineteenth-century phenomenon. See Marc Ventresca, *When States Count: Institutional and Political Dynamics in Modern Census Establishment, 1800–1993*, Ph.D. Diss., Stanford University, 1996, 50.

[22] Fredrick Barth, *Ritual and Knowledge among the Baktaman of New Guinea* (New Haven: Yale University Press, 1975), 217. I thank Maurice Bloch for this reference.

[23] On this point, see Michel Rolph Trouillot, *Silencing the Past: Power and the Production of History* (Boston: Beacon, 1995). On the relationship between state-formation and archival production, see Michel Duchein, "The History of European Archives and the Development of the Archival Profession in Europe," *American Archivist* 55 (Winter 1992): 14–25.

the case in his study of South Africa's Native Affairs Commission, when he notes that "the real seat of power" in modern states is "the bureau, the locus of writing," but it is an insight that Weber shared and that many students of colonialisms would subscribe to, as well.[24] Systems of written accountability called for elaborate infrastructures. Paper trails of weekly reports to superiors, summaries of reports of reports, and recommendations based on reports all called for systematic coding systems by which they could be tracked. Colonial statecraft was an administrative apparatus to gather, draw together, and connect—and disconnect—events, to make them, as needed, legible, insignificant, or unintelligible as information. Striking in this accumulation process is how much of what was collected was made irrelevant to what state officials decided, both to what they acknowledged they could do in practice and what about the Indies they claimed to know.[25]

Nowhere was this process more evident than in the form of state-sponsored commissions of inquiry. Colonial commissions reorganized knowledge, devising new ways of knowing while setting aside others. One implicit task was to reconstruct historical narratives, decreeing what past events were pertinent to current issues and how they should be framed. Sometimes commissions were responses to catastrophic events and extended periods of crisis.[26] As responses they generated increased anxiety, substantiating the reality of "crisis," the wisdom of pre-emptive response, foreshadowing that new directives were demanded, as were the often coercive measures taken to ensure their effect. By the time most commissions had run their course, political signposts were set in place: "turning points" were identified, precedents established, causalities certified, arrows directed with vectors of blame—if not action—sharply aimed.

Just as often they attested to what a commission had set out to show in the first place—that is, if the commission knew what it was after.[27] As

---

[24] See Andrew Ashforth, *The Politics of Official Discourse in Twentieth-Century South Africa* (Oxford: Clarendon, 1990), 5.

[25] For a richly subtle analysis of the production of such commissions as a critical feature of modern governing processes, see Oz Frankel, *States of Inquiry: Social Investigation and Print Culture in Nineteenth-Century Britain and the United States* (Baltimore: The Johns Hopkins University Press, 2006).

[26] On investigatory commissions as an "emergency apparatus of government," see Jonathan Simon, "Parrhesiastic Accountability: Investigatory Commissions and Executive Power in an Age of Terror," *Yale Law Journal* 114 (6) (April 2005): 1419–57, 1430.

[27] See Fred Block and Margaret Somers, "In the Shadow of Speenhamland: Social Policy and the Old Poor Law," *Politics and Society* 31 (2) (June 2003): 1–41, 5. Oz Frankel notes that social activists like Beatrice and Sydney Webb regarded royal commissions as political tools to "promote preconceived policies or to put thorny issues on the shelf, peddling official passivity as action" (Frankel, 139).

Dutch anthropologist Frans Husken notes of colonial commissions in Java, "when nothing else works and no decision can be reached, 'appoint a commission' was a favorite response of colonial authorities."[28] Commissions could reactivate knowledge but also stop it in its tracks. As technologies of delay, they could effectively mobilize interest and satisfy it, as well as arrest decision. They were primed to distract. Pathos and statistics may seem a strange pairing but both were at the political heart of state inquiries. Some commission reports were searingly detailed; some were impressionistic and abstract. Vignettes about the unnamed and anecdotes of the everyday established the truth-claims of local officials, their local knowledge and ethnographic authority.

Such commissions, as we shall see in chapter 5, were also consummate producers of social kinds. The European Pauperism Commission of 1901 reassigned clusters of people for state scrutiny and in so doing revised and overwrote what was to count in ascriptions of race. Ways of living were congealed into "problems," subject persons were condensed into ontological categories, innocuous practices were made into subjects of analysis and rendered political things. Statistics, historical narrative, and anecdote were made ready at hand, mutually corroborating evidence for commission-making projects. Proof of the difference between destitute whites and Indo-European paupers was construed by identifying distinct sorts of persons, with specific dispositions and states of mind. Details of the everyday were elevated to reliable proof of character. Neglect of children, indifference to work, succumbing to native standards were affective states not captured in numbers; condemnations of the sensory world in which poor whites lived afforded more palpable and convincing evidence of what colonial agents already thought they knew about the sorting of people and how race shaped distinct habits and inclinations.

Like statistics, commissions were common tools of statecraft forged by social reform–conscious nineteenth-century states. As instruments of moral science, statistics used deviations from the mean to identify deviations from the norm. Commissions joined those numbers with prototypic cases to measure gradations of morality and the gradations of unfreedom that went along with them.[29] That so many commissions were convened in the late nineteenth century was part of a technology of state practice

[28] Frans Husken, "Declining Welfare in Java: Government and Private Inquiries, 1903–1914," in *The Late Colonial State in Indonesia*, ed. Robert Cribb (Leiden: KITLV, 1994), 213.

[29] See Arjun Appadurai on numerical representation in colonial India as a "key to normalizing the pathology of difference" in "Numbers in the Colonial Imagination," in *Modernity at Large: Cultural Dimensions of Globalization* (Minneapolis: University of Minnesota Press, 1996), 114–38.

that spanned the imperial globe.[30] In metropole and colony, these were high-profile promises of public accountability that in turn identified the commensurabilities on which international colonial conferences thrived. In the Indies they garnered moral authority both through the specific *comparisons* they sought to make between their "mixed blood problem" or their "poor white problem" and those in South Africa, Australia, and elsewhere in the imperial world.

This was a politics of comparison in which biopolitical assessments of differential racial capabilities and character were key features of social technology.[31] Those commissions, like the European Pauperism Commission or the South African Carnegie Commission on Poor Whites thirty years later, explicitly linked domestic relationships—between parent and child, nursemaid and infant—to the security of the state. Relations between people and objects—to clothing, furnishings, room arrangements, and window-openings—were invoked, as well. Eyewitness testimonies to intimacies of the home had become data of a particular kind, critical to the state's audit of its commitment to the public good, to racial differentiation, and to its own viability.

Not least, these commissions were quintessential "quasi-state" technologies that were in part authored and authorized by persons of stature outside it. If modern states gain force by creating and maintaining an elusive boundary to civil society, such commissions exemplified that process.[32] "Outside" experts verified both the state's right to assess the public interest and its commitment to objectivity. Commissions, in short, demonstrated the state's right to power through its will to the production of truth.

Ethnography in the Archives

> [Ethnographic work] is neither a matter of piling on theoretical antecedents nor a matter of going where no one has been before. I would put it rather that *we need to go precisely where we have*

[30] Royal commissions have a longer history still. See, for example, David Loades, "The Royal Commissions," in *Power in Tudor England* (New York: St. Martin's, 1997), 70–82. On statistics and state building, see Alain Desrosières, "Statistics and the State," in *The Politics of Large Numbers* (Cambridge, Mass.: Harvard University Press, 1998), 178–209. For the twentieth century, see William J. Breen, "Foundations, Statistics, and State-Building," *Business History Review* 68 (1994): 451–82.

[31] On the use of the comparison as an instrument of statecraft, see my "Tense and Tender Ties," in *Haunted by Empire*, ed. Ann Laura Stoler (Durham, N.C.: Duke University Press, 2006), esp. 23–58.

[32] Timothy Mitchell, "The Limits of the State," *American Political Science Review* 85 (1991): 77–96.

> *already been*, back to the immediate here and now out of which
> we have created our present knowledge of the world. That
> means constructing a mode of enquiry which will enable a re-
> turn to fields of knowledge and activity in the hindsight of un-
> predicted outcomes, and which will thus enable recovering of
> material that investigators were not aware they were collecting.
> The ethnographic method . . . with its insistent demands of im-
> mersement, begins to look extremely promising.
> —Marilyn Strathern, "The Ethnographic Effect"

A convention in the study of colonial governance is to treat state bureaucracies as information-hungry machines, ambitiously taxonomic, bent on
categorical claims about those social differences that mattered and those
that did not. Scholars of the colonial have become deft at identifying the
distance between those normative, imposed categories of social difference
that so contrast with the more mobile social and intimate relations in
which people lived. If one no longer needs to argue, as Sally Falk-Moore
did twenty years ago, that fieldwork should be treated as "current history," the case might still need to be made that archival productions
should be treated in more registers as ethnography.[33]

Students often ask what and where is ethnography in the colonial
archives: is it in what, where, or how we approach these gatherings of
documents? Is it in the issues addressed or their treatment? What would,
and should, what Marilyn Strathern calls "immersement" look like for
the ethnographer on historical-colonial ground? One could respond that
the ethnographic space of the archive resides in the disjuncture between
prescription and practice, between state mandates and the maneuvers people made in response to them, between normative rules and how people
actually lived their lives.

But, as the last decade of historical ethnography suggests, no single answer will do. Ethnography in and of the colonial archives attends to processes of production, relations of power in which archives are created,
sequestered, and rearranged.[34] If ethnographies could be treated as texts,
students of the colonial have turned the tables; to reflect on colonial documents as "rituals of possession," as relics and ruins, as sites of contested
cultural knowledge. Here I treat archives not as repositories of state power
but as unquiet movements in a field of force, as restless realignments and

---

[33] Sally Falk-Moore, "Explaining the Present: Theoretical Dilemmas in Processual Ethnography," *American Ethnologist* 14 (4): 727–36.

[34] Trouillot's *Silencing the Past: Power and the Production of History* is the most explicit
and noteworthy example.

readjustments of people and the beliefs to which they were tethered, as spaces in which the senses and the affective course through the seeming abstractions of political rationalities.[35] I take sentiments expressed and ascribed as social interpretations, as indices of relations of power and tracers of them.

The case need no longer be made that "sources" are not "springs" of colonial truths.[36] Distinguishing fiction from fact has given way to efforts to track the production and consumption of facticities as the contingent coordinates of particular times and temperaments, places and purposes.[37] As some of the best of this work now recognizes, filing systems and disciplined writing produce assemblages of control and specific methods of domination.[38] More than ever, new studies of archival production tackle the politics of colonial knowledge and the "arrested histories"—those histories suspended from received historiography—that are its effects.[39] Ethnographic sensibilities have led us to ask how oral and vernacular

---

[35] See Patricia Seed, *Ceremonies of Possession in Europe's Conquest of the New World, 1492–1640* (New York: Cambridge University Press, 1995), and Roberto Gonzalez-Echevarria, *Myth and Archive: A Theory of Latin American Narrative* (New York: Cambridge University Press, 1990).

[36] Ranajit Guha, "The Prose of Counter-insurgency," in *Culture, Power, History: A Reader in Contemporary Social Theory*, ed. Nicholas Dirks, Geoff Eley, and Sherry Ortner (Princeton: Princeton University Press, 1994), 336–71. Greg Dening, *The Death of William Gooch: A History's Anthropology* (Honolulu: University of Hawaii Press, 1995), 54. See also Nicholas Dirks, "Annals of the Archive: Ethnographic Notes on the Sources of History," in *From the Margins: Historical Anthropology and Its Futures*, ed. Brian Axel (Durham, N.C.: Duke University Press, 2002), 47–65.

[37] Carlo Ginzburg, "Clues: Roots of an Evidential Paradigm," in *Clues, Myths and the Historical Method* (Baltimore: The Johns Hopkins University Press, 1989), 96–125, and David William Cohen, *Burying SM: The Politics of Knowledge and the Sociology of Power in Africa* (Portsmouth, N.H.: Heineman, 1992); Richard Price, *The Convict and the Colonel* (Boston: Beacon, 1998). See also Axel, esp. 1–44.

[38] On filing systems, see Ilana Feldman, *Governing Gaza: Bureaucracy, Authority, and the Work of Rule (1917–1967)* (Durham, N.C.: Duke University Press, 2008). On the nature of "documentary government," see Keith Breckenridge's insightful essays, "From Hubris to Chaos: The Making of the Bewsyuro and the End of Documentary Government," "Flesh Made Words: Fingerprinting and the Archival Imperative in the Union of South Africa, 1900–1930," paper presented at the History and African Studies Seminar, History Department at the University of KwaZulu-Natal, Durban, South Africa, 2 October 2001.

[39] See Carole McGranahan, "Arrested Histories: Between Empire and Exile in 20th-Century Tibet," Ph.D. Diss., University of Michigan, 2001, and idem, "Truth, Fear, and Lies: Exile Politics and Arrested Histories of the Tibetan Resistance," *Cultural Anthropology* 25 (4) (November 2005): 570–600. See also Javier Morillo-Alicea, " '*Aquel laberinto de oficinas*': Ways of Knowing Empire in Late Nineteenth-Century Spain," in *After Spanish Rule*, ed. Mark Thurner and Andres Guerrero (Durham, N.C.: Duke University Press, 2003): 111–40. Attention to how states shape and efface personal memories has placed emphasis on how those alternative accounts are retained as preserved possibilities for future claims and political projects. See Joanne Rappaport, *Cumbe Reborn: An Andean Ethnography of*

histories cut across the strictures of archival production and refigure what makes up the archival terrain.[40] They prime us to look for arrogant assertions of know-how couched in unacknowledged native expertise.[41] Such sensibilities have opened to a broadening array of genres of documentation, to representational practices that impinge on received canons of inscription, to collages of memory that at once deface official writing as they provide new forms of historical evidence.[42] Methodologically, they pose a challenge to conventional historical narrative, inviting students of the colonial to take critical license with "sources," with what counts as context, and creative license with form.[43]

If every document comes layered with the received account of earlier events and the cultural semantics of a political moment, the issue of official "bias" opens to a different challenge: to identify the conditions of possibility that shaped what warranted repetition, what competencies were rewarded in archival writing, what stories could not be told and what could not be said. Such queries have invited a turn back to docu-

---

History (Chicago: University of Chicago Press, 1994); Sarah Nuttall and Carli Coetzee, eds., *Negotiating the Past: The Making of Memory in South Africa* (Capetown: Oxford University Press, 1998); Keith Breckenridge, "Confounding the Documentary State: Cape Workers' Letters on the Early Witwatersrand," paper presented at the History and African Studies Seminar, University of KwaZulu-Natal, Durban, South Africa, 30 May 2000; and Keith Breckenridge, "Verwoerd's Bureau of Proof: Total Information in the Making of Apartheid," *History Workshop Journal* 59 (Spring 2005): 83–108.

[40] See Shahid Amin's fine analysis of this mix in *Event, Metaphor, Memory, 1922–1992* (Berkeley: University of California Press, 1995).

[41] See Nicholas Dirks's exemplary treatment of this issue in "Colonial History and native Informants: Biography of an Archive," in *Orientalism and the Postcolonial Predicament: Perspectives on South Asia*, ed. Carol Breckenridge and Peter van der Veer (Philadelphia: University of Pennsylvania Press, 1993). On the critical labor performed by Africans in the study of local law and the making of colonial jurisdiction, see Benjamin Lawrance, Emily Osborn, Richard Roberts, eds., *Intermediaries, Interpreters, and Clerks: African Employees in the Making of Colonial Africa* (Madison: University of Wisconsin Press, 2006).

[42] For a unique ethnographic history of personal archives, local historians, and the power of their historiographies (as well as an excellent review of recent work on archives), see Penelope Papailias, *Genres of Recollection: Archival Poetics and Modern Greece* (New York: Palgrave, 2005). On the relationship between amateur photography, technology, and archival practice as a site of political critique, see the subtle work of Karen Strassler, *Refracted Visions: Popular Photography in Postcolonial Java* (Durham, N.C.: Duke University Press, forthcoming). See also the excellent contributions to Antoinette Burton, ed., *Archive Stories: Facts, Fictions and the Writing of History* (Durham, N.C.: Duke University Press, 2006).

[43] Among such innovative historiographic operations I think of Richard Price's *Convict and Colonel: A Story of Colonialism and Resistance in the Caribbean* (Boston: Beacon, 1998); Donna Merwick's *Death of a Notary: Conquest and Change in Colonial New York* (Ithaca: Cornell University Press, 1999); and Martha Hodes, "Fractions and Fictions in the United States Census of 1890," in *Haunted by Empire*, ed. Ann Laura Stoler (Durham, N.C.: Duke University Press, 2006), 240–70.

mentation itself, to the "teaching" task that the word's Latin root, *docere*, implies, to what and who was being educated in the bureaucratic shuffle of rote formulas, generic plots, and prescriptive asides.

COLONIAL COMMON SENSE AND ITS EPISTEMIC FRAMES

> The archive does not have the weight of tradition; and it does not constitute the library of libraries, outside time and place—it reveals the rules of practice . . . its threshold of existence is established by the discontinuity that separate us from what we can no longer say.
> —Michel Foucault, "Archaeology of Knowledge"

In this book, ethnographic sites emerge in the space between prescription and practice, but more pointedly elsewhere. I look for the pulse of the archive in the quiescence and quickened pace of its own production, in the steady and feverish rhythms of repeated incantations, formulae, and frames. I pursue it through the uneven densities of Dutch archival preoccupations and predicaments: where energies were expended, what conditioned the designation of an event, what visions were generated in the pursuit of prediction, which social groups garnered concern and then did not.

One of those densities, not surprisingly, thickens around social categories themselves. Here I track them through, what I call their "social etymologies." Social etymologies trace the career of words and the political practices that new categories mark or that new membership in old categories signals. Most importantly, social etymologies attend to the social relationships of power buried and suspended in those terms.[44] Such etymologies index how social kinds were produced and what kinds of social relations were construed as plausible evidence of membership. Social etymologies, then, are not just about words. They trace practices gathered into intelligible forms. They seek those histories that have found quiet refuge in them.[45]

They might also register how new social categories gained relevance as they annulled designations no longer sufficient to make the distinctions relevant to current reformist projects. In the successive waves of

---

[44] On "social etymology" in the analysis of imperial formations, see Ann Laura Stoler and Carole McGranahan, "Refiguring Imperial Terrains," in *Imperial Formations*, ed. Ann Laura Stoler, Carole McGranahan, and Peter Perdue (Santa Fe: School of American Research, 2007), 4.

[45] I thank David Bond for developing this point with me.

commissions that addressed the problem of European pauperism, discussed in chapter 5, state visions sometimes were contested by those persons whose personal histories they rewrote and remade. Persons clustered into an administrative category that joined "pauper" and "white" rejected the stigma of the designation "pauper," the state's assessment of their living conditions, and the government aid designed for them

But the career of categories is also lodged in archival habits and how those change: in the telling titles of commissions, in the requisite subject headings of administrative reports, in what sorts of stories get relegated to the miscellaneous and "misplaced." Attending to "words in their sites" and the conceptual weight they bear, the authority with which they are endowed, I ask how people think and why they seem obliged to think, or *suddenly find themselves having difficulty thinking*, in certain ways.[46] It is, then, not just *any* words that matter, but rather those "that revolve around different focal points of power," that are "set in play by a particular problem" as they gather around them debate and the provisional terms of convention.[47]

If Foucault's conception of archaeology joins "the lesson of things, and the lesson of grammar," as Deleuze claims, it is also an "audiovisual archive" that combines two forms of stratification—a "practical assemblage" of the visual and the verbal in any historical formation. On the terrain of race that "audiovisual" archive is key. It attends to "the lesson of things" to measure the "multisensory complexes" of *unseen* racial attributes, as well.[48] Throughout these archives racialized categories are shuffled, reassigned, and remade. In chapter 4, "Developing Historical Negatives," that category of *"Inlandsche kinderen"* (who were neither natives [*inlandsche*] nor children [*kinderen*], as a literal translation would suggest) could mark those of mixed background, those of illegitimate birth, or, just as easily, those Europeans whose attachments to, and familiarity with, things Javanese were considered dangerously unsuitable for a colonial situation.

Debates on the *Inlandsche kinderen* were driven by implicit notions of racial decorum, and anxious concern over the nonvisual criteria of racial membership. If easily distinguished from both well-heeled Europeans and the native and Chinese population, there was less consensus about who they were. Sometimes the term *Inlandsche kinderen* was used for those Europeans born in the Indies (as the term *los hijos del pais* was used in the

---

[46] Ian Hacking, "Two Kinds of 'New Historicism' for Philosophers," *New Literary History* 21 (2) (Winter 1990): 343–64, 359.

[47] Gilles Deleuze, *Foucault* (Minneapolis: University of Minnesota Press, 1992), 17.

[48] Ibid., 50.

Philippines for Spaniards born in the colony);[49] elsewhere it served to designate the impoverished mixed blood population, but there is no consistency. Sometimes those of "mixed race" (*gemengd ras*) were not included, the term implicitly being reserved not for all Europeans born in the colony but for destitute whites whose circumstances and cultural affiliations marked them as not quite European.

But the term disappears almost as abruptly as it came into use. Whatever politics of identification and guardianship might have animated its currency in the late nineteenth century when unpublished commissions on white impoverishment were written, by the time of the published commission in 1902 the term was in decline, and by the 1920s, with racialized distinctions increasingly codified, largely abandoned.[50]

Such discrepancies are neither misrecognitions nor cultural "mistakes" to be set aside. They provide a diacritics of the patent and latent distinctions that marked the colonial epistemology of race.[51] Actively under scrutiny throughout the second half of the nineteenth century, by the 1920s the term *Inlandsche kinderen* had morphed into other designations. Newly fashioned taxonomies that more clearly identified the covert attributes of racial membership, eclipsing the earlier term. It is precisely those moments of difficulty, the "breach of the self-evident," by which Foucault designates an "event." It is such "uncertainty" in the order of things that enlists us to locate such sites for ethnography and problematization.[52]

Ethnographic sensibilities guide my forays into the nature of Dutch colonial rule and its archival formations in what I take to be another basic way; namely, in attention to what the philosopher C. S. Peirce calls the "habit-taking" processes by which people align themselves with forces that are already there. Habit-taking works off colonial conventions and their common sense and is part of their making. These were the "grids of intelligibility" that made certain conventions acceptable, obvious, and

---

[49] See Paul Willem Johan van der Veur, "The Eurasians of Indonesia: A Problem and Challenge in Colonial History," in *Journal of Southeast Asian Studies* 9 (2) (1968): 191–207. Van der Veur holds that in the mid-nineteenth century the term was synonymous with the "colored" (*kleurlingen*), though such a broad definition was rarely used. He also underscores that *Inlandsche kinderen* "was used to designate Eurasians *and* Dutchmen born in the Indies during this period"[ibid.; emphasis in original]. See also idem, *Introduction to a Socio-Political Study of the Eurasians of Indonesia*, Ph.D. diss., Cornell University, 1955.

[50] Compare, for example, A. van Delden's "Nota's over de *Inlandsche kinderen*" from 1872 and the published reports of the European Pauperism Commission in 1901–1902.

[51] On the "patent and latent" attributes of racial assessments, see my "Racial Histories and their Regimes of Truth," *Political Power and Social Theory* 11 (1997): 183–206.

[52] Paul Rabinow, *Anthropos Today: Reflections on Modern Equipment* (Princeton: Princeton University Press, 2003), 41–42.

familiar—or discordant and strange. My concern is with the *conditions of epistemic choice and chance*, of inculcation and innovation. I ask how people charged with large-scale management and local situations imagined they might identify what they knew they could not see, what common sense they used to assess racial belonging or political desires that were not available to ocular senses, how they distinguished politically motivated passions from private ones.

Anthropology has no privileged claim on the study of common sense nor the epistemologies that underwrite it. But as Michael Herzfeld argues, anthropology may have special purchase on how to go about its *comparative* study.[53] I am less sure we can really make that claim. For such expertise in common sense we would need to become far more proficient at studying the *changing parameters* of common sense, how common sense is rendered *uncommon*, and how people know it. Michael Polanyi refers to a "tacit dimension," Mary Douglas to "implicit meaning," Pierre Bourdieu to "habitus," Charles Taylor to an "implicit understanding,"—the distilled dispositions and trained capacities that work through bodies and on them.[54] Each, with different emphasis, identifies those habits of heart, mind, and comportment that derive from unstated understandings of how things work in the world, the categories to which people belong, and the kind of knowledge one needs to hold unarticulated but well-rehearsed convictions and credulities.

But what constitutes common sense is at once historical and political; colonial contexts teach us clearly that dispositions are trained and disciplined and not without deliberation. Like habitus, they are neither uniform nor uncontested. Dispositions emerge out of a habitus that is rejected, accepted, or uneasily accommodated. Dispositions are not given, they are interpretations, discerned and made.[55] Nor were they always below the threshold of reflective surveillance.[56] To my mind, this shaping of common sense, and the reigning in of uncommon sense, together make up the substance of colonial governance and its working epistemologies. By Bourdieu's account "habitus is that presence of the past in the

[53] Michael Herzfeld, *Anthropology: Theoretical Practice in Culture and Society* (Malden, Mass.: Blackwell, 2001), 1.

[54] See Michael Polyani, *The Tacit Dimension* (Garden City, N.Y.: Anchor, 1967); Mary Douglas, *Implicit Meanings: Essays in Anthropology* (London: Routledge and Kegan Paul, 1975); Pierre Bourdieu, *Outline of a Theory of Practice* (Cambridge: Cambridge University Press, 1977); and Charles Taylor, *Modern Social Imaginaries* (Durham, N.C.: Duke University Press, 2004), 26.

[55] Clifford Geertz, "Common Sense as a Cultural System," in *Local Knowledge: Further Essays in Interpretive Anthropology,* (New York: Basic, 1983), 73–93.

[56] William Connolly, *Why I Am Not a Secularist* (Minneapolis: University of Minnesota Press, 1999), 28.

present."[57] What I call "epistemic habits" are steeped in history and historical practices, ways of knowing that are available and "easy to think," called-upon, temporarily settled dispositions that can be challenged and that change. Epistemic habits share some of the properties that Hacking's assigns to "rock-bottom givens"—they produce "permanent momentary items of [implicit] fact."[58]

Rather than treating epistemology as a domain of the foundational, architectural, and fixed (I think here against Richard Rorty's claim that "time will tell but epistemology won't"), I start from a premise shared by students of historical and social epistemology: that epistemic considerations are neither transcendent nor abstract.[59] They are of the colonial world and squarely in it. Colonial governance entailed a constant assessing and recapping of what colonial agents could know and how they could know it. Central to all the chapters in this book, then, is an engagement with this disquiet: with colonialism's unevenly shared epistemic formations, the varying uneasiness and differential discomforts about what could be assumed to be communicable and circulated—or unrepeatable and not subject to the economy of official exchange. Epistemic formations "provide us with the possible, with the thinkable, with the constellations of concepts that are in question, what people assume to know about their worlds and how they disagree over them."[60]

Affective Strains

But even these terms of "debatability" may be up for grabs.[61] Chapter 3, "Habits of a Colonial Heart," explores the messy space between reason and sentiment, the sort of elusive knowledge on which political assessments were dependent and often had to be made. One is reminded of Weber's contention that bureaucracies excise those domains they cannot measure, that

---

[57] Pierre Bourdieu, "Social Being, Time and the Sense of Existence," in Bourdieu, *Pascalian Meditations* (Stanford: Stanford University Press, 1999), 210.

[58] Hacking (2002), 13.

[59] Richard Rorty, *Philosophy and the Mirror of Nature* (Princeton: Princeton University Press, 1979), 4. It is not really "epistemology," as I use it here, to which Rorty's attack is aimed but at a philosophy that imagines itself endowed as the foundational and privileged "tribunal of pure reason," unfettered by history.

[60] Margaret Somers, "Where is Sociology after the Historic Turn?," in *The Historic Turn in the Human Sciences* (Ann Arbor: University of Michigan Press, 1996), 71. Somers is not among those included in Ian Hacking's review of a growing corpus of literature on historical epistemology. For her perceptive work that has paralleled and sometimes preceded the authors he cites, see also Somers, "The Privatization of Citizenship: How to Unthink a Knowledge Culture," in *Beyond the Cultural Turn*, ed. Victoria E. Bonnell and Lynn Hunt (Berkeley: University of California Press, 1999), 121–61.

[61] Arjun Appadurai, "The Past as a Scarce Resource," *Man* 16: 201–19.

"bureaucracy develops . . . the more completely it succeeds in eliminating from official business love, hatred, and all purely personal, irrational, and emotional elements which escape calculation."[62] By Weber's criteria, the Dutch colonial bureaucracy was at best an imperfect success. "Emotional elements," personal grudges, long-harbored resentments, whether assaults should be taken as acts of personal affront or political subversion, might have escaped calculation but they were deeply part of what Douglas Holmes has called the "para-ethnography" of the lay world—queries and details of the everyday that had to be sensed and could not be measured by enumeration.[63]

Managed hearts were critical to colonialism's political grammar. Imperial projects called upon specific sentiments, and assessed racial membership, in part by locating appropriate carriers and recipients of those feelings. To whom one expressed attachment as opposed to pity, contempt, indifference, or disdain provided both cultural and legal "proof" of who one was, where one ranked in the colonial order of things, and thus where one racially belonged.

Colonial statecraft required the calibration of sympathies and attachments, managing different degrees of subjugation both among its agents and those colonized. Being a taxonomic state meant more than setting out categories; it meant producing and harnessing those sentiments that would make sense of those distinctions and make them work. Reason may be the "public touchstone of truth," but it is anchored in sensibilities, as Kant insisted, and in affective states.[64]

Sentiments are not opposed to political reason but are at once modalities and tracers of it. Here I treat sentiments as judgments, assessments, and interpretations of the social and political world.[65] They are also incisive markers of rank and the unstated rules of exemption. How and to whom sentiments of remorse or rage, compassion or contempt were conveyed and displayed measured degrees of social license that colonial rela-

---

[62] Weber (1946), 975.

[63] Douglas R. Holmes and George E. Marcus, "Fast Capitalism: Paraethnography and the Rise of the Symbolic Analyst," in *Frontiers of Capital: Ethnographic Perspectives on the New Economy*, ed. Melissa Fisher and Greg Downey (Durham, N.C.: Duke University Press, 2006), 34–57.

[64] Immanuel Kant, *Political Writings*. ed. Hans Reiss and trans. H. B. Nisbet (Cambridge: Cambridge University Press, 1970), 146.

[65] Similar points have been eloquently made by others. See, for example, Robert Solomon, "On Emotions as Judgments," *American Philosophical Quarterly* 25 (1988): 183–91, and, more recently, Martha Nussbaum, "Emotions as Judgments of Value," in Nussbaum, *Upheavals of Thought: The Intelligence of Emotions* (Cambridge: Cambridge University Press, 2001), 19–88.

tions so inequitably conferred.[66] To underscore this crucial point: expressions of sentiment depended on situated knowledge and thus relational know-how about rank—where and to whom one displayed one's range of feeling within that prescriptive world. Archival documents participate in this emotional economy in some obvious ways: in the measured tone of official texts; in the biting critique reserved for marginalia; in footnotes to official reports where moral assessments of cultural practice were often relegated and local knowledge was stored.[67] Not unlike Steven Shapin's tracking of the social history of truth in the seventeenth century, I ask who and what was granted epistemological virtue, with what cultural competencies, and by what social criteria.[68]

If colonial archives were nurseries of legal knowledge and official repositories of policy, they were also repositories of good taste and bad faith. Scribes often wrote out the final, clean copy but not always. "Semi-official" correspondence, and certainly personal letters, could be directly penned by their authors. Reports to the Governor-General in Batavia and to the Minister of Colonies in The Hague were composed by men of letters whose status was enhanced by reference to Greek heroes and French bons mots. Such proof of competence and good judgment was demonstrated in no small part by configuring events into familiar and recognizable plots. In empire's "lettered cities" of administrative work, virtue was defined by limited and selective familiarity with the Indies.[69] Those with too much knowledge of things Javanese were penalized, as were those with not enough.[70]

But administrative anxiety was also rightly riveted on those affective states of European colonials that could not be easily gauged, on those not within the state's reach to manage or assess. The public demonstration by European and creole whites in Batavia in May 1848, when family attachments threatened to crash against the demands for state loyalty, underscored

---

[66] On contempt, condescension, and insolence as markers of social rank, see Don Herzog, "The Politics of Emotions," in *Poisoning the Minds of the Lower Orders* (Princeton: Princeton University Press, 1998), 202–43. On contempt as "what the honorable have the right to show for the less honorable," see William Ian Miller, *The Anatomy of Disgust* (Cambridge, Mass.: Harvard University Press, 1997), 206–34, 225.

[67] On footnotes as the lines that lead into moral communities and their claims to truth, see Anthony Grafton, *The Footnote: A Curious History* (Cambridge, Mass.: Harvard University Press, 1997).

[68] Steven Shapin, *The Social History of Truth: Civility and Science in Seventeenth-Century England* (Chicago: University of Chicago Press, 1994).

[69] On the "lettered cities" of early colonial Latin America, see Angel Rama's exquisite rendition of the power of written discourse among the "*letrados*" in the making of Spanish rule in Rama, *The Lettered City* (Durham, N.C.: Duke University Press, 1996.)

[70] See Fanny Colonna, "Educating Conformity in French Colonial Algeria," in Colonna, *Tensions of Empire* (Berkeley: University of California Press, 1997), 346–70.

that those in charge of the city and the colony knew how much habits of the heart could not be contained as the "private"; they could as easily spiral into a political field not in the state's control. At issue was the contagious, transient quality of sentiment and its portability. Whether certain sentiments were politically dangerous because they were local or because they were smuggled in on the last mail boat via Paris newspapers and by word of mouth, they really did not know.

If epistemology was once the term given to *formal* theories of knowledge and their systematic study, students of social and historical epistemology have since taken it in a very different, worldly direction. Armed with a vocabulary of (epistemic) community, (epistemic) culture, (epistemic) crisis, and (epistemic) practice, more emphasis is now placed on the procedures and activities on which certain ways of knowing rely, not unlike what De Certeau called historiographic "operations."[71] While such a lexicon is more commonly reserved for the study of scientific communities of experiment and expertise, such an approach offers productive ways of thinking about governing practices that, too, depended on how much conviction, experience, and expertise were shared, and the extent to which architects and agents of rule could count on that common ground.

The epistemic practices of science and colonial governance have something else important in common: a preoccupation with the taming of chance."[72] Much as classical probability theory was to measure the incertitudes of a modernizing world, colonial civil servants were charged to do the same.[73] Both ventures approach the conventions and categories of analysis as neither innocuous nor benign. As interpretive communities, both depend on rules of reliability and trust, on an assumed common sense about what was likely, that allow prediction and direct the political projects that those plausibilities serve.

Both are also communities of expectation. If the sciences participate in "a permanent process of . . . reshuffling . . . the boundary between what is

---

[71] See Michel de Certeau, "The Historiographic Operation," in de Certeau, *The Writing of History* (New York: Columbia University Press, 1988), 56–85. On epistemic cultures, see, among others, K. Knorr-Cetina, "Epistemics in Society: On the Nesting of Knowledge Structures into Social Structures," in *Rural Reconstruction in a Market Economy*, ed. W. Hijman, H. Hetsen, and J. Frouws, Mansholt Studies 5 (Wageningen: Mansholt, 1996), 55–73, and Knorr-Cetina, *Epistemic Cultures: How the Sciences Make Knowledge* (Cambridge, Mass.: Harvard University Press, 1999.) On epistemic crisis, see Alisdair Macintrye, "Epistemological Crises, Dramatic Narrative and the Philosophy of Science," *Monist* 60 (4) (October 1977): 453–72.

[72] Ian Hacking, *The Taming of Chance* (New York: Cambridge University Press, 1990).

[73] See Mary Poovey, *A History of the Modern Fact: Problems of Knowledge in the Sciences of Wealth and Society* (Chicago: University of Chicago Press, 1998); and Lorraine Daston, *Classical Probability in the Enlightenment* (Princeton: Princeton University Press, 1995).

thought to be known and what is beyond imagination," colonial governance did much the same.[74] Sound conjecture and expectation can make governing strategies work, or as anticolonial movements have amply demonstrated, make them violently fail. And like scientific communities, new objects emerge between what one does "not quite yet know" and that for which there is not yet a name. Such epistemic objects are produced in the haze of what historian of science Hans-Jorg Rheniberger calls "a mixture of hard and soft," or, as Michel Serres puts it, "object, still, sign, already; sign still, object already."[75] The making of colonial categories shares this ambiguous epistemic space. New social objects were the archives' product as much as subjects of them.

The notion that "granting epistemic warrant is a covert way of distributing power" underwrites colonial studies in some of the field's most productive projects, which trace both veiled epistemic authority as well as blatantly assertive forms of control.[76] But just how that warrant was granted, how firmly entrenched, and how much debate accompanied that process is less often pursued. Some of the problem may be with an overcommitment to Foucault's vocabulary. An "episteme" has come to index a scale, longevity, and hardening of thought-formations that can set us astray. A "regime of truth" suggests a durability of distinctions, a finite field of truth-claims that colonial knowledge-production would never attain.[77] As I will argue in chapter 3, understanding "what happened" in May 1848 calls on different vectors of intelligibility, alternate causalities and attributions of affect that crossed and met. I use the terms "grids of intelligibility" and "regimes of truth" cautiously, with the caveat that both mark epistemic habits and ways of knowing cut through with competing investments and altering claims. As these archives of the Indies' colonial agents and architects evince, it was not epistemic clarity but epistemic uncertainty that generated the densest debates and the longest paper trails that wound their way through a range of seemingly unrelated subjects. Like imperial formations themselves, colonial truth-claims were provisional and subject to change.

[74] Hans-Jorg Rheinberger, *Toward a History of Epistemic Things: Synthesizing Proteins in the Test Tube* (Stanford: Stanford University Press, 1997), 11.

[75] Michel Serres, quoted in ibid., 28–29.

[76] Quoted in Steven Fuller, *Social Epistemology* (Bloomington: Indiana University Press, 2002), 10. See Dipesh Chakrabarty's *Provincializing Europe* (Princeton: Princeton University Press, 2000), which cogently makes the case for "documenting how [European] 'reason,' which was not always self-evident to everyone, has been made to look obvious far beyond the ground where it originated," 43. As I argue here, lack of the "self-evident" permeated the tissue of imperial governance, producing confused policies born of epistemic anxiety among European colonials themselves.

[77] Among the many places Foucault invokes "regimes of truth," see "Truth and Power," in Foucault, *Power/Knowledge* (New York: Pantheon, 1980), 132.

Tracing the Archival Turn

If "the transformation of archival activity is the point of departure and the condition of a new history," as De Certeau has argued, we are clearly in a new moment.[78] The warning of E. E. Evans-Pritchard in 1951 that anthropologists tended to be "uncritical in their use of documentary sources" had little resonance then.[79] So, too, did F. W. Maitland's earlier dictum that anthropology had "the choice between being history or being nothing."[80] Both pronouncements read as fairly quaint today.[81] Among historians, literary critics and anthropologists, archives have been elevated to new analytic status with distinct billing, worthy of scrutiny on their own. One might be tempted to see this as a Derridian effect of the last decade that followed on the publication of *Archive Fever*.[82] But the archival turn has a wider arc and a longer durée. *Archive Fever* compellingly captured that impulse by giving it theoretical stature, but Jacques Derrida's intervention came only after the "archival turn" was already being made.

This move from archive-as-source to archive-as-subject gained currency across the richly undisciplined space of critical history and in a range of fields energized by that reformulation.[83] The sheer number of volumes devoted to "the archive" is staggering: in film and literary studies, in analyses of truth commissions or the human genome project,

[78] De Certeau (1988), 75.

[79] E. E. Evans-Pritchard, "Anthropology and History," in Evans-Pritchard, *Social Anthropology and Other Essays* (Glencoe, N.Y.: Free Press, 1962).

[80] F. W. Maitland, *Selected Essays* (Cambridge: Cambridge University Press, 1936). 249. It was later famously quoted by E. E. Evans-Pritchard in "Social Anthropology: Past and Present, The Marett Lecture, 1950," in Evans-Pritchard (1962), 152.

[81] Some might argue that anthropology's engagement with history has been less a "turn" than a return to its founding principles, an enquiry into cumulative processes of cultural production but without the typological aspirations and evolutionary assumptions once embraced. Others counter that the feverish turn to history has represented a significant departure, a new kind of rupture with anthropology's complicity in colonial politics. Both might agree that the move signals a new way of thinking about the politics of knowledge, what a "colonial legacy" means in practice—the categories, conceptual frame, and practices of colonial authorities that have permeated anthropology's central concerns.

[82] Jacques Derrida, *Archive Fever: A Freudian Impression* (Chicago: University of Chicago Press, 1995).

[83] Sonia Combe, *Archives Interdites: Les peur françaises face à l'Histoire contemporaine.* (Paris: Albin Michel, 1994.) Dominick LaCapra, too, notes that the "problem of reading in the archives has increasingly become a concern of those doing archival research" in La-Capra, "History, Language, and Reading: Waiting for Crillon," *AHR* 100 (3) (June 1995): 807. See also a special issue on "The Archive," *History of the Human Sciences* 11 (4) (November 1998), and *Penser l'Archive: Histoire d'Archives-Archives d'Histoire*, ed. Mauro Cerutti, Jean-Francois Fayet, and Michel Porret (Lausanne: Antipodes, 2006.)

from rereadings of histories of colonialism to those of gay rights.[84] "Reading" here is an agentive act, one squarely focused on what we know and how we know it. Focus on the politics of knowledge is a methodological commitment to how history's exclusions are secured and made.

One could argue that "the archive" for historians and "the Archive" for cultural theorists have been wholly different analytic objects: for the former, a body of documents and the institutions that house them, for the latter a metaphoric invocation for any corpus of selective collections and the longings that the acquisitive quests for the primary, originary, and untouched entail.[85] Those differences might suggest sharply defined domains, but the blurring that is so common today is hardly a recent intervention.[86] For, indeed, something resembling the broader social life of an archive, what might be called "ethnography in an archival mode," has been around for some time. Carlo Ginzburg's microhistory of a sixteenth-century miller, like Natalie Davis's use of pardon tales, drew on "hostile" documents to reveal "the gap between the image underlying the interrogations of judges and the actual testimony of the accused."[87] Both questioned "how people told stories, what they thought a good story was, how they accounted for motive." In Davis's notion of "fiction in the archives," she worked through pardon tales to reveal both the "constraints of the law" and its popular manipulations, both the terms of argumentation and the broader set of literary forms invoked to support or undermine those claims.[88] Still, these were not ethnographies *of* the archive, but in it.

Archivists have been thinking about the politics and history of archives in ways that increasingly speak to a broader community of

---

[84] Among many others, see Carolyn Hamilton, Verne Harris, Jane Taylor, Michele Pickover, Graham Reid, and Razia Saleh, eds., *Refiguring the Archive* (Capetown: David Philip, 2002), and references throughout this chapter.

[85] For this metaphoric move, see the two special issues of *History of the Human Sciences* devoted to The Archive (11 [4] [November 1998] and 12 [2] [May 1999]). Derrida's valorization of "the archive" as imaginary and metaphor is predominant in both. On the archive as metaphor, see also Allan Sekula, "The Body and the Archive," *October* 39 (Winter 1986): 3–64.

[86] See, for example, Patrick Geary, *Phantoms of Remembrance: Memory and Oblivion at the End of the First Millennium* (Princeton: Princeton University Press, 1994), esp. 81–114. On contemporary forms of documentation see, Annalies Riles, ed. *Documents: Artifacts of Modern Knowledge* (Ann Arbor: University of Michigan Press, 2006).

[87] Carlo Ginzburg, *The Cheese and the Worms: The Cosmos of a Sixteenth-Century Miller* (New York: Penguin, 1982), xvii, xviii.

[88] Natalie Davis, "Fiction in the Archives," in Davis, *Pardon Tales and Their Tellers in Sixteenth-Century France* (Stanford: Stanford University Press, 1987), 4.

scholars.[89] What marks the past decade are the new conversations between archivists and historians about documentary evidence, record keeping, what features of archival form and content can be retrieved, and how
decisions should be made about historical significance and preservation.[90]
As storage technology revamps, both question what information matters,
what tacit narratives inform contemporary archival practices, and what
should be retained as archives' physical forms change.[91] All are asking what
new accessibilities and connections are gained—and lost—when parchment
and paper gave way to digital recordings.

Colonialism's Archival Grains

> Genealogy is gray, meticulous and patiently documentary. It
> operates on a field of entangled and confused parchments, on
> documents that have been scratched over and recopied many
> times.
>
> —Michel Foucault, "Archaeology of Knowledge"

If one were to characterize what has informed a critical approach to the
colonial archives, it would be a commitment to the notion of reading

---

[89] On the history of archives and how archivists have thought about them, see Ernst Pos-
ner, "Some Aspects of Archival Development since the French Revolution" [1940], in *A
Modern Archives Reader*, ed. Maygene Daniels and Timothy Walch (Washington, D.C.: Na-
tional Archives and Record Service), 3–21. See also *Les Archives*, in the series *Que Sais-Je?*
(Paris: Presses Universitaires de France, 1959). See also Eric Ketelaar, *The Archival Image:
Critical Essays* (Hilversum: Verloren, 1997).

[90] See Marlene Manoff, "Theories of the Archive from Across the Disciplines," *Libraries
and the Academy* 4 (l) (2004): 9–25; Richard Berner, *Archival Theory and Practice in the
United States: An Historical Analysis* (Seattle: University of Washington Press, 1983); Kenneth E. Foote, "To Remember and Forget: Archives, Memory, and Culture" *American
Archivist* 53 (3) (1990): 378–93; Terry Cook, "Mind over Matter: Towards a New Theory
of Archival Appraisal," in *The Archival Imagination: Essays in Honour of Hugh A. Taylor*
(Ottawa: Association of Canadian Archivists, 1992), 38–69; James M. O'Toole, "On the
Idea of Uniqueness," *American Archivist* 57 (4) (1994): 632–59. For some sense of the
changes in how archivists themselves have framed their work over the last twenty years, see
the *American Archivist*, and, most recently, *Archives, Documentation and Institutions of
Social Memory: Essays from the Sawyer Seminar*, ed. Francis X. Blouin Jr. and William G.
Rosenberg (Ann Arbor: University of Michigan Press, 2006) and "Archives, Records, and
Power," a special issue (2 [1–2] [2002]) of *Archival Science*, guest-edited by Terry Cook and
Joan M. Schwartz.

[91] Terry Cook, "Electronic Records, Paper Minds: The revolution in information management and archives in the post-custodial and post-modernist era," in *Archives and Manuscripts* 22 (2) (1994): 300–329. See also Eric Ketelaar, "Tacit Narratives: The Meanings of
Archives," *Archival Science* 2001 (1): 131–41.

colonial archives "against their grain" of imperial history, empire builders, and the priorities and perceptions of those who wrote them. Schooled to think "from the bottom up," students of colonialism located "structure" with colonizers and the colonial state, and "human agency" with subalterns, in small gestures of refusal and silence among the colonized.

In reading "upper-class sources upside down," we sought to read against the languages of rule and statist perceptions. "Un-State-d" histories were to demonstrate more than the warped reality of official knowledge, to elucidate their textual properties and the violences condoned by such political distortions. In Ranajit Guha's influential formulations, colonial documents were rhetorical sleights-of-hand that erased the facts of subjugation, reclassified petty crime as political subversion, or located violence and unreason as inherent to the colonized.[92] The analytic tactics pursued have been those of inversion and recuperation, recasting colonial subjects as agents who made and make choices and critiques of their own.

Insistence on the link between what counts as knowledge and who is in power to record their versions of it has since become a founding principle of colonial ethnography. Such analyses invite other, more challenging pursuits. In treating archival documents not as the historical ballast to ethnography, but as a charged site of it, I see the call for an emergent methodological shift: to move away from treating the archives as an *extractive* exercise to an ethnographic one. That call has been taken up differently: sometimes hotly pursued, other times merely a nod in that analytic direction. For some it represents a turn back to the powerful "poetics of detail."[93] To others the archival turn provides a way to cut through the distorted optics of colonial historiography and the distinctions that cordone off fiction from authorized truths.[94]

---

[92] See Ranajit Guha, *Dominance without Hegemony: History and Power in Colonial India* (Cambridge, Mass.: Harvard University Press, 1997), where some of Guha's early essays published between 1988–1992 are collected.

[93] See Greg Dening, *The Death of William Gooch: A History's Anthropology* (Honolulu: University of Hawaii Press, 1995).

[94] Trouillot, 6–10. See also David William Cohen, *The Combing of History* (Chicago: University of Chicago Press, 1994). Foucault's insistence that the archive forms a system of enunciabilities rather than all the texts that a culture preserves or those institutions that store them guides Thomas Richards's treatment of the British imperial archive as "the fantastic representation of an epistemological master pattern." See Thomas Richards, *The Imperial Archive: Knowledge and the Fantasy of Empire* (London: Verso, 1993), 11. For Richards, Hilton's *Lost Horizon* and Kipling's *Kim* are entries in a Victorian archive that was the "prototype for a global system of domination through circulation, an apparatus for controlling territory by producing, distributing and consuming information about it." See also Michel Foucault, *The Archaeology of Knowledge* (1972), 79–134. On the archives as an "instituting imaginary," see also Achille Mbembe, "The Power of the Archive and Its

Michel-Rolph Trouillot noted with consummate clarity that "historical narratives are premised on previous understandings, which are themselves premised on the distribution of archival power."[95] More importantly, he offered neophytes to archival work a way to tackle what De Certeau meant by "historiographic operations" by distinguishing the archival power lodged in moments of creation from practices of assembly, retrieval, and disciplinary legitimation.[96] If Trouillot urged students to distinguish among these different operations, Nicholas Dirks' call for "a biography of the archive" insisted on examining who was performing that labor by showing to what extent early colonial officials cum historians in British India were dependent on native informants who did the work of collection and cultural translation for them.[97] But "mining" for treasures rather than immersement is still a prevalent approach to archives and an all too expedient research mode.

Feminist historians have long sought out creative ways of demonstrating how, what Bonnie Smith aptly dubbed, "male prowess" shaped archival production, the initiation rites of historiography, and the absence of agentive histories of women excised from documents and excluded from subsequent texts.[98] On colonial terrain the challenge to locate women as subjects continues to critically stretch the scope of the archive in ways that redefine what kinds of reading and writing are historically germane.[99]

Limits," in Hamilton et al., 19–26. Roberto Gonzalez Echevarria's subtle analysis of the grounding of Latin American literary narrative in the early Spanish colonial state's styles of documentation also bears that stamp. See Roberto Gonzalez Echevarria, *Myth and Archive: A Theory of Latin American Narrative* (Cambridge: Cambridge University Press, 1990). Both Richards and Gonzalez Echevarria take the archive as a template that decodes something else, and both push us to think differently about "archival fictions," though they reserve their analyses for literature rather than colonial archives themselves.

[95] Trouillot, 55.

[96] Ibid., 54.

[97] Nicholas Dirks, "Colonial Histories and Native Informants: Biography of an Archive," in van der Veer and Breckenridge, 279–313. See also Christopher Bayly, *Empire and Information: Intelligence Gathering and Social Communication in India, 1780–1870* (Cambridge: Cambridge University Press, 1996), whose attention to the British intelligence service's work through native channels similarly highlights the local purveyors of knowledge to which Europeans were so beholden.

[98] Bonnie G. Smith, "Gender and the Practices of Scientific History: The Seminar and Archival Research in the Nineteenth Century," *American Historical Review* 100 (4–5) (1995): 1150–76.

[99] Antoinette Burton, *Dwelling in the Archive: Women Writing House, Home and History in Late Colonial India* (New York: Oxford, 2003); and Betty Joseph, *Reading the East India Company, 1720–1840: Colonial Currencies of Gender* (Chicago: University of Chicago Press, 2004). See also Durba Ghosh, "Decoding the nameless: gender, subjectivity and historical methodologies in reading the archives of colonial India," in *A New Imperial History*, ed. Kathleen Wilson (New York: Cambridge University Press, 2004), 297–316; Anjai Arondekar, "Without a Trace: Sexuality and the Colonial Archive," *Journal of the History of Sexuality* 14 (1–2) (January–April 2005): 10–27; and Stoler (2006).

My own first sense of what I call here "the pulse of the archive" came decades ago when I found myself confronted with reports on the horrific mutilation and murder of a European planter's wife and children in 1876 on Sumatra's East Coast. Multiple reports were collected on the murder, preceding attacks, and speculation on both the most immediate affronts and distant uprisings to which the murder might be linked. Even detailed accounts sometimes were unfettered by specific knowledge of the assault. In an earlier version of chapter 6, I explored how rumor ricocheted between planters and the workers they feared and the insurgents they ignored, undoing facile distinctions between reliable and conjured information, between fact and fantasy, between mad paranoia and political reality.[100] The contrast between neat copy and hurried hand, tidy statements and quick-paced query and response, enraged and tempered narrative, fine-grained knowledge and unabashed ignorance—all struck me as startling testimonies to the workings of empire and to what we still did not know about it.[101] Those challenges remain at the heart of this book and with me today.

Most students of the colonial, who now work with archives in a reflective mode, treat "the archive" as something in between a set of documents, their institutions, and a repository of memory—both a place and a cultural space that encompass official documents but are not confined to them. Some of the most creative work branches out to the range of scripted and performed practices that bear the psychic and material stamp of colonial relations.

Here I do something else: several chapters stay largely within the state's purview by attending to documents viewed by state officials but not always produced by them. As I use the term, the Dutch colonial "archives" were both a corpus of statements and a depot of documents, both sites of the imaginary and institutions that fashioned histories as they concealed, revealed, and contradicted the investments of the state.[102] Power and control, as students of archiving are quick to point out, are fundamental to the

---

[100] Ann Laura Stoler, "In Cold Blood: Hierarchies of Credibility and the Politics of Colonial Narratives," *Representations* 37 (1992): 1–18. For an innovative treatment of the work of colonial rumors as the site of the fantastically real, see Luise White, *Speaking with Vampires; Rumor and History in Colonial Africa* (Berkeley: University of California Press, 2000).

[101] Those challenges prompted the 1996 Lewis Henry Morgan lectures I gave on "Ethnography in the Archives" and years of subsequent seminars bearing that title.

[102] This link between state power and what counts as history was long ago made by Hegel in *The Philosophy of History*, as Hayden White points out: "It is only the state which first presents subject-matter that is not only adapted to the prose of History, but involves the production of such history in the very progress of its own being." White, *The Content of the Form* (Baltimore: The Johns Hopkins University Press,1987), 12.

etymology of the word "archive" and should need no iteration.[103] Moralizing stories mapped the scope of state vision, the restricted limits of government responsibility, and what were defined as its beneficent missions.

Nor were they to be read in any which way. Issues were rendered important by where they appeared, how they were cross-referenced, where they were catalogued, and thus how they were framed. Official exchanges between Governors-General and their subordinates, between Governors-General and Ministers of Colonies, and between the latter and the King served as reference guides to administrative thinking; they were abbreviated "cheat sheets" of what counted as precedent and what properly fell under "concerns of state." Some reports were meticulously scrutinized, others were carelessly read and set aside. Archival convention, however, dictated that all were abundantly cross-referenced in ways that produced paths of precedent and mapped relevance. Citation also served, not unlike footnotes, to affirm the import of one's observations, choice of historical context, and implicitly the legitimacy of one's selected narrative.[104]

Some would argue that the grand narratives of colonialism have been amply and excessively told. On this argument, students of colonialisms often turn quickly and confidently to read "against the grain" of colonial conventions. One fundamental premise of this book is a commitment to a less assured and perhaps more humble stance—to explore the grain with care and read along it first. Assuming we know those scripts rests too comfortably on predictable stories with familiar plots. Such a stance leaves intact the assumption that colonial statecraft was always intent on accumulating more knowledge rather than on a selective winnowing and reduction of it. The assumption may accept too quickly the equation of knowledge to power and that colonial states sought more of both.[105] Not least, it leaves unaddressed how often colonial categories reappear in the analytic vocabulary of historians rather than as transient, provisional objects of historical inquiry that themselves need to be analyzed, if not explained.[106]

Colonial archives were sites of command—but of countermand as well. "Factual storytellings"—a phrase Hayden White uses to define what

---

[103] From the Latin *archivuum*, "residence of the magistrate," and from the Greek *arkhe*, "to command." See Gonzalez Echevarria, 31–34, for a detailed etymology of the term, and see Derrida (1995), 1–3, for his characteristically exquisite treatment of the conceptual entailments of "the archive" as that which commands, shelters, and conceals itself as it gathers together signs.

[104] On footnotes as the pathways into moral communities and their claims to truth, see Grafton.

[105] For a careful treatment of this culling project, see Amin.

[106] For a discussion of this issue, see my "Caveats on Comfort Zones and Comparative Frames," in Stoler, *Carnal Knowledge and Imperial Power: Race and the Intimate in Colonial Rule* (Berkeley: University of California. Press, 2003), 205–17.

counts as history—did not always prevail.[107] Perturbations in the form of discrepant accounts, dissenting voices, and extraneous detail could disable action, unhinge the "facts," and forestall response. Archival power was no more monolithic than the governing practices that it enabled and on which it was based. Subjugated knowledge erupts in contested ontologies of peoples and things. Countervailing interpretations of what compromised danger and threat could send ripples through imperious states and the polished surface of their writerly modes.

As such, I am drawn to think about archival events with and against Foucault's compelling invitation to treat them as "reversals of a relationship of forces, the usurpation of power, the appropriation of a vocabulary turned against those who had once used it."[108] Such an approach undoes the certainty that archives are stable "things" with ready-made and neatly drawn boundaries. But the search for dramatic "reversal," "usurpation," and successful "appropriation" can hide "events" that are more muted in their consequences, less bellicose in their seizures, less spectacular in how and what they reframe. Here I treat archival events more as moments that disrupt (if only provisionally) a field of force, that challenge (if only slightly) what can be said and done, that question (if only quietly) "epistemic warrant," that realign the certainties of the probable more than they mark wholesale reversals of direction.

The Watermarks of Empire

Most of these chapters treat specific government archives of the nineteenth-century Netherlands Indies and the problems their authors and collators sought to avoid or address. The final chapters are written in a different register, one which responds to lives that slip in and out of the official colonial archives and their instrumental narratives. (Indeed, some readers may want to turn directly to these last two chapters that trace the biographies of empire, and may find it more compelling to read them first.)

In chapter 7, "Imperial Dispositions of Disregard," I question how much we who study the work of empire know about the dispositions of those it empowered. It wrestles with those habits of heart and comportment recruited to the service of colonial governance but never wholly subsumed by it. More directly, it identifies a "politics of disregard," what psychological and political machinations it takes to look away for those who live off and in empire, as Valck did, and as many of us might find

[107] See White, esp. 26–57.
[108] Michel Foucault, "Nietzsche, Genealogy, History," in *Language, Counter-Memory, Practice: Selected Essays and Interviews by Michel Foucault*, ed. Donald Bouchard (Ithaca: Cornell University Press, 1977), 139–64, 154.

ourselves inadvertently doing now. Here I take the story of Frans Carl Valck as told through government archives (chapter 6) and as it appears from a private archive (chapter 7) of a very different sort—the family papers housed in a genealogical bureau established decades after Valck's death by one of his scholarly descendants.

The story of his failed career appears here as a palimpsest, erupting at the tender and fraught center of his relationship with his only child, a daughter from whom he remained estranged for most of their lives. Sometimes the course of his Indies career as a colonial civil servant is centrally framed; sometimes it is irrelevant and only partially visible; elsewhere it is utterly absent, delicately unacknowledged, discreetly erased. Viewed from these differences of time, tone, and place, I imagine what it might take to write a history of empire "in a minor key," through a register that conveys the confused sensibilities that cut across Valck's official record, inflecting the collision and collusion between his personal and public lives. It is thus chapter 7 that opens most directly to one way of thinking a colonial history of the present.

When historical ethnography was just coming into its own, John and Jean Comaroff urged us to "create new colonial archives of our own."[109] Some students of empire have sought new kinds of sources. Others have looked to different ways of approaching familiar archives with questions not yet asked and readings not yet done. In this book, it is unexplored fault lines, ragged edges, and unremarked disruptions to the seamless and smooth surface of colonialism's archival genres over which I linger and then attempt to track. My attention is on the field of entangled documents that have been "scratched over" and crossed-out many times. But it is as much on repetitions, what Edward Said reminds us is always about "filiations" pursued or abandoned. "Repetition cannot long escape the ironies it bears within it," or the histories upon which it calls.[110] In these colonial archives, these repetitions join the disparate, enlist the counterintuitive, and provide the vectors of recuperations and ruptures by making familiar what colonial agents sought to know.

De Certeau defined the science of history as a redistribution in space, the act of changing something into something else. Archival labor, he warned, must do more than "simply adopt former classifications"; it must break away from the constraints of "series H in the National Archives," to be replaced with new "codes of recognition" and "systems of expectation."[111] But such a strategy depends on what we think we already know.

[109] Jean and John Comaroff, *Ethnography and the Historical Imagination* (Boulder, Colo.: Westview Press, 1992).

[110] Edward Said, "On Repetition," in Said, *The World, the Text, and the Critic* (Cambridge, Mass.: Harvard University Press, 1983), 111–25, 125.

[111] See De Certeau, *The Writing of History*, 74–75.

For students of empire, colonial codes of recognition and systems of expectation remain at the elusive center of imperial rule, its implicit plots and its deflecting and resilient narratives.

When Robert Darnton some twenty years ago identified "history in the ethnographic grain" as what cultural history should be about, he had in mind how people make sense of the world and "thought about how they thought."[112] Epistemic anxieties are precisely about that reflection. Here the ethno-graphic is about the graphic, detailed production of social kinds, the archival power that allowed its political deployment, and the grafting of affective states to those inventions. Reading along the archival grain draws our sensibilities to the archive's granular rather than seamless texture, to the rough surface that mottles its hue and shapes its form. Working along the grain is not to follow a frictionless course but to enter a field of force and will to power, to attend to both the sound and sense therein and their rival and reciprocal energies. It calls on us to understand how unintelligibilities are sustained and why empires remain so uneasily invested in them.

[112] Robert Darnton, *The Great Cat Massacre and Other Episodes in French Cultural History* (New York: Vintage, 1984), 3.

PART 1

Colonial Archives and Their Affective States

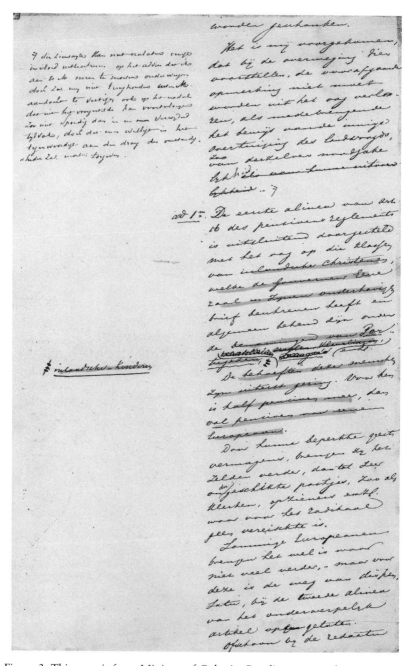

Figure 3. This page is from Minister of Colonies Baud's report to the King. Here is a striking example of how difficult it was at the time to fix terminology to specific social kinds. In his report on who participated in the 22 May 1848 demonstration, the terms *"creolen"* and *"kleurlingen"* were added, then crossed out and substituted with *"Inlandsche kinderen"* in the left margin.

CHAPTER THREE

Habits of a Colonial Heart

MUCH OF COLONIAL STUDIES over the last decade has worked from the shared assumption that the mastery of reason, rationality, and the inflated claims made for Enlightenment principles have been at the political foundation of colonial regimes and should be at the center of critical histories of them. We have looked at what colonial authorities took to be indices of reasoned judgment and the political effects of policies that defined rationality in culturally narrow and prescribed ways—at the epistemological foundations of received categories as much as the content of them. Students of the colonial consistently have argued that the authority to designate what would count as reason and reasonable was colonialism's most insidious and effective technology of rule—one that, in turn, would profoundly affect the style and strategies of anticolonial, nationalist politics.[1]

Viewed in this frame colonial states would seem to conform to a Weberian model of rationally minded, bureaucratically driven states outfitted with a permanent and assured income to maintain them, buttressed by accredited knowledge and scientific legitimacy and backed by a monopoly on weaponed force.[2] Similarly, they have been treated as contained, if not containable, experimental terrains for efficient scientific management and rational social policy, "laboratories of modernity," information-hungry

---

[1] For a sophisticated account of the authority of scientific reason, and colonial and anticolonial claims to it, see Gyan Prakash. *Another Reason: Science and the Imagination of Modern India* (Princeton: Princeton University Press, 1999). See also Ranajit Guha, who describes the "advent of a ruling culture" committed to an "unfolding of Reason" in *Dominance without Hegemony: History and Power in Colonial India* (Cambridge, Mass.: Harvard University Press, 1997), 12. For earlier examples, see Lewis Pyenson, *Empire of Reason* (Leiden: Brill, 1989) and Michael Adas, *Machines as the Measure of Man* (Ithaca: Cornell University Press, 1989). On reason and anticolonial politics, Partha Chatterjee, in *Nationalist Thought and the Colonial World: A Derivative Discourse* (Minneapolis: University of Minnesota Press, 1986), and *The Nation and Its Fragments: Colonial and Postcolonial Histories* (Princeton: Princeton University Press, 1993), has most influentially pressed the view of African and Asian nationalisms as "prisoners of European post-Enlightenment rational discourse." S. P. Mohanty works through the play of reason in cultural relativist arguments in "Us and Them: On the Philosophical Bases of Political Criticism," *Yale Journal of Criticism* 2 (2) (1989): 1–31.

[2] W. G. Runchiman, ed., *Weber: Selections in Translation* (Cambridge: Cambridge University Press, 1994), 40–41.

machines that neither emergent European states nor capitalist enterprises in Europe could yet realize or afford.[3] In both accounts it is the conceit of reason and the celebration of rationality on which imperial authority has been seen to rest—and eventually—to fail and fall.[4]

In this chapter I question continued confidence in that model and what suppositions have supported such claims. For if an homage to reason was a hallmark of the colonial, it was neither pervasive nor persuasive, nor was it empire's sole guiding force.[5] As striking in the nineteenth-century Dutch colonial archive—in its more public as well as its secreted documents, official and private correspondence, commissioned reports, guides to good health and household management, as well as programs of economic reform, primary education, and belles-lettres—is not the rule of reason but what might be (mis)construed as its very opposite: namely, a discursive density around issues of sentiment and their subversive tendencies, around "private" feelings and their political consequences, around racial attribution to sensibilities, and around assessments of affective dispositions and their beneficent and dangerous political effects.

Dutch colonial authorities were troubled by the *distribution* of sentiment, by both its excessive expression and the absence of it; of European fathers too attached to their mixed blood offspring; of Indies-born European children devoid of attachment to their (Dutch) cultural origins; of European-educated children, who, upon return to the Indies, held sympathies and sensibilities out of order and out of place.[6] Administrative debates over social policy were strained over the extent to which the affective attachments colonial agents and subjects held for family, language, and homeland were at odds and whether they should—and could ever—be under the

[3] Gwendolyn Wright, *The Politics of Design in French Colonial Urbanism* (Chicago: University of Chicago Press, 1991).

[4] See Frederick Cooper, "The Dialectics of Decolonization," in *Tensions of Empire: Colonial Cultures in a Bourgeois World*, ed. Frederick Cooper and Ann Laura Stoler (Berkeley: University of California Press, 1997), 406–35. For an earlier period, Sabine MacCormack, in "The Heart Has Its Reasons: Predicaments of Missionary Christianity in Early Colonial Peru," *Hispanic American Historical Review* 65 (3) (1985): 443–66, argues that missionaries moved from an early model of colonization based on persuasion and faith to one of reason and force.

[5] The first rendition of this chapter was delivered at the Comparative Studies in Societal Transformation Conference on "Power in the Disciplines," University of Michigan, 1991. Other versions were given as the 1996 Lewis Henry Morgan Lectures at the University of Rochester, and also at the University of Melbourne, Johns Hopkins University, Stanford University, and Barnard College. A much condensed version without citations was published as "Affective States," in *A Companion to the Anthropology of Politics*, ed. David Nugent and Joan Vincent (Malden, Mass.: Blackwell, 2004).

[6] See my *Carnal Knowledge and Imperial Power* and "Tense and Tender Ties: The Politics of Comparison in North American History and (Post) Colonial Studies," *Journal of American History* 88 (3) (2001):829–65, 893–97.

state's control. Which states of mind and sentiment might be considered concerns of state were questions revisited by those who governed from up close and afar. It pitted Governors-General against Ministers of Colonies, local officials against their superiors, and civil administrators charged with enforcing state directives against the colony's most prominent European city fathers. Here I argue that the "political rationalities" of Dutch colonial authority—those strategically reasoned forms of administrative common sense informing policy and practice—were grounded in the management of such affective states, in assessing both appropriate sentiments and those that threatened to fly "out of control."[7]

The suggestion that fantasy should be resituated "at the heart of our political vocabulary," that the term "state" had a "psychological meaning long before its modern-day sense of polity," is a useful reminder.[8] Students of colonial history would agree, by now well-schooled to take social imaginaries and imagined communities as key concepts for thinking about imperial projects.[9] Fewer have pursued a key correlate: such construals of the social were productive of, and produced by, specific sentiments that were fundamental to the vocabulary of colonial states, and as consequential as was the imperative of "reason" to a "modern-day sense of polity."

Here I consider the management of these "states of sentiment" to be critical to the arts of governance and to which kinds of knowledge of peoples and their passions were required for "reasons of state."[10] While the formal styling of the official archives of the nineteenth-century Dutch East Indies can be read as discourses devoted to the supremacy of reason and rationalized rule, in the first part of this chapter I suggest that they yield a different sense of the colonial when read for the doubts and debates about what was deemed central to administrative practices, which sorts of self-mastery and sensibility were cultivated among their civil servants, which empathies were enlisted, and which sorts of impassioned as

---

[7] David Scott offers a succinct colonial parse on Foucault's notion of political rationality as "those ways in which in which colonial power is organized as an activity designed to produce effects of rule," focused on those "targets of colonial power (the point or points of power's application; the object or objects it aims at; and the means and instrumentalities it deploys in search of these targets, points and objects)" in *Refashioning Futures: Criticism after Postcoloniality* (Princeton: Princeton University Press, 1999), 25.

[8] See Jacqueline Rose, *States of Fantasy* (Oxford: Clarendon, 1996), 4–8, where she argues that "the private and public attributes of the concept 'state' are not opposites but shadows—outer and inner faces precisely—of each other."

[9] See Charles Taylor, *Modern Social Imaginaries* (Durham, N.C.: Duke University Press, 2004), and Benedict Anderson, *Imagined Communities: Reflections on the Origin and Spread of Nationalism* (London: Verso, 1983).

[10] On "reason of state" as an "art" and "technique" of governance, see Michel Foucault's "Omnes et Singulatim," *The Tanner Lectures on Human Values 1979*, ed. Sterling M. McMurrin (Cambridge: Cambridge University Press, 1981), 225–54.

well as disinterested stories they crafted. Colonial states "kept watch" through a fuzzier set of conceptual distinctions than the rubrics of "reason" versus "passions" imply—through a blurred rather than a sharp Cartesian lens. Here I ask how sentiment has been dislocated in colonial studies, and why it has been relegated as the embellishment to, rather than the substance of, governing projects.

Part 2 of this chapter offers a challenge to that analytic convention. It looks to an unprecedented protest on Java, in Batavia—the seat of Dutch authority in the Indies—in May 1848, coinciding with the surge of revolutionary actions on the European continent. In Java it was a protest remarkably organized and attended by both European-born and creole whites—many of whom were themselves respected agents of the state. Its immediate target was clear: a highly restrictive, deliberate, and discriminatory educational policy for the Indies that firmly assured that only those youths schooled in the Netherlands would be eligible for the colony's most coveted civil service posts. But the target was not confined to education alone. It was equally about the racial constraints on rights and representation that aggravated familial bonds and patriotic affiliations. These tensions in turn produced affective surplus that political rationalities could not wholly contain.

The demonstration, its staging, its aftermath, and the arresting accounts of it that circulated in the colony, the Netherlands, and among empire-watchers beyond opens to at least two broader questions: (l) how colonial authorities imagined the *portability* of affective knowledge in a shrinking world with global resonance, in which riots in Paris could be imagined to unseat Dutch rule in Java; and (2) how those same authorities construed the strained relationship between parental dedication and political allegiances (of their agents and potential adversaries) and what urgent efforts they made to educate the affective habits of both.

PART 1: SENSE AND SENSIBILITY IN COLONIAL STUDIES

If, as I claim, a discourse that both speaks of and expresses sentiment is everywhere in the colonial archives, why then has that relationship between its management and colonial governance been so easily sidestepped and so awkward to pose among students of colonial history? At one level the answer may seem obvious.[11] Critical analyses of colonial authority have often treated the affective as a smokescreen of rule, as the ruse masking the dis-

---

[11] A preoccupation with the role of reason in governing practices is not specific to students of colonial studies. As Neil Smelser has noted, "stirrings in the psychology and sociology of emotions . . . are flickers in relation to the larger trends toward rationalization" as dominant "perspectives in the social sciences." Smelser, "The Rational and the Ambivalent," *American*

passionate calculations that preoccupy states, the persuasive histrionics rather than substance of politics, the moralizing self-presentation of the state as itself "a genre of political authority."[12]

One view construes an age of empire in which imperial states and their bourgeois subjects celebrated the story that humanitarian social reform was empire's *raison d'être* and driving force. At home and abroad, agendas motivated by "compassion," "pity," and "empathy" motivated reformist zealots who swarmed the underworlds of Amsterdam, London, Paris, and their colonial "Other Worlds" overseas."[13] Echoing Bernard Shaw in his 1907 play *Major Barbara*, students of colonialism have waged political war on such moralizing missions and their "do-good" bourgeoisies, mocking "uplift" projects and their redemption-seeking advocates.[14] Impatient with benevolent, sentimental imperialisms—both U.S. and European variants—and their self-serving justifications, critical historians have looked more to the "rational" categories "behind" moral panics, to the irrationalities of rule, to pathos as a political contrivance of the strategic disciplinary social reforms that followed.

Others have avoided a focus on sentiments altogether, dismissing the attribution to colonized people of rampant unreason and overcharged passions as insidious and transparent features of colonialism's reductive racist ideologies. In this view a more rational actor better captures the

---

Sociological Review 63 (1998): 1–16. Anthropologists have long argued against a generic Western psychosocial theory where "thought" and "emotion," "reason" and "passion," "cognition" and "feeling" are treated as distinct epistemic sites and where "civilized" reason "evacuates" affects from it. See Vincent Crapanzano, "Réflexions sur une anthropologie des émotions," *Terrain* 22 (March 1994): 109–17. Marxist critiques of political economy have treated the psychological, and sentiment in particular, as a poor and misleading substitute for a "real" political analysis rather than as a potentially powerful means to understand the cultural frame in which relations of power work. Whether modeled on Marx's commitment to a rational science of capitalist logic and predictions for its demise, such key concepts as "alienation" often remain the outcome of capitalist relations of production and sociality, not the complicated subject of them. Even where strategies of labor control are mediated through "habits of the heart," the *state*'s part in structuring sentiment is rarely the subject of analysis. On "alienation" in political economy as a given, see Lewis Feuer, "What is Alienation? The Career of a Concept," in *Sociology on Trial*, ed. Maurice Stein and Arthur Vidich (Englewood Cliffs, N.J.: Prentice Hall, 1963), 127–47; and Daniel Bell. "The Debate on Alienation," in *Revisionism: Essays on the History of Marxist Ideas*, ed. Leopold Labedz (New York: Praeger, 1962, 195–211).

[12] See Sally Falk Moore, ed., *Moralizing States and the Ethnography of the Present* (Washington, D.C.: American Anthropological Association, 1993), and especially John Borneman's contribution therein.

[13] For critical views on this moralizing mission, see Anna Davin, "Imperialism and Motherhood," and Susan Thorne, "Missionary Imperialism and the Language of Class in Early Industrial Britain," in Cooper and Stoler, 87–151, 238–62, respectively.

[14] George Bernard Shaw, *Major Barbara* (London: Penguin, 1982 [1907]).

nature of agency across the colonial divide: attachments and affections—
tender, veiled, violent, or otherwise get cast as compelling human elements
that make vivid the dislocations and distresses of empire, but are canceled
out as distractions from both the "real" workings of colonial authority,
its underlying agenda, and its true plot.

Some might rightly argue that this view caricatures, or at least overstates,
the case. Early critical witnesses to colonial distress have identified the psychic injuries of empire, what Frantz Fanon and Homi Bhabha following
him, cast as the "weeping wounds," the "avenging anger," the "psychic violence" imposed on the colonized.[15] Aimé Césaire, Albert Memmi, and
Ousmane Sembene, among others, have singled out the insecurities of those
Europeans taught to rule and the violences that followed from the prescriptions imposed upon, and weakly or fiercely embraced by, them.[16] Michael
Taussig and I, each in our own ways, have sought to track the production
of fear so fundamental to colonial labor relations.[17] Veena Das takes on
Jacques Donzelot's notion of a "tactical collusion" between the order of
families and the order of states to ask whether something other than collusion took place.[18] Still, how sentiments have figured in and mattered to the
shaping of *statecraft* has remained largely marginal to studies of colonial
politics. What has been barely addressed are those habits of the heart and
the redirection of sentiments fostered by colonial regimes themselves.[19]

Again colonial print culture points in a different direction: official
archives, belles-lettres, the press, and epistolary history register "structures
of feeling" of political import—emergent sites of critique, inchoate common and unarticulated expectations, what Raymond Williams described as

---

[15] Homi Bhabha, *The Location of Culture* (New York: Routledge, 1994), 43, 44, 63;
Frantz Fanon, *The Wretched of the Earth* (New York: Grove, 1979 [1961]).

[16] Albert Memmi, *Portrait du Colonisé précedé du Portrait du Colonisateur* (Paris: Payot
1973 [1957]; and Aimé Césaire, *Discourse on Colonialism* (New York: Monthly Review,
2000 [1955]); Oyono, Ferdinand. *Houseboy*, trans. John Reed (London: Heinemann, 1975
[1966]).

[17] Catherine Lutz and Lila Abu-Lughod, eds., *Language and the Politics of Emotion*
(New York: Cambridge, 1990), 14, have credited both Taussig and me with showing that
"emotion discourses may be one of the most likely and powerful devices by which domination proceeds." But the attribution was more generous than either of us deserved. Like many
cultural accounts of the colonial, these, too, engaged a predictably narrow affective range:
fear, awe of, dependence on, and ambivalence toward the Other have been called on to make
sense of excessive responses, of particular and peculiar governing practices, rather than to
address how political regimes define the grids of intelligibility in which humiliations, disdain, sympathies, or compassions can be safely expressed.

[18] Veena Das, *Critical Events: An Anthropological Perspective on Contemporary India*
(Delhi: Oxford University Press, 1995), 57.

[19] For an important exception, see Johannes Fabian, *Out of Our Minds: Reason and
Madness in the Exploration of Central Africa* (Berkeley: University of California Press,
2000).

interpretive labor barely within the semantic and political reach of their authors.[20] The categories of affect and reason may have been available and relevant but, as we shall see, confidence in their clarity and content was not.

It is not just that private passions had public consequences, a point that has been made often and well. Nor is it that the metaphors of feeling culled from other intimate, trusted, and well-established communities of sentiment shored up the ties between ruler and ruled, as Lynn Hunt cogently argues in her analysis of the "family romance" of the French Revolution.[21] Nor is it, as Melvin Yazawa contended with regard to the early American Republic, that "the conception of a polity that combined restraint with affection . . . [drew on] the traditional familial paradigm of patriarchal authority."[22] These analyses focus on the practical power of paternalistic *metaphor* and familial *analogy*, less on the sorts of governing practices that directed and reworked the affective bonds within families themselves.[23]

My argument is that the Dutch colonial state's concern over sentiment, the state's assessments of the intensity of "feelings," "attachments," and senses of belonging—prompting loyalties to race over family, or family over state—were not metaphors for something else. These administrative apprehensions were instrumental as "dense transfer points" of power in themselves.[24] Such concerns informed virtually every aspect of racial policy, political calibrations, and the tone and tenor of the archives produced about them. William Connolly's claim that public reason depends on "a visceral register," "on culturally formed moods, affects, [and] sensibilities," begins to address the issue: that the management of colonial agents

---

[20] Raymond Williams, *Marxism and Literature* (London: Verso, 1977), 128–35.

[21] Lynn Hunt, *The Family Romance of the French Revolution* (Berkeley: University of California Press, 1992). Philip Corrigan and Derek Sayer similarly have argued that "the family . . . has been (as it continues to be) a major organizing metaphor of state." Corrigan and Sayer, *The Great Arch: English State Formation as Cultural Revolution* (Oxford: Blackwell, 1985), 12. See also Mabel Berezin, "Political Belonging: Emotion, Nation, and Identity in Fascist Italy," in George Steinmetz, ed., *State/Culture: State Formation After the Cultural Turn* (Ithaca: Cornell University Press), 355–77, who argues that "the language of emotion structured fascist public narrative" and that the family was a "vehicle of emotional attachment" (366–67).

[22] Melvin Yazawa, *From Colonies to Commonwealth: Familial Ideology and the Beginnings of the American Republic* (Baltimore: The Johns Hopkins University Press, 1985), 19.

[23] On family ties as the site of the political and/or as a source of political agency, see Julia Adams, "The Familial State: Elite Family Practices and State-making in the Early Modern Netherlands," *Theory and Society* 23 (1994): 505–39; see also Michael Grossberg, *Governing the Hearth: Law and the Family in Nineteenth-Century America* (Chapel Hill: University of North Carolina Press, 1985).

[24] Michel Foucault, *The History of Sexuality. Volume I: An Introduction* (New York: Vintage, 1978), 103, uses "a dense transfer point for relations of power" to identify the "instrumentality" of sexuality as a "linchpin" in the strategies of knowledge and power.

and subjects depended on reformatting the visceral—and mediating family affections, as well.[25]

Debates in the Dutch East Indies on educational reform, the need for orphanages, citizenship requirements, marriage laws, and the appropriate entrance requirements for civil servants were charged with a shared tension. Each was riveted on what sorts of institutions and policies would produce *sensibilities* that were fitting, *aspirations* that were appropriate, *dispositions* that would confirm the explicit and implicit entailments of social membership and the truth-claims that distinguished ruler from ruled.

Evidence of rationality, reason, and progress were invoked to affirm privilege and station, but European colonials policed their borders, imposing what Bourdieu referred to as "common principles of vision and division," by appealing to other criteria, attended to with equal and studied care.[26] European legal status for the Indies-born of mixed parentage, as I have long argued, was accorded based upon the display of a familiarity and proficiency with European cultural styles that required proofs of estrangements from other social kinds—evidence of feeling "distanced" from that "native part of one's being," "of "feeling no longer at home" in a native milieu.[27] Racial membership was as much about the cultivation of culturally trained moral virtues and character as it was about the hue of skin, producing a quest for measures of those sensibilities as well as protracted debate about how they "safely" might be rendered inaccessible to some and by others easily obtained.[28]

Investment in the distribution of sentiment was equally apparent in the bureaucratic protocols of governance—in the "emotional standards" that policymakers imagined their agents needed in order to rule.[29] Evaluations of affective comportment—evidence of integrity, reserve, and trustworthiness—generated and motivated the density of the colonial state's archival production, its empathetic or intemperate narrative tone, and the scope of bureaucratic labors.[30] Steven Shapin argues that "good character"

---

[25] William E. Connolly, *Why I Am Not a Secularist* (Minneapolis: University of Minnesota, 1999), 27.

[26] Pierre Bourdieu, "Rethinking the State: Genesis and Structure of the Bureaucratic Field," in George Steinmetz, *State/Culture: State Formation after the Cultural Turn* (Ithaca: Cornell University Press, 1999), 53–75, 61

[27] See Stoler (2003), 79–139.

[28] Ibid.

[29] See Peter and Carol Stearns, "Emotionology: Clarifying the History of Emotions and Emotional Standards," *American Historical Review* 90 (1985): 813–36; and Peter N. Stearns, "Historical Analysis in the Study of Emotion," *Motivation and Emotion* 10 (2) (1986): 185–93.

[30] William Reddy, *The Invisible Code: Honor and Sentiment in Postrevolutionary France, 1814–1848* (Berkeley: University of California Press, 1997), 114–83, eloquently makes a similar point.

measured more than one's degree of civility and respectability in the world of seventeenth-century science—precisely because it appraised one's claims to be convincing and worthy of trust. It concisely assessed whether one could speak the truth—and therefore whether one was competent to assess the character and claims of others.[31] In the nineteenth-century Indies, assessments of sentiment similarly determined how truth-claims were made and whose accounts were reliable. Appeals to self-sacrifice, social empathy, family honor, and parental affections guided the rhetorical strategies of bureaucratic reports, both the credibility and future advancement of their authors.

Entrance exams for the Indies civil service, like those for its counterpart in British India, were meant to measure character as much as bookkeeping skills—"self-denial, diligence, temperance and self-control" were coveted bureaucratic traits.[32] As Weber so well understood, the "structures of domination" that bureaucracies have embraced, called for, "cultivated men" with "cultural quality" more than specialized expertise.[33] These "qualities of life conduct" that included feelings of sympathy and compassion are more often associated with eighteenth-century "masculine sensibility." But those "moral sentiments" that concerned Adam Smith—what Julie Ellison calls the "core curriculum of liberal emotion" that embraced "emoting across the empire"—extended well into the political life of the nineteenth century.[34] Thomas Haskell makes a strong case for just that. He compellingly argues that the market gave rise to "new habits of causal attribution that set the stage for humanitarianism" by making trust and breach of promise central to the character of capitalist social relations.[35] Similarly, affective criteria went into the racialized categories of colonial rule, on the implicit causal argument that a person's affective profile, rather than

[31] Steven Shapin, *A Social History of Truth: Civility and Science in Seventeenth-Century England* (Chicago: University of Chicago Press, 1994).

[32] Thomas Osborne, "Bureaucracy as a Vocation: Governmentality and Administration in Nineteenth-Century Britain," *Journal of Historical Sociology* 7 (2) (1994): 289–313, 306.

[33] By Weber's account, in *Economy and Society: An Outline of Interpretive Sociology*, ed. Guenther Roth and Claus Wittich (New York: Bedminister, 1968), 1001–1003, the tension between bureaucratic demands to produce "cultivated men" or those with expert knowledge were struggles that "affect[ed] the most intimate aspects of personal culture."

[34] See Julie Ellison, *Cato's Tears and the Making of Anglo-American Emotion* (Chicago: University of Chicago Press, 1999), 10. On "Whig Sentimentalism," see Kenneth Silverman, *A Cultural History of the American Revolution* (New York: Columbia, 1987), 82–87. On race and sensibility in the nineteenth-century United States, see Shirley Samuels, ed., *The Culture of Sentiment: Race, Gender and Sentimentality in 19th century America* (New York: Oxford University Press, 1992).

[35] Thomas L. Haskell, "Capitalism and the Origins of the Humanitarian Sensibility, Part 1," *American Historical Review* 90 (2) (1985): 339–61, and "Capitalism and the Origins of the Humanitarian Sensibility, Part 2" *American Historical Review* 90 (June 1985): 547–66.

physiology, measured self-mastery, moral integrity, habituating the "invisible bonds" of race. As such, affective criteria could and did serve as the exclusionary basis for educational advancement, claims to citizenship, and social entitlements.[36]

"Men of character" and "cultural quality" were, by definition, men of reasoned feeling—attributes that both silently indexed social origins and that were built into racialized grammars of social worth. Amit Rai rightly argues that compassion and sympathy both marked and created colonial inequalities of the British Empire in India.[37] The schooling of such sentiments also produced standards of comportment and taste that distinguished the quality of citizens, citizens from subjects, as well as their disparate entitlements.[38] Nor did colonial authorities imagine emotional excess and its inappropriate display as confined to the colonized side of the imperial divide, with reason and rational action on the other. If sentiments can be taken as "settled dispositions," and reason as "the internalization of public procedure," as historians of emotions suggest, then both shared a charged space of governance.[39] For it was through these settled dispositions and practices

[36] On how Dutch authorities made that argument in demarcating who would have access to European equivalent status and European standards of education, see Stoler (2002), 79–111.

[37] Amit S. Rai, *The Rule of Sympathy: Sentiment, Race and Power, 1750–1850* (New York: Palgrave, 2002). On Adam Smith and Edmund Burke's very different understanding of how sympathy worked politically, see Luke Gibbons, *Edmund Burke and Ireland: Aesthetics, Politics, and the Colonial Sublime* (Cambridge: Cambridge University Press, 2003), 83–120. I thank Katarzyna Bartoszynska for directing me to this piece. On the affective economy that joins compassion, race, and empire today, see my essay "On Degrees of Imperial Sovereignty," *Public Culture* 18 (1) (2006): 125–46, where I argue that "compassionate imperialism and the distributions of pity it produced and condoned did not constitute objections to empire. . . . Sympathy conferred distance, required inequalities of position and possibility, and was basic to the founding and funding of imperial enterprises—these were core features of empire that the elaboration of such sentiments helped to create" (134). See also Didier Fassin, "Compassion and Repression: The Moral Economy of Immigration Policies in France," *Cultural Anthropology* 20(3) (August 2005): 389–405, and Luc Boltanski, "The Politics of Pity," in Boltanski, *Distant Suffering: Morality, Media and Politics* (New York: Cambridge University Press, 1999), esp. 5–13, who follows Hannah Arendt's distinction between compassion, as "mute" and local, versus pity, as "loquacious" and endowed with the capacity for generalization. Within colonial relations, on the contrary, pity was both local and socially distant while compassion could also be very loquacious, as Arendt defined it—"to be sorry without being touched in the flesh." See Hannah Arendt, *On Revolution* (New York: Viking, 1965), 53–111, 80.

[38] See in particular Uday Mehta, "Liberal Strategies of Exclusion" in Cooper and Stoler, 59–86; see also David Goldberg, *Racist Culture: Philosophy and the Politics of Meaning* (Oxford: Blackwell, 1993), and Stoler, *Race and the Education of Desire: Foucault's History of Sexuality and the Colonial Order of Things* (Durham, N.C.: Duke University Press, 1995).

[39] Richard Peters, quoted in Francis Dunlop, *The Education of Feeling and Emotion* (Boston: Allen and Unwin, 1984), 14.

of European officials and their families that colonial regimes secured loyalties by reordering relations within those families themselves.

In the nineteenth-century Indies, preoccupation with the making of virtuous selves prompted recurrent debates over where the cultivation of those selves should take place and who should be charged with responsibility for it: in state institutions or in families; at isolated hill-station boarding schools or carefully guarded urban orphanages; with European parents (however impoverished or ill-educated) or surrogate providers; by virtue of residence in the colonies or in Europe; via proximity to parents or through removal from the home. Policymakers, parents, doctors, and teachers stumbled repeatedly over the same question, whether what it took to be European required the instilling of specific formal knowledge or less tangible ways of being and feeling about the (Javanese) worlds they did not know, and feelings of belonging in the European milieus in which they lived. For nearly a century, between the 1830s and 1930s, Dutch authorities called on experienced and expert counsel to determine how best to provide European children in the Indies with a sense of national belonging and racial affiliation and to gauge the extent to which an education of the sentiments could be mobilized for both purposes. They understood what anthropologist Janis Jenkins has underscored in a different context: that states do more than control emotional discourse, they attempt to "culturally standardize the organization of feeling" and produce as well as harness emotional discourse within it.[40]

STATECRAFT AS AFFECTIVE MASTERY

> The truth, of course, is that the distinction between reason and the passions is as suspect and ultimately as misleading as the dichotomy between East and West.
>
> —Robert C. Solomon,
> "The Cross-Cultural Comparison of Emotion"

The nineteenth-century colonial states of England, the United States, the Netherlands, and France may have agreed about the centrality of their moralizing missions, but did not share a common notion of what "morality"

---

[40] Jenkins sets her sights on violently coercive states that justify their brutality through a "political ethos." Her astute treatment of the "social production of affective disorders" attends to the state's part in producing mental illness, not in ordering what is moral and respectable as part of the *normal* and normalizing technologies of noncrisis rule. Janis Jenkins, "The State Construction of Affect: Political Ethos and Mental Health among Salvadoran Refugees," *Culture, Medicine, Psychiatry* 15 (1991): 139–65.

was or how to measure it. While colonial authorities were not moral philosophers in disguise, the questions their political concerns pushed them to pose about the cultivation of the moral were strikingly similar. Namely, whether morality was the "work of reason" or the "work of passion," whether it hinged on the "affections" and feelings or on reasoned judgment. These questions were at once the musings of philosophers *and* the very grist of colonial politics.

This is not to argue that these philosophical debates "account for" colonial politics and that the latter derived from them. A more plausible claim might be that it worked the other way around: that philosophical queries were generated out of historically specific political contexts.[42] The making of the moral and the ambiguities over which sensibilities it required were at the center of political debates on colonial ground.[43] Whether morality was taken as a matter of rational judgment, affective disposition, or some combination of the two determined whether state funds would be devoted to formal schooling (*onderwijs*) of European children, to their upbringing (*opvoeding*) in nurseries and kindergartens, or to their even earlier rearing in the home. Opponents of the former two options opined that better schools would confer few benefits if European children remained in the care of native servants and if children of mixed parentage were exposed and attached to the sensibilities of their native mothers.

As we shall see in chapter 4, proposals in the 1860s, 1880s, and again at the turn of the century to set up artisan schools (and the failed attempts to do so) for orphan children of mixed unions turned on the belief that proper habits of the heart were instilled by specific kinds of labor. "Mixed blood" youths who refused manual work—labor that "full-blooded" Europeans disparaged as sullying their status and hands—were seen as arrogant, impudent, and politically dangerous.[44] "The language of reason" was an "idiom of power," as Gyan Prakash claims, but relations of subordination were equally secured by assessing those sensibilities deemed virtues when displayed by some (Europeans), or politically dangerous and "contagious," when embraced by (mixed blood and native) others.[45] At issue was "the emotional economy" of empire, and how colonial states intervened

---

[42] For a powerful and influential analysis that pursues this argument, see Susan Buck-Morss, "Hegel and Haiti," *Critical Inquiry* 4 (6) (Summer 2000): 821–65. See also Mary Louise Pratt, *Imperial Eyes: Travel Writing and Transculturation* (New York, Routledge, 1992), who contends that European romanticism moved from the colonies to Europe and back again.

[43] An exploration of the moral components of colonial politics through a social history of early modern moral philosophy is an important project that I do not pursue here.

[44] See chapter 3 in the present volume.

[45] Prakash, 9. On the "contagious," "communicative" quality" of sentiment, see David Hume, *A Treatise of Human Nature* (New York: Oxford, 2000) 605, book 3, part 3, §3,

in shaping which feelings mattered, who had a right to them, and how they were politically framed.[46]

If Weber is often credited with having identified rationalization and reasoned management as the hallmarks of modern European states, it is Durkheim who is seen to have insisted that they were "supremely the organ of moral discipline."[47] These positions need not be seen as contradictory. In the colonies, Weber's reasoned state, staffed by "cultivated men," complemented Durkheim's moralizing one. Colonial states were in the business of "engineering morality," both among their agents and among those they ruled. As such, both Weber and Durkheim attended to a register of governance neither explicitly named: the harnessing of affect in the state's shaping of what constituted morality and who had the right to assess it.[48]

Such a focus opens to another possible premise: that the role of the state is not only, as Antonio Gramsci defined it, in the business of "educating consent."[49] More basically, such consent is made possible not through some abstract process of "internalization," but by shaping appropriate and reasoned affect, by directing affective judgments, by adjudicating what constituted moral sentiments (that is, affectively informed good reason)—in short, by educating the proper *distribution* of sentiments and desires.[50] Michelle Rosaldo has rightly argued that "affective life has more to do with social morality (and rationality) and less with passive irrationality than has often

and Adela Pinch's nuanced treatment of this motility in *Strange Fits of Passion: Epistemologies of Emotion, Hume to Austen* (Stanford: Stanford University Press, 1996). Julie Ellison, in *Cato's Tears and the Making of Anglo-American Emotion* (Chicago: University of Chicago Press, 1997), 1, 7, productively extends Pinch's insight to argue for the imperial "itinerary of feeling" through a reading of "scenarios of inequality" in literary texts.

[46] Don Herzog, in *Poisoning the Minds of the Lower Orders* (Princeton, Princeton University Press, 1998), 203, 206, points in precisely the right direction by treating emotions as "richly cognitive," dependent on "background beliefs" that serve "as "contestable sources of authority, buttressing or undercutting the appeals of various partisans." Catherine Lutz's observation that emotions "exist in a system of power relations and play a part in maintaining it," and Michelle Rosaldo's claim that "emotions . . . may be understood . . . as the creation of particular sorts of polities" have been appreciated for sometime but with little impact on colonial ethnographies. Catherine Lutz, *Unnatural Emotions: Everyday Sentiments on a Micronesian Atoll and Their Challenge to Western Theory* (Chicago: University of Chicago Press, 1988), 54, and Michelle Rosaldo, "Toward an Anthropology of Self and Feeling," in *Culture Theory: Essays on Mind, Self and Emotion*, ed. Richard Shweder and Robert LeVine (Cambridge: Cambridge University Press, 1984), 141–42.

[47] Quoted in Corrigan and Sayer, 5.

[48] For a fascinating account of the tension between the rational model of political behavior for which Weber is so well known and the strong presence of the emotive in his thinking, style, and analytic work, see Alan Sica, *Weber, Irrationality and Social Order* (Berkeley: University of California Press, 1988).

[49] Antonio Gramsci, *Selections from Prison Notebooks* (London: Lawrence and Wishart, 1978), 259.

[50] Stoler (1995), 143.

been assumed."[51] As a starting point, both premises anticipate questions that much literature on state-formation has long left unaddressed. Why is it easier to imagine, as Benedict Anderson writes, that "millions of people . . . willingly die for [nations]" but not for states?[52] How is it that a citizenry can accrue virtue by sacrificing their lives for nations, even though people are killed not by nations but by states? "Nation" and "sentiment" are often treated as an obvious pairing while "state" and "sentiment" are not. How is it that states are commonly viewed as institutional machines that squelch and counter passions, while nations are envisaged as culturally rich producers of them?[53] Why does that pairing of "state" and "sentiment" read as an oxymoron?

It is certainly not because the dissonance of that pairing has always been so inharmonious. Attending to the relationships between affective disposition and political control, between the art of governance and the passions, between politics and sentiment were defining concerns of philosophy and a "broader preoccupation" throughout the seventeenth and eighteenth centuries.[54] Moral and political philosophers of the "long" eighteenth century were deeply intent on identifying connections between the two. The relationship between what Bernard Mandeville in 1714 called the "private vices" and "publick benefits," between affective life and political life, between individual passions and social welfare, was central to the philosophical queries and concrete agendas of Bacon, Spinoza, Locke, and Hume, and lesser luminaries such as Mandeville, Hutcheson, and Shaftesbury.[55] Students of seventeenth-century philosophy are increasingly prepared to argue, with Susan James, that the passions have been systematically ignored as "a central topic in the heartland of early modern philosophy." It is precisely the fact that the passions were seen to serve the interests of political power that captures a critical impulse of European culture in the early-modern period.[56]

---

[51] Michelle Rosaldo, "The Shame of Headhunters and the Autonomy of Self," *Ethos* 11 (3) (1983): 135–51, 136.

[52] Anderson, 16.

[53] Among those who deftly make the case for the relationship between affect and the nation (not for sentiment and the state), see Doris Sommer, *Foundational Fictions: The National Romances of Latin America* (Berkeley: University of California Press, 1991), and Lauren Berlant, *The Anatomy of a Nationalist Fantasy: Hawthorne, Utopia, and Everyday Life* (Chicago: University of Chicago Press, 1991), on "the harnessing of affect to political life through a national fantasy" (5).

[54] See Susan James's accessible account of how the passions were treated in this period in *Passion and Action: The Emotions in Seventeenth-Century Philosophy* (Oxford: Clarendon, 1997), 2.

[55] The title of Bernard Mandeville's *The Fable of the Bees: or, Private Vices, Publick Benefits*, quoted in Albert Hirschman. *The Passions and the Interests: Political Arguments for Capitalism before Its Triumph* (Princeton, Princeton University Press, 1977), 18.

[56] James, 15.

It was Francis Bacon (philosopher cum statesman) who so finely articulated why the governance of states should be conceived of as something akin to "the government within." Both, he claimed, required knowing "how affections are kindled and incited; how pacified and refrained, . . . how they disclose themselves, how they work, how they vary, how they gather and fortify, how they are enwrapped one within another."[57] For those following Bacon, the role of the state was increasingly clear: namely, to curtail the dangerous and combustible passions of ordinary men. *Statecraft was not opposed to the affective, but about its mastery.* Like Foucault's notion of "governmentality," statecraft joined the care and governing of the polity to the care and governing of the affective self.

These earlier philosophers debated not only the state's responsibility to check unruly passions but to *harness* them in the interests of the public good.[58] Albert Hirschman's observation that the nineteenth-century modern state would later be "called upon to perform this feat . . . as a civilizing medium" alerts us to a crucial point: that what is now taken as intuitively incompatible in the heyday of colonialism—namely, a state devoted to reason *and* defined by its efficacy in producing countervailing passions and affections—was once not thought to be so.[59] Foucault may be credited with reminding us that all sentiments have their histories, but it was Norbert Elias and Hirschman who suggested in their own ways that tracking a sentiment's history is an inspired way to trace the changing form and content of what constitutes the subject and terrain of politics.[60] The seventeenth-century notion that states should be called upon to harness individual passions, to transform and civilize the sentiments of their subjects through counteracting ones, as Hirschman recognized, was "to prosper as a major tenet of nineteenth-century liberalism."[61]

Hirschman's compelling history of the passions suggests another historical frame for understanding what shaped the strategies of colonial rule.

---

[57] Bacon's *Collected Works*, vol. 3, quoted in Hirschman, 22. As Hirschman notes, Bacon's view was neither influential at the time nor was the statement above directed at statecraft per se.

[58] Hirschman, 16.

[59] Ibid.

[60] Michel Foucault, "Nietzsche, Genealogy, History," in *The Foucault Reader*, ed. Paul Rabinow (New York: Pantheon, 1984), 76. For Foucault on "governmentality," statecraft, and affective self, see, among other titles, *Naissance de la biopolitique: Cours au Collége de France, 1978–1979* (Paris: Gallimard, 2004). Norbert Elias's two-volume historical work, *The Civilizing Process* (New York: Pantheon, 1982), esp. 229–50, directly engages the relationship between state-formation, the "affective," and "patterns of self constraint," arguing that as states developed, the restraint on sentiment and "civilized" conduct was a crucial part of their task. In his repressive model of history, states invested more in quelling desire than, as Foucault might have argued, in actively nurturing and producing it.

[61] Hirschman, 19.

It would not be a history that starts with the supremacy of reason in the nineteenth century and then traces it back to the roots of rationality in the Enlightenment. It would rather set out another genealogy of equal force—and of as long a *durée*. Such a genealogy might register the incessant flux in political theory in the seventeenth and eighteenth centuries over what morality was (either a "natural sense" or a "cultivated taste," as it was for Shaftesbury).[62] It would look to that eighteenth-century "culture of sensibility" that tied material power and moral weight to the taste and character of cultivated and lettered men.[63] It would register that sustained oscillation between reason and sentiment rather than the final dominance of the one and their definitive severance. It might take up William Reddy's claim that modernity's early moments in the "age of reason" could as accurately be characterized as an "age of sentiment."[64] It would register the recurrent attack on what constituted reason and political rationality in the eighteenth century.[65]

Nor would such a genealogy track a rule of reason (veering on or off course) with an undercurrent of emotional strain. Rather it might resituate the art of governance as one modeled after an earlier genre that took as its project the art of knowing oneself as part of the "art of knowing men" (*"l'art de connaître les hommes"*).[66] As Alasdair MacIntyre writes in his history of moral theory: "Virtues are dispositions not only to act in particular ways, but also to feel in particular ways. To act virtuously is not to act against inclination; it is to act from inclination formed by the cultivation of the virtues. Moral education is an '*éducation sentimentale.*' "[67]

The Indies' colonial authorities would have agreed. Placing colonial governance in this broader frame makes more sense. A joint commitment to reason and affective knowledge was central to nineteenth-century imperial polities and a basic tension within them. Gary Wilder refers to "colonial humanism" as a new way of exercising political authority in

---

[62] Stephen Darwall, *The British Moralist and the Internal "Ought," 1640–1740* (Cambridge: Cambridge University Press, 1995), 186.

[63] On cultural sensibility and what Shaftesbury, Mandeville, Hume, and Smith had to say about it, see G. J. Barker-Benfield, *The Culture of Sensibility: Sex and Society in Eighteenth-Century Britain* (Chicago: University of Chicago Press, 1992), esp. 104–53.

[64] Reddy's prolific work on the subject includes *The Invisible Code: Honor and Sentiment in Postrevolutionary France, 1814–1848* (Berkeley: University of California Press, 1997), and *The Navigation of Feeling: A Framework for the History of Emotions* (New York: Cambridge University Press, 2001).

[65] As traced in Frederick C. Beiser, *The Fate of Reason: German Philosophy from Kant to Fichte* (Cambridge, Mass.: Harvard University Press, 1987).

[66] James, 2.

[67] Alasdair MacIntyre, *After Virtue: A Study in Moral Theory* (Notre Dame: Notre Dame University Press, 1981), 149.

early twentieth-century Greater France.[68] In the Indies the notion that men in authority were to train their own sentiments and guide those of their subordinates—to be men of certain feelings—intervenes in the political life of colonial rule by the 1830s and 1840s; in debates over nurseries; mixed marriages; European pauperism; and, not least, in how these men positioned themselves in debates about whether and how access to a Dutch education and elite civil service posts would be pegged to wealth and race.

Thus to return to an earlier question: What makes students of colonialism declare with such conviction that "colonialism became the mode of universalizing the rule of reason" in the nineteenth century?[69] Why have those who study colonial authority and its representations largely ignored Hirschman's striking observations?[70] As we shall see, it is not official archives that bracketed sentiment from their cultures of evidence and documentation, but our pre-emptive readings of them.

PART 2: POLITICS AND PATHOS IN COLONIAL JAVA

PARENTAL FEELINGS AND TORN HEARTS: DEMONSTRATIVE CITY FATHERS

> Education is used to train members of a class and to divide them from other men as surely as from their own passions.
> —Raymond Williams, *Marxism and Literature*

On 22 May 1848, a Monday evening when most members of Batavia's European community otherwise would have been comfortably settled in their clubs, refreshed from their late-afternoon naps, there occurred an extraordinary meeting unprecedented in the history of the Dutch Netherlands Indies. Between five and six hundred people (that authorities later identified as "European," "creoles," and "colored") gathered on the steps of the exclusive Harmonie Club to register their deep dissatisfaction with a specific set of government policies and to make a specific set of demands. At the top of their strategic list was growing resentment toward a government decree of 1842 that produced a monopoly on senior posts in the colonial civil service exclusively for those who could attain the *Radikaal* certificate that only an education at the Delft Academy in the

---

[68] Gary Wilder, "The Politics of Failure: Historicizing Popular Front Colonial Policy in French West Africa," in *French Empire and the Popular Front*, ed. Tony Chafer and Amanda Sarkur (New York: Palgrave, 1999), 33–55.

[69] Prakash, 5.

[70] Hirschman, 19.

Netherlands conferred. Those with too many children to support and who thus could not afford to send their sons to Delft, or chose not to do so, were barred from the higher administration and confined to minor posts with meager salaries and pensions slashed by half.

The ruling sent a confused message about privilege and race, for while it blatantly discriminated against the middling Indo-Europeans whose sons were confined to the lowliest civil service jobs, it was also perceived as a direct affront to both the Dutch-born and creole Dutch who were unwilling or unable to pack their sons off to Europe for a decade of their lives. Those gathered at "the Harmonie," as it was called, charged the government with discriminatory pension allocations to civil servants trained in the Indies and condemned an educational policy that forced estrangement from their sons. Later reports described, among those gathered, several hundred "colored" who were "well-to-do," "coloreds" of more modest means arriving in carriages they could not have afforded to rent on their own. Among the group were many and equal numbers of senior Dutch civil servants, high-placed administrators of justice, finance, and religion, as well as those considered respected "city fathers."[71]

It was an extraordinary event but not a spontaneous one. As we learn from the rapid-fire exchange of letters, announcements, reports, and circulated petitions, J. J. Rochussen, Governor-General between 1845 and 1851, was informed directly by the gathering's advocates and by his own agents on several occasions why, when, and where the assembly would take place. In the heady rush of the four preceding days, Batavia's Resident Pieter van Rees urgently met with Rochussen several times; the gathering's organizers met with Van Rees; and the vocal Protestant minister of Batavia's Malay congregation, Wolter Robert Baron van Hoëvell, considered to have spearheaded the protest, was summoned by Rochussen.

In the city, according to later testimony before the Resident, verbal and written forms of news and rumors were spreading fast. People accosted one

---

[71] AR, KV 317x ("zeer geheim"), 5 August 1848, from the Minister of Colonies and Navy to the King, is an 11½-page report based on two lengthy reports (nos. 157x and 158x) three times that length from the Governor-General that were sent on 26 May (no. 158x), several days after the event. The Governor-General's report no. 158x contains a calculation of the number of native and European soldiers available (583 native officers and foot soldiers and 712 European infantry), as well as a detailed listing of all the weaponry (pistols, bayonets, swords, carbines, and gunpowder) available at the Batavia, Semarang, and Soerabaja military installations. Governor-General Rochussen's report is included as exhibitum 5 August 1848, no. 317 zeer geheim, in a subsequent verbaal that the Minister of Colonies sent to the King five days later. The Minister's verbaal provides an overview of the demonstration, communications from the leaders of the demonstration to Batavia's Resident van Rees and to the Governor-General prior to the event, the petition sent by the demonstration's organizers directly to the King, as well as correspondence between the Resident and the Governor-General.

another on the streets, hailed one another on horseback, detained one another's carriages to exchange opinions or information. According to Van Rees, little got done in government offices the day before the event: people were too busy passing notes from desk to desk. Others called on one another at home, outside conventional early-evening visiting hours. In this condensed and charged time the "gathering" transformed into a demonstration that exceeded the well-mannered planning of some city fathers.

On 17 May, Van Hoëvell met with the Governor-General to discuss what issues would be raised. On 19 May J. T. Cantervisscher, Director of the Chamber for Orphans and Estates, arrived in person at the Resident's office to request permission to issue a written public summons to the gathering, sure that the Governor-General could not refuse. That same day, the now-agitated Resident van Rees met with Rochussen to report the visit, describing Cantervisscher in "a very excited, almost wild mental state." Batavia's "mood is not calm," he tells Rochussen of "an uproar" (*oproer*) of its inhabitants over "social issues."[72]

In the early hours of the following day Rochussen received a yet more agitated Van Rees, this time carrying a "highly improper and inappropriate" letter he had gotten the prior evening from President of the High Court, P. C. Ardesch, bluntly stating that he would be among the attendees and would not confine himself to "minor topics." Referring to himself as a "liberal-minded Dutchman, like the King," served as a not subtle reminder that the Indies was no longer under autocratic rule but was now a liberalizing nation.[73] Only then, with Ardesch's letter in hand and now aware of new rumors that the gathering would issue a proclamation, does Rochussen wonder if more is afoot than he originally thought. As Van Rees reports to the Minister of Colonies, only then does he realize that Van Hoëvell was exerting more influence than he had imagined. That same afternoon Van Rees learns that the meeting's venue had been changed from a private home to the more spacious central hall of the Harmonie Club to accommodate the growing number who conveyed their intention to attend. Worse still, he learns that Van Hoëvell was offering to provide transport to anyone from the Dutch-speaking community and, more alarmingly, from Van Hoëvell's Malay-speaking Indo congregation.

To "avert the storm," on 20 May Rochussen concedes to allow the gathering as long as it does not encourage "disorder" or "impropriety," explaining to his subordinates that he would not prohibit a well-planned

---

[72] The term "*oproer*" can be translated as "disturbance," "uproar," "insurrection," "revolt," or "sedition." In this context I opt for "uproar" not because it is more literal but because this was how authorities initially imagined the severity of the complaints. They were to revise that assessment as the numbers participating increased and the "social" issues could not be contained as nonpolitical ones.

[73] AR, KV 317x, 19 May 1848x, bijlage B.

gathering by "moderate and reasonable" men, "stolid inhabitants and city fathers."[74] Calming the fearful Van Rees, Rochussen tells him that the gathering will take place. There was simply no other course of action— "their father hearts were bleeding too much" (*hun vaderhart te zeer bloedde*) to be refused.

Together, the principal organizers—Van Hoëvell, Ardesch, and Cantervisscher—persuade the Governor-General that "parental feelings" and the hardship parents experienced by having to school sons afar were not "matters of state" (*staatkundige zaken*) but "social" issues that posed no political threat. Rochussen's subsequent account of why he granted the permission suggests that the organizers were convincing and their strategy a partial success. After meeting with Van Hoëvell, Rochussen wrote to the Minister of Colonies:

> Feeling that here [with respect to the *Radikaal* certificate and secondary education] I was on less favorable terrain, I answered [Van Hoëvell] that with regard to this question, in which the parental feelings and the financial interests of city fathers were so closely concerned, I did not consider these of a purely political nature and if any respectable citizens and city fathers wanted to raise this with moderation and discretion, I would not be opposed but would present their petition to the King.[75]

While the organizers might have appeased Rochussen, rumors of broader political dissent were spreading fast and not all parties were in accord with Van Hoëvell's plan. In the meantime Van Hoëvell, in the newly minted magazine of which he was publisher and editor, *Tijdschrift voor Nederlandsch Indië*, wrote an article about "matters of state" that Rochussen expressly had asked him not to publish. In the afternoon of that same May twentieth, Rochussen would receive cause for alarm from other quarters. At a benefit held at the local racing club his speech was greeted with "more than usual" enthusiasm but he was disconcerted that around the building were many "coloreds" (*kleurlingen*) waiting to accost the carriage of J. C. Reijnst, a much disliked member of the Indies' Advisory Council, who was publicly and in print openly hostile to the *Indische*, the Indies-born and -bred European population.[76]

Copies of Ardesch's letter, with the names of prominent Europeans appended, were by then circulating more widely among the "colored" popu-

---

[74] Ibid. Although Cantervisscher earlier had agreed not to send around a printed circular and instead to make known the gathering's convening by word of a mouth among a small number of well-respected Europeans, he must have decided not to wait for permission because he had a packet of at least one hundred circulars with him.

[75] AR, KV 317x, exh. 5.

[76] Hostility to Reijnst was fierce: his son-in-law reported to Rochussen that stones had been thrown at his father-in-law's house later that evening.

lation, though Ardesch later claimed to have no idea how it got into so many hands. On Sunday the twenty-first, the day before the public gathering, Van Hoëvell made a last effort to articulate the nature of the discontent to the Governor-General, "to neutralize any biased and false rumors Your Excellency might have heard." Again he stated that the cause of their collective disquiet was "the backward state of education in the Indies which has made it absolutely necessary for those Europeans born here to separate themselves from their children at a tender age and forever break the bond between parents and their offspring."[77]

Other matters of state reluctantly had been shelved. Among these were demands for parliamentary representation, a reduction of the "autocratic" power of the Minister of Colonies, and freedom of the press. All of these items were removed from the agenda, at the Governor-General's request, on the grounds that they were too overtly political and potentially incendiary for a public *colonial* forum.

Meanwhile a group of self-proclaimed *"inboorlingen"* (to whom the Governor-General officially referred by the designation *"Inlandsche kinderen"* but privately by the pejorative *"liplappen"*) delivered to Rochussen a petition of their own. It called for Reijnst's immediate dismissal from the Advisory Council; their legal parity with *"echte* Hollanders" (true Dutchmen); abolition of the existing civil service exam (the *Radikaal*); and improved higher education in Java for those of European descent. Only the last two demands would remain on the agenda.[78]

Upon receiving Van Hoëvell's letter, Rochussen was increasingly agitated and let it be widely known that he would hunt down the European ringleaders to make sure those not of "goodwill shook with fear." To demonstrate his tenacity he also made it known that military forces were readied in the nearby barracks with loaded guns, live cartridges, and pointed cannons.[79] Apparently afraid that such a gathering might

[77] AR, KV 317x, from Governor-General's report 158x, Bijlage F, 22 May 1848, Van Hoëvell to Governor-General Rochussen.

[78] Paul van 't Veer, in a study of five nineteenth-century Dutch "radicals," among whom he counted Van Hoëvell, cites three petitions that came out of the gathering: (1) Van Hoëvell's; the petition of Ardesch (discussed below); and a petition signed by the *"inboorlingen,"* of which he thought there was no trace. He opined that the latter group must have "swiftly backed off when, under official pressure, they were refused." In P. Van 't Veer, *Geen blad voor de mond: Vijf radicalen uit de negentiende eeuw* (Amsterdam: Arbeiderspers, 1958), 104–5. He was wrong on both counts. There was a trace (it ended up in the bundles of documents sent to the Minister of Colonies and on to the King) and at least two of the demands were pursued that evening.

[79] As Governor-General Rochussen was to write former Minister of Colonies Baud on 27 May, "I have not strengthened the [military] posts, no soldier has shown himself. But I did have everyone ready in the barracks with loaded guns and cannons." *De semi-officiële en particuliere briefwisseling* (Assen: Van Gorcum, 1983), 364.

embolden the wider Javanese and Chinese populations, four companies of European and native artillery troops, 1,300 men in all, were commanded to wait on Batavia's outskirts.

As a demonstration of force, the spectacle was geared to Europeans inside the city and to the wider Javanese and Chinese populations imagined to be watching from within and outside the city's borders. He did not make public the two very detailed orders to the Military Commander to be executed at eight o'clock that evening: the first was that, under no circumstances, should the troops fire upon the demonstrators "other than in a situation of great distress and increasing danger," and then only "after *three* warnings"; the second, contingent upon "disorder and insurrection" in the old city, permitted the artillery "to turn against them [the crowd] and to fire until quiet and order was restored." Rowdy Europeans were to be arrested. Rowdy Javanese and Chinese were to be shot.

THE GATHERING: AVERTING THE STORM

"What happened" at the Harmonie Club that evening was reported in wildly contradictory abbreviated narratives based on third-hand knowledge, often in synoptic form. But it has also been recounted in vivid detail in testimonies by those present in a set of transcribed narratives, which were never referred to in any published accounts that I have read. Eight days after the event, Governor-General Rochussen still did not know what had actually transpired. Nor was there any sign that Resident van Rees knew better. Pleased, however, that "calmness reigned" in Java's other major cities of Semarang and Soerabaja (where he feared disturbances might have, but did not, spread), and that his prohibition on public assemblies had been honored in the week following the demonstration, Rochussen, having to answer to the Minister of Colonies and the King for his own actions, asked Van Rees to report immediately to him.

He decided not to make a further showing of "stern measures," concerned that the government might be seen as "vindictive," thereby inciting more general support, if only "out of pity," for those who participated in the demonstration. By order of the newly convened Indies' Supreme Court, on 29 May, Rochussen instead ordered Van Rees to provide "a detailed account of what happened on 22 May," to mount an investigation, and to answer as quickly as possible four questions: (1) By what means and by whom were the so called *Inlandsche kinderen* informed about taking part in the assembly? (2) Is it true that many of those who came were armed with daggers and sticks and that the latter were sold to them by Chinese? (3) Who took care of the arrangement of the Hall and who paid the expenses for the lighting? (4) Is it true that wanton violence against the Indies Advisory Council member, J. C. Reijnst, was carried out on that day and by whom?

The questions themselves were strange. Did Rochussen really need to wait a week to verify that Reijnst's house was stoned? And how much did it matter that Chinese, who owned so many shops in Batavia, had sold walking sticks with concealed blades? (As it turned out, the only ledgers that Van Rees's police officers could collect were those for some twenty to thirty "*tongkat yang pedang*" [cudgels with scabbards] sold to a few named [and more unnamed] persons two years earlier.)[80] And given that so many high officials were involved, did it really matter who paid for the lighting?

Van Rees wasted no time. Within two days the investigation had begun. Still, as he pleaded to Rochussen, it was no easy task. The police had never had to deal with such an event. He insisted that in the prior thirty-three years the Indies had shown itself to be a "jewel of the Dutch crown"; there had never been a gathering of certainly seven hundred Europeans and *Indische* Christians in any public place intent to treat subjects of a political nature.

Van Rees himself was shocked to find many of his close colleagues among the most vocal instigators. Instead of conducting a public inquiry, he made the decision to carry out a "secret investigation to discover those acts carried out by high-placed officials and people, colleagues and compatriots who I have always held in esteem and for whom I always had felt kindness." Van Rees summoned more than fifty men to appear in person before him between 31 May and 19 July 1848, to describe what they saw, what they did, who was present, and what was said.[81] Some were interviewed in Dutch, some in Malay. Most strikingly, the transcripts were verbatim, conveying vibrant movement, rumors careening across the city, people accosting one another on horseback and on foot about whether they planned to go to the gathering, and what they understood it to be. Some clearly acknowledged that they were excited by the prospect, others that they were curious, and still others that they went under threat. Some directly denied "with passion and impertinence" that they had actually carried out the actions attributed to them. Others simply crafted their accounts to place blame for their presence on what they were told would happen if they failed to show.

---

[80] "*Tongkat*" can be translated as a "truncheon," "cudgel," or "stick." A "*pedang*" is translatable as "scabbard," "saber," or "blade." In the Resident's report, however, they are referred to in Dutch as "walking sticks" with concealed "*keris*," a hand-crafted blade or sword worn by Javanese elites.

[81] Entitled "Maartse buien op Java in 1848" ("The March Squall on Java in 1848"). This is Pieter van Rees's report to the Governor-General, including over 200 pages of testimony by those Van Rees had, for the most part, personally interviewed and a 100-page report of 9 June 1848 on what he did in preparation for and response to the demonstration.

Here the "pulse of the archive" beats hard and fast. Documents and petitions passed quickly among the city's stolid citizens, while plans were made among "the youth" to damage the homes and ransack the property of officials. The Indies "house of glass" threatened to be shattered from inside, by those who Pramoedya Ananta Toer would have included among his "devils of the darkness," and from outside by those long excluded from the inner sanctum.

Lighting, chairs, and sofas had been arranged in the early morning of 22 May, the day of the meeting, by an underling of Colonel Dr. W. Bosch, head of the Department of Health, a medical officer who supported the demands. A green table was set up as a podium for the organizers. By six in the evening there were already flocks of carriages and pedestrians on their way to the Harmonie Club. By seven o'clock the club was completely full. By acclamation of those present, Van Hoëvell was appointed President. He, in turn, proposed to appoint a committee made up of several prominent officials to author a petition and bill to the King. He finished the task quickly, but expectations for the agenda seem to have been higher and the promise of a committee working on the bill in private was not enough. Whether Van Hoëvell was alarmed by the turnout or by the mood of the crowd, to the surprise of those later asked to testify he quickly called for an adjournment.

According to those present, this more immediately met with angry shouts from the crowd: "Treason! We weren't called for this nor was this why we came!" Van Hoëvell was reported to have seemed startled and "looked nervous and visibly started." Van Rees says he literally had a "nervous attack from the effort of speaking" to such a huge and tense crowd. Ardesch shouted from the floor, "This doesn't suit us." Others shouted insults and more frustrated condemnations:

We don't want to be treated in this way.
We don't want a president who treats us like disruptive, angry rascals.
Out with Van Hoëvell!
The committee must be dissolved! We dissolve it and protest what has happened.

Saved by someone in the crowd who called out "This is a president with courage and strong nerve," Van Hoëvell and some of the assembly left while a smaller group (that included Ardesch and two prominent lawyers, L. J. Tollens, and H. C. A. Thieme) remained for another hour.

How many were actually shouting is hard to say. The voices of Ardesch, Tollens, and Thieme were heard, as was that of a retired official turned wealthy storekeeper. According to Van Rees's most reliable informant, the government official R. van Nauta (who the assembly had appointed to Van Hoëvell's committee to draw up a bill), the scene had degenerated into a

Figure 4. The Harmonie Club in Rijswijk, Batavia, where the 22 May demonstration took place, as seen from across the canal. *Source: KIT 60025068.*

"Polish beer garden" with everyone talking at the same time, "in groups, on chairs, behind and in front of the table" set up for the steering committee. Someone pushed through the crowd to say that the coastal trade, in the hands of Arabs, had totally ruined him, a point he wanted addressed in the petition. Tollens and Thieme insisted on a free press and presented lists to sign. Only a few people did. Ardesch called for another public assembly and "pledged his word as an honorable man" that it would take place. He would later take full credit for what he claimed was a strategic move to disperse the "unruly crowd" of "*Sinjos*" (a term of address for Eurasian and Europeanized native young men). With loud hurrahs, the roar subsided and the remaining crowd dispersed into smaller groups. It was after nine. The doors of the Harmonie Club were closed by ten that night. Arrests were not made at the time, nor were shots ever fired.[82] The gathering was never to be

[82] In Rochussen's detailed report to the Minister of Colonies, J. C. Rijk, he claims that there was such confusion the night of the gathering that he was not sure what actually went on and promised to send a more detailed report when he had one. It eventually came from Resident van Rees in June.

repeated again. Despite its uniqueness and vancor, it has rarely received more than passing mention in Dutch colonial historiography.[83]

A Slip of the Pen

On the face of it, this was neither a radical nor particularly revolutionary event. But if the gathering remained relatively tempered and contained, the events that surrounded it, the interpretations of what it represented, and the sentiments that traveled and were attributed to those who took part were not. Rochussen's later assessment of the situation was very different than it had been a week earlier. He wrote Baud the next day, expressing outrage that his permission for a temperate meeting of a few well-placed citizens in a private house turned into what he called "a public assembly of many hundreds of persons of different rank, unknown to one another; some with the explicit aim of discussing matters of state and the basic principles of governance."[84] That same day, he banned all public meetings "concerning matters of government and of common interest," giving notice that armed force would be used if his order was disobeyed.

The ban was not challenged but the sentiment behind it remained. Instead of leaving their petition to the King, available for signing at the Harmonie Club, it was circulated from hand to hand throughout the rest of the day. The next morning Rochussen received it in the name of "the *Dutch* inhabitants of the Indies" living in Batavia. But this was not the original wording of the petition which so many had signed. As Van Rees was to write in his June report, the first petition that he had received from Cantervisscher on the morning of 19 May was a sealed document of several lines that read:

*Meeting of inhabitants of Netherlands Indies,
on next Monday March 22nd*

---

[83] Rob Nieuwenhuys, *Mirror of the Indies: A History of Dutch Colonial Literature* (Amherst: University of Massachusetts Press, 1982), notes that with the fall of the cabinet in the Netherlands and proposals for constitutional amendments, "a number of high officials, Van Hoëvell among them, took the initiative to use the upcoming reviews of the constitution to press the wishes of those in the Indies." Nieuwenhuys is one of the few to note that the demands for better education were not only in the name of those who "stayed on (the *blijvers*) are those thousands of Eurasian half-castes, or *liplaps*, who made up far and away the majority of European society"—but in the name of the "higher-ups" as well, whose "families were torn asunder" such that "everyone suffered the consequences of estrangement" (60). On Van Hoëvell as a pioneer of colonial liberalism, see Herman Stapelkamp, "De rol van Van Hoëvell in de Bataviase mei-beweging van 1848," in *Jambatan* 4 (1986): 11–20. Classic histories of the Netherlands rarely accord it more than two (confused) lines. See P. J. Blok, *Geschiedenis van het Nederlandsche Volk*, 4 (Leiden: Sijthoff, 1906), 402–3.

[84] AR, KV 1848 no. 493. Batavia, no. 158/x., Appendix H, 23 May 1848.

Cantervisscher withdrew and returned later to say that Ardesch had thought the convocation was too general and instead opted for a much more limited invitation that read:

Meeting of Dutch inhabitants of Batavia

Van Rees changed the request in pencil above the original phrase. Between pencil and print were hundreds of thousands of people at issue: a "meeting" versus a call for multiple demonstrations across Java, a contained demand versus a racially transgressive call to protest slipped between those amended words. When Van Rees opined to Cantervisscher in a conciliatory gesture that the former printed words were "a slip of the pen" (*schrijffout*), Cantervisscher stiffened and denounced the sham. He drew from his pocket a printed convocation flyer with the uncorrected phrase. Indeed he had hundreds of copies on his person. In addition, he refused to sign the amended document.

But many others did. When the final petition arrived at the Resident's office, there were nine appendices with the signatures of over two hundred male supporters. Even with its tempered amendments, the petition was a bold document, forceful in its demands. After praising the King's decision to call for constitutional reform in mid-March, it read:

> We would like to turn your Majesty's high attention to an institution that has already wounded so many parents deep in their heart; that has made so many children born in the Indies unhappy; has destroyed the future of all who receive their upbringing in [the Indies]; and is horribly affecting the moral and religious state of society. . . . [The Royal Decree of 1842 forces parents to send] their children away some thousands of miles from them at a very early age and to entrust them to the care of strangers and to exclude themselves from contributing to their moral formation, education and intellectual development. Experience has taught what the consequences of this are and many of the undersigned have all too painfully felt this most insufferable parental grief.[85]

For Rochussen, parental sentiments and the sorrow of a father's heart now looked much more like "political" issues and concerns of state. As he was to write to the Minister of Colonies in the following days, his deepest fear was not of outside foreign enemies but treason: with "nearly every member of the judiciary," as well as "chief military officers" implicated, "what measures could be taken if there was no purity within?"[86] What counted as "within" is hard to say: "within" the government, "within the colony,"

---

[85] AR, KV 317x, no. 493, no. 158/x., Appendix I.

[86] "[M]aar als *het van binnen* niet zuiver is, wat dan?"[my emphasis]; AR, KV 317x, no. 493, no. 158/x., Appendix I.

or "within" the community of Europeans among whom he counted his loyal supporters? Was it white sedition among the high-placed Europeans or revolt among those more lowly mixed bloods (*liplappen*) who had attended "armed with hidden daggers and walking sticks concealing their swords"? Or were these all the excesses of his overly primed colonial imagination? As those present at the meeting wryly noted, the daggers were not hidden. And walking sticks were what sensible people carried at night to protect themselves from petty thieves and more commonly from packs of dogs. Among those Europeans who came with pistols, they claimed to have armed themselves because of rumors that the urban underclasses (*stadslui*) were planning to make trouble.[87]

Marginalia on the petitions, annotations on subsequent reports, and confusion over the population to which it referred—and how to refer to them—were scribbled across page after page. In question was both the "real" nature of the complaints and the racial identity of those involved. Demands to improve the pension allotment were seen as pertaining principally to the "*Inlandsche Christenen*" ("native Christians") but the Minister of Colonies report to the King that September suggests that the identity of the participating population was less than clear. In it, the terms "*Portugezen*," "*creolen*," and "*kleurlingen*" ("colored") were added. Later, the latter two were crossed out, substituting "*Inlandsche kinderen*" in the margins.[88] If there was considerable ambiguity surrounding what to call the lower rungs of the mixed population, the evaluation of their inherent shortcomings was much more certain. As the Minister of Colonies put it: "The needs of these people are very few. For them, the half of a pension is more than the full pension for a European. Because of their limited mental capacities, they seldom get further than subordinate positions such as clerks, overseers, etc. for which the Radikaal is not required."[89]

Whether Rochussen himself feared that the *liplappen* might revolt en masse and "bring the Chinese into play," as he wrote to Baud, he considered it a plausible rationale to avert the "incalculable consequences" that might otherwise follow. It did not help that the day after the gathering Rochussen received reports that rumors were spreading among the native Javanese population in the outlying Bantam district of a "*perang di Batavia*" ("war in Batavia").

In subsequent months, hundreds of government documents assessed the social makeup of the Indies' European community, its resentments

---

[87] AR, KV 8 January 1857, no. 27, titled "Maartse Buien," testimony 22.

[88] AR, KV 317x, Governor-General no. 158/x, bijlage K, Petition to the Governor-General of the Netherlands Indies from "the native inhabitants of Java," 25 May 1848.

[89] AR, KV 327x, Minister Baud's report to the King, 10 August 1848, Letter. A.

Figure 5. Inside the main hall of the Harmonie Club, some twenty years after the May 1848 demonstration, in which several hundred people filled the same hall. *Source*: KIT 60089128, c. 1870.

and its liberal political currents, identifying those already inclined to rebel and which others might potentially join them. The gathering's organizers were to be dismissed from their posts and banned from ever returning to Java. By the time news of the event reached The Hague a month later, secret government missives were steeped in talk of treason, the imminent threat to peace and order, and outrage at the backhanded stab at metropolitan rule—assaults on the very sustainability of Dutch authority and the Netherlands' jewel of empire.

But who and what comprised the threat was not clear, certainly not in Governor-General Rochussen's letter to Baud four days after the gathering: was there subversion among the well-to-do, European-born city fathers, led by liberals like Van Hoëvell, or among the more extreme "hotheads" who stayed on at the Harmonie Club that night after the bulk of the crowd had retired? Was it a creole uprising among the Indies-born and -bred Europeans or a seditious bid to break off from the Netherlands by destitute "coloreds" with nothing to lose? As Van Hoëvell later pointed out in a series of detailed articles published in the *Tijdschrift voor Nederlandsch Indië* (replete with the citation of reference numbers in the official correspondence), Rochussen must have known almost nothing of what had gone on that night, since it was only a few days later that he requested the Van Rees make a detailed report of the events.

Rochussen's report described an "extremely agitated" public mood, while his letter to Baud—where he characterized his own position as "becoming extremely difficult"—displayed troubled and confused personal feelings. He was unsure of the scope of Van Hoëvell's support and how far it extended beyond him.[90] He wondered how Van Hoëvell could have printed the flyers without access to a government press and without the complicity of those who knew how to run them. Worse still was Van Hoëvell's betrayal in publishing a "disobligingly rude" article in which he had the audacity to cite confidential government documents. And interspersed with these comments, Rochussen's account would repeatedly circle back to the rumors in white Batavia, to the stir among lettered people in the lettered city about revolution in Europe and to the bravado, entitlements, and liberal thinking that the mail boats were bringing from Marseille.[91]

Some authorities apparently believed the gathering was the prelude to a revolutionary overthrow among liberal-minded colonials with a communist bent influenced by the events in Paris and Amsterdam two months earlier. More saw it as a refusal to accept what even the Governor-General assured the Minister of Colonies was an unjust privilege and that without abolition of the *Radikaal*, the colony would never have "a lasting peace." But the danger was also more immediate and threatening still. It was not generated by an impassioned outburst of a few, but by a critique lodged in

[90] As it turned out, some did go much further. Ardesch, Tollen, and Thieme, who had stayed on at the Harmonie Club after Van Hoëvell adjourned the meeting, sent a petition directly to Parliament on 26 June 1848 making those demands that had been shelved in the petition to the King by Van Hoëvell and his supporters. These included freedom of the press; limiting power to the Governor-General; an end to the monopoly of the *Nederlandsche Handel-Maatschappij* (the Dutch Trading Company); reform of the monetary system; and establishment of a new bank to stand alongside the government-controlled Java Bank. They also condemned the slave trade, "not only by Chinese and Arabs, but even by members of the Indies Advisory Council and directors of government ministries," what they called "the immoral selling of bodies and souls" (AR, KV 391x). Baud sent the petition on to the King, advising that "although some of the demands were not unfounded, the tone in which it was composed was so offensive against authority and the colonial administration, that for such persons to remain in the Indies was very dangerous for the peace and order of Java." He recommended that they be permanently expelled. And they were (AR, KV 391x, exh., 23 September 1848).

[91] Fasseur describes a route via the Isthmus of Suez, opened after 1844, that connected an overland route with a English steamship mail service, reducing the journey from the Netherlands to Java to just under two months. Post could then be sent monthly by "landmail," which in fact went via Marseille, Southhampton, or Trieste, and Alexandria and was collected from Singapore by a Dutch government steamship. See Cornelis Fasseur, *The Politics of Colonial Exploitation: Java, The Dutch and the Cultivation System* (Ithaca: SEAP, 1992), 17.

the *sustained distress* of parents who refused that their sons' careers should be contingent on an education in Europe, on four thousand miles of distance and at least eight years of separation from their mothers and fathers. Van Hoëvell would later describe what he obviously intended to portray as a heart-wrenching scene: in a Batavia living room, a mother, "Mevrouw van der Poot," sitting on a sofa, following with her eyes her seven-year-old son as his *babu* fed him his last slice of sugared butter and bread before departing for the ship that would take him to school in the Netherlands: "[she was] weeping and sobbing[;] with a vague and dark feeling, she said . . . that she would never again hold her child in her arms and press him close to her heart."[92] She was not to see him again for fifteen years. Colonial authorities may have little political weight to such singular stories as "Mevrouw van der Poot's," but the cumulative strain that such distress produced was in part what the administrative alarm was about. On the line was the Dutch regime's ability to assess the import of such sentiments—to predict and contain its visceral and, what Hume and Van Hoëvell understood so well, "contagious" quality.

CONTAGIOUS SENTIMENTS AND MARSEILLE MIASMAS

In May 1848 Victor Hugo was to write from Paris:

> From February to May, during these four months of anarchy in which the collapse was felt on all sides, the situation of the civilized world has been unparalleled. Europe feared a people, France; this nation feared a part of it, the Republic; and this part feared a man, [Auguste] Blanqui. The ultimate word for everyone has been fear of something or someone.[93]

The revolutionary fervor that swept through France in February 1848 resonated throughout Europe, but, as Victor Hugo observed, who and

---

[92] AR, KV 327x, Minister Rijk's report to the King, 10 August 1848, Letter A. *De demonstratie der ingezetenen van Batavia*, op den 22 Mei 1848. Van Hoëvell published no less than fourteen installments between 1848 and 1849. His more searing account of the indictment against him and those who participated in the 22 May demonstration appeared a year later as *De beschuldiging en veroordeeling in Indië, en de regtvaardiging in Nederland* (Zalt-Bommel: Joh. Noman, 1850).

[93] Juin Hubert, *Victor Hugo: Choses Vues. Souvenirs, Journaux, Cahiers, 1830–1885* (Paris: Gallimard, 2002), 552. The French text reads:

> De février à mai, dan ces quatre mois d'anarchie où l'on sentait de toutes parts l'écroulement, la situation du monde civilisé fut inouie. L'Europe avait peur d'un peuple, la France; ce peuple avait peur d'un parti, la République; et ce part avait peur d'un homme, Blanqui. Le dernier mot de tout était la peur de quelque chose ou de quelqu'un.

what was at risk and under attack was not everywhere the same. Demonstrations, petitions, and pamphlets in Vienna, Prague, Milan, Berlin, Frankfurt, and Dresden were about civil rights, representation in parliament, workers' councils, and workers' benefits. That which motivated a disenfranchised French middle class in February was not what made the working classes take to the streets in May. People talked of revolution and the abolition of slavery in Guadalupe in late April but at the very proclamation, as Hugo snidely observed, a white proclaimed it, a mulatto held his parasol, and a man of color carried his hat.[94]

And what did this have to do with the reverberating unease within the house of glass? Some authorities thought everything. Some saw the Harmonie Club demonstration as a colonial, Indies issue, spurred on, but not motivated by, European events. High authorities imagined a connection between political events in Europe and those in Batavia but were unsure of its nature. One thing is clear. They feared less an uprising modeled after the violently impassioned French and German ones than another sort of uprising—a creole revolt against a metropolitan stronghold on Indies policy, against what one petition called "the Russian autocracy" of colonial rule, against a civil service structure that imposed what Van Hoëvell characterized as "eternal familial estrangement" and steep financial burden as prerequisite for advancement to a lucrative career. The outrage was not only among the dispossessed but among the respected and "respectable" against a system that assured loyalty to the Dutch state rather than the Indies through a distorted circuit of knowledge-production—one that valorized and required for promotion competence in a removed, Netherlands-filtered knowledge of Java.[95]

Although students of the colonial are now more ready to accept the argument that metropole and colony should be treated as one analytic field, there is less consensus on what those contingencies look like on any specific historical ground. We remain confounded by the direct and indirect ways in which metropolitan practices shaped the face of empire and the other way around. But the conundrum is not ours alone. Working out the contingencies of confluence and commensurability, scope and scale, what bound a "community of sentiment" and what did not, were the very dilemmas of rule and what the tools of statecraft were designed to, but could only poorly, assess.

---

[94] Ibid., 551.

[95] As Rochussen added at the bottom of his letter of 27 May 1848 to Baud: "I just received a malicious petition from the *Inlandsche kinderen* about assimilation in all respects with the Dutch[-]born Hollanders. They are very much against Reijnst (who they had planned to plunder), and are also not well-disposed toward you." *De semi-officiële*, 365. It was, after all, Baud who as Governor-General in 1842 had imposed the original requirement for a Delft degree.

Authorities in Batavia spent the weeks and months after the May demonstration struggling to clarify the causes and meaning of the event. They questioned whether it was a home-grown colonial liberalism that had seized white Java, parental sentiments that were turning the state's very agents against it, the clamor for constitutional reform in the Netherlands echoed in the archipelago, or revolutionary fervor transported by print, passengers, and rumor via Trieste and Marseille. Rochussen's report was confused about what was a risk, and what and who was to blame. When February's overland post arrived in Java on 23 March, he reported no mention of the "new popular revolution and the fall of the crown" for the post had left The Hague on the twenty-third of February, the very day before the monarchy fell in Paris. But by mid-April private French tradesmen came with news of increased "communist thinking" spreading among Europe's working poor. Still, that news came a month *after* the rapid-fire shift in political direction in France. What had been accomplished in Europe in February and March "evaporated" by May.[96] By June the workers' national councils were abolished, with thousands killed or arrested. The bourgeoisie was in ascendancy and the workers' movement was in shambles.[97]

Radicals in Amsterdam did sing the Marseillaise and the International in March as they had in Paris, but with more muted vigor and with little effect. On Amsterdam's central square facing the palace, the Dam, it was sung by a small group of political activists, with little influence on (or participation by) a large constituency of the Dutch working class. Revolution in the Netherlands never seemed to have a chance.[98] Street slogans of "long live the Republic" were quickly channeled into more temperate demonstrations and meetings for constitutional reform.[99] The monarchy in France fell in February and by mid-March, King Willem II pre-empted the liberals by himself calling for broad constitutional reform. With parliamentary rule and ministers resigned, the *burgerij*—the stolid bourgeoisie—came into partial power. How partial these political maneuverings were is not hard to assess: over the next twenty-five years,

[96] William Sewell, *Work and Revolution in France: The Language of Labor from the Old Regime to 1848* (New York: Cambridge University Press, 1980), 272.

[97] Roger V. Gould, *Insurgent Identities: Class, Community and Protest in Paris from 1848 to the Commune* (Chicago: University of Chicago Press, 1995), 5–7.

[98] J. C. Boogman, "De politieke ontwikkeling in Nederland, 1840–1862," in *Geschiedenis van het moderne Nederland* (Den Haag: De Haan, 1988), 78–80. According to Boogman, the few score of workers that did demonstrate in Amsterdam in March were led by Dutch communist groups and order was so quickly "restored" that "the order-loving citizens in the Netherlands could rest at peace: the 'danger' of a real revolutionary development was doused" (80).

[99] M. J. F. Robijns, *Radicalen in Nederland (1840–1851)* (Leiden: Leiden Universitaire Pers, 1967), esp. 256–60.

eighty of the one hundred government ministers remained of patrician origin.[100] For the colonies, however, the reform was crucial. The Constitution of 1848 limited the Crown's power and assigned to the States-General, for the first time, a "real share" in legislating colonial policy in the overseas possessions.[101]

Events in Java were clearly part of a global historical moment in the mid-nineteenth century, but the public mood had its own impetus and took its own direction. Like the political banquet of 22 February in Paris, whose banning was said to have set the French insurrection in motion, Batavia had one of its very own. On 1 May Rochussen, in addressing a banquet of over one hundred guests on the occasion of inducting a new Indies Supreme Court, quickly realized that the applause that followed his toast to the King was "due more to the conviction and warmth with which I gave my speech than to approval of what I was saying."

Generalized disquiet among the European population was already evident in early 1848 but gained momentum in May. By 14 May—only eight days before the demonstration—Rochussen described a scene so dissonant with current historiography of colonial Java that it is hard to imagine that it took place. He described hundreds of people gathered at dawn in the old city's customs house to await the Batavia steamship from Singapore carrying their subscriptions to the European press. He too had come down from Buitenzorg to wait in the nearby government hotel. When the bundles were opened, along with the regular post were masses of newspapers, thick bundles of press clippings, and literary extracts addressed to many of the European inhabitants—himself included—who had neither requested nor had subscriptions for them. Upon reading that the King had conceded to a new governmental reform that would begin in March, people burst into applause. As Rochussen's report of 26 May to the Minister of Colonies detailed, throughout the crowd were cries that "the boom has fallen, the day of freedom has arrived for the colonies' inhabitants also to air their grievances and have their desires heard." And there was more to come, as we have already seen, less than two weeks later.

"DOWN WITH THE *RADIKAAL*?"

The night before the Harmonie Club gathering, the public mood was one of excitement and increased agitation in both the old and new city. Local police reports in Batavia from that night described something stranger

[100] Siep Stuurman, *Wacht op onze daden: Het liberalisme en de vernieuwing van de Nederlandse staat* (Amsterdam: Bert Bakker, 1992), esp. 135–70, 147.
[101] Fasseur, 103.

still—a charivaresque scene in the colored quarters of the old city, where small groups were heard shouting what authorities took to be a password, "*Samoanja radical,*" accompanied by music on large copper kettles. Carriages were unharnessed and pulled by men in the crowd. As they moved through the streets, a rowdy group made its way to the home of that much disliked member of the Indies Advisory Council, J. C. Reijnst, who in their petition they had named as "an enemy of the people" and called for his deportation. The crowd jeered as they passed, throwing stones at his house. Perhaps what was most unsettling to Rochussen in the reports of that night was the "fraternizing" of Eurasian and European youth with Chinese and the "popular classes" (*volksklasse*), reminding him, as he put it, of what had happened a century earlier—an uprising of Chinese in 1734 that ended in bloodshed.

But what was this outcry, "*Samoanja radical,*" which seems to have captured a bilingual *jeu de mot,* a Dutch Malay play on words, embedded in the phrase? The Malay word "*samoanja*" (or *semuanja*) literally means "they're all," or "everything is," which is clear enough. But "*radical,*" in mid-nineteenth-century Indies Dutch had two distinct referents: one, to "radical," in the more familiar political sense; and two, to the "*Radikaal*" (sometimes spelled "*radicaal*"), the despised diploma for entry into the elite ranks of the civil service, granted only by the academy in Delft. It was of course abolition of the *Radikaal* that was the principal subject of the next day's planned assembly. Whether "*Samoanja radical,*" as shouted on the streets of Batavia in 1848, meant "everything is about the diploma," or "everyone should be able to get the diploma," or "they're all radical" (the most unlikely) is impossible to say. There was no further mention of the phrase. It disappears from the archive, as does the rich ambiguity of Indonesia's colonial history buried in that bivalent phrase.[102] Nor did the Governor-General's report bother to explain the phrase to his friend, now the ex-Minister Baud, also a former Governor-General himself who (was it presumed?) knew what it meant.

It is not clear that Rochussen himself did.[103] In his report to the Minister, he wrote it as "*radical*" without the double *a* and without the *k* of

---

[102] Kathryn Woolard, in "Simultaneity and Bivalency as Strategies in Bilingualism," *Journal of Linguistic Anthropology* 8 (l) (1999), 3–29, uses "bivalence" to describe bilingual code-switching, "simultaneous messages of communication in the contact zone (and by extension . . . in almost any imaginable social zone of communication)."

[103] In fact, when Van Hoëvell resigned that July and returned to the Netherlands, in an issue of the *Tijdschrift voor Nederlandsch-Indië,* which he continued to edit and publish, he pointed out that Rochussen actually knew nothing about the gathering and submitted his report to the King *without* having received a *relaas* (detailed account) of the gathering from Resident van Rees, whose report came on 9 June, two weeks later. *Tijdschrift voor Nederlandsch-Indië* 1848 (l): 84–85.

Radikaal. His narrative moved from concerns over high officials "liberally expressing themselves in an unseemly manner" to an understanding that more was at issue than a "momentary outburst of feeling." His impressionistic day-by-day account of the events leading up to the demonstration jumped from Batavia to Paris and back again, interrupted by a long exegesis on the Indies population so negative in its appraisal that it suggested a colony primed for a creole-led revolt—certainly not one that would mount an independence movement with such a different composition a hundred years later. The picture Rochussen painted was dismal to say the least: in his profile were "the Javanese without any attachment to us," the Arabs who "hate us," "the Chinese who cherish only money and sensual pleasures," and a European population with increasing numbers of liberal thinkers made up of "the most energetic but not the most moral part of the nation."

Still more disturbing to him were increasing numbers of "coloreds" so "reduced to poverty they could only hope for a change and had nothing to lose." Here was a population, he argued, growing in proportion to the number of Europeans, and potentially dangerous given the increased "scientific" knowledge available to them. Discontent with regard to the low-ranking civil service posts they had long occupied and considered their own, they now saw even those positions threatened by more Dutch youths coming to Java. These "colored," Rochussen insisted, "were despised by natives and Europeans, but what most marked them was something else: They were people who were deprived in their youth *of parental love*, nameless or with names that branded them as illegitimately born, and with their hearts and souls full of hate for Europeans." Nor did the Governor-General miss the point that, among those most resented by the illegitimately born and abandoned, were their own fathers.[104]

Parental love (*ouderliefde*), too much of it (among creole whites) or not enough of it (among mixed bloods), seems to come up at every turn. Demand for parliamentary representation in Holland was a problem, but the "more dangerous grievances" were those perceived as broadly spread among the established *Indische* Europeans, among old timers and newcomers, creoles, and the colored: what they all wanted was an end to the privileges of the Delft monopoly and the obligatory *Radikaal* certificate that denied careers to their offspring.

Worse, still, was this forced separation, the feelings it engendered and what it did to people's lives. Rochussen punctuates his narrative with three searing tales that were plastered across the local European press: the case of a Dutch mother who went into shock and was rendered mad for several months after her two young sons departed for Europe; a father ruined by

[104] AR, KV 317, 5 August 1848 [my emphasis].

debt, forced to sell his furniture and broken by his efforts to pay for his son's schooling in Holland; and, perhaps most poignant, the story of an educated young man returning to Java after ten years' leave, whom we might imagine poised on the dock as his ship landed and scanning the sea of faces, wondering "which of these ladies is my mother?" Rochussen's defense of his action—granting permission for the gathering in sympathy with those "father hearts" bleeding too badly to be restrained or refused— was less convincing to the King. Dismissing Rochussen's distinctions between parental feelings and politics, he took the former to be no less dangerous than the latter because they were heartfelt *and* directed against the metropolitan monarchy and the emergent colonial state.

Historians of the Indies have alluded to the "disturbance" but the machinations that surrounded it and the political threat envisioned at the time garner little space in Dutch colonial historiography.[105] The prominent historian Cees Fasseur makes passing mention of the newspaper coverage of the maddened mother and ruined father as evidence that "pathos was not eschewed" and in fact inflated in the press.[106] But government authorities at the time took seriously the political force of affect and undoubtedly would have deferred from Fasseur's minimization of these sentiments. For decades after, a central, if unresolved, question remained: which sorts of domestic and pedagogic environments could instill loyalty to Dutch rule, and which sorts would nurture affective attachments dangerous to it?[107]

In subsequent months, the authorities hardened their conviction that a European education was critical to "the necessity for close ties between the motherland and colony" and the need for it to counter a prevailing trend: namely, "that with European children raised in the Indies those ties had come unbound and European parents too had estranged themselves from the motherland." Family rearing was important but only if mediated by other sorts of apprenticeship defined by state priorities. While some proposals were made to establish secondary schools "in healthy highland areas of Java separated from the Indies world" (on a "European footing" and with only European servants), more powerful voices demurred. The latter argued that the mothering styles of native and Indo-European women were turning their children toward native sensibilities rather than "cultivating" in them the energetic self-discipline that emerged in an authentic Dutch milieu. In the end, European higher education in the Indies was extended to Java but heavily policed for the mixed population on three foundational

---

[105] Michel-Rolph Trouillot, *Silencing the Past: Power and the Production of History* (Boston: Beacon, 1995), esp. 72–94.

[106] Fasseur, in *De Indologen: Ambtenaren voor de Oost, 1825–1950* (Amsterdam: Bert Bakker, 1993), 120–30, 121, discusses the demonstration under the subheading "Revolutionary Batavia" in the context of the expansion of the Indies civil service.

[107] On both points, see Stoler (1996), 137–64; (1995), 137–64; and (2002), 112–39.

grounds: that Indies mothers were incompetent to rear their young as true Europeans; that the "personality traits of the *Inlandsche kinderen* formed a hindrance that as a rule could not be overcome"; and that in contrast prolonged residence in the Netherlands would "awaken love of the fatherland" for those Indies-born children so sorely deprived of it.[108] The Minister of Colonies made the latter case:

> Raising and educating Europeans in the Indies will stand in the way of a desirable civilizing of the native and this upbringing will have the result that these children so frequently suckled with the breast milk of Javanese wet nurses along with their own native children, at a more advanced age, will lack any sense of unity with Europeans. They become haughty, imperious, lazy and lascivious. They will learn from their youth to mistreat and denigrate servants; they become, in male adulthood, still greater despots than now is the case with the native rulers themselves.[109]

At issue was *not* the insubordinate sentiments of the colonized, but rather the inappropriately expressed aspirations of those "out of character" and "out of place": "haughty" referred to those mixed bloods who refused to do manual labor; "imperious" to those creoles who claimed their right to the status of "full-blooded" Europeans; "lascivious" to those whose sexual desires were seen as misdirected toward those above their racialized standing and class. This was an "emotional economy" of affective relations of production and exchange that tied the senses and their expression to the worth of human kinds.[110]

This fear of contagious emotions prompted another fear: that those who remained too attached to the Indies would see themselves more as "world citizens" (as they were fearfully labeled) than as patriotic partisans of Dutch rule. Over the next seventy years Dutch authorities continued to battle over when and how to intervene in the education of school-age children and in the formative rearing of the very young. Crucial to this understanding was the idea that local knowledge should never be too local and that familial attachments were to be mediated and reworked through concerns of state, filtered through a fine sieve, through the ears of Dutch categories, distilled into European typologies, and reconfigured as sanctioned knowledge in usable form. That could conceivably be done in Indies schools run on European principles by Europeans. But success was easier to achieve from the distance of the Netherlands—where social categories were tethered to specific racialized traits. Not least, parental love required separation

[108] *Het Pauperisme onder de Europeanen in Nederlandsch-Indië*, Part 1 (Batavia: Landsdrukkerij, 1902), 20.

[109] AR, KV 389x, 22 September 1848.

[110] Herzog, 202–43.

from one's offspring. Most importantly, local knowledge would be digested through institutions of learning in Europe and only then re-served as qualified knowledge about Indies "customs," "cultures," and "peoples," ideally shorn of touch and taste and no longer local at all.

AFFECTIVE REGISTERS IN THE PUBLIC SPHERE

Colonial scripts prompt us, their distant readers, to imagine that concern with the affective was centered on unbridled passions, irrational outbursts, or at least the unpremeditated affective states their bearers embraced. These scripts make it plausible to imagine that what European authorities feared most was that "hidden force" so powerfully described at the turn of the century, by the Dutch novelist Louis Couperus as that to which the colonized had access and colonials unknowingly could be subject, a display of sentiments that evinced more powerful mystic and mental states.[111] But, as the public assembly of 22 May suggests, this may not have been the case. Rather than extemporaneous passions was the threat of *sustained* sensibilities, resentments against ongoing unfreedoms, and the political standards which they called into question. Outbursts were manageable. It was those durable sentiments, those of parental distress and the wounds of estrangement, that expressed judgment and critique. These were (un)colonial dispositions and expectations with high political stakes.[112] Colonial authorities, not unlike moral philosophers, understood sentiments to be moving and sensory, "richly cognitive," deeply felt appraisals.[113] Some sentiments mattered not because they were in conflict with reason but because they demanded "specific sorts of reason" that indicated social knowledge of expectations and a rich evaluative vocabulary.[114] The "hatred" that Dutch authorities so feared arising among disenfranchised mixed blood youths (what the Governor-General Baud

[111] Louis Couperus, *The Hidden Force* (*De stille kracht*) (Amherst: University of Massachusetts Press, 1985).

[112] Quoted in Francis Dunlop, *The Education of Feeling and Emotion* (London: George Allen and Unwin, 1984), 7.

[113] In philosophy, judgmentalism views emotion as "involv[ing] a moral judgment . . . an appeal to moral standards and not merely personal evaluations." See Robert Solomon, *The Passions* (Garden City, N.Y.: Doubleday, 1976), 185, and Allan Gibbard, *Wise Choices, Apt Feelings: A Theory of Normative Judgment* (Cambridge, Mass.: Harvard University Press, 1990), esp.126–35.

[114] Justin D'Arms and Daniel Jacobson note in "The Right Way to Feel" that "envy, anger, pride and the like each come with a built-in epistemology that demands specific sorts of reason for feeling the emotion, and requires others to accept certain reasons as rational grounds for it." I thank Allan Gibbard for sharing this manuscript. See also Jon Elster, *Alchemies of Mind: Rationality and the Emotions* (Cambridge: Cambridge University Press, 1999).

referred to as the "*liplappen*"), the threat of "patricide" envisioned by colonial authorities and called by that name, were affective states that were moving, dispassionately reasoned, and often rejections of standardized "European" norms.[115]

What colonial officials feared was not the *economic* costs of providing education for Europeans in the Indies (undoubtedly cheaper for the state), but the disparate cultural, economic, and political investments of those families who sought to bring up their children in the Indies and dared to think of the Indies as their "fatherland." If postcolonialism has produced a "fax nationalism," as Benedict Anderson suggests, colonialism produced its own distorted, long-distance variant. Colonialism in the Indies was only viable if local affinities were kept subordinate, if the pleasures of the colonial remained a "hardship allowance" but the colony itself was not home. The colonial difference was key. As Rochussen bluntly put it, those Europeans who wanted to enjoin the full freedoms that a constitutional democracy embodied should return to the Netherlands. For those who had decided to raise their families and make their fortunes in the Indies, they had to accept the constraints of a colonial situation. Freedom of the press, freedom of assembly, and representation in parliament were universal "rights" only in a European context and those who wanted them were advised to return home.[116]

Immanuel Kant's reason-based account of moral thinking and practice might well have informed imperial policy, but so, too, did Locke's contention that moral thinking was embodied in the dispositions of the every-

---

[115] Nor were all of these unstated, tacit judgments. In a published and powerful defense of Van Hoëvell, the learned liberal Pieter Johannes Veth (1814–1895) noted that it was Van Hoëvell who was among the few willing to put in print that Dutch colonial authorities considered the peoples of the Indies not "thinking, reasoning, independent individuals suited and destined for development but as a mass," who would and should always remain as they were, a "steam engine that once started up needs no further care other than supervision." It was Van Hoëvell who accused "this huge machine of the state administration in the Indies" of resisting change by condemning those who sought to promote it as "noxious and pernicious." Pieter Johannes Veth, *Bijdragen tot de kennis van den politieken toestand van Nederlandsch-Indië* (Amsterdam: P.N. van Kampen, 1848), 5.

[116] But as Van Hoëvell noted a year later, colonial legislation actually changed the definition of who was a foreigner and for whom the Indies could be considered home. What Van Hoëvell called "the barbaric system" that forced Indies European inhabitants to send their children to the fatherland undid the notions of belonging and home. Quoting a cruel exchange in 1847 between Resident van Rees and a distressed father, whose nineteen-year-old son, born in Soerabaja, upon returning to his parents' "home" from study in Amsterdam was deemed a "foreigner" (*vreemdeling*), Van Hoëvell writes that Van Rees, in a terse letter, ordered the son to make a formal request to remain in the Indies (with a duplicate notarized birth certificate in hand), pay a fine of several hundred guilders, or leave the colony within a week. Van Hoëvell queried, as did the father, how a child born in the Indies could be a foreigner? *Tijdschrift voor Nederlandsch-Indië* 1849 (l): 290–95.

day, in the habits of comportment that had to be learned.[117] It was also not unlike that of Hume, for whom "sentiments" and "passions" were seen to "treacherously cover both feeling and thought."[118] Like Locke, colonial experts debated the sensibilities that endowed certain individuals with the "capabilities" to exercise freedom, to be responsible as citizens capable of progress, to be deemed actors who were "rational men." To be reasonable, as Max Horkheimer once noted, not be obstinate, to conform "with reality as it is."[119] Those city fathers, government officers, those men of class and character who gathered in the evening on the streets of Batavia in May 1848 (and worse still, those who lingered later into the night) were deemed "unseemly" and unreasonable if not "irrational"— and therefore unsuitable colonial men. To be reasonable was to master one's passions, command one's sensibilities, and abide by proper invocation and dispersal of them.

What could be taken for a failed creole nationalist impulse—a hardening conflict of interest between the Indies-born Dutch and those of the Netherlands—accentuated debates over who were full-fledged citizens and who were marginal variants. It also underscored a critical feature of the colonial state's early formation—its commitment to consolidating a more clearly delineated politics of race. Max Müller's observation that the British colonial state in India was devoted to a "conquest of the heart" might now seem obvious, but the fact that those arts of suasion were as firmly directed at distinguishing among colonizing agents as among colonized subjects is less so. Appropriate sentiment structured advancements within the bureaucratic apparatus and the affiliations outside it. But the boundaries between those spaces inside and out were porous and often redrawn.[120] Imputed sentiments, ascriptions of affective negligence, or excess were among the measures that differentiated mixed blood from pure blood, Indies- from Netherlands-born, and children tinged with native blood from their pure blood European age mates. Who displayed which sentiments, and when and where such display occurred, were purported to distinguish the coveted attributes of the European-born and -bred elite from

---

[117] See Uday Mehta, *The Anxiety of Freedom* (Ithaca: Cornell, 1992), 127–54, who examines Locke's understanding of the malleability of the child's mind, an understanding that leads him to detail the everyday practices required to make a child into a cultivated being.

[118] Quoted in Annette Baier, *A Progress of Sentiments: Reflections on Hume's Treatise* (Cambridge, Mass.: Harvard University Press, 1991), 181.

[119] Max Horkheimer, *The Eclipse of Reason* (New York: Seabury, 1974 [1947]), 10.

[120] Timothy Mitchell, "The Limits of the State: Beyond Statist Approaches and their Critics," *American Political Science Review* 85 (March 1991): 77–96, argues that "producing and maintaining the distinction between state and society is itself a mechanism that generates resources of power"; and see Akhil Gupta, "Blurred Boundaries: The Discourse of Corruption, the Culture of Politics and the Imagined State," *American Ethnologist* 22 (2) (1995): 375–402 .

those Indies-born Europeans who dared to suggest that they were as fully Dutch as those Dutch who held fast to their right to rule.

Ascribed sentiments indexed entitlements and rights, as well as adherence to the cultural standards of appropriate behavior, reasonable expectations, and acceptance of racialized limitations.[121] Attribution of sentiments mapped what was "out of character" and "out of place." Mixed bloods could only be called "too proud" because they expected more than they were granted: better jobs than those given to "natives," access to the better-paid and well-pensioned civil service ranks. They were deemed "self-aggrandizing" because they refused to do manual labor, as we shall see in the next chapter. Creoles could only be called "imperious" in a political system in which they expressed political commitments to issues that mattered less to those Dutch-born Europeans for whom the Indies was but a temporary home. Native women who thought to outfit their mixed blood daughters in European dress in the hope of securing their entrance into better schools could be called "duplicitous" and "conniving." Such attributions both reflected controversies about social hierarchies and consolidated those distinctions. This emotional economy was a forceful reminder of social prescription and of where people belonged. As Ian Hacking reminds us, such systems created the very realities they ostensibly only described.[122]

Historian Christopher Bayly, in a thoughtful analysis of the information order of British India, has argued that the mastery of "affective knowledge" was an early concern of the British colonial state that diminished during the nineteenth century as that state became more hierarchical and governing became a matter of routine.[123] I have argued here that affective knowledge was at the core of political rationality in its late-colonial form. Colonial modernity hinged on a disciplining of one's agents, on policing the family, on Orwellian visions of interventions in the cultivation of compassion, contempt, and disdain.

---

[121] See Herzog, 241.

[122] Ian Hacking, "The Looping Effect of Human Kinds," in *Causal Cognition: An Interdisciplinary Approach*, ed, D. Sperber, D. Premack, and A. Premack (Oxford: Oxford University Press, 1996), 351–83.

[123] Christopher Bayly, *Empire and Information: Intelligence Gathering and Social Communication in India, 1780–1870* (Cambridge: Cambridge University Press, 1996), 365. Bayly uses the term "affective knowledge" to describe a more specific range and source of knowledge than I do here: "The knowledge gained through participation in communities of belief and marriage, through religious affiliation and association with holy men, seers, astrologers and physicians . . ." (17). He refers also to the "deep knowledge" that came from the "sense of inhabiting the same moral realm. In the early days of conquest the gap was not so apparent. Britons married Indian wives and communicated through contacts of mixed race. . . . The British, however, were not very interested in affectionately savouring the delights of the land. They sought instead a textual and quantified understanding of the country in order to make it 'progress' and pay" (55).

The accumulation of affective knowledge was not then a stage out of which colonial states were eventually to pass. Debates on poor whites and child-rearing practices nearly a century later make that point again and again. Deliberations over the quality of upbringing, of whether abandoned mixed blood children could be placed in the "care of the mother" (*moeder-zorg*) or care of the state (*staatszorg*) put the responsibility for the formative production of sentiment at the heart of political agendas. In deliberations over how best to secure "strong attachments" to the Netherlands among a disaffected and growing European population, "feeling" was the word that crops up repeatedly. At stake were disquieted reflections on what it took to make someone "moved" by one set of sensory regimes—of sounds, smells, tastes, and touch—and estranged from another.[124]

Dutch authorities never agreed on how to cultivate European sensibilities in their young, and just how early in a child's development they imagined they needed to intervene. But as a broader history of child rearing would show, these were not idiosyncratic colonial concerns. Seventeenth-century philosophers, eighteenth-century medical experts, and nineteenth-century purveyors of domestic science rehearsed the same set of questions: whether affective dispositions were filtered through a wet nurse's milk, the tone of a lullaby, or in the moral makeup of a pregnant mother.[125] In the nineteenth-century Indies, too, colonial coffers, time, and energy were expended on devising education and social policy that would provide their own children and those of their creole counterparts with proper "feelings" and "attachments" to things Dutch and to imbue them with a "disaffection" for that which was native—or at least a disinterested sympathy for it.

Architects of colonial rule saw familial attachments implicated in political security in nuanced ways. They not only sought to intervene in the secreted domestic arrangements of European homes, but worried over whether weak—or excessively strong—personal attachments would trump political loyalties. George Orwell's futuristic fantasy in *1984* of a thought-police that staked out interior family spaces was undoubtedly based on the specter of totalitarian European states, but it was equally motivated by another manifestation of those states that Orwell and generations of his family knew more intimately, the British Empire.[126]

---

[124] On sensory regimes in memory-work and the making of race, see Stoler (2002), 162–204.

[125] On the relationship between character, race and breast milk, see Stoler (1995), 162–63, and the references therein. On childcare and the philosophy of the emotions, see James, 7–8.

[126] See Raymond Williams, *George Orwell* (New York: Columbia University Press, 1971), 1–2, who was among the first of his biographers to address Orwell's multigenerational family history in the colonial service (his paternal grandfather was in the Indian Army, his maternal grandfather was a teak trader in Burma, and his father was in the Indian civil service). Orwell himself served in the Indian Imperial Police for nearly five years until 1927, when he resigned.

The colonial state could only be selectively panoptic; it was directed less at the internal dynamics in domestic spaces of the colonized than on the minute movements and psychological perturbations of their white and not quite white agents—in their clubs, offices, with their children, at school and at home. Reading Orwell's *Burmese Days*, or his even more arresting short story "Shooting an Elephant," beside *1984* suggests a colonial order of things in which sentiments were effects of political systems, not metaphors for them.

MORAL STATECRAFT: STATISTICS AND SENTIMENT

Students of colonialism have focused on those features of statecraft that measured, classified, and controlled the movements of colonized populations—on those features that could place them in a hierarchy of human kinds. We have come to see censuses, cartography, ethnological surveys, and statistics as forms of knowledge collection that epitomized state commitments to large-scale rationalized reform based on predictive and comprehensive scientific knowledge.[127] Such technologies are seen to emphasize the rationality of human behavior and the efficacy of precision tools that could measure the probability that one could be counted on to follow social norms. But statistics enjoyed its "distinctive reputation" as the "science of the state" not only because it claimed this authority.[128] Its force also resided in its principal subject—the study of deviance, abnormal behavior, *moeurs*, and mental states. Referred to as "the mental science" and the "moral science," respectively, in late-eighteenth- and early nineteenth-century Britain and France, its practitioners sought "ratios of deviancy" (much as they did "laws of mortality") that would both describe and prescribe thought and action.[129]

---

[127] See Benedict Anderson, *Imagined Communities*, 2d ed. (London: Verso, 1991) esp. 163–86; Bernard Cohn, *Colonialism and Its Forms of Knowledge: The British in India* (Princeton: Princeton University Press, 1996). Peter Pels, "The Anthropology of Colonialism: Culture, History, and the Emergence of Western Governmentality," *Annual Review of Anthropology* (1997) 26: 163–83.

[128] Alain Desrosières, *The Politics of Large Numbers: A History of Statistical Reasoning.* (Cambridge, Mass.: Harvard University Press, 1998), 19.

[129] Ian Hacking, "How Should We Do the History of Statistics?" in *The Foucault Effect: Studies in Governmentality*, ed. G. Burchell, C. Gordon, and P. Miller (Chicago: University of Chicago Press, 1991), 181–95. I thank Peter Pels for sharing his manuscript, "The Politics of Aboriginality: Orientalism and the Emergence of an Ethnology of India, 1833–1869." On moral science as prescriptive, see Lorraine Daston, *Classical Probability in the Enlightenment* (Princeton: Princeton University Press, 1988), esp. 296–369. See also Nikolas Rose, *The Psychological Complex* (London: Routledge and Kegan Paul, 1985), who holds that "moral management" referred to the"emotions and the will rather than the body" (23).

Indies authorities embraced these measures of the moral in their efforts to distinguish human kinds. Commissions of enquiry on European destitution in the colonies, on the moral ecologies that produced concubinary arrangements between native women and European men, mixed blood orphans and their "inclination" to crime—all plotted a politically dangerous set of affective microenvironments. Authorities sought to identify habits of the heart, to assess the presence of resentment, rancor, impudence, and disdain, the degrees of and potential for affective intensity, amidst those categories of people whose dispositions were thought to incline toward danger.

How sentiments articulate with state projects can be imagined in several ways, some more developed than others. In one perspective, states are in the business of controlling the passions of their subjects and citizens, setting up rules to ensure they are penalized for transgressions and remain subject to a rule of reason and a rule of law. In this model, affect is outside the state; reason is the means to sort out irrational ends. Alternately, knowledge of affect may be seen as an art of the individual politician's craft and his or her mobilizing rhetoric. Tapping into what people consider their "private" aspirations presumes a fine-tuned empathy, both more and less than people want those who rule to know. Here a knowledge of sentiment is seen as a ruse of politicians, not something internal to the structure of states. Others, such as William Reddy, offer keen insight into how specific sentiments drive bureaucracies, their recruitment procedures and meritocracies. Here affective knowledge is that on which states depend in their pursuit of "the art of knowing men."

There is yet another interpretive strategy, the one I have attempted to describe here. Sentiment is the negative print of the colonial archive's reasoned surface, the ground against which the figure of reason is measured and drawn. Archived missives between Governors-General and Ministers of Colonies, lawyers and parliament, city fathers and local police all plot "structures of feeling," residual and sedimented into the artifacts of debates, emergent as they sprawl across dry reports in which they would otherwise seem to have no proper place.

The supremacy of reason did figure prominently in the making of rule and its statist projects but its distinction from the affective never constituted a stable epistemic ground. Parenting practices, nursery rules, and sleeping arrangements were not archival marginalia. These were understood to be key sites where self-regulating habits were formed, where dispositions to race and empire were made "second-nature." "Unseemly" sentiments indexed mismanagement of the polity and mismanagement of the self.

A genealogy of colonial morality would not be a search for what was moral and what was not. Rather, it would address the social etymologies of the moral, its unstable vocabulary and political coordinates. It might look at imperial interventions in the emotional economy of the everyday. Not least, it would ask why colonial authorities knew what we are only beginning to grasp: that the viability of colonial regimes depended on middling masters struggling to predict and prescribe which sentiments would be contagious and portable across the globe—and which would not.

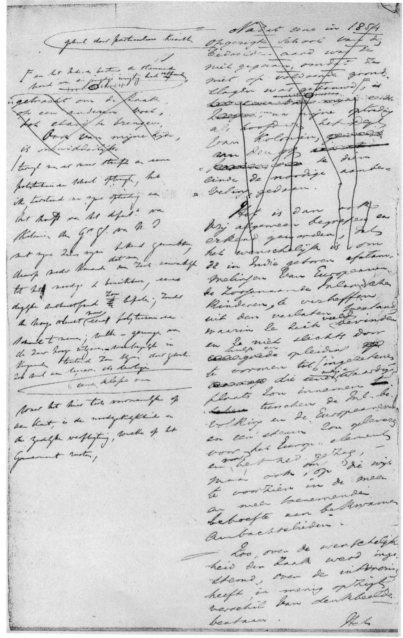

Figure 6. A draft of the Minister of Colonies' *verbaal* to the King concerning the establishment of an artisan/craft school in Soerabaya. Here one can see how much revision, addition, and deletion went into producing a final document. Note reference in the middle of the page to the fact that the school would not only uplift the "*zoogenaamde* [so-called] *Inlandsche kinderen*" but provide support for the "European element and for Dutch authority," as well as meet the "ever more increasing need for skilled craftsmen."

CHAPTER FOUR

Developing Historical Negatives

> We do not want to create imitation Europeans, we just need
> perfected natives.
>
> —AR, KV 28 March 1874, no. 47M

THE ABOVE CAPTURES BOTH the arrogance of Dutch colonial authorities and a delusional confidence in their projects. Who the "we" were went easily unstated, just as the possibility of social engineering was assumed. But to whom did this slip between the mimetic and the perfected apply? To whom was this contempt for the ersatz attached? It was *not* to the indigenous population, as students of colonialism might expect—not to the Indies' Javanese, Batak, or Balinese. This scrutinizing gaze of reform was cast elsewhere, across the dimly discerned outlines of another population—those who occupied the racial corridors of Indies society—who were poor and light skinned, and most often mixed blood descendants of Europeans.

They are not called Eurasians, or "half-bloods," or "metis"—all racialized assignments by which a mixed racial positioning might be conferred. The reference to so-called *Inlandsche kinderen* in official parlance marks the unease in administrative circles about how they might be named and who they actually were. That discomfort never detaches from the noun "children," from the adjective "native," from the qualified prefix "so-called," creating at once a suspect naming and a disparaging official distance that refuses to relinquish or release the term. For, as we already know, those denoted by this category were neither "native" (*inlandsche*) nor necessarily "children" (*kinderen*). The sense of *inlandsche* here is perhaps better captured by its connotation of "home-grown": that is, Europeans born and bred in the colony, the yield of its native soil.

"Children" (*kinderen*) is ambiguous but with this inflection it too makes vernacular sense. As the offspring of European men and native women—often abandoned by their fathers—or paupered whites of European birth, the term "children" may speak to a tender age but as often implies a subordinate and dependent status, the neediness of an underclass born out of colonial contact, an ill-fated group more akin to what "children" connotes in the biblical expression "children of god." Orphaned or abandoned status, economic destitution, and racial ambiguity joined to make them objects of pity, disdain, and threat.

By the 1840s the term *Inlandsche kinderen* was already endowed with pejoratives. The Governor-General could confide to the Minister of Colonies, with colloquial pleasure, that he (of all people) was no "liplap lover."[1] Conceived to be "white-haters" (*"blanken-haters"*), who might later become colonial dissidents, it was the state's fantasy that under proper tutelage and rigorous reform, the *Inlandsche kinderen* could one day be the most loyal vanguard of a modern and stable colonial rule.

BLUEPRINTS OF DISTRESS

This chapter turns to documents of a specific kind; those in which colonial officials thought about and envisioned specific concrete responses to what they saw as the disturbing increase of those persons strewn across the colonial divide over the course of the second half of the nineteenth century. But it is more the *subjunctive mood* of official imaginings and the affective temperament of their archived inscriptions that interest me here. The sheer volume of documents dedicated to the remaking of the *Inlandsche kinderen*, the profusion of proposals conceived to deal with their affective malaise, turns us to the nature of the archive that disquiet produced. For this is a genre of archival production lodged less in "what happened" than in the anticipatory, the foreseen, and the possible— fantasies that, as Jacqueline Rose has suggested, threatened "political composure."[2] These are narratives not about what might *have been*—as counterfactuals are—but more about what *might yet be*.

Such imaginings are not usually the stuff of our histories. But the archival space of the Dutch colonial state swells with them, a site of both the phantasmic and the assiduously concrete. State fantasies careen between the detailed and ethnographic, the theoretically conceivable and the fearfully abstract. What they are not is "events" in the conventional sense that historians attach to a discrete occurrence and its documented occasion. On the contrary, they make up an ethnographic archive recording the non-eventful: in drafts of proposals, in unrealized and unrealizable plans, in short-lived experiments, in liabilities and in failed projects. They are rather templates of the present and visions of the future. They are the archival traces that only sometimes congealed into full-blown debates: more often they are filled with innuendo, exchange opinion, and observations that shaped governing taxonomies and gave substance to colonial politics.

[1] *Liplap* here has the distinctly pejorative sense of "half-breed." See *De semi-officiële en particuliere briefwisseling*. The Governor-General uses the term throughout his correspondence, explaining that while he is "no lover of the *liplappen*," he sees that something must be done to ameliorate the conditions producing discrimination toward them.

[2] Jacqueline Rose, *States of Fantasy* (Oxford: Clarendon, 1998), 5.

It is the "non-eventful" quality of these archives that this chapter pursues and from which we may take our analytic cue. Rather than beginning from the notion that the colonial "facts of the matter" might be found in the actual "events" that made up social reforms that were carried out, this archival form resides in the conditional tense. Such unrealized and improbable plans were accretions of official knowledge that we can read as a political diagnostic. These were reflective discernments filtered through a lens at once microscopic and wide-angled, at once about the Netherlands (on the cusp of a diminishing agrarian base, an as yet emergent industrial future), and a colonial utopia obliquely expressed.

Metropolitan Transparencies and Colonial Negatives

> *negative* (photog.), n., Image on glass with reversed lights and shadows from which positive pictures are drawn.
> —*Concise Oxford Dictionary*

> *transparency*, n., Picture . . . shown up by light behind.
> —*Concise Oxford Dictionary*

These visions highlight the politics of race through tone and hue, through frames of different scope, and contrasts of different intensity. The stark glare of the present casts shadows across a foreboding future: the unsettling dispositions of what were referred to as "wavering" colonial classes, whose future might forecast the underside of what things might someday be. Some proposals had their referents in Europe, others in the Indies, still others in colonial contexts further afield. Together they map circuits of knowledge-production of varied scale and unexpected breadth. Colonial officials both created and called up a set of transnational equivalencies between "their" indigent Europeans and those elsewhere. What was produced was less often viable social policy than anxious efforts to identify an elusive social category available for cross-colonial comparison. Not least, these administrative recitations bear witness to how analogies were fashioned, and how the casual narratives that tied racial membership, class belonging, and impoverishment accumulated, gained, lost, and regained credibility when they were cross-referenced and (re)stored.

These "colonial utopias" then were not so much "paradigms of conquest" as they were blueprints of distress.[3] They make up what Frederic

---

[3] Cf. with Steve Stern, "Paradigms of Conquest: History, Historiography, and Politics," *Journal of Latin American Studies* 24 (1992): 1–34, in which the conquistadors' "contending paradigms of utopias" are used to describe the colonizing project in sixteenth-century Latin America (6).

Jameson might designate as the horizons of the "political unconscious," the disjuncture between what was possible to think and impossible to implement in and Indies' context and a colonial world.[4] Such a focus presents an analytic and methodological quandary: how much historical weight should be assigned to such a set of improbable visions that were, for the most part, never implemented? How should we treat the history of what was deemed possible but remained unrealized? What can we learn about colonial cultures and the states they sustained from their aborted projects, from proposals whose circulation was interrupted, from (blue)prints that were ultimately scrapped?[5]

This is not a return to a history of ideas, mentalities, or representations. Instead my attention to "non-events" takes as its subject the uneven presence of what was imagined as the possible, the tension between what was realizable and what was romance, between plausible plans and implausible worlds. At issue here is not the relationship between "text" and "context," but the changing force fields in which these proposals were produced. I think here of a space for "developing historical negatives." The analytic shift from the high-gloss print of history writ-large to the space of its production, the darkroom negative: from direct to refracted light, from "figure" and "field"—that which is more often in historic relief—to the inverse, grainy texture of "surfaces" and their shifting "grounds."

Although the *Inlandsche kinderen* confounded the statistics of the colonial state and were indeed largely invisible to numeration, they appear everywhere in the state's archives: in reports on public education and health, in discussions on the colonial economy, in debates over political unrest, and in commissions on social welfare. This oscillation between presence and absence marks a social kind whose content was malleable, whose membership was reshuffled as state visions of what we might call a "domesticated race" shifted and changed.

Romances of the Modern in the Colonial Archives

I treat these visions as historical negatives whose reverse-images traces disturbances in the colonial order of things, whose shadows trace the lineaments of potential dissent and current distress. As prose they are

---

[4] On Jameson's notion of political and semantic horizons of possibility, see Fredric Jameson, *The Political Unconscious: Narrative as a Socially Symbolic Act* (Ithaca: Cornell University Press, 1981), esp. 74–93.

[5] I thank political scientist James Johnson for his comments on an earlier version of this chapter and for pointing me to Geoffrey Hawthorn, *Plausible Worlds: Possibility and Understanding in History and the Social Sciences* (Cambridge: Cambridge University Press, 1991).

uninspired, but as political narratives they read as strangely compelling, even as utopian romances. As visions of colonial futures, they were what Foucault might have called "political dreams"—"figures of political technology" that were judged to be "impractical" yet central to colonial design, both in and out of place.[6]

Most obviously they were imagined and imaginative, offered to enlist their readership in new visions, and not least to persuade. Some were schematic, but many were attuned to the details of the everyday. Painstakingly penned, they were ethnographic reflections that called up the definition of "romance" as something of a "moving nature."[7] All were characterized by studied attention to the affective states of those persons they sought to remold: to what habits of the heart might accompany a trade, to the "character" qualities of craftsmen, to the moral sensibilities that environment and handwork might bestow, to *the management of sentiment as well as the management of labor.*

Like those sentiments discussed in the preceding chapter, these colonial romances were relational, dependent on situated knowledge, and thus have histories of their own. Three stand out, not because they are wholly distinct in vision or chronology (they, in fact, work around and through one another's visions in recursive rather than linear ways), but because they refract different referents with respect to what served for each as precedent, context, and relevant model. One could be called an "artisanal romance," dating from the 1840s. Promoted during a moment of expanding social reform in the Netherlands, it coincided in the Indies with the consolidation of the European colonial community and its administrative apparatus. Its advocates imagined the making of European foremen, craftsmen, and artisans who would meet the demand for competent craft labor and serve as a dependable lower-middle class (*middenstand*).[8]

This artisan class (*ambachtstand*) was to embody new competencies and fulfill new economic desires. To be trained as piano tuners, clockmakers, tailors, saddle makers, and cobblers, they were to service the consumption needs and the cultural distinctions of a European enclave, fecund in cultural capital and proliferating with material prosperity. The list of crafts is telling in itself. It anticipates the demands of a growing European elite and longings for acquisitions and services that the majority of the Indies' Dutch inhabitants neither had nor would ever have the means to afford.

---

[6] S.v. "utopia," as derived from "nowhere, from Gk *ou*, not + *topos*, place" (*Concise Oxford Dictionary*). On "political dreams," see Michel Foucault, *Discipline and Punish* (New York: Vintage, 1977), 117.

[7] S.v. "romance" (*Concise Oxford Dictionary*).

[8] "*Middenstand*" and "*middelstand*" were used interchangeably in these mid-nineteenth-century documents.

An "industrial romance" complemented and competed with the earlier vision. Promoted in the 1860s and 1870s, its advocates called for the making of an industrial labor force from an unskilled, illiterate poor white–mixed blood class. Here, Indies-born sons would become the new "subordinate technical personnel" for a modernizing colony, a labor aristocracy armed with limited European practical training and a selective local knowledge.[9] They were to be schooled as land surveyors, telegraph operators, post office workers, and skilled mechanics for heavy machinery. They would operate both the communication network and productive forces of an expanding, technologically advanced, capitalist colony foreseen on the near horizon.

A "rural romance" prevailed over a longer period and was at once the most nostalgic, the most utopian, and the most embattled of all these imagined futures. Here was envisioned an ironic return to the land for those who had never lived upon it, a reclamation of a mode of existence that might forge a new settler colonialism out of those who were not really "settlers" but born in the colony and considered only "quasi-European." At its heart was the fantasy of a placated and placid population of small-scale truck farmers, living off a modest but productive agrarian base. The vision was for the Indies but its nostalgia and yearnings were grounded elsewhere. In part, its source was the Netherlands, where an extensive landed yeomanry was in attrition and such a way of life becoming less possible.[10]

But that rural romance was also part of a reformist vision across the colonial globe. It is what I call here the *carceral archipelago of empire*. Explicitly, its blueprints were drawn from early nineteenth-century models of agricultural colonies fashioned to reform Europe's impoverished urban youth through bodily discipline and love of the soil. The most famous and relevant example for colonial authorities was based on the 1840 rural penal colony in Mettray, France, and the experiments that it inspired. In its Indies variant such children's colonies would produce future generations to serve as choice cultural brokers and political middlemen, at once adept in native know-how but committed and beholden to Dutch supremacy and its enduring rule.

These disparate and competing visions marshaled different sorts of comparative colonial knowledge, local familiarity, and scientific expertise. Not least, they registered different interpretations of a usable past, divergent assessments of present risks, and conflicting visions of the future.

[9] AR, KV, 9 July 1860, no. 13, Konsideratiën en advies van de Direkteuren van het marine establissement en de fabriek voor de marine te Soerabaja, 24 November 1858.

[10] On changes in the nineteenth-century Netherlands' laboring classes with the introduction of large industry, see I. J. Brugmans, *De arbeidende klasse in Nederland in de 19e eeuw* ('s-Gravenhage: Martinus Nijhoff, 1929).

Each refigures the appropriate sociological terrain for comparison; some speak in a language of racial attributes, others in a language of class. Each posits a different assessment of the relationship between political disposition, productive work, and inner character. Each, too, represents a slightly different political aperture, a different "cropping" of relevant knowledge—neither the same framing nor "ground."

These alternative visions conceive differently how *Inlandsche kinderen* would best fit in the Indies landscape. But they also carve out alternative senses of what roles they might play in a modernizing colony, what sentiments might guide them, what kinds of political subjects they might become. Some planners had visions that resonated with Dutch experiments in social welfare planning. Others drew their blueprints from models of reform, containment, and colonization tried out in other contexts and in other parts of the imperial world. In turning to Australia, the Caribbean, and India, authorities reviewed experiments that were known to have gone dangerously awry or to have met with success.

In what follows I describe an exemplary moment—neither the first nor the last—in which colonial projects were weighed and evaluated in an international field, across colonies and across national borders. The frequency and urgency with which British, French, and Spanish experiments were invoked as viable comparisons mark the expanding breadth of imperial imaginaries to include new comparative knowledge of colonizing missions, of mistakes they could learn from, statistics they would now need to gather, and pedagogic failures they could avoid or redress. As far-flung colonial contexts were refocused through an Indies lens, so too were metropolitan ones, reminders of the fact that nineteenth-century social reform and its concomitant solutions to pauperism, poverty, and undisciplined workers were not only being played out on a global imperial field. Indeed such practices created the commensurabilities that constituted that imperial field itself.

Reframing Dissent and Distress

The notion that the Dutch administration *could*, if it so desired, craft "imitation Europeans" (*nagemaakte Europeanen*)—or that this was what the *Inlandsche kinderen* sought to become—begged certain questions. If many were legally classified as European, then how could they be "imitations," "defective" versions of what they already were?[11] Alternately, how could they be made into "perfected natives" if a founding colonial

---

[11] When this 1874 statement reappeared in the 1901 report of the European Pauperism Commission, the crucial modifying adjective did not remain the same: "*naggemaakte*" (imitation) European was replaced by "*gemankeerde*" (defective) European, underscoring how

premise construed them as a group who should never ally with, feel affiliation to, or take their cultural cues from the native population?

At the heart of these proposals, too, were a set of different answers to
similar questions: could and should this mixed underclass be shaped into
an enlightened working class or a middle class of modest means (*middenstand*)? Could the latter be formed on the basis of skilled manual
labor? Could manual labor (*handenarbeid*) ever be "honorable" for
those who saw them themselves as white? Could one remain Dutch and
poor in the colonies or was this a dangerous oxymoron? Answers to these
questions hinged, in part, on the frame of reference. Those fixed on a
colonial economy in need of technological upgrading and expertise
feared the political consequences and financial burden of providing such
education to any but *echte* (true) Europeans. Others looked to an Australian settler model, asking whether mixed bloods should participate as
full-fledged members or as second-class citizens confined to its service
sector.

Some contributors in these debates saw earlier labor policies in the Indies as cautionary tales taking not only their warnings from them, but as
we shall see in the next chapter, rewrote those histories in vivid color—
tales of astounding failure or tepid success. Others staged their tableaus
with different backdrops—concerns about industrialization in the Netherlands, the fate of its craft industry, and of Dutch artisans who might not
survive the competition of Europe's new technologies. Other aspects of
the debates were triggered by new negotiations in the mid-nineteenth-
century Netherlands over private charity and public assistance—whether
care for the poor was a responsibility of private citizens or the newly installed parliamentary state. A Dutch *burgerlijke* class that had long
prided itself on its philanthropic stance toward the less fortunate was rethinking its obligations to the indigent members of a modernizing soci-

---

much an "imitation" was indeed a "defective" product. See *Het Pauperisme onder de Europeanen in Nederlandsch-Indië. Derde Gedeelte. Kleine Landbouw* (Batavia: Landsdrukkerij, 1901.) The phrase was reworked yet again in a 1916 report on education that
recommended segregated schools for the *Inlandsche kinderen* (separating them from Europeans and from the Javanese) in the following way:

> If people want the native (*den Inlander*) in general to share in Western civilization,
> then one should guard against fostering imitation-Europeans [*imitatie*], hybrids with
> no inner strength, useless in the Netherlands as in the East-Indies itself. . . . What the
> Indies needs is not a generation of imitation-Europeans, but of developed natives who
> along with a broad knowledge of the old Indies civilization and culture have learned
> as much as possible from Western culture, who would appreciate its benefits without
> losing contact with their own people.

See *Praeadvies omtrent punten van den agenda van het Koloniaal Onderwijs -
Congres,* den Haag, 28–30 August (Leiden: Van Vollenhoven Instituut, 1916).

ety.[12] In both cases, the debates did not underscore the hegemonic self-assuredness of a ruling class. Rather, this was a class wrestling over how best to secure its status in a lucrative and growing imperial economy and an increasingly powerful colonial apparatus.

These protracted debates were not limited to official circles alone. "Expert witness" was provided by ex-colonial officials and metropolitan advisors, as well as those in the fields of education and healthcare, industry and military establishments. School headmasters, religious leaders, directors of orphanages, naval factory supervisors, and small businessmen were called on to offer their opinions, produce qualified knowledge, and demonstrate their expertise. Their conclusions reflected different assessments of the inherent capabilities of the *Inlandsche kinderen* and what could be expected of them.

By some accounts, the *Inlandsche kinderen* were pauperized whites, subaltern soldiers, widows with meager pensions, fair-skinned children conceived in the army barracks whose comportment, speech, and habits were locally learned and singularly Javanese. These included myriad sorts of impoverishment: children of mixed parentage who were educated in state-run schools; children "given up" by their well-born Dutch fathers; the offspring of soldiers (*soldatenkinderen*) of commoner European origin. Some were included because of their absence from the municipal civil registers, others because of where or how they lived.[13]

Destitution was not the only concern. Some architects of colonial policy were as worried about those who were approaching the lower-middle class and the political sensibilities that might accompany that status. This was not taxonomic trivia. Different rehabilitative visions of what they could become were contingent on these varied assessments of what kinds of political sensibilities different forms of labor might nurture. Fundamental disagreement remained about how dissent and discontent might be curbed and groups within the colonial underclass already harbored these inclinations.

Equally dissonant as the content of the projects were the lilliputian scales on which they were attempted and the gargantuan scales on which they

---

[12] The Dutch were not alone in reconsidering this role. See, for example, Peter Mandler, ed., *The Uses of Charity: The Poor on Relief in the Nineteenth-Century Metropolis* (Philadelphia: University of Pennsylvania Press, 1990), and Felix Driver, *Power and Pauperism: The Workhouse System, 1834–1884* (Cambridge: Cambridge University Press, 1993).

[13] See, for example, two recent studies of urban colonial society in Soerabaja and Semarang in which the "Indo" and impoverished Europeans go unmentioned. See Allan Cobban, "Kampungs and Conflict in Colonial Semarang," *Journal of Southeast Asian Studies* 19 (2) (1988): 266–91, and William Frederick, "Hidden Change in Late Colonial Urban Society in Indonesia," *Journal of Southeast Asian Studies* 14 (2) (1983): 354–71.

were conceived. As early as the 1850s, proposals to train a few dozen youths in a craft school in Soerabaja were ridiculed for their too modest scope. Similarly in the 1860s local officials criticized high-government sponsored initiatives, contending that there were "not hundreds, but thousands of such children whose inclination to become an artisan class needed awakening."[14] In contrast others scoffed at such panic-inflated concerns estimating only a handful of dysfunctional youths who could be easily absorbed into the native milieu. By 1872 there were reports of a "staggering increase of pauperism," tens and thousands of "embittered" paupers, scattered throughout the urban landscape, squatting in the European enclaves and miserably housed on their edges.[15] As the Governor-General was warned in 1881, European pauperism was not new. But news of it increased within government circles and the press, which broadcasted at high volume that impoverishment was "felt more and increasing by the year."[16] Others painted a more sinister canvas still: an uncountable underclass spanning generations, cultural chameleons alternately seen as racial impostors, misplaced natives, disaffected Dutchmen, and defective and fictive Europeans.

Fashioning European Artisans in an Indies World

Of all the reformist visions that captured the imagination of Dutch colonial authorities in the nineteenth-century Indies, none generated more intense debate and exchange of paper than that which centered on the creation of an artisan and craft-based training school—an *ambachtschool* in east Java's large port city of Soerabaja. It was not an implausible choice of location. Soerabaja had long housed a shipbuilding complex, a military installation, civil service employees and civilian Europeans. In the eighteenth century it was home to what has been considered "the first vaguely 'modern' manufacturing establishments" in the Netherlands Indies. Along with shipyards and defense installations first established by the Dutch East India Company, in 1851 there was a military arsenal outfitted with metalworking and machine shops manned with European labor.[17] Soerabaja also housed a large population of subaltern soldiers, low-ranking civil servants, and private profiteers, whose most often lived with local women and their mixed blood children.

[14] AR, KV 9 July 1860. Governor-General's summary report to the Minister of Colonies concerning "Inrichting van een ambachtschool te Soerabaja."

[15] AR, KV 28 March 1874.

[16] AR, KV, MR 904/x, 14 April 1876. Letter from the Director of Education to the Governor-General, 18 September 1881.

[17] See H. W. Dick, "Nineteenth-Century Industrialization: A Missed Opportunity?" in J. Th. Lindblad, ed. *New Challenges in the Modern Economic History of Indonesia* (Leiden: PRIS, 1993), 123–49.

One could approach the vision of this artisanal romance by tracing the events that led to the succession of schools that quickly opened and closed over a period of some fifty years. In 1853 the first school was opened under private initiative and faltered three years later under the strain of insufficient governmental backing and little financial support. In 1857 the school reopened as a state-run institution for "industrial" training. With dwindling enrollments, it, too, closed in less than a decade. In the 1870s and again in the early 1880s the craft school vision was deemed a "fiasco," out of touch both with the colony's labor demands and with the employment aspirations of those who had invested their sons' futures in it.

One might also look to the number of students that passed through its doors. In its first year there were 41 youths, 81 two years later, and 51 when it closed. Under the state's aegis, numbers were smaller still. Although more than 70 students were enrolled between 1862 and 1864, 50 soon dropped out, leaving but 20 who finished the course. In any one year, there were no more than 13 students. Just before its third closing in 1872 there were none. Upon reopening once again in the 1880s as a school for continuing "refresher" education (*herhalingschool*), in the years following it often had no enrollment at all.

By most historical standards, Soerabaja's craft school merits no mention. It failed on any measure of success. But debates about the school's openings and closings speak to something more. Embedded in the specifics of curriculum, food expenditures, building costs, and the preparedness of its prospective pupils were the calibrations of other "costs." At issue was the racial scope of social reform (who should be included), the moral scope of the state (who it should assist), and not least how the management of affect figured in the crafting of subjects and social policy. Nor did the state's repeated return in the archive to the school's failure always correspond to the actual realization of specific projects. As Van Hoëvell noted in 1858, debates in the Dutch parliament about the school's merits continued long after, oblivious to the fact that the school itself had already been closed.[18] Conflicting assessments over the composition of the *Inlandsche kinderen* tied every discussion of reform to expectations about what racial membership would mean to the *kind* of modern colony the Indies could become, to what should constitute the relationship

---

[18] By 1864 the prospects of the school looked even worse. By December of that year only 4 students were prepared to sit for the exam in the graduating class. The 1865 report was the first to acknowledge the school's failure, noting that graduates were finding it extremely difficult to find suitable employment, principally because manual labor held so little attraction for them. With little knowledge of Dutch and no further education, they had no chance of being promoted. Van Deventer opined that they needed real technical training in electricity and magnetics. not lessons in a manual craft (AR, KV, 18 August 1868, letter from the Resident of Soerabaja to the Director of Education).

between metropole and colony, and thus to how racial distinctions would figure in imperial politics. These reformist debates were grounded in racial categories, as were the taxonomic tensions that produced them.

A Colonial Oxymoron: European Status and Manual Labor

Colonial officials did not *always* need a colonized population to turn their mimetic fabulations and fears into a mockery of those fantasies, as Homi Bhabha has schooled us so well to imagine.[19] In and outside the sheltered space of the state's archive they were gifted at deploying these anxieties in biting critiques among themselves. The subjunctive mood produced wit and nostalgia. But it also animated irritable irony as officials contested one another's knowledge of the Indies and its menace, about what they claimed to know and could not.

"Should [*Inlandsche kinderen*] be made into a self-supporting middle class or into a working class, skilled and distinguished from the natives?"[20] As it turned out, the question was moot from the start, as the Director of Soerabaja's marine workshop was quick to point out. In a letter to the Governor-General, he mocked the fiction that they could become the "core of future trade and industry," much less an "independent *burgerlijke* class." Their "advanced age," "illegitimate unions," "abuse [of] hard drink," and tendency to "languish with neither will to work nor vitality" counted against them from the start.[21] Nor could they be made into "useful citizens" if barred from a middle-class existence. What kind of work could they possibly perform, he asked, to make them a "respectable working class"?

Solutions hinged on definitions of character, disposition, and race. Some authorities argued that the *ambachtschool* should train only Indies-born European orphans. Others held that since many "pure-blood" European children were living off church charities, their need for skilled training was just as great. Those who in the early 1860s supported providing "scientific" and "theoretical" knowledge rather than "practical" training were opposed by others who argued that the former "exceeded their needs" and "went too far."[22] Here was an epistemological Taylorism *avant le lettre*: the *Inlandsche kinderen* were not only to be schooled just for the

---

[19] Homi Bhabha, "Of Mimicry and Man: The Ambivalence of Colonial Discourse" *October* 28 (1984): 125–33.

[20] AR, KV 9 July 1860, no. 13. Konsideratiën en advies van de Direkteuren van het marine establissement en de fabriek voor de marine te Soerabaja, 24 November 1858.

[21] Ibid.

[22] AR, KV 9 July 1860. No. 13. Summary Report, Governor-General to Minister of Colonies. Note that throughout these documents, "scientific" and "theoretical" knowledge are used interchangeably.

"parts" instead of the "whole," but for the parts out of which no whole could be made.

Central to the debate was whether those of European descent could be instilled with a "desire to work" if that work was manual labor. Conversely, even if officials were convinced that true Dutchmen were imbued with a suitable work ethic, there remained the question whether those classified as European should have to perform manual labor. Access to scientific knowledge was more dangerous still, since it would prompt a desire for political entitlements that *Inlandsche kinderen* were not to be granted and were unqualified to possess.

Such debates were not limited to the Indies context alone. Other colonial regions offered ample evidence that Europeans were ill-adapted to physical labor in tropical climates. But acclimatization was not what these debates were about.[23] From the 1830s to the 1930s those in and outside the international scientific community repeatedly were asked to assess whether Europeans could survive in the tropics, the health risks of manual labor, and to speculate about the political consequences of allowing colonial whites to work with their hands.[24] The debate was transnational and transcolonial. Physiological limitations were less important than what certain kinds of labor meant for the distinctions of race and the development of moral character.

In question was not whether Europeans could perform physical work in the tropics, but whether those of *partial* European descent were, by temperament, "disinclined" to do so. Some critics held that *Inlandsche kinderen* had their sights set only on clerical and civil service jobs, and refused any employment resembling that performed by natives. Some saw this

[23] On the preoccupations of the British state with poor whites in South Africa, see Colin Bundy, "Vagabond Hollanders and Runaway Englishmen: White Poverty in the Cape before Poor Whiteism," in *Putting a Plough to the Ground: Accumulation and Dispossession in Rural South Africa, 1850–1930*, ed. William Beinart, Peter Delius and Stanley Trapido (Johannesburg: Raven, 1986), 101–28. See also *Die Armblanke-Vraagstuk in Suid-Afrika. Verslag van die Carnegie-Kommissie* (Stellenbosch: Pro Ecclesia-Drukkerij, 1932). In India, proposals made in the early 1800s to recruit impoverished Scottish farmers imbued with "Saxon energy" to populate and protect Britain's prize possession were defeated in the British parliament and never carried out, as David Arnold explores in "White Colonization and Labour in Nineteenth-Century India," *Journal of Imperial and Commonwealth History* 11 (2) (1983): 133–58.

[24] As the debate was framed, there was no reference to the fact that European men had ever worked in the Indies doing manual labor. But this was not the case. In the late seventeenth and eighteenth centuries Batavia had a specially designated *ambachtskwartier* (artisans' quarter) populated by slaves, freemen, and nearly 400 Europeans working, among other things, as carpenters, shoemakers, smithies, glass makers, cabinetmakers, and woodcutters. There are no accounts that document what happened to these European artisans when Daendels, Governor-General during the brief British interregnum, abolished the ambachtskwartier in 1809. See *Oud Batavia*, Part 1 (Batavia: G. Kolff, 1922), 356–60.

disdain for manual labor emanating from false vanity, haughtiness, and pretentious claims to European descent. In this view, refusal to do manual labor was *not* because they were indeed European but rather because they were really not, because of "fabricated" European affinities among those of native origin. Some explanations focused more on the racial attributes of mixed bloods, others more on the class culture of subaltern Europeans. Others identified a more general phenomenon, a disinclination "shared among the *Inlandsche kinderen*, and *mestizen* in general, and more specifically by those of the lower and needy class."[25] Partisans on both sides shared the belief that indolence and insolence could produce one another and had to be checked. For some the *Inlandsche kinderen* were inadequate workers because they were native in temperament and body. For others they were inadequate workers because they were at heart Europeans.

One person saw these debates as a distraction from what was the real concern of authorities. Van Hoëvell, that outspoken and seasoned critic of the Indies administration, characteristically veered from the normative discourse and turned the story on its head. He contended that the government had systematically sabotaged the first craft school in Soerabaja from the start.[26] The school was closed *not* because it was failing but because it promised to be a resounding success. He described a flourishing experiment in 1853, enthusiastically supported by the then Governor-General Duymaer van Twist. There were more private donors each year, a stream of committed and energetic students, and evident confidence in the pedagogic venture among the families whose sons were enrolled.

In any event, the school lacked one crucial ingredient—agreement from the Indies administration that it would honor the school's diploma and employ students who had earned its degree. Neither was forthcoming. In fact, when former Minister of Colonies Pahud replaced Duymaer van Twist as Governor-General, he confirmed this: in 1856 his first decree limited state subsidies to the school. Not surprisingly, private donors, following Pahud's lead, withdrew their support. Students and their parents, who had slowly come around to acknowledge the school director's insistence that artisanal work could be "honorable" for Europeans, dropped out. Others, disillusioned, did not bother to enroll.

As just noted, Van Hoëvell claimed that support for the school was withdrawn not because it was not working—Java's European press lavishly praised the experiment—but precisely because of its promise. The

---

[25] AR, KV 9 July 1860, No. 13. Summary Report, Governor-General to Minister of Colonies.

[26] See Van Hoëvell's sharp criticism of government policy toward the school in "De Ambachtschool te Soerabaja," *Tijdschrijft voor de Nederlandsch-Indië* 1 (1858): 129–49.

administrative debate was focused on the political danger of a subaltern class whose resentment was born out of their poverty, but Van Hoëvell thought the Dutch administration's fear lay elsewhere: in the perceived danger that access to education and skills would produce in a population with a sense of independence and self-worth. A mixed blood class of modest means and autonomy was just what the Indies' governing body feared and refused to permit or endorse.

Educating Hearts and Minds

> You can only start seeing—this was Freud's most basic insight—
> when you know that your vision is troubled, fallible, off-key.
> The only viable way of reading is not to find, but to disorient,
> oneself.
>
> —Jacqueline Rose, *States of Fantasy*

Van Hoëvell's analysis was prescient and probably correct, but it went unheeded by government authorities who were working in a different political frame and from a different timetable. A state inquiry into the creation of a government-backed industrial school was in the making even before the first private initiative for the school had failed. Writing to the Governor-General in 1854, the Minister of Colonies gave his support for an industrial-technical school that would train needy descendants of Europeans to become land surveyors, tailors, shoemakers, carpenters, and wagon makers, among other trades. Students would be drawn from the local orphanage and do on-the-job training in Soerabaja's naval workshops. Training was to consist of formal classes and apprenticeship with skilled European craftsmen.[27]

As so often was the case in colonial deliberations over the cultivation of new kinds of moral selves and political subjects, age was key. Whether children should begin attending the industrial school at 10, 12, or 14 years of age, a point of dispute nominally about the physical stamina such work required. Of more concern was the age at which such institutions could "awaken the *inclination* to become an artisan class [*ambacht-stand*]."[28] "Inclinations," as officials themselves knew, were physical, affective, and cognitive dispositions that were hard to assess. The recognition that children acquired habits of being and thinking in their early years turned them repeatedly to the formative, familial environments in

---

[27] AR KV 22 July 1854, no. 7. Minister of Colonies to the Governor-General.

[28] AR, KV 9 July 1860, no. 13. Konsideratiën en advies van de Direkteuren van het marine establissement en de fabriek voor de marine te Soerabaja, 24 November 1858.

which children lived, to the moral landscape that would foster stable domestic arrangements, political loyalty, and industrious adult lives. Convinced that a "desire to work" (*werklust*) was the proclivity lacking, it was sentiment, not opportunity, that had to be kindled and redirected, not employment possibilities that needed to be changed.

A "competent" workforce was one that recognized its proper racial affinities and knew where it belonged. Advice on how to shape these dispositions came from one Heer de Bruijn, a high-ranking civil engineer in the Department of Roads, Bridges, and Canals. Long resident in Soerabaja, while his experience was local, his knowledge of artisanal training was Europe-wide. He described how "capable bosses and manual workers" (*knappe bazen en handwerkslieden*) were trained in England, Germany, The Netherlands, and France, and why, in the Indies, such a system was bound to fail. Apprenticeships with skilled European supervisors were not feasible because Javanese workers needed "constant supervision."[29] There was no time for training and not nearly enough European technicians to do it. Moral contamination would be a problem, as well: close contact with those Javanese already employed in the workshops would do little to improve the Indo youths and their moral selves.

Addressing the Minister of the Colonies' desire for "more than simply a manual labor force," he proposed what he called "the Spanish model." There, orphans under 12 years of age were sent to the motherland so that the girls might be brought up in cloisters and the young men taught a skill of their choice. Upon returning to the colony, the girls married Spanish workers from the craft industries and the young men wed Spanish girls. De Bruijn neither elaborated on where this had been implemented, or whether it had actually worked. Instead he appealed to a language he may have imagined the Governor-General already embraced and could comprehend:

> The boys, married to Dutch women, would considerably improve the race, there would be more Dutch ways of thinking and the language of the *Inlandsche kinderen* would be purified, while the Dutch mothers would have influence on developing the moral sensibilities and the desire to work of their children.

Here was a colonial utopia in which European women were key actors and staged to take charge: as wives, mothers, and moral instructors. It was a futuristic picture haunted by what officials most feared: the influence of native nursemaids and native mothers. Taken with De Bruijn's sketchy plan, the Governor-General quickly passed it along to new Minister of Colonies Pahud, pointing out that it accomplished two goals. It re-

---

[29] AR, KV 9 July 1860, no. 13, 28 February 1855.

duced the danger of a displaced and discontent population and facilitated the "improvement of the race of European" descent. Embellishing De Bruijn's sketch, he in turn filled in its imagined local coordinates. The Indies would send hundreds of orphan children to be raised in municipal orphanages in the Netherlands each year. The appeal of the plan again spoke to more than the acquisition of specific labor skills. This was a formula for shaping appropriate sentiments and limited desires.

But the "Spanish model"—advocating racial mixing—was seen as fatally flawed. The possible benefits of mixed marriages were summarily dismissed by Minister of Colonies Pahud, as was De Bruijn's expert knowledge; the former unilaterally vetoed its consideration before the suggestion could be aired or discussed. He insisted that Indies youths schooled in Holland would lag behind their Dutch cohort and be subject to ridicule for their crude manners and *Indische* ways. Exclusion was converted into compassion. For their protection, he recommended that they be kept in the Indies to "improve the race."[30]

A second attempt to establish a craft school in Soerabaja also failed. Resident van Deventer of Soerabaja blamed low enrollments and high attrition on the school's recruitment strategies. The school was simply not training those "lower classes and illegitimately born" needing public assistance, and for whom it was ostensibly designed.[31] Instead it was gearing itself to Indies-born families who were enrolling their sons to avoid costly schooling in Holland, the requirement for higher civil servant posts that most could not afford—what had in part prompted the unprecedented Batavia demonstration in May 1848. When the school reopened in 1862, enrollments were low for good reason, he claimed. There were not enough children from these families to fill the school. Little effort had ever been made to recruit the really needy from the local European orphanages.

Some middle-class families initially enrolled their sons as an alternative to the civil service. But, as Van Deventer recalled, within a few years of the school's opening "rumors had spread" that after completing the three-year course, opportunities were limited to menial jobs as tailors and shoemakers. Those few graduates who had gained employment complained that so much instruction had not served them well. They were overqualified. Others fared worse, with jobs as the "upper class of manual laborers" (*boven klasse der handwerksleiden*). In short, the school was producing skilled manual workers, but the students "lacked both the desire and suitability" for such jobs. The school's 1867 annual report

---

[30] Ibid.

[31] AR, KV 18 August 1868. Resident van Deventer to Director of Education, 31 October 1868.

concluded that without "the sort of private industry of Birmingham and Manchester," it was "natural" that many youths upon completing the course looked on such labor with distaste. This was a different picture altogether. It was Europeans of comfortable, if modest, means, who had become disillusioned with the school's limited prospects, not the orphaned children for whom the school was designed and who never even got through the door.[32]

The decision to change the name from "craft" to "industrial" school just ten months after its opening—an appeal to well-off (*gegoede*) families who previously had been unwilling to place their children in a school for trades involving manual labor—had its intended effect. It ensured that only children of the European *middenstand* would enroll. But even those youths from the "small Indies *burgerstand*" were deemed unfit to pursue study. In Van Deventer's view, they were so "morally and intellectually backward" that the possibility of acquiring theoretical knowledge was "wholly killed off" in their early years.[33] The school's annual reports repeatedly returned to their "neglected upbringing" and "unsuitability for any education." But it was with colonial "common sense" about language use that Van Deventer most forcefully made his case. The cognitive rigor assigned to the complexity of the Dutch language and the mental dexterity it required were unfavorably contrasted with the crude market Malay that many officials knew. Thus he could confidently state that their "undeveloped skills at reasoning" were derived from "their exclusive use of the most narrow-minded and confining language of Malay."[34]

Language use was a piece of another story. The most serious fault lay with the parents—and especially the children's native mothers—so ignorant of the "first and weightiest of principles: that upbringing and education must begin at birth." The school could succeed if these children were properly raised. But what was the point if the destitute it intended to "uplift" were the ones excluded, he asked? Training them as "skilled workers and factory supervisors" was all wrong. Their accumulation of scientific knowledge was "useless" and "too comprehensive." Instead, Van Deventer proposed limiting the school's scope to those who would remain in the Indies. State funds would be better invested in sending "five suitable and capable" students each year to the Netherlands for seven years of training and apprenticeship. But even this token effort, he admitted, might be unrealistic because of the children's "aversion" to manual work and uncertain job prospects when they returned. In the end, he recommended that

---

[32] Ibid.

[33] Ibid.

[34] Quoted by Resident van Deventer from the 1864 Annual Report of the Soerabaja *ambachtschool*.

the *ambachtschool* be replaced with a "general training college" (*kweekschool*) where pupils could acquire skills for specific jobs as office workers, telegraph operators, shipping agents, and archivists.

Van Deventer's appraisal was more articulate than most and more detailed than many, but the basic premises were widely shared. The notion that children should be sent to the Netherlands, not just to learn a craft or trade, but to change the social environments in which they lived, to change "their thoughts about the world," was based on a common contention: that the colony's economic and political viability were contingent upon educating the hearts and minds of those who were a danger to it, on managing their aspirations in the Indies world. Van Deventer captured a sentiment that usually went unstated because it was colonial common sense; youths sent to the Netherlands "must not [conceive of themselves as] *heeren* (bosses/masters). They must not be burdened with more skills than they need . . . but only practical know-how for the tasks to which they are geared."

Van Deventer's focus on skills, sentiments, and aspirations was loosely shared among most authorities, but those to whom he presented his plan considered his conclusions impractical and the scope of his vision absurd. "How," asked Minister of Education de Waal, "could we possibly uplift an entire class of people . . . without building an institution on a colossal scale?"[35] Students with "free time" would easily evade the school's control. Nor was there any assurance that upon completing the proposed training as inspectors, telegraph operators, and box-office clerks that they would even find jobs. Who and what purpose would the school serve? And if the school's graduates were not going to get jobs, as he was convinced they would not, would the state then support them or just send them back to their home villages?[36]

De Waal's objections were based on a simple fact: as he warned his high-placed readers, Java simply had "no need for craftsmen in the major cities, since even skilled European-born and trained craftsmen in the smaller towns could not find sufficient work." Reminding the city officials that the school's purpose had been to uplift the *Inlandsche kinderen*, he urged that it be tied—and remain so—to the needs of the Soerabaja orphanage.[37] His objections to sending youths to the Netherlands were stronger still: If just 10 were sent a year, the costs of housing, clothing, and food for 40 students for four years would be prohibitive. Instead, De Waal came up with two alternatives: conversion of the Soerabaja craft school into an industrial one and creation of a continuing educational institution attached to

[35] AR, KV 13 March 1869. Department of Education to the Governor-General.
[36] Ibid.
[37] AR, KV 22 January 1868. Director of Education to Resident van Deventer.

the public elementary schools in Java's three major urban centers. In his vision, a portion of the Indies budget would be allocated to poor relief and nurseries for needy *Inlandsche kinderen* in the same three cities. His recommendation was at once prescient and tardy, too early and too late. A decade earlier such a nursery had opened and failed; four years later the same proposal, this time made by the 1872 Commission on Needy Europeans, was rejected. It would take three more decades for nurseries and kindergartens to again be proposed to counter the disaffection and despair among Indo youth.[38]

INDUSTRIAL ANXIETIES AND ILLUSORY FUTURES:
  LESSONS FROM ELSEWHERE

The Indies' "home-grown" Europeans were targets of reform, discipline, and domestication. But they were also envisaged as important actors in a future racial order that would buttress the colony's stability as it fostered a move to the modern. Some imagined a modernized technology manned by *Inlandsche kinderen* as subordinate technicians within industry. Others sought to provide limited practical training but not the analytic knowledge and advanced education that proper industrial schools would provide. Over and again, colonial authorities warned one another against schools that might prompt "illusions about the future."[39] In short, this was a population that was to provide the amenities and comforts of a European bourgeois lifestyle for a growing colonial community that they themselves, reared in austere institutional environments, would never *want* to attain, or expect to afford.[40]

Early debates over their technical and skill training not surprisingly looked to the Netherlands, sometimes as a model to emulate, other times as one to avoid. Still, many of these social designers would not have seen themselves as "looking" to Holland at all. The Netherlands was the transparency on which their models of colonial reform were drawn, explicitly or as a backdrop that set their plans in sharper relief. How craftsmen in the Netherlands would adapt their skills to increasingly competitive production

---

[38] See Ann Laura Stoler, *Carnal Knowledge and Imperial Power: Race and the Intimate in Colonial Rule* (Berkeley: University of California Press, 2002), 124–27.

[39] AR, KV 31 October 1868. Resident van Deventer to the Director of Education, 18 August 1868.

[40] Such visions resonate with the politics of racial accommodation and acquiescence that were typified by Booker T. Washington's Hampton Institute (opened in 1868) and the Tuskegee Institute (opened in 1888) in the United States. All of these institutions share a language of "uplift" and respectability. Each was designed to turn historically laden resentments into sensibilities that would maintain a domesticated race and a respectable working class.

in industrializing Europe was partly echoed in the Indies-based debates. But it is not always clear in which direction the anxieties about modernizing labor forces flowed. Debates in the Indies around craft schools that began in the 1830s probably did not prefigure similar debates in Holland but they did precede the widespread creation of such schools in Dutch cities.[41]

Craft guilds had long been abolished in the Netherlands, yet craft and vocational schools were slow to replace them. A French writer could still observe in 1851 that industrial training in Holland was the least developed among the Western European states.[42] The expansion of modern industry came with new demands in the 1860s for vocational schools in the Netherlands. Whether they were designed to train artisans in traditional crafts, or more ambitiously to "retool" them for modern industry, is a point on which historians tend not to concur.[43]

Some historians have argued that these schools had another purpose altogether: namely, to deter working-class youth from the growing trade union movement.[44] Here too assessments of indolence and insolence converged. Not infrequently, supporters and critics of the Indies *ambacht* initiative noted a working-class "preference for leisure" and lack of work-drive (*werklust*) in the Netherlands, as well.[45] Authorities who questioned whether the Netherlands was up to the technical and motivational challenge of industrialization saw the pairing of "insolence" and "indolence" as a dangerous political expression of the Dutch working class.[46]

Tailoring and shoemaking, which had "already become predominately sweated trades by around 1850" in the Dutch economy, were precisely the crafts that the Indies administration sought to promote for destitute Europeans in the same period.[47] Thus the appeal of the craft romance in the Indies, strongest during the 1850s and 1860s, and in sharp decline by

[41] I. J. Brugmans, *De arbeidende klasse in Nederland in de 19e Eeuw* ('s-Gravenhage: Martinus Nijhoff, 1929), 174.

[42] Ibid.

[43] Van Lente notes that one of the early vocational schools in Den Haag opted to strengthen the crafts while allowing them to be competitive with large-scale industry. Offering courses for electricians, gas fitters, and motor mechanics, it advocated a renewed appreciation of craft-produced articles, and not necessarily a modernization of the production process. See Dirk van Lente, "The Crafts in Industrial Society: Ideals and Policy in the Netherlands, 1890–1930," *Economic and Social History in the Netherlands* (2): 103–5.

[44] See Brugmans, 86.

[45] Joel Mokyr, *Industrialization in the Low-Countries, 1795–1850* (New Haven: Yale University Press, 1976), 215.

[46] Mokyr notes the fear "that a large number of unemployed, who were reported to be teeming in the Dutch cities, may have been to a large extent voluntary rather than involuntary unemployment," citing a late eighteenth-century periodical complaining that Dutch workers seemed to "prefer the austere living that they can make from alms to a richer existence they could enjoy if they had been willing to work. Mokyr, 194.

[47] Van Lente, 101.

the 1880s, may have reflected these debates about Dutch craft industries more than the actual feasibility, demand for, and desirability of their promotion overseas. It could not have escaped even a casually observant Dutch town dweller in Java that Chinese craftsmen were poised to take over these positions with an apprenticeship system long in place.[48] In Van Deventer's account, as in others, Dutch metropolitan and colonial visions collided and converged. To some advisors, nineteenth-century Dutch society was the dominant "figure" against the backdrop of Java. For others, concerns about the rate of industrial developments in Holland were less relevant than the colony's emerging industrial needs. If some Indies proposals sought to prepare prospective students for jobs in modern private industry, the preferred model was one that would limit their training to work as "artisans or machinists, *not as engineers*."[49] However obliquely stated, that distinction between practical and conceptual knowledge— between "artisans" and "machinists" on the one side, "engineers" on the other—set out who could expect to be accorded the future privileges of colonial prosperity and to whom they would be categorically denied.

Expert knowledge did not always confirm state fantasies. Two factory managers whose advice was sought on the craft-based initiative held that the real problem was not, as most authorities insisted, the youth. The *Inlandsche kinderen* with whom they had worked shared little of the pejorative profile that so prevailed. They were neither lazy nor incompetent but "industrious and well-behaved," eager to learn skills but lacking opportunity and stimulation that would push them in that direction. Nor were they wanting when compared to European recruits. These managers saw the *Inlandsche kinderen* as preferable to them—if, that is, they received the proper training.[50] But here, too, "preferability" was in part an affective measure: modest aspirations, gratitude for such jobs, zeal that would stop short of the demand for entitlements. As they wrote, "the *Inlandse kind* [already had] knowledge of the language, population, customs and climate while the European would need an acclimatization period. [He] would feel attached to the enterprise established in his fatherland's interest. Not belonging to the favored class of Indies society, his expectations and sense of entitlement will not be high." It was this population that could provide what the colony needed, "a ready supply for the [maritime] industry of subordinate technical personnel."[51] If the Indies really wanted to think of itself as a modernizing colony, one or two industrial schools could not possibly accommodate the fast-growing

---

[48] Ibid.

[49] AR, KV 9 July 1860, no. 13. Konsideratiën en advies van den Direkteuren van het marine establissement en de fabriek voor de marine te Soerabaya, 24 November 1858.

[50] Ibid.

[51] Ibid.

demand for skilled workers. The managers contended that a bolder and grander vision was required—industrial training on a much larger scale.[52]

Viewed from the workshop floor, they saw the real problem with the quality of workers from Holland, who were far inferior candidates than were the Indies youth. They described a Dutch lower-class population that was generally older, dissipated by liquor, with neither "vitality" (*levenskracht*) nor a moral compass. The idea of creating an independent *burgerklasse* out of these men, they opined, was pure fantasy. Their argument anticipated a theme that Van Deventer was to bring up a decade later—that the creation of a "subordinate but technologically skilled personnel" would need to target a broader population, "the entire expanding class of European descent." He too saw a population no longer content to remain office scribes and factory hands but one that sought "work that they could judiciously and independently carry out." Self-worth in labor, dignity in employment, and political independence were seen to go dangerously hand in hand.

The industrial vision did not remain a romance for long. By 1872 it was considered a "total fiasco." The Commission on Needy Europeans mounted in that year insisted in each of its reports that the "cultivation of *skilled craftsmen* will no longer be our exclusive priority."[53] Instead, attention turned to the "upbringing of the child," nurseries, good elementary education, and opportunities in agriculture. The Soerabaja craft school's state subsidy had dropped from 30,000 gulden in 1861 to 5,000, then l,000, and finally to 300 gulden by 1872, when it closed.[54] One instructor who learned of the school's "temporary" closing while he was on leave in Holland nailed the coffin by testifying to the school's inviability: the school's problems stemmed from a basic misapprehension. Government authorities persisted in imagining that the students were getting "practical know-how." That was a delusion, he insisted. They had working knowledge of nothing that could serve them, no practical knowledge at all.[55]

If the 1872 Commission on Needy Europeans rejected the artisan initiative, this did not end the desperate efforts to make it work. When in 1882 the Soerabaja craft school was reopened as an "evening school"

[52] AR, KV 9 July 1860. Governor-General to the Minister of Colonies.

[53] AR, KV 28 March 1874, no. 47.

[54] AR, MR 904, 18 September 1881. Director of Education Stortenbeker to the Governor-General. According to Stortenbeker, the school's annual report for 1862 lists 31 students initially enrolled in the school; by the end of that year only 14 remained. How many of these were from the orphanage is not indicated. The school's annual report the following year lists 35 matriculating students; by year's end 23 remained. Some of the attrition is explained by some students having left for jobs, but many more dropped out because they were "ill-prepared" to follow the course.

[55] AR, KV 21 January 1872, no. 5.

(*burgeravondschool*) under new direction, again the Director of Education posed the question raised thirty years earlier: could the "so-called *Inlandsche kinderen* really be made into a true artisan class?" His answer was an emphatic no, noting that "laziness, unwillingness, and indifference" among the "indolent *indische* youth" was evident in the 1860s and remained the case.[56] But he too was not entirely convinced that indolence was the problem. He professed to know scores of Indo youths with energy and a will to work. It was "haughtiness" (*hooghartigheid*) and "false pride" that got in their way and would continue to hamper them "as long as our society has the peculiar character it does." What he had to say next was both commonplace and unthinkable. Everyone "knew" that mixed blood youth were too proud to do the same work as natives. What few could recognize was that they *did not aspire* to be placed alongside working-class Europeans: "The *inlandse kind*, above all else, is fearful and apprehensive of being confused with natives and would not choose to be part of a European *ambachtstand*. . . . [They] are ashamed of their work clothes, and of the company they keep in their workplaces."[57] It was the "company" of lowly Dutchmen for which they had disdain.

Of the 123 orphans sent to the Soerabaja school, only 28 made use of their specialized training: 9 became machinists, 11 were overseers, 3 worked in the military atelier, 4 became smiths, and 1 a technical engineer. Forty others became office clerks and scribes, 17 joined the military, and 10 "disappeared." The Director of Education again blamed the failure to make them into a laboring class (*handwerksklasse*) their aversion to manual work. They could not compete with the sort of fine-tuned apprenticeship that Javanese and Chinese workers were able to find in their "free time." More importantly, the latter were willing to work for far lower wages. The "Indo-European manual laborer," he concluded, "was on precarious terrain."

This did not stop some state advisors from persisting in pushing the same artisan vision again. Director van Schouwenberg of Semarang's *hoogereburgerschool* could still opine that "nothing could more benefit Indies society than that it go about forming a class of industrious citizens (*burgers*) [exclusively for Indo-Europeans and Europeans] who, through honest and honorable *manual labor* would provide for their own needs and those of the colony." It was "the severed link between the races of foreign rulers and native ruled" that he imagined they would mend.[58]

---

[56] AR, KV 29 June 1882, no. 8852. Director of Education to the Governor-General.
[57] Ibid.
[58] AR, KV 21 September 1883, no 49. Director of the Hooger Burgerschool, Semarang, 22 December 1881.

And this is perhaps what so many of these visions were about in the end. Nevertheless, his proposal was impatiently dismissed out of hand. Van Schouwenberg's own *burgeravondschool* had not come close to the mark. It was neither a craft nor industrial school, nor were there "children from the Indies' better classes who had any interest in learning a craft or taking such jobs." In exasperated prose, the Director of Education threw up his hands: the only alternative was to orient the school to train "bosses" and foremen, not to provide technical skills.

By 1883 state authorities had come to four conclusions: (1) the Indies badly needed technicians, whoever it ending up training for those jobs; (2) education of the *Inlandsche kinderen* should be limited to practical know-how, as they had no need for more and anyway the costs were too high; (3) European students should not be turned into common workers but into persons suitable as managers, supervising the work of others; and (4) the practically trained Indo and European youths should be provided with the opportunity to enter low-ranking government positions for which exams were not required. Some of these plans were fleshed out unevenly and with varying degrees of success. The school that replaced Soerabaja's *ambachtschool* counted 265 students by 1901. European youths were no longer recruited for manual jobs, and "scientific" training of *Inlandsche kinderen* was abolished across the board.[59]

Retrospectively, Soerabaja's craft school was seemingly unrealistic, utopian, and doomed from the start. But "what happened" to it is less to be found in the events surrounding its openings and closings than in the distorted imaginaries of its visionaries as to the space and subjects they sought to mold. They explained away its failure as the fault of a population blocked by its own false vanities, by refusal to sit at a "carpenter's bench" rather than a desk. But as we have seen, not everyone agreed. Van Hoëvell's assessment in the 1850s had been correct. The school was not a "natural" disaster but made a disaster, and was pointedly undermined by state authorities.

What is striking in these conflicting and confused arguments during this seventy-year period is how much the visions changed. *Ambacht* schools, heralded in the 1860s, were seen as badly misguided twenty years later. By the 1880s both the artisanal and industrial romances had been largely abandoned, only to resurface at the turn of the century in revised form. But by then the size of the poor European and Indo population had grown even more. The attention of the 1901 Pauperism Commission, as we shall see in the following chapter, like that of the Indo-European population itself, had turned elsewhere.

---

[59] *Koloniaal Verslag 1902–1903* (Den Haag), 186.

Tracing the Rural Romance

> Were I to fix the date of completion of the carceral system, I
> would choose not 1810 and the penal code, nor even 1844,
> when the law laying down the principle of cellular internment
> was passed. . . . [T]he date I would choose would be 22 January
> 1840, the date of the official opening of Mettray. In the arrange-
> ment of a power-knowledge over individuals, Mettray and its
> school marked a new era.
>
> —Michel Foucault, *Discipline and Punish*

The "rural romance" that gained momentum in the 1870s was a direct response to the failures of the artisan-based reform effort. But it was also responsive to what the Indies administration saw as a "terrifying increase"
of European pauperism, with Europeans and their descendants "living in
wretched conditions" in virtually all of Java's main cities—Batavia, Soerabaja, and Semarang, the latter "probably the worst of all."[60] The fact that
the rural vision outlined a much more limited set of financial responsibilities for the state conferred on it broad government appeal.

The small-scale proposals made for industrial schools in the 1860s now
seemed totally out of line with the numbers at risk. By the time of the
1872 commission there was widespread official agreement that the *Inlandsche kinderen* were neither "inclined nor suitable for manual labor,"
and that the plan to make them into craftsmen had failed. Instead, recommendations turned to nurseries and children's agricultural colonies. The
emphasis was less on remolding the recalcitrant than on the shaping of
children at an earlier stage.

The Carceral Archipelago of Empire

Projects were proposed to remove the *Inlandsche kinderen* from urban
slums and relocate them in contained rural settlements where they would
learn self-sufficiency and remain out of sight, if not out of place. But the
model on which authorities drew took advantage neither of local conditions
nor expertise. Their sights were not really on the countryside and rural settlements but what came to be one of the most famous pan-European experiments in disciplined social reform. This was the agricultural colony at Mettray, France, on which other reformatory-prison colonies were fashioned in
the Netherlands, England, Belgium, and France. Mettray was the reform
project that Foucault singled out "as the most famous of a whole series of

[60] AR, KV 28 March 1874, no. 47.

institutions which, beyond the frontiers of criminal law, constituted what one might call the 'carceral archipelago.' "[61]

The Mettray model had been raised by colonial authorities earlier. In 1854 the Indies Advisory Council had already recommended that the Soerabaja craft school follow its lead.[62] Mettray fulfilled colonial fantasies in several ways. It was a prison colony whose inmates would be rehabilitated through agricultural labor. Education and bodily discipline were at the center of its transformative vision of reform. Docile subjects would be the product of dociled bodies and dociled minds. Agricultural work would reshape the wayward young and the revolutionary potential of the urban poor.[63]

For Foucault, Mettay was part of a "carceral archipelago" that was "beyond the frontiers of criminal law." But it was really a *carceral archipelago of empire* that connected penal colonies to agricultural relief and to reformatories. It connected strategies of confinement from metropole to colony and across the imperial world. Mettray's inmates were called *colon* (a term that could mean "member of a colony" but also "settler"), not only because they were nested within an enclosure and were to subsist by their own agricultural labor. Mettray's inmates were part of a much broader set of midcentury projects designed in part to provide colonists for Algeria and other French possessions overseas.[64] Here was social engineering on both macro-and micro-imperial scale, an overarching solution to multiple social and political problems that had set off the revolutions of 1848. It was also a solution that erased the state's obligation for social welfare just at the very moment when public assistance was on the docket across Europe and poor relief threatened to be reassigned from private to state coffers. Orphans, abandoned urban youth, and political dissidents would be trained and recruited to settle the expanding reaches of empire. At Mettray the inmates practiced maneuvers on a ship placed in the center of the courtyard and could only leave the colony before the age of 21 if they joined the French Foreign Legion.[65]

---

[61] Foucault (1977), 297.

[62] AR, KV 16 April, 1856, no. 3.

[63] Ceri Crossley, "Using and Transforming the French Countryside: The 'Colonies Agricoles' (1820–1850)," *French Studies* 44 (l) (1991): 36–54.

[64] Alphone Cerfberr de Medelsheim and J. H. Detrimont, *Project de colonisation d'une partie de l'Algérie par les condamnés liberés, les pauvres and les orphelins* (Paris: Plon, 1846). On the varied meanings of "*colon*," see Ann Laura Stoler and Carole McGranahan, "Refiguring Imperial Terrains," in *Imperial Formations*, ed. Ann Laura Stoler, Carole McGranahan, and Peter Perdue (Santa Fe, N.M.: School of American Research, 2007), 3–7.

[65] I thank Katrina Amin for sharing her reading of the Mettray archives in Caen on these points. See also Sophie Chassat, Luc Forlievesi, Georges-Francois Pottier, eds., *Eduquer et Punir: La colonie agricole et penitentiare de Mettray, 1839–1937* (Rennes: Presses Universitaires de Rennes, 2005).

In its French variant one minutely conceived plan, outlined in 1854, envisioned "preparatory colonies" of young orphan children who would then be transferred to "colonies of transition" for those aged 12–14, where an adolescent would be "bronzed by the sun in Provence, Roussillon or Langeudoc" and finally transported to the "colonies of application" in Algeria where those aged 14–21 would learn proper cultivation of the soil and of the self. Out of this progression of children's agricultural colonies would be the future colonists of North Africa's French homesteads.[66] Some of these plans were indeed carried out, though never with the order and detail of their paper visions.

The discrepant and confused accounts of the numbers of *colon* who left for Algeria between 1848 and 1851—and the conditions under which they did so—is itself instructive. By some counts, 14,000 "Parisian workers" were sent by decree in September 1848, followed by 3,000 "republicans" after the 1851 coup d'état of Louis Napoleon.[67] "Disorder" in Paris led to 450 political deportations to the Algerian penal colony of Lambese, and deportations to at least six former *colonies agricoles* (agricultural colonies) newly converted into *colonies penitentiaires* (penal colonies). Thousands were recruited as well under an intensive colonization program to make *colon* out of a toxic mix of unprepared urban poor, alternately referred to as the unemployed (*les sans-travail*), as insurgents (*les révoltés*), and as the rootless and dispossessed (*les déracinés*). How many of those from Mettray were included within the intensive deportation-cum-colonization project is hard to say. But what this amalgamation of colonizing projects underscores is the extent to which *colonies agricoles, colonies penitentiaires*, and European colonial settlement were conceptually and politically tethered projects. This was a carceral archipelago of confinements, detentions, and cordoned-off space that cut across the imperial globe.

Mettray, however, was not the first experiment in outdoor relief or disciplinary charity. The Dutch Benevolent Society had created an earlier version in 1818 for criminals, beggars, orphans, and paupers.[68] France, too, in the 1820s, prior to Mettray, had turned to agricultural reform colonies.

---

[66] See Le Comte A. De Toudonnet, *Essais sur l'éducation des enfants pauvres: des colonies agricoles d'éducation*, vol. 1 (Paris: P. Brunet, 1862), 26, and a discussion of them in Stoler and McGranahan, 3–7.

[67] Jeanne Verdes-Leroux, *Les Francais d'Algérie* (Paris: Fayard, 2001), 195. See also J. P. T. Bury, *France, 1814–1940* (London: Routledge, 1989), 77, and Catherine Belvaude, *L'Algérie* (Paris: Karthala, 1991), 36.

[68] See Albert Schrauwers, "The 'Benevolent' Colonies of Johannes van den Bosch: Continuities in the Administration of Poverty in the Netherlands and Indonesia," *Comparative Studies in Society and History* 43 (2) (April 2001): 298–328, where he argues that Van den Bosch's agricultural colonies in the Netherlands were inspired by his short experiment in plantation management between 1808 and 1810 in Java (301). See also Jan Lenders, *De Burger en de Volksschool* (Nijmegen: SUN, 1988), 73.

What set Mettray apart from these efforts was the rigorous and meticulous structuring of psychological, bodily, and spatial disciplines. It focused on mock-family arrangements, close comaradery, and the details of the everyday. In Europe young vagrants and urban delinquents were to be taught respect for religion, family, and labor.[69] In the Indies, Mettray principles were easily adapted, but cast in a local, colonial frame:

> To develop religious sensibilities in the hearts of the youth through unceasing surveillance of their behavior, allowing them to resist their tendencies to indolence and to develop their skills and character. [Only then would they form an] esteemed and cultivated *middenstand* who would make up a solid element and support European colonisation.[70]

The Mettray model responded to the failed industrial vision in other ways. First, the children would be taken when they were very young, not at 10–12 years of age, as with the craft-school model, but at the more "kneadable" age of 3–4 years. Second, the agricultural colonies would promote modest aspirations, provide only simple clothing, and a spartan lifestyle. Girls were to be outfitted with "nothing more than a blouse (*kebaja*) and sarong," with a special outfit for holidays. It was in this context that reformers expressed their chilling vision that begins this chapter, one so radically different from the goals they more commonly professed, "not to create imitation Europeans . . . just . . . perfected natives."

Cultivating spare needs addressed a third shortcoming of the earlier craft-based efforts. If their "haughtiness" and insolence (which "excessive" education was thought to encourage) would stand in the students' way, here was an organic antidote to it built on an artful plan. The agricultural colonies were *to curb frustrations by curbing desires*; these were to provide environments that neither animated those sensibilities nor prompted youth to think of themselves as *deserving* parity with "full" Europeans. This was more than a project in harnessing the passions; it was a project designed to starve the growth of those desires and remove the conditions for their production.

Children were to be schooled in those tasks that would allow them to become a farming class (*boerenstand*) and embrace the honest values that

---

[69] On the pan-European exchanges of information and excitement generated by Mettray, see Crossley, as well as Jeroen Dekker, "Transforming the Nation and the Child: Philanthropy in the Netherlands, Belgium, France and England," in *Charity, Philanthropy and Reform: From the 1690s to 1850*, ed. Hugh Cunningham and Joanna Innes (New York: St. Martin's, 1998), 130–47. On "Dutch Mettray," see Jeroen Dekker, *Straffen, redden en opvoeden: Het onstaan en de ontwikkeling van de residentiële heropvoeding in West Europa, 1814–1914, met bijzondere aandacht voor "Nederlandsche Mettray"* (Assen: Van Gorcum, 1985), 14.

[70] AR, KV 16 April 1854. Report of *Raad van Indië* to Governor-General, 20 October 1854.

a rural, family-based lifestyle required. As at Mettray, the children's agricultural colonies were to assign "mothers" and "fathers" to orphan
groups, providing both discipline and measured affection.[71] Poor widows,
otherwise unable to provide for their own children, would be enlisted as
supervisors with their children maintained at the colony's expense.[72] Finally, such rural institutions would remove the children from the contaminating influence of natives, something that the craft-school programs had
perilously allowed. The children would produce their own food, learn
about agriculture, and "be separated from all natives, even servants."
They were to be kept strategically distant and removed from both the
temptations of native proximities and, conversely, the allures (and self-
contempt) that were assumed to accompany excessive exposure to and
contact with full Europeans.

The *Raad van Indië* enthusiastically endorsed the plan for Mettray-
style colonies that would yield "competent farmers"—"both the less fortunate as well as others working for a wage." On coming of age, state assistance would provide the colonies' residents with a parcel of land and a
cash advance. Such colonies would work along with state institutions to
train the young for work in crafts, factories, and industry. Public and private charities would continue their relief efforts.

If the rural romance was promising to some colonial reformers in its
elaborate paper version, in practice many were dissappointed. Critics saw
these isolated agricultural children's colonies, so lauded as ideal sites to
nurture independence and self-sufficiency, as a harsh and punitive means
to reform the colony's European poor. Director of Education Stortenbeker, writing in 1876, was amazed that many authorities could construe
the Mettray model as benign. He preferred to name it what he thought it
really was:

Such plans force a question. Are we speaking of a school of correction
or of a penal colony, i.e., a depot for delinquents? People want to place
young people of both sexes on an uninhabited and deserted island that
has no housing; at the same time the land will be brought into cultivation by this brigade of chained youths! What a joyless life for which
these youths will be prepared. Seeing no other human beings but their
comrades and guards, they must live in the small confines of the garden
where the institution is established; bound to a forced labor which is

---

[71] Mettray founder F. A. Demetz, after touring European reform schools in 1838, wrote
how impressed and enthusiastic he was about the Prussian reform school at Horn, where
"delinquent children and vagabonds" were sent off as "*colon*" in families of a dozen, under
the authority of a "*chef de famille*" and a housekeeper. See Raoul Leger, *La Colonie Agricole et Penitentiare de Mettray* (Paris: Harmattan, 1997), 114.

[72] AR, KV 28 March 1874.

entirely against their inclinations. What an existence! What is the difference between such an establishment and a penal colony?[73]

The notion that children would develop a taste for agriculture and take pride and pleasure in their new fatherland struck him as equally preposterous: "But no, this is not what will happen. They would use their freedom to return to their native places. There they would be without any help in strange surroundings. The young women would service the Chinese and Europeans, the boys would end up in jail." In short, they would fall back into the destitute conditions from which they had come. The proposal that children's colonies (*kindercolonie*) should be established on "wasteland" outside of Java struck him as equally misguided. Instead he proposed that the children be raised on Java, agreeing with Van Delden that they should be "isolated but certainly not cut off from European surroundings. The choice of place is very important if the goal is an improved race and if we want to include as many children as possible."

Others in contrast found Van Delden's plan to gather 750 children in a rural orphanage as ludicrous. How, Stortenbeker asked, could they possibly educate such large numbers in practical rural work without a hugely expanded personnel? And even if it were conceivable, it would do nothing for the "hundreds of children who remain badly cared for and without supervision in the villages" and who belonged in the school. Maintaining the quality of food, education, and child care would be impossible. Such oversized orphanages would only make matters worse. With that characteristic impatience officials reserved for their inferiors, he dismissed the whole plan.

Nevertheless the Director of Education was not convinced that Mettray and similar such agricultural colonies in Europe had ever really worked. He noted that they had produced more soldiers than farmers; the largest of them, rural orphanages, were breeding grounds for "prisoners and whores." The most successful system in Europe was adoption of orphan children, but this was not viable in the Indies, where suitable families were in short supply. In any event he was convinced that private initiatives were the only answer since the state could not provide subsidies on such a scale.

Other European institutions of discipline and confinement were pulled up as models, but almost as quickly rejected. The proposal to set up workhouses (*werkhuizen*) for Indos on Java, like those in the towns and smaller cities of Europe, enjoyed favor for a short time. But once again Stortenbeker upbraided the commissioners who had proposed it for being out of touch with local reality, ignorant of the nature of the European workhouses and what had become of their charges. Work-provisioning programs

[73] AR, Mr. 904, 14 April 1874. Report of Minister of Education Stortenbeker.

in Europe had a poor record of success. If in Europe the impoverished looked upon the workhouses as a last resort, in the Indies "such institutions would be more humiliating still," and the perception worse. Instead, he urged the creation of agricultural schools on a Froebel model for nursery school–age children to "train them in agriculture, animal raising, butter and cheese production, and in the making and tending of orchards."[74]

Mettray was not, then, the only blueprint on which colonial visionaries would draw. The notion that rural, agrarian-based activities could reshape the minds of the very young prompted the *kindergarten* movement of the mid-nineteenth century. Later in the century the "orphan trains" that farmed urban youths out to the rural western region of the United States played off a similar fear of urban life and the redemption promised by a rural one.[75] The self-sufficient agrarian colonies of the socialist utopian movements may have been called upon, as well. While these communities were designed to replace the need for property, marriage, and religion, in the Indies these were the very values that rural colonies were designed to nurture and maintain: to encourage marriage, imbue religious belief, sexual morality, and a respect for private property that would serve the youths as independent farmers when they grew up. But the ethos of self-sufficiency that underwrote these rural nostalgias produced conditions that were often as dismal as those they were supposed to replace. William Cobbet criticized these utopias as "parallellograms of paupers." Lewis Mumford described Robert Owen's model projects as ones that had "more of the flavor of a poor colony than that of a productive human society."[76] In the Indies, the *kindercolonies*, too, were viewed as punitive pauper colonies on more than one occasion. They remained as blurred negatives of punitive confinement. As images, they were neither worth developing nor blowing up.

Where utopian and colonial visionaries differed was in how they conceived of the moral and cultural training of the young, where it should occur, under whose aegis, and at what age. In the Indies, children's agricultural colonies, industrial schools, nurseries, and various apprenticeship programs were envisioned as sites for learning one's proper racialized place; self-discipline, limited expectations, and the spartan conditions of labor and living that would serve these ends. Most similar projects in the Indies were stifled before they were tried on the lament that few of the Indies mixed blood population would be content "behind a plough." Detailed

---

[74] Ibid.

[75] See Stephen O'Connor, *Orphan Trains: The Story of Charles Loring Brace and the Children He Saved and Failed* (New York: Houghton Mifflin, 2001). As O'Connor notes, many of the 250,000 children subject to this "out-placement" were not without parents but removed because of what the Children's Aid Society deemed "immoral influences" (xvii, xx).

[76] Lewis Mumford, *The Story of Utopias* (New York: Boni and Liveright, 1922), 123.

proposals offered to the European Pauperism Commission, as we know, were never carried out. Nor were revised proposals in the decades that followed. In 1929, as seventy years earlier, the failure was attributed to the lack of "fitness" of the Indo "lower classes" for small-scale agriculture.[77]

The commitment to recuperating an agrarian space for those awkwardly positioned in Indies society played upon nervous premonition and vague senses of loss, on both rural nostalgia and industrial anxiety. Such sentiments were shared by others beyond the colonial authorities. The vision of a white settler society, or a farming class made up of *Inlandsche kinderen*, held political appeal for many who were not part of the delusional colonial decision-making apparatus. "Land to the tiller" was an early platform at the turn of the century for an emergent Indo-European political movement whose adherent were discontent with the European-born monopoly on economic resources, social status, and political rights.[78] It was also a platform of the strongly conservative Fatherland's Club in the 1930s. Many political projects were galvanizing around it. The political stakes were high. And authorities knew it. Virtually every proposal to alleviate what in the twentieth-century came to be called the "Indo problem" through agriculture, though repeatedly offered, was defeated before it got off the ground.

Fear and fantasy joined in these visions to paralyze implementation in just about every way. The fear that the Indo poor *could be* more than office clerks and scribes, perform more than rote jobs was, for some of the colonial elite, more disquieting than the dangers of their continued impoverishment. And in this archive of implausible futures, authorities enjoyed little consensus among themselves. Over the course of nearly a century there was hardly a moment when impoverished Europeans and their descendants were not the object of some combination of sympathy, pity, and disdain that served to confine their movements and seal their fate. The political dreams were different but elements remained the same: to make of them modest but respectable loyalists whose political claims would be contingent on continued denial of native rights, whose investments in a racial hierarchy would remain strong, but whose sense of entitlement would be limited to legal European equivalency, not equal social or political status.

As such, the Indies administration at once embraced reformist gestures but withdrew financial support, declaring plans defunct before they were

---

[77] J. C. Kielstra, "The 'Indo-European' Problem in the Dutch East Indies," *Asiatic Review* (1929): 588–95.

[78] On the Indo-European movement's bid for land (and its conservative Dutch political allies), see P. J. Drooglever, *De Vaderlandse Club* (Amsterdam: Franeker T. Wever, 1980), and Johan Winsemius, *Nieuwe-Guinee als kolonisatie-gebied voor Europeanen en van Indo-Europeanen*, Ph.D. Diss., University of Amsterdam, 1936.

tried. They devised and just as quickly disassembled projects that might allow those Europeans with "native blood" to man a modernizing state but not to manage it; to work in new industry but not to gain control over new channels of communication, information, and technology. In an angry article on the "Indo question" and "racial hatred" (*rassenhaat*) published in one of Java's noted European newspapers, an anonymous writer snidely noted that the Indo half-bloods might well serve as "uplifted go-betweens of European capital" but they were no more than foremen and they were to remain that nonetheless.[79] Racialized understandings were imminently "modern" but how those discriminations would be mobilized was unclear in a colony in which racial categories had been muddied all along. Demands for a skilled labor force were defeated by fears that a well-educated mixed blood labor force would press for more than a colonial situation could and should ever allow.

Accusations of "indolence" and "insolence" were substitutable codes for those unsuited and unworthy of political entitlements. Converting the former into usable labor and breaking the political will of the latter not only produced a gridlock on reform. It animated more intense administrative anxiety about the coding of race. Debates about character and capability flourished in this reformist period, in which few projects were implemented and little "happened." The craft, industrial, and rural romances rose and fell as reams of plans swelled the state archives, justifying why little, despite the state's good intentions, could be safely carried out. Some proposals died as Governors-General, Ministers of Colonies, and regional Residents were reshuffled and relocated for short tenures that altered political priorities before projects were tried.

These visionary narratives were colonial negatives in more than one sense: they were cropped and re-cropped. Some were never developed. Some faded as they were overexposed to what was transpiring in the Indies. Others were blown up and distorted out of all proportion to the social realities in which people lived. Most are absent from the historiography because they appear to be colonial debris, unfulfilled visions discarded in process. But as a pulse on the tensions and uncertainties that pervaded these moments, such refracted images command attention. As blueprints of distress they underscore what was deemed to have gone awry in the Netherlands, what was imagined to be wrong with Dutch colonial society, what might be excised from that picture, and what could not be redeveloped or touched up. What such an archive "produced" was not specific reform, but a new compendium of expert, if uncertain, knowledge. It

---

[79] "Het Indo-vraagstuk en rassenhaat," *De Indische Gids* (Part 1) 34 (1912): 73–76, whose author describes himself as "neither a conservative nor a friend of capitalism, neither a civil servant nor a totok [a Dutch-born colonial]."

made the problem of mixed bloods and that of poor whites a specialized colonial field, one that drew Indies officials into a comparative dialogue with colonial situations elsewhere. Not least, as we shall see in the next chapter, it produced implicit but prolific commissions about *whether race was really about a kind of people or whether it was an index of a particular state into which people could fall.*

In their densities these documents registered distributions of administrative concern that gained cumulative and historical weight. Archives could arm the state with evidence and, in so doing, justify inaction, reduce allocations, and abort policy. In this sense, they are archival events, not non-events, of capacious quality. They register the conditions of possibility in which colonial authorities operated. They tell us about how implausibility was measured, about the constrictions in which plausible colonial truths were framed. Not least, they suggest how keenly authorities attended to the ascription of affective states in managing the present and envisaging a future of the colonial modern.

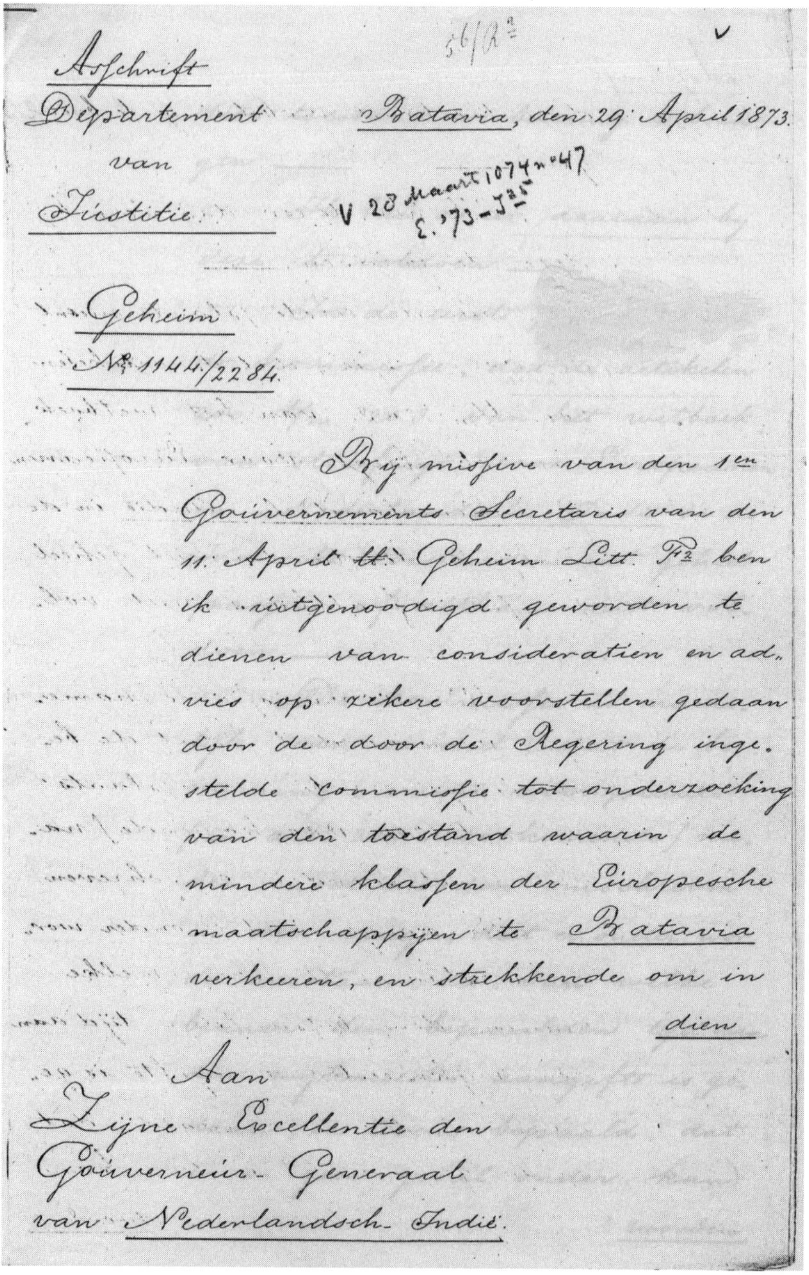

Afschrift

Departement   Batavia, den 29 April 1873.

van

Justitie

V 28 Maart 1874 n° 47
E. '73 – J 25

Geheim

N° 1144/2284.

Bij missive van den 1en
Gouvernements Secretaris van den
11. April ll. Geheim Litt. F2 ben
ik uitgenoodigd geworden te
dienen van consideratien en ad.
vies op zekere voorstellen gedaan
door de door de Regering inge.
stelde commissie tot onderzoeking
van den toestand waarin de
mindere klassen der Europesche
maatschappijen te Batavia
verkeeren, en strekkende om in
dien

Aan
Zijne Excellentie den
Gouverneur-Generaal
van Nederlandsch-Indië.

Figure 7. Control of European beggars on the streets of Batavia was no secret but it was the subject of this secret missive of 29 April 1873 from the Department of Justice to the Governor-General, in which a specific interpretation of what constituted "permanent residence" and "homelessness" for Europeans was spelled out with respect to the existing civil code.

CHAPTER FIVE

Commissions and Their Storied Edges

When is the time that Dutch youth read? Is it on a Saturday of a
beautiful spring or summer day, or indeed in the morning of a
winter month when the rivers run full or the street is thick with
snow?
——AR, KV 28 March 1874, no. 47. Nota van den Heer R.
Weijhenke, Bijlage, no. 6

SUCH NOSTALGIC MUSINGS over the lost leisures of childhood as in the
epigraph are the stuff of embarrassing memoirs and bad fiction. It would
hardly be worth quoting did this cozy evocation not emerge from another
sort of sentimental space. It appeared in the Indies European Pauperism
Commission's report of 1874, the melancholic contribution of one of its
esteemed board members, Heer Weijhenke, charged to analyze the causes
of increasing destitution among Batavia's Europeans and their descendants. For Heer Weijhenke and his commission colleagues, an investigation by way of survey and statistic was not how they interpreted their
task—nor did the Governor-General give them time to do so.

But no matter. For some commissioners the causes were ones they already knew. The answers were evident and ready at hand. They could be
found in the psychic space of "character." For Heer Weijhenke the distress of the Indies' European poor could be traced to a deeply impoverished cultural milieu. The desire to curl up with a good book had to be
awakened, as did strivings of other kinds—thus his recommendation to
establish children's libraries in the orphanages for abandoned Indo youths.
Unrealistic proposals were subject to criticism, and sometimes ridicule.
Weijhenke's idyllic vision of orphan children, redeemed by reading and
made content with their racial lot through books—even in the conjured
world of colonial authorities so evident in the last chapter—was discreetly
ignored. Chortled coughs might have accompanied the reading, but Heer
Weijhenke was sincere and well meaning. Rather, chuckles of recognition
would not have been out of place.

State commissions of inquiry are curious beasts. They are both of the
state and authorized by notables outside their jurisdiction, forms of inquiry
whose "solutions" were often preordained and agreed upon before they
were carried out. As morality tales, they powerfully sanction the limits of

state responsibility as they reached into intimate and other social spaces that extend the state's authority. As genres of documentation, they tended to employ certain writerly conventions, techniques of persuasion, and forms of evidence that combined a passion for numbers with the numbing bulk of repetition and the pathos of vignette.

Such commissions were neither unique to the nineteenth century nor to the colonies. But those devoted to poor relief, poverty, and pauperism were specific to a particular European moment of intensified social reform and of righteous state confirmations of commitment to it. In the Netherlands the first such commission of 1815 launched a flood of commissions that followed.[1] In Britain the Poor Law Commission of 1834 provided the template for 74 more inquiries in the 1850s alone.[2] If Jeremy Bentham's dictum, "banish poverty, you banish wealth," captured the moral calculus of this commission-making impulse—devoted to sharply distinguishing the deserving from the undeserving poor—in the colonial heartlands of empire, such as Java, the emphasis was elsewhere. Bentham's warning, as the two preceding chapters should make clear, might easily have read: "Banish race, you banish wealth."

The two major Commissions of Inquiry on European Pauperism, initiated in 1872 and 1901, the subject of this chapter, could be read as testimonies to the state's commitment to social reform. They are replete with recommendations for more and better schools, improved heathcare, and increased pensions for those on the lower rungs of the colonial civil service. Such proposals bulk up these commissions with thousands of pages, but quandaries about race divert their authors' musings and shift their preoccupations elsewhere. These are less focused on impoverishment than on the task of distinguishing among "an *amalgama*" of racial groups, their ontological status, their political aspirations, and their changing spatial coordinates.[3] Nor did they have an easy time making these assessments. Both commissions were riveted on that vague population they assumed to know and could only loosely name: while the category of so-called "*Inlandsche*

---

[1] On the Netherlands Poor Relief Commission, see Frances Gouda, *Poverty and Political Culture: The Rhetoric of Social Welfare in the Netherlands and France, 1814–1854* (Lanham, Md.: Rowman and Littlefield, 1995), 221–22. See also Piet de Rooy, "Armenzorg in Nederland," in *Geschiedenis van opvoeding en onderwijs*, ed. Bernard Kruithof, Jan Noordman, and Piet de Rooy (Nijmegen: SUN, 1982), 96–104.

[2] On the British royal commissions, see Felix Driver, *Power and Pauperism: The Workhouse System, 1834–1884* (Cambridge: Cambridge University Press, 1993), 27, and Oz Frankel, *States of Inquiry: Social Investigation and Print Culture in Nineteenth-Century Britain and the United* States (Baltimore: The Johns Hopkins University Press, 2006), 139–72.

[3] *Uitkomsten der Pauperisme-Enquête. Algemeen Verslag* (Batavia: Landsdrukkerij, 1902), 15. As in 1848, there was still the fear that out of this "amalgama" "could be born as an independent state, entirely detached from the Netherlands."

kinderen" was still in use in 1872, it no longer adequately covered the unwieldy range of those who so provoked administrative anxieties. The seemingly protective and benign connotations of the term, which merged Indies-born Europeans with those of mixed descent, couched distinctions that the state sought increasingly to make: "colored" reappeared from earlier use; "Indo" became more common in official and vernacular parlance; and "Indo-European," as in British India, slipped between designations of a population that was mixed and one for whom both parents were born in Europe but who themselves were often not. Among those deemed to cast a longer and more ominous shadow than ever before were "Europeans" of all sorts: vagrants, light-skinned beggars in native dress, dismissed soldiers living in native neighborhoods, indignant Indo youths rejected from civil service jobs that advertised for "pure Europeans," and a growing civilian class that was either unemployed or reduced to meager incomes and pensions.

At one level, the social semantics of these commissions would seem to offer few surprises. Their scripts are honed, as are the stereotypes to which they subscribed. They mirror even as they produce the prevailing idioms of colonial common sense. The phrases are stock and formulaic— faithful to the truth-claims of racialized rule. And the "causes" of distress among a "lesser class of Europeans and their descendants," as we saw in the last chapter, are contradictory but invariably the same: they target the moral turpitude of native mothers incapable of instilling their mixed blood children with European sensibilities; parental ignorance and indifference account for absenteeism in mixed blood schools; destitution is the fault of lower-class European men who populated the army barracks with their native partners and with illegitimate children bereft of religious training and knowledge of Dutch. They identify a population unwilling to perform skilled manual labor and too proud to undergo the necessary training for it. They fixate on the inherent resentments of a population at once misinformed about their racial entitlements and disdained. Not least, commissioners worried in secret missives (whose sentiments were echoed loudly and publicly outside the official texts) about the potent political force of a disaffected class whose native attachments threatened "the Indies' enduring and peaceful development."[4]

But these incantations on the character of social kinds were not all that these commissions rehearsed.[5] It is on their storied edges that the fault lines

---

[4] AR, KV 28 March 1874, no. 47 E 27 1873 G5, Wilkens to the Governor-General, 30 December 1872.

[5] See my *Carnal Knowledge and Imperial Power: Race and the Intimate in Colonial Rule* (Berkeley: University of California Press, 2002), 122–39, and *Race and the Education of Desire: Foucault's History of Sexuality and the Colonial Order of Things* (Durham, N.C.: Duke University Press, 1995), 95–164.

of colonial ethnography may more fully reside, in the interstices of sanctioned formulae, in the descriptions of what it meant to say that some Europeans were *not* "out of place" in native villages and of those places where some Europeans were not supposed to be. Details pierced the formulaic. Vignettes persuaded but could also disrupt. Even well-honed clichés could jar the calm of tacit common sense when adjectives broke loose from the social categories to which they were attached and made to "belong."

Such commissions summoned archival power in part by what they accumulated around them: a report from the director of an orphanage, from a district officer, from the manager of a shipbuilding factory who took on the training of Indies youths. Such documents slipped easily between what "went without saying" about racial capabilities and moral character and what statements about social groups merited repeating again and again. Sometimes studied ignorance and assumed understanding went hand in hand. The space of the commission not only made room for both. It depended on the fact that its schooled readers would find the vignettes appealing and could easily complete the pathos of snippets stories with truncated narratives.

If the pauperism commissions provide sites where shared understandings were justified and rehearsed, the discrepant assessments of what counted as *European* impoverishment in a specifically *colonial* context pulled at the seams of common sense in unintended ways. It did more than reveal the flimsy fabric of racial categories. It exposed a centralized colonial state whose departments and divisions were not in touch. It called to discussion the intricate stitching and sloppy patchwork of educational policy, residence laws, pension stipulations, and labor ordinances that contradicted one another as they differently defined what rules would hold for a colonial underclass neither fully of the rulers nor wholly of the ruled. If destitution of Europeans and their mixed descendants was the problem, what mattered to the "solutions" was how those who decided policy (and those who carried it out) imagined they could and should know race. Racial epistemologies were at issue. Epistemic politics and its practical consequences pushed the accumulation of paper. It was the political effects of how race should be assessed that had to be sorted out first.

In the Indies, the pauperism commissions did something more. They activated the colonial archive; called upon documents long left to rest; brought back into circulation promises not kept, resolutions shelved, earlier commissions found lacking, initiatives that had faltered or failed. Such sources merited long quotations and frequent reference. Thus the 1831 declaration of Minister of Colonies van den Bosch that the Indies government would care for its abandoned mixed blood youth was a requisite citation over the next eighty years—whether state aid to the *Inlandsche kinderen* was supported or not. Similarly, confidential recommenda-

tions offered in the 1872 commission report provided the grist for the secret commission of 1880, and did so again two decades later, in 1901,
when the unseemly underside of European society in the Indies was to captivate the press. For the Netherlands' public, when the untranslatable term
Inlandsche kinderen morphed into "Indo" and European pauperism
achieved its own name, the problem still remained distant, but more difficult to ignore.

Activation of the archive and an expansion of its breadth occurred both
within the official domain and in the accumulations that gathered on its
contested edges. Thus those who opposed or endorsed the public 1901
commission had accounts to convey and stories of their own to tell; newspapers reported on the creation of the commission and the nature of opposition to it; articles appeared in the Indies press and scholarly journals
by those claiming firsthand knowledge of the white pauper class. Poignant
anecdotes aimed at metropolitan readers called up a range of sentiments
that moved quickly between sympathy and disgust.

Novels, short stories, and dramas staged by local theater groups pulled
at the heartstrings of their audiences with compassionate portrayals of
abandoned children (*kinderen*), if not of those "children of the soil"—
Inlandsche kinderen—who were already adults. Others nourished economic, sexual, and political fears of imperial subjects that might strike
back, led by an entitled, embittered, and more "conscious" (*bewuste*)—
but only loosely European—underclass. In the affective economy of empire the European poor and their mixed blood descendants were at the
center of a racialized field of force, and at the vortex of administrative
labors that far outweighed their numbers.

None of this would have been so surprising if the 1872 commission
had not concluded—after seven months of meetings, opinion papers, and
secret reports—that there were no more than 39 Europeans in Batavia
with no means of livelihood, just one-third of the number of commissioners called on to do the investigation: 26 were in the military, 2 of whom
were ranked military officials; 6 were sailors; 1 was a carpenter; 1 was a
steersman; 2 were typesetters; and several were unspecified. Divided according to background, 16 were "of lowly origin," 9 with a "good education," and 14 substantially of "the middle class." In all, 17 men were
heavy drinkers, of which 7 were in trouble with the police: the remaining
22 gave "no immediate cause for complaint." The figures were arbitrary,
as were the categories for analysis, suggesting to some that pauperism was
underestimated, to others that it was inflated, and to still others that there
was something seriously flawed in the investigation.

Why was so much time and labor devoted to a population that would
not have filled a small hamlet in a colony that counted the native dispossessed in the hundreds of thousands? Commissioner King was one of many

confused by the numbers when he noted the 6,500 Indies-born Europeans counted by the 1870 government gazetteer. If approximately 1,600 were in civil service, 2,150 in industry, and nearly 400 more in trade or the plantation industry, he asked, were the remaining thousands simply vagrants ("*rondloopende personen*")? What kind of contact had they with needy?[6] But the more delicate and divisive question that rustled on the discursive margins was whether the criteria used to describe "European" was appropriate—and therefore whether the criteria of "needy" was accurate.

The 1874 Secret Commission on "a Certain Class"

As a commission of inquiry, what appeared in 1872–74 shared few of the attributes common to that genre. Most commissions are destined and designed for public consumption, yet none of this commission's reports were made public at the time. After two years of work by the 16 members, and two subcommissions, the findings were deemed inconclusive and problematic. The commission affirmed the increase of destitute Europeans but still had no idea how many there were. Secondly, the commission was instructed to report only on Batavia and had little to say about the rest of Java. Limited to one city, the sample was considered too small, the "data" inadequate. Nor were statistics collected. Despite the hundreds of pages transcribed and the number of expert witnesses enlisted to share their views—school directors, doctors, heads of orphanages, and religious leaders—neither surveys of the impoverished nor interviews with those in contact with them were carried out.

A striking feature of the royal commission was not its secret nature but that its confidentiality thwarted any systematic investigation. At its first gathering in June 1872, its appointed Chairman convened the group to ask if an actual investigation should be made concerning the education, lifestyle, and attitudes of the *Inlandsche kinderen* (one of the key questions the Governor-General had asked that they address.) None of the commissioners supported doing so, on the argument that it would countermand their order to work in secrecy, signal the commission's existence to those "outside," and thus undermine their goal.[7] It took another twenty-five years for the European Pauperism Commission of 1901 to ask about what its members, too, assumed they knew. As we shall see, this new commission was quicker to learn—from the vehement intensity of the response to their queries—that what they feigned not to know was dangerous and that what they thought they knew, they did not.

---

[6] AR, KV 28 March 1874, no. 47, Bijlage 1, Nota van den Heer E. King.
[7] AR, MR 4 January 1873, no. 23, Nota's der vergadering gehouden op 5 June 1872.

Structured Zones of State Abandonment

If statistics and surveys were beyond the mandate of the 1872 commissioners, the real focus seemed to be a critique of those prior state policies seen to have led up to the current situation. Taking their charge literally, to "speak frankly," "freely," and "not to hold back a single one of our proposals," they explicitly identified long-standing areas of state neglect. Most of the 16 commissioners each filed a "nota," sometimes on a specific topic assigned by the commission's chairman, André Wilkens, and at other times on their assessment of the general situation.[8] In striking detail, and because they defined "European" and "the needy" in different ways, their individual reports chronicled a wide-ranging population at risk. By their appraisal, whole sectors of the lower rungs of the colonizing population had been, and continued to be, systematically rendered ineligible for state support and positioned beyond the legal reach of government aid.

Some commissioners made the point that subaltern soldiers commanded wages too low to afford the urban housing districts where most Europeans with more substantial incomes chose to live. Others noted that native women living with European men out of wedlock were not entitled to widows' pensions. Even those widowed European women with pensions could not subsist on the state's inadequate subsidies and automatically lost them upon remarriage. Children not legally recognized by their European fathers had no access to European schools. Moreover, free healthcare that was, in principle, available to all lower civil servants "and their families" was considered a "gross fiction," when those families included "native companions" (*huishoudster*, literally housekeeper), the mothers of their illegitimate children, who were categorically excluded from state subsidies. As the commission remarked, health care for the native population was more "generous" than that designated for those who were *partially* European.

The commission made its point strongly by enumerating these seemingly disparate "findings" in a unified picture of sustained inequities. But few of their observations were novel, nor did they ever rise to the level of official disclosures; the colonial archives were full of missives on every

---

[8] All of these *nota* appear in KV 28 March 1874, no. 47. Those consulted here are from the following: E. King, A. C. Claessens, I. van Steeden , R. Weijhenke, W. van Ommeren, A. Van Delden, I. Storm van 's-Gravesande, R. van Goens, and D. Steestra Toussaint. Some are only a few pages. Weijhenke's was lengthy (forty-one pages), as was Van Delden's (over sixty pages). No dates are provided for the writing of the individual *nota*. Other commissioners included Kelijn, Klein, and van Berckel Bik. André Wilkens, chair of the commission and a member of the *Raad van Indië*, summarized their confidential findings in a nearly one hundred page report to the Governor-General of 30 December 1872, also included in the same verbaal.

one of these issues.[9] Governors-General, Ministers of Colonies, and their underlings had crafted those policies themselves. These were not areas of state inattention or oversight. These were enduring zones of state abandonment, structured by successive administrations' refusals to recognize kinship that transgressed race and to include within their charge the native kin of "a certain class" of Europeans. These were the public secrets of the Indies and the commission set them out in exacting terms.

Still, the compassion of the commissioners was conservatively husbanded and not directed everywhere. It extended most directly to "the full-blooded European element" forced to live in "decent poverty" ("*fatsoenlijke armoede*"), a poverty they esteemed "harder to bear than the kind suffered openly"; that is, by those of mixed descendants, who they seem to have imagined suffered impoverishment with lesser shame.[10]

Rather than carrying out a detailed investigation, the commission worked off what its members claim to have heard, incidents of which they "knew," sometimes what they witnessed themselves, but more often what was "commonly" known and said. Godlessness, neglectful upbringing, and concubinary relations provided the holy trinity of evils whose stories the commissioners knew by heart. Their first meeting, two weeks after the commission was created, set the tone of what was to follow. Pastors wrote about the lack of religious instruction, men of industry described Chinese workers replacing the less energetic labor of Indos. School directors, as we saw in the last chapter, wrote about the disinclination of the *Inlandsche kinderen* to labor or learn.

Most commission members agreed that the *Inlandsche kinderen* were afflicted not so much by a poverty of opportunity as much as a "poverty of imagination and ideas" (*armoede van denkbeelden*). But not everyone agreed. Commission member and state medical officer, Dr. Abraham Steenstra Toussaint, who had worked in Java for thirty years, distinguished his own contribution as a "proper critique," which, he implied, the government needed and sorely lacked.[11] He condemned the state's neglect of healthcare, the lack of sanitary drinking water, and the absence of a sewage system in the poorer quarters where *Inlandsche kinderen* lived. Few of these criticisms were mentioned in the final report, nor did they surface again. Instead, the point on which all board members concurred was that the *Inlandsche kinderen* needed proper upbringing, and that the

[9] Nor was this the first report on the situation of needy Europeans. Governor-General J. Loudon notes in a classified missive to the Minister of Colonies that such a report was filed twenty years earlier. He provided no description of it, only noting that, by comparison, the "situation has not improved, but lost ground." AR, Mr. 4 January 1873, no. 23, 30 December 1872, Geheim.

[10] AR, KV 28 March 1874, no. 47, Wilkens' report to the Governor-General.

[11] AR, KV 28 March 1874, no. 47, 1873G5.

future of the colony was in jeopardy unless early education was taken out of their ill-equipped hands.

The commissioners were pleased with their results and recommended that all, or at least parts, of their report be printed and made available for "public criticism." Their rationale was clear: given the "prevailing spirit of discontent," people needed assurance that they were not being "overlooked." The Minister of Colonies, I. D. Fransen van den Putte, conservative and highly protective of state interests and funds, thought otherwise. On reading the report, he not only forbade its publication. He criticized nearly every recommendation made, accusing the commission of placing all blame on the government.[12] His advisory board, the *Raad van Indië*, did not uphold his position, instead concluding that "a huge number of descendants of Europeans [were] drudging through miserable lives with no means of existence." He ignored their conclusion and questioned the claim.[13] With a lack of statistics, he quipped, what did the commission really know about the livelihoods of the nearly 8,000 Indies-born Europeans that only Commissioner King had bothered to mention? (The fact that Van den Putte's figure was a good 1,500 people more than Commissioner King's was an artifact of the problem with the category itself and who was included in it.)

But it was an even touchier issue that foreclosed publication: the commission's unanimous recommendation to institute mandatory entry of *Inlandsche kinderen* and European children in nurseries (*bewaarscholen*) and preparatory schools. Nursery schools per se were not at issue—as we have seen, these were in the offing for decades. What the board had the temerity to assail was the sacred retreat of the colonial state from broad public assistance. Instead, the commission insisted on the government's obligation—not that of private and religious organizations alone—to provide financial support for early rearing (*opvoeding*) of small children, not just education (*onderwijs*) in later years. The retort of the Minister of Colonies was sharp and clear: *staatszorg* (state care) was not to replace *moederzorg* (mothercare). Education was in the state's jurisdiction, upbringing of small children was not. Enraged at the report's tone, he accused some commissioners of revealing "bitter and hostile feelings toward the Government."[14] In their "commendable zeal," they had gone "too far."

Other recommendations were considered equally ill-conceived. Workhouses on a European model would humiliate their charges and offend

---

[12] This refusal to publish the commission was not endorsed by the *Raad van Indië*. It recommended publication, arguing that doing so would allow the government to better respond to the Indies' European press, which would surely write about it whether it was published or not. AR, KV 28 March 1874, no. 47, MR. 260, Advies van den Raad van Nederlandsch-Indië, de vergadering van den 7 March 1873.

[13] Ibid.

[14] AR, KV 28 March 1874, no. 47.

the Dutch community in good standing; a proposal to establish European beggar colonies throughout Java was rejected on similar grounds. The plan to create rural colonies of *Inlandsche kinderen* on the remote island of Ternate was dismissed, as well. But the Minister's irritated refusal to publish the commission's reports was driven by more than his contention that the colonial state was not in the business of expansive social welfare. He, like others, claimed not to be sure who these destitute were, suggesting that among them were persons claiming a European status that was not rightly theirs. As to those living in native compounds, they had not maintained a manner of being and living to be considered part of a ruling class and forfeited their rights as Europeans.

Given this reception, there is little surprise that few of the 1872 commission's proposals were attempted. Both a confidential review of its findings in 1881 and the public commission of 1901 remarked that little was turned into policy. In fact, the 1872 commission was crippled from the start by two opposing goals. On the one hand, its task was to "improve the lot of needy Europeans." On the other, there was prevailing common sense among the colonial elite that those needy Europeans most "discontent with their lot" included those of suspect legal status, and who therefore had no legitimate right to complain. The built environment of social separation had produced a thick corridor of state neglect and it was the durability of that zone over which officials fought in the commission—some sought to dissolve it, while others took it as the bulwark of empire to be guarded and maintained.

Vagrant Movements and Beggar Europeans

The failures and false starts of social reform took reams of paper to explain away. These explanations fostered evidentiary vignettes and the richly (ethno)graphic on their storied margins. Even in its impressionistic mode, the commission provided testimony to the changing geography of race. In this molten social landscape, people were transgressing both moral and spatial boundaries, living where they were said not to be "at home," where fair-skinned adults and children "did not belong." Below the purview of government surveillance and its documentary practices—birth certificates, housing permits, and legal declarations of male paternity—had emerged a muddled social space occupied by men and women with "light hair," and by "blue-eyed" children who were vagrants or beggars, living homeless or in hovels on the outskirts of European neighborhoods or in native compounds.

Whether there were many more in the 1870s, or just more who were noticed, was still hard to say. When Minister of Education Stortenbeker secretly wrote up a review of the 1872 commission's findings nine years later, he insisted that pauper Europeans were in even greater numbers than authorities had thought, an "entire class" spread across urban Java.[15] Others had observed the same. Then why was there so little attention paid to them in the histories that colonials then and later wrote? And why is there a virtual absence of this "entire class" from the postcolonial historiography of Indonesia? For colonial observers they were a blight and too present; for postcolonial historians they remained peripheral to the colonial stories they have chosen to tell. Yet in the archives they are in both obvious and unexpected places: in the fixed frames of colonial history, they emerge and submerge, get "lost" in changing nomenclatures and sometimes cannot be "seen" at all.

Nevertheless, virtually every year, from the 1840s onward, reports from some officials, perhaps recently transferred to a new post, remarked to a superior—a district officer to the region's Resident, a Resident to the Governor-General, the Governor-General to the Minister of Colonies—on the "alarming increase" of vagrant whites."[16] The commission of 1872 repeatedly if obliquely alluded to their inappropriate locations at every turn, and noted that reports of ten and twenty years earlier had done the same.[17] Sometimes they pointed to abandoned mixed blood children wandering the cities and towns. Elsewhere reports made reference to adult Europeans and their descendants begging on roads into the cities, squatting in the European quarters, or hiding in the back alleys of Batavia. An even larger number were said to have retreated even further into "the remote corners of the native neighborhoods [kampongs] of Semarang, Batavia and Soerabaja," where they could avoid all other Europeans.[18] Ashamed "descendants of

---

[15] AR, Mr. 904, Director of Education Stortenbeker to the Governor-General, 14 April 1876.

[16] Signs of "the problem" were detected even earlier: in 1753, when the Indies was still under the VOC, an orphanage was established in Cheribon to prevent what the Governor-General then referred to as an increase of "the many poor bastards and orphans of Europeans, running free and roaming about." S.v. "Pauperisme," Encyclopaedie van Nederlandsch-Indië (Den Haag: Martinus Nijhoff, 1917), 366.

[17] Thus Wilkens notes that "De Regering" (the government or ministry here) had received similar reports, a classified report of 1851 and one of A. van Pers of 1863 that returned to the same subject; see AR, KV 28 March 1874, no. 47, exh. 1873 G5, 30 December 1872.

[18] AR V 28 March 1874, no. 47. Fifteen years later the same point could still be made—in Soeria Soemirat, the weekly of an association created in 1887, devoted to the welfare of needy Europeans in the Netherlands Indies—that "even well-educated persons don't apply for a humble and meager salaried job; they indeed want to work but find no opportunity; and who will count them, the hundreds, among which are descendants of distinguished families, who hide in the kampongs, drudging through a wretched and unworthy existence for a European." Soeria Soemirat was the first association to demand repeal (unsuccessfully) of the prohibition on paternity suites established by the Napoleonic Code. See Mededeelingen der Vereeniging "Soeria Soemirat," 1891, nr.1, 10.

distinguished families" were said fifteen years later to be similarly hiding in native quarters. Some were too poor to afford clothing or footwear to send their children to school, a "finding" the commission noted had been made a good decade earlier.[19] Others did not seem to have a home. Some slept in empty lots, some in abandoned buildings, others in unoccupied houses of Europeans on leave in Holland, or those who had moved or simply left their properties temporarily vacant.

Intrusions into the European enclaves put stress on the law and strain on the administrative apparatus. With a native police force that was considered unsuitable to apprehend (even poor) Europeans, place and race were not in sync, people were displaced and locating themselves across racial lines. With formal sumptuary laws long rescinded, conventions regarding some social categories of people were no longer easily fixed to speech, housing, and dress.[20] Materiality became an unreliable index of these "wavering" classes and of specific social kinds.

These issues were neither the primary subject of the 1872 commission nor of those that followed. The discussions, however, registered disquieting displacements in the social order of colonial Java. In the margins of these reports are seemingly offhand references to commonplaces that defied new racial decorum. Jarring practices and perceptions erupt from the shadows of casual remarks. Some could be said in passing because they were common sense and the associations they made were deemed innocuously evident; other remarks—obtuse or overt—registered how alien they were to the sense and logic of what were thinkable ways of being in a colonial situation.

Nowhere was this juxtaposition of the commonplace and the unusual more striking than over the question of European beggars. Although commission members claimed that the number of vagrant Europeans was insignificant, debates about legally regulating their movements suggested otherwise. The precise transgressions that were at issue were identified with circumspection, often in the guise of extended debates about what counted as trespassing, who had residency permits, and what it meant to have a "permanent residence." Thus the commission questioned what to do with European vagrants who might stay "this week in this native *kampong*, the next in another" or with those "who passed the night on the front verandah of a native house?"

How common such white squatters were, and how long such practices had been going on, is hard to gauge. They may have represented relatively

---

[19] AR, KV 28 March 1874, no. 47.

[20] Jean Taylor, in *The Social World of Batavia: European and Eurasian in Dutch Asia* (Madison: University of Wisconsin, 1983), 68–69, notes that the VOC's sumptuary laws were revoked in 1795 and new ones were re-established in the nineteenth century.

recent developments since it was only two years before the commission began meeting that the new Agrarian Law of 1870 dramatically altered the spaces that poor Europeans could inhabit. The law forbade for the first time the permanent alienation of land by Europeans from the native population.[21] The poor mixed population who were classified as "European" and unable to afford housing in the European quarters were pushed to the outskirts of towns, often on the most undesirable, low-lying, flood-prone land.[22] The most "radical solution," the commission opined, would be simply to forbid Europeans from living in native neighborhoods. But even advocates of this proposal thought it unwise "since many people of *otherwise irreproachable conduct*" were forced into the native slums, unable to afford housing elsewhere. To "chase" them out was deemed "a too harsh measure."

With whom was the commission worried about being "too harsh"? Some paupers were seen as a class apart. Others deserving of more compassion, those brought to conditions of disgrace through no fault of their own. Even those who sought to live "unknown or hidden as much as possible" so as not to expose smuggling and other illegal pursuits garnered some sympathy. The commissioners' refusal to treat punitively those forced to retreat to the *kampongs* suggests that this may have been the only option for many more Europeans, not just those who were "poor Indos." Loose interpretation of the term "permanent residence" to include those who frequently moved their domiciles from European to native neighborhoods, may indicate that a lenient interpretation of "permanent residence" was considered the only appropriate recommendation.

Reticence to use harsh measures was not always sustained. If sympathy for downtrodden compatriots was sometimes evident, it receded in other passages. European beggars earned the commission's special attention. What to do, they asked, about a European who begged in the courtyards of European dwellings? How to legally exclude their entry but not that of itinerant Chinese traders and Javanese hawkers, a mainstay of Dutch households, who plied their foodstuffs and wares in the backyards where gates were opened to the street most of the day? Were poor whites guilty of trespassing for showing up there, as well—or were they only if they stepped *inside* a home? The subcommission's carefully worded example made their case. "[A] European vagrant . . . made his way to the back veranda of a house occupied by some old Dutch *dames*: the male occupants

[21] While this was an ostensible effort to "protect" native land rights, in practice it marked a massive appropriation of rural land for agricultural industry with creative long-term—ninety-nine–year—leases and rental agreements.

[22] Charles Fisher, "The Eurasian Question in Indonesia," *International Affairs* 23 (4) (October 1947): 522–30, 527–28.

had just left for work. The intruder only departed after exacting money from the harassed and frightened women." Since no one had refused him entry, there was no infraction. The full commission thus endorsed a proposed revision of the trespassing laws to include a house and "its premises"—that is, the land that made up the compound.

Unexpected social practices that defied colonial racial decorum emerged in the show and tell of commission narratives. For example, the subcommission was concerned with Europeans who they suspected of begging in bad faith. Here was apparent distress that provoked the distrust of the commission and the greed of others. The commission refers to those supposedly "in dire need" ("*in broodsnood*," literally, in dire need of bread) who nonetheless kept a servant to take around their beggar letters (*bedelbrief*) for them. The beggar letters warrant no surprise in these documents; only their improper use brought forth a response. When were such beggar letters first distributed in Java by needy Europeans and why do we know so little about them?[23] Was it so improbable that servants (who could easily have worked for as little as the rice they were fed) might still be employed by those in "need" and called upon to do what their shamed employers could not? And what conventions of humiliation and obligation were activated through these social arrangements? There are no answers: as an issue these practices lacked repetitive traction and the matter was never raised again.

Begging entrained other concerns about practices of which the commission was skeptical, but on which it reported nonetheless. The commission described enterprising neighbors who, in the name of a needy widow, might send their own servants to prey "on the purses of good hearted neighbors."[24] Again, the practice of writing such letters elicited no comment—only that others profited from a widow's name. Finally, to curb the presence of needy Europeans, the subcommission proposed that residence cards only be given to those with firm, written proof of a skill and training, to be verified by a local district officer.

To students of the colonial Indies, this would seem trivial stuff in a colony where coerced labor was still prevalent, where indentured labor was enforced, and where thrashings of estate workers were still the order of the day. It was just a few years later in 1876 that Frans Carl Valck would accuse Sumatran planters, those "so-called pioneers of civiliza-

---

[23] *Bedelbrieven* were common in eighteenth- and nineteenth-century Holland but not in the Indies. In contemporary Dutch dictionaries the term is still translated as a "begging letter," but is more widely used to mean a written "plea," not necessarily for charity; the term remains in active use today,

[24] AR, KV 1874, no. 47, Nota van den Heer van Goens, Steenstra Toussaint, and en Van Slooten, Bijlage 12, 1873 G5.

tion," of killing Javanese workers "in cold blood." But in Batavia, such unseemly intrusions were not trivial. The commission's recommendations were forwarded to the Minister of Justice, with comment by the *Raad van Indië* to the Governor-General, and finally with comment by the Minister of Colonies himself. The late-colonial state was well versed in dealing with recalcitrant civil servants and with the native population. It was far less adept at doing so with Europeans veering off racial course— impoverished widows of "good name," tradesmen who fell on hard times, retired clerks, discharged soldiers—and the descendants of each.

The Minister of Justice concluded that the proposals were unnecessary, rejecting them across the board. The recommendation that civilians be required to demonstrate proof of a trade or craft was dismissed as ludicrous—one of those rare moments when authorities acknowledged the glass ceiling for this "certain class"—since nothing would ensure their gainful employment, however much they could demonstrate skills. The *Raad* concurred, noting that in a colony with so many former soldiers and officers, "a number of beggars and vagrants" were "to be expected and posed no threat."[25] Nor did the *Raad* deem it prudent to send such a destitute (and often aged) group back to the Netherlands to burden local charities, as at least one commissioner urged. Further discussion of that possibility took another twenty years. In the meantime, the Indies *Raad* "commended" the Director of Justice for his thoughtful and "courteous" rejection of the commission's proposals on European vagabonds, reminding all involved yet again of how foolish and implausible the recommendations were.[26]

The European Pauperism Commission of 1901

On the face of it, the commission on *Inlandsche kinderen* of 1872 and the European Pauperism Commission of 1901 had little in common. One was replete with statistics, the other had none. The 1901 commission sent out a detailed questionnaire to district officers, whereas in 1872 the commission did not bother. The 1901 commission was Java-wide and included the eastward island of Madura. Its regional reports promised local knowledge and plenty of it. The 1872 commission was confined to hundreds of pages of classified reports to the Minister of Colonies and focused only on Batavia. The 1901 commission's printed report filled five thick volumes—on Education, Small-holder farming, Agricultural Credit, Concubinage, Vagabondage, Pensions, and a "monograph" on Orphanages

---

[25] AR, KV 28 March 1874, no. 47, Nota van den Heer van Goens, Director of Justice van den Heer van Goens to the Governor-General, no. 1144x/2284, 29 April 1873; and advice of the *Raad van Nederlandsch-Indië*, 17 May 1873.

[26] Ibid.

and State Poor Relief for Europeans. With supplements that included regional studies, penultimate briefs, and final results, there were ten volumes, their total pages numbering in the thousands. The 1872 commission was not divided into sections or organized into them later.

The two commissions differed stylistically as well. Unlike the earlier commissions, the report of the European Pauperism Commission of 1901 was a history-rewriting project, one that called up the past in selective and strategic ways. For one, it was heralded as a landmark public statement, committed to objectivity, to fact-collection and comparison—the earlier commission made no such claims. Secondly, it extensively reviewed earlier reports and confidential missives. One can imagine a bevy of subordinates following the detailed cross-referencing of antecedent communications by date and number that official documents always required.[27] Indeed, some volumes in the 1901 commission report were devoted entirely to assessments of earlier initiatives. The initial volume thus signaled its new critical approach with an 1850 report of Batavia's Resident on "the considerable increase in recent years of impoverished *Inlandsche kinderen*"—to which he did not see authorities giving adequate attention.[28] Other volumes provided historical introductions, as did the one on education that described every private and state school opened (and closed) over the preceding hundred years.

It was history-making in another sense: these commissioners imagined themselves as progressive and modern men, enlightened and less constrained by the colonial rubrics of race. A. S. Carpentier Alting, a prominent Protestant cleric and member of the elite society for arts and letters, spoke for many board members when he wrote to the commission Chair, "One can no longer speak of ruler and ruled in this time, as people are all the same. That a European has greater needs than a native, cannot be claimed. *It certainly cannot be said of those Europeans, who by descent and character stand so very close to the native.*"[29] The first and last sen-

---

[27] As noted above, the head of the 1872 commission did refer to several earlier alerts about the situation of poor Europeans, but did so more or less in passing. On the other hand, sometimes he included the earlier documents of decades earlier.

[28] *Het pauperisme onder de Europeanen in Nederlandsch-Indië. Eerste Gedeelte. Algemeen Overzicht* (Batavia: Landsdrukkerij, 1902), 1.

[29] POE (*Het pauperisme onder de Europeanen*), Nota van het lid der commissie, den Heer A. S. Carpentier Alting, Batavia, 16 October 1902, 4; italics added. The note continues:

> There are scores of so-called Europeans who consider themselves far above the native and therefore make so many higher demands, who are only counted as European because a European recognized him and gave him his name, but did nothing further for the upbringing of the person recognized, who in thought and in inclination is fully like the native, yes often even beneath him. Why do people now judge one of the two by another standard? The question can have no answer.

tences may read as contradictory but within the context of the colonial Indies were not. Both lines captured the moralizing spirit of the commission and the racial order of the day. More pointedly, the elision of race in the first line prepared the way for a strategic undercutting of the social claims of certain Europeans in the second. Together they evince how much class disdain inflected and twisted racial narratives.

The commission's timing was significant, as well. Mounted during what was considered a liberal moment of moral reckoning, the commission of 1901 coincided with the much hailed "Ethical Policy," a campaign and set of principles designed to acknowledge publicly and with much fanfare the Netherlands' moral obligation and financial debt to the Indies.[30] Both the commission and the Ethical Policy were pursued in the same year. Both celebrated a more progressive Netherlands and a modernizing imperialism at the "heyday" of its most expansive growth.[31] But the target of the Ethical Policy was "native welfare" of a particular sort: that of a clearly defined subject population. The social welfare of those neither fully subject nor fully citizen commanded little space. One inquiry was applauded. The other, which scrutinized the minutiae of life on the far fringes of colonial comforts, provoked dissent and distaste.

For the European Pauperism Commission touched intimately on more than the dispositions of those clearly in distress. It also implicated those who preferred not to publicize that they were barely getting by or badly in debt, or, worse still, that the offspring of their unacknowledged intimacies lived in the native slums while they and their "proper families" were comfortably apart in their European enclaves and homes. How many family genealogies cut across these residential quarters and for how many generations is impossible to assess. Statistics collected during the 1930 census estimated that three-quarters of those classified as European were of partial native origin.[32] But this still does not speak to the destitution into which many people fell, or to the numbers of European men who completely cut ties to their own children and companions and who were swept back into the native quarters and bore no *legally recognized* European connection or trace. But it could not have escaped the political unconscious of many colonial Europeans who remained in the colony and who had long since

[30] The Ethical Policy (supported by progressive liberal and social democratic circles) has a rich historiography. See H. W. van den Doel, *De stille macht: Het Europese binnenlands bestuur op Java en Madoera, 1808–1942* (Amsterdam: Bert Bakker, 1994), 165–66. And on "ethical imperialism" in its Indies variant, see Elsbeth Locher-Scholten, *Ethiek in Fragmenten* (Utrecht: HES, 1981).

[31] Elsbeth Locher-Scholten, "Dutch Expansion and the Imperialism Debate," *Journal of Southeast Asian Studies* 25 (1) (March 1994): 91–111, 93.

[32] See A. van Marle, "De groep der Europeanen in Nederlandsch-Indië, iets over ontstaan en groei," *Indonesië* 5 (1951–52): 314–41.

left that their severed "kin" were the refuse that social reform endeavored to uplift even as those policies kept them in their place.

Opposition was raised to both the 1872 and 1901 commissions, but in vastly different ways. In 1874 it was the Minister of Colonies who squashed publication. In 1901 it came from many more quarters—from those who felt seared from afar as well as from those scorched up close. Both commissions were forced to confront the ambiguous terms of white privilege and who had rights to claim it. Moreover, what had remained a secreted debate on whether it should be the state's obligation to pay for poor relief in 1872 emerged at the center of public debate in 1901 over whether social welfare would be forged—or would flounder—on the intimate politics of kinship, family, and race.

The Questions

The European Pauperism Commission of 1901 was ordered by official decree as a response to the "repeatedly expressed complaints" about increasing European impoverishment in the Indies. On 26 June 1901 lengthy circulars were sent throughout Java. Regional government offices were instructed to collect detailed statistics. The 16 basic questions were generic and seemingly innocuous: the more specific ones, which sought to specify how and with whom one lived, were not. This time around, "good and reliable" statistics would codify distinctions earlier reports had discerned but not described: Indies-born Europeans versus those Europe-born Europeans, Indies-born Europeans versus those with native roots who were European only in name. Concubinage, one focus of the earlier commission, was here the cornerstone on which other issues were to revolve and from which the final recommendations followed, for it was concubinage, especially as practiced in the military barracks, that had produced families in which native mothers were "unequipped" to properly rear their wayward Indo young.

The causal narrative was already evident in the historical account the commission chose to convey, one in which racial characteristics were durable and impervious to historical change. It was a story that began with the VOC in 1715 forbidding the *"mixiste inboorlingen"* [*sic*] (mixed Indies-born Europeans) from company positions; with British Governor Daendals in 1808 urging an end "to the neglect . . . of bastard children"; with the observation that even then, the "well-known characteristics" of the descendants of mixed bloods were present "to this day," along with their "lack of mental willpower . . . and their inability to uplift themselves."[33] These were accepted as "facts of the matter" from the

---

[33] *Het pauperisme onder de Europeanen in Nederlandsch-Indië. Eerste Gedeelte. Algemeen Overzicht* (Batavia: Landsdrukkerij, 1902), 3–4.

start. The questions were grounded in an epistemology of race that conjoined a physical definition of race (hair-, skin-, and eye color) with one that relied on comportment, disposition, and moral character.

Local officials carring out the questionnaires asked about the marital status (married, widowed, or in concubinage) of individuals with child dependents whose income was less than one hundred guilder per month (for those without child dependents, the threshold was set at fifty guilder). Those in "temporary" need were excluded from the survey. Age, sex, birthplace, nationality, and "social position" of one's parents, and age at marriage of household head were to be tabulated, as well. Number, age, sex, and occupation of one's children; employment; income; children's schooling; "life style"; religion; health; housing conditions; schooling; knowledge of Dutch; army service and rank; "probable causes of social decline"—questions on all of these topics followed.

On the face of it, these were standard questions. That was not so for the more precise inquiries under each general heading. Under "past and present life style," the inquiry asked about opium and liquor use, prostitution, profligacy, and gambling. Local religious teachers were to verify "the sort of people with whom [the needy] mingled," "whether [they] lived as Europeans or mixed with the Native population," whether the person in question "lived apart from the native population or in the *kampong*s or *desa* [village] among them." On Dutch-language competence, parents were asked about their children's fluency, a question that people quickly recognized as one that would be interpreted to assess how, and among whom, they lived and raised their young. European women in relations with native, Arab, or Chinese men were asked about "their nationality," the age at which they entered concubinage, and whether they had borne children *not* belonging to their present family.

By any calculation, these more specific inquiries were difficult questions to answer and to ask. Some were to be addressed to the "less well-off" themselves; others were to be answered by state officials. District wardens, chaplains, neighbors, and school teachers were called on to help. In principle, local state officials were to carry out the surveys. In dense European centers like Batavia and Soerabaja, a committee was appointed of local civil, religious, and government authorities, who ostensibly knew the needy and were trusted—those who could answer for the needy or more easily encourage them to answer for themselves.

How the data was *actually* collected was a different matter. Sometimes the Residents wrote opinion papers based on their own prior knowledge, sometimes their Assistent Residents wrote the reports for them. Local committees were used in some places, but not in others. Who actually spoke with those deemed disadvantaged is hard to say. The commission insisted that it was through "personal contact with the needy themselves" that the data was to be gathered, and "as necessary, through neighbors and acquaintances." "As necessary" turned out to be quite often in districts where people refused the inquiry. "Common knowledge" was liberally written into the commission's report, as was gossip when individuals were pressed to divulge and report on the intimate lives of neighbors.

In some places district wardens (*wijkmeester*) were entrusted with the task: in Semarang that worked; in Batavia and Jogjakarta they were uncooperative. District officials eager to please central authorities provided "written and oral testimony . . . hoping they could be of help in some way." House visits were done in Salatiga, duly noted as an exception, and seemed to have been rare elsewhere. In some districts the committees sent forms to household heads, which were to be returned by mail or in person to district bureaus. Sometimes authorities simply completed the forms.

Vignettes appeared throughout the regional reports and were often cited in the commission's final summation, but their provenance was never clear. The vignettes read as stories about the needy, but not by them. In many cases they seem not to have been consulted. What the commission, in the end, collected were starkly different forms of knowledge: on the one hand, a compendium of elite beliefs about racial types, and received common sense about Indos and lower-class whites; on the other hand, details of survival and material need that pierced the conventions of the prescribed narratives.

Refusals and Affronts of Many Kinds

Opposition emerged even before the commission got off the ground. One particularly avid critique came quickly from one Otto Knaap, born in Cheribon in 1866 of an Indo-European mother and a Dutch father employed in the plantation industry. Schooled in Leiden, self-fashioned as a promoter and critic of the arts, he had just returned to Java at twenty-nine years of age, a few years before the commission was announced. His articles in the Indies press had already shown him to be an agile and ardent commentator on the parochial pretensions of Indies society, so it was fitting that he was among the first to pan the investigation.[34]

Writing in the *De Amsterdammer* in January 1902, Knaap did three important things: he published the entire set of questions that were being posed by the European Pauperism Commission, warned that the circular

[34] Rob Niewenhuys holds that Otto Knaap was one of the very few to write in support of one of the most infamous attacks on the social snobbery and provincialisms of the Indies' European society—that of Bas Veth's *Life in the Netherlands* (1900)—when everyone else was outraged by Veth's cutting portrayal of colonial Batavia. See Rob Nieuwenhuys, *Mirror of the Indies: A History of Dutch Colonial Literature* (Amherst: University of Massachusetts, 1982), 139–40.

would be badly received by just about everyone involved, and, most importantly, he predicted what the commission would conclude no matter how much new "data" was gathered.

First, he opined that the district officers would be disgruntled to have so much work foisted upon their understaffed offices. And he was right. As the commission itself acknowledged, for a variety of reasons the inquiries were stymied at every step. The number of Europeans in question was more than the commissioners had expected, and regional offices complained of insufficient manpower and sometimes reluctant help from church, medical, and other local authorities. Despite the extensive instructions, local officials were confused about what "line of action" to take, and who they should be counting: whether to focus more broadly on disadvantaged (*minvermogenden)* inhabitants or, more specifically, on paupers.[35] Some reports were terse, no more than "brief summaries," showing what the commissioners disappointingly interpreted as "insufficient interest" in the matters at hand.[36] There were considerable delays in reporting, especially in returning the statistical data: at the end of 1901 only a score of districts had done so. Despite numerous reminders, the rest only came in six months later. More pointedly, many officials were themselves uncomfortable asking questions of such a "touchy" nature.

Secondly, Knaap predicted that most of those approached would never agree to be interviewed about precisely those issues the commission most sought to know. Calling upon racial common sense, he reminded the commission that "the" Indo was "well known" to be excessively timid and reticent, with a strongly developed, if sometimes "misplaced," sense of pride. He renounced the circular as "absurd" and derided its directive. Point by point he dissected its "unbelievably immodest and indiscreet" questionnaire, providing a list of the intrusive, personal questions to be asked.[37] *How long have you lived out of wedlock? How many illegitimate children do you have? With whom have you had them? How often do you pray? How often do your children skip school? Do you speak with them in Malay? Have you ever engaged in prostitution? Do you sleep on a bed, a mat, or the floor? Was your mother a concubine? What charity do you depend on? How many of your natural children do you not support? Why were you dismissed from your last job? Have you*

---

[35] *Uitkomsten der Pauperisme-Enquête. Algemeen Verslag* (Batavia: Landsdrukkerij, 1902). See, especially, the subsection entitled, "Objections found with the investigation," 2–4, 8.

[36] Ibid.

[37] Otto Knaap, "Pauperisme onder de Indo-Europeanen," *De Amsterdammer*, 26 January 1902, 1–2.

really sought others? Were your parents paupers? Why do you think you are in such a distressed situation?

Such invasive questions were not unusual for poor commissions. What made these so charged was the category of "pauper" itself and who was reckoned—and who reckoned themselves—to be included in it. The commission, by its own admission, was never about poverty per se. It was designed to identify Europeans living in a style and at a level that was *not commensurate with how Europeans should live in a colonial situation.* "Needy" was a relative term and those who were cast in that category saw themselves subjected to inquiries unbefitting their station: pauperism and scrutiny of their private lives was to define their place in the politics of race.

As the commission itself realized, the investigation was very "unpopular" among "many" European residents: "the Indo-European population in the Indies" was "especially" uneasy and "suspicious" of the inquiries. And authorities were convinced that the press, and those like Knaap, made it worse. Nor were those most needy necessarily the most offended. More embarrassing to all, and especially to the ruling elite, were the numbers of subaltern civil servants in government offices whose own incomes were lower than the level at which pauperism was calculated to start. The commissioners lamented this "misunderstanding" and misconstrual of their intention by those questioned, among whom were lowly clerks in those very offices charged to carry out the investigation.

Repeatedly, the commission reissued statements to affirm that it was not after "the details of people's lives," but rather wanted a "global approximation" of the conditions of the less-advantaged: "Those Europeans who, though not in a strict sense belonging to *personae miserabiles*," of European society, [those] seen as needy in relationship to the circumstances and the proper quality of life demanded of the European race and who have not yet sunk to the level of the lesser Natives."[38] These were not to be considered "pauper statistics in the strict sense of the word," as so many thought, but merely the "broad limits" within which pauperism might be considered and framed. "These figures are not meant to say that the persons within the stated limits are 'paupers' per se, but only that they, considering their nationality, can be regarded as 'less well-off.'"

Those "broad limits" were unacceptable to many. Irate colonial Europeans stamped the investigation an "inquisition" and the Indies administration an "inquisitionary state."[39] One commission member who acknowledged being "an Indo and friends with many of those interviewed" excused himself from the commission so that he could do the

---

[38] *Rapport der Pauperisme-Commissie* (Batavia: Landsdrukkerij, 1903), 7.
[39] "Het Handelsblad over Pauperisme in Indië," *Indische Gids*: 619.

questionnaire on himself. He claimed not to find it truly "grievous" but made the point that it "surely would have been extremely painful" had there been a tactless interviewer. In central Java, the Assistent Resident of Bojolali reported that the investigation was met everywhere with "distrust, reluctance, and irritation" ("*wantrouwen, weerzin, wrevel*").[40] Elsewhere in the residency, the reception was worse. Questions, especially about income and life style, were "dodged." Rumors were so rampant in Sragen that one Assistent Resident reported a respondent pleading with him to fill out an "act of legal recognition" before 1 January 1902 for the children he conceived with his native companion because he had heard rumors that after that date it would no longer be allowed. The committee in Djoewana considered the task of asking "the most utterly intimate" questions "delicate," to say the least. Some of those approached would not comply with the survey and baldly stated why. Some skipped town and could not be found. Others who refused to have themselves described as paupers "simply refused to fill out the forms."[41]

A few commissioners claimed to have been greeted with a warm reception. They were pleased to learn that the questions were "politely received" and the information "most willingly provided." In Semarang a trusted warden replaced the individual appointed by the commission. In Salatiga house visits were made to verify the statements of those whose own reports of destitution were not trusted and to check on the actual "degree of reduced circumstances."

In Batavia the surveys were recognized as a failure and the statistics as unreliable. There the committee complained that if they had had to use a general yardstick of "poverty, "then there were hardly any paupers to be counted." But "the simple character of poor relief" meant nothing in a colonial situation. As a chaplain in Preanger explained,

> The definition of pauper—a term which has become an accepted term in everyday speech here—we use in its wider meaning, i.e., in the sense of people, *albeit not in great hardship*, who by circumstances, dependent or not of their own free will, have fallen into a situation which is unsatisfactory for the future, and for the family, *considering the place that one would want the European elements to have within the native society.*[42]

But how was it that a "European" *should* live? And did it matter what kind of European they were? Was the same measure to be used both for those who were mixed, descendants of Europeans, and for those Europe-born?

---

[40] *Uitkomsten der Pauperisme-Enquête. Gewestelijke Verslagen*, 2, Soerakarta (Batavia : Landsdrukkerij, 1902), 1.

[41] Ibid., Pasoeroean, 6.

[42] Ibid.

These were charged issues and Otto Knaap eagerly played out their political implications. Knowing the class fears of his adversaries, he warned
that their inquiry could easily backfire on their do-good intentions in ex-
plosive and unintended ways. Those already politicized and inclined to a
communist bent, "*de proletariërs*," would become further embittered—
precisely that group the 1872 commission had been concerned to quell,
and those whom Batavian authorities in May 1848 feared might have
been behind the demonstration of "city fathers and coloreds" led by Van
Hoëvell. Again, Knaap had identified what was to be a strong undercurrent in the commission's subjacent enterprise.

The commission repeatedly had stated its intention to investigate the
spread of pauperism among a European population that was sometimes
regarded as negligible in number and sometimes vividly depicted as
"rogues and dangerous elements for the state."[43] In response, questions
were answered that the commission never directly asked. No, reported
the Resident of Preanger, there was no "learned proletariat" (*geleerd proletariat*) poised to storm the palace gates. In Soerabaja the committee
noted that paupers were "calm and moderate" and "content with their
lot." Semarang officials remarked that the paupers lived "calm and
sober[ly]" amongst themselves. The Pasoeroean committee concurred
that "socialism has not penetrated . . . and that there was still respect for
higher status and social place."[44] In short there was no "bad blood,"
"many were content with their daily plate of rice, not hankering for lux-
urious or costly clothing or dwellings."

But if this romance of "shared poverty" and impoverished content was
part of the scripted narrative of some reports, it did not pervade them
all.[45] Other district officials saw "inveterate indolence" hiding something
else. As the Assistent Resident of Semarang put it, the "temporary success
of the Filipino revolution had gone to [the] heads" of bitter, unemployed
Indo young men, who "fancied themselves as potential firebrands, as

[43] *Het pauperisme onder de Europeanen in Nederlandsch-Indië. Eerste Gedeelte*, 8.
[44] Ibid.
[45] "Shared poverty" was the term Clifford Geertz famously used to describe how Javanese peasants managed the onerous extractions to which they were subject during the
colonial period and after. See *Agricultural Involution* (Berkeley: University of California
Press, 1963). Numerous critics, most notably the anthropologist Benjamin White, have
questioned Geertz's benign characterization, pointing out that Geertz did not work with
colonial archives but uncritically off the historiography and categories that were derived
from them. See especially, Benjamin White, "Agricultural Involution and Its Critics: Twenty
Years Later," *Journal of Concerned Asian Scholars* 18 (1983): 18–31, and "Clifford Geertz:
Paradoxcial Genius of Interpretive Anthropology," *Development and Change* (forthcoming), where White explicitly points to Geertz's unfamiliarity with Dutch archival documents; see also Jennifer and Paul Alexander, "Shared Poverty as Ideology: Labor Relations
in Rural Java," *Man* 17 (4) (1982): 597–619.

'Aguinaldos in the making.' "[46] While they were "resentful of full-blooded Europeans," the Assistent Resident counseled calm since they were still only "bickering" and not yet seriously organizing among themselves.[47] Fear, compassion, and class contempt underwrote these interpretations. District officials wrote of those Indos who saw Natives as being far beneath them while living amongst them as imperious and exploitative taskmasters—"the sort of Europeans who are the cancer of the Indies."

Knaap carefully chose his epithets with the social pretensions of the commissioners and colonial European elite carefully in mind. The investigation was not just a "useless concoction," he claimed. It "lacked *savoir faire*." And who, he asked, could possibly imagine that queries about one's daily prayers, placed in a "question box," were an effective and enlightened means to investigate social misery! By Knaap's account, paupers could not be studied "from above" but only by those who "more or less" had grown up with them (or had provided needy young Indos with gratis Dutch lessons, as had he). "Pauperism in the Indies is a more complicated, intricate phenomenon than in Europe. In Europe it is almost exclusively a question of livelihood and housing; in the Indies it is about the distance that separates ruler from ruled."

But Knaap also targeted the hypocrisy of Dutch compassion and its racially circumscribed character. Why was there such an outpouring of interest and sympathy for the South African Dutch (*de Boeren*) admittedly devastated by the Boer War, he asked, while the dismal fate of European paupers in the Indies left his Leiden neighbors "utterly cold?" He accused them of needing "high drama to stir their feelings," whereas the "tragedy of quiet distress and submissive social misery escaped them all."

Finally, he rightly predicted what the gentlemen commissioners would conclude: that there really was no white pauperism in the rich colony because those counted as needy were not really European. As he snidely put it, "Mountains of paper will be filled to the profit of the paper factories in the Netherlands." There would be lots of documents, but no results. By way of conclusion, he conjured another fanciful scenario with pointed barbs:

> If only the clemency of the Governor-General goes so far that he might sometime hide himself incognito among the paupers, speaking familiarly

[46] "Aguinaldo" is a reference to the young Chinese mestizo revolutionary Emilio Aguinaldo (1869–1964), one of the leaders of the war of independence against the Spanish in 1896 and who became president of the Philippines' first republic. From the quiescent distance of the Indies, Aguinaldo may have seemed radical to Dutch authorities, but it was he who had executed in 1897 the far more incendiary Andres Bonifacio, leader of the underground Katipunan anticolonial brotherhood, and he who swore fidelity to the United States in April 1901 (reportedly on the condition that his own life be spared).

[47] *Uitkomsten der Pauperisme-Enquête. Gewestelijke Verslagen*, 1, Semarang, 7.

and confidentially with them, and promising his support. . . . But such things only happen in fairytales. What reasonable person would willingly want to leave the splendid palace of Buitenzorg, even for a brief moment, on the proletariat's behalf!

Knaap's attack elicited a quick response. J. E. de Meyier, the editor of *De Indische Gids* and a loyal backer of the government, came to the Governor-General's defense, criticizing Knaap's "spiteful tone," his ignorance of how high state officials operate, and his failure to see the difference between an actual Governor-General and a *"khalif"* from *A Thousand and One Nights*.[48] Knaap snapped back that De Meyier displayed his own inept art of reading if he thought to take the comparison between the Governor-General and a despotic Muslim ruler literally: anyone who had lived in the Indies for decades and had prolonged contact with the Indo poor would recognize his meaning and intent. Again Knaap stated his case: that an investigation into pauperism should be done by educated Indos, those who knew the land where they were born as newly appointed European civil servants could not. More pointedly, Knaap tore into De Meyier's claim that state underlings would find their wages sufficient if they only knew how to save and "curb their needs." As Knaap insisted, countless among them already lived so simply that there was nothing else to cut. What else do you do without "when you live in miserable hovels, have insufficient food, always in want," and on a starvation wage (*hongerloon*)? What more did they have to be wanting, he asked, for De Meyier, who apparently had never seen poverty up close, to be satisfied?

Knaap was not alone in denouncing the commission's premise and the content of its questionnaire. The *Tijdschrift voor Nederlandsch-Indië* (which, as noted above, Van Hoëvell had started in 1848, just prior to his forced departure from Java) also reprinted the questions, noting that "exposing the intimate lives of the greater part of the population . . . was not the job of an enlightened government." In a letter of public protest a group signing themselves "those dispossessed from life's banquet" reproved the commission's methods and goals. They claimed that the investigation invaded and exposed their private lives to public scrutiny and violated their most basic human rights. They demanded to know how

---

[48] Otto Knaap, "Pauperisme onder de Indo-Europeanen," *De Indische Gids*, 27 March 1902. The reference to *A Thousand and One Nights* might allude to the fact that Otto Knaap regularly wrote reviews of the *komedie stamboel*, a popular form of itinerant theater at the turn of the century with many Indo-Eurasian among the actors and audience, for which nearly 90 percent of the performances were based on *A Thousand and One Nights*. See Matthew Isaac Cohen, *The Komedie Stamboel: Popular Theater in Colonial Indonesia, 1891–1903* (Athens: Ohio University Press, 2006), esp. 45–49.

questions about church attendance and knowledge of the catechism would further the commission's endeavor. And why was a question about "interest in worship" ("exclusively between a person and his conscience") the state's business? Such an "inquisitional investigation" was deemed inappropriate, all the more so for a Protestant government.[49]

The Political Arithmetic of Race

Admitting the results to be "not completely favorable," the commission published the statistics nonetheless, despite confusion about who had asked the questions and who had answered them; the large numbers who were noncompliant; and the fact that in some districts the "less well-off" demanded to be distinguished from paupers and excluded from the inquiry, whereas elsewhere they did not. So how many paupers were there? With all of the "misunderstandings" and with all the state's caveats that it was simply striving to gain a general picture, the figures were authoritative—not rounded but exact.

And some figures, as we shall see, carried more weight than others. According to the commission's final report, out of a total of 53,584 Europeans "and their equivalents," there were 9,381 disadvantaged, or 17.5 percent of the European population.[50] Of these, 5,935 were paupers, 3,234 of whom were children. These were large numbers for any colony, but especially for a nonsettler one. In some residencies the broader category of "the disadvantaged" made up only 10 percent, but in Madiun it reached 24 percent and in Preanger 31 percent. In some districts the more

[49] Anonymous, "Eene circulaire over het pauperisme in Indië," *Tijdschift voor Nederlandsch-Indië* 5 (1901): 627–34.

[50] The convoluted racial classifications of the Dutch East Indies are one of the strongest testaments to the quixotic and nonbiological basis of colonial racial taxonomies. Europeans "and their equivalents" (the latter referred to as "Official Europeans," since European status was conferred by ordinance) was based on Artikel 109 of the *Regeeringsreglement* (the Indies government regulations) of 1854 that excluded native Christians from the category, thereby removing the religious criterium that had been used earlier. By the time of the ordinance of 1883 requests for European equivalence could only be made by those who were in legal possession of a "family name" (*geslachtsnaam*) "or who had taken a [European] family name with the consent of the Governor-General." Not surprisingly, there were very few persons who requested and received that consent. The descendants of Europeans with European fathers were included as "equivalents" in 1854, but this was short-lived. By 1898 the new mixed-marriage regulations reassigned children of European fathers and native mothers to the legal status of their mothers. Christian Arabs and Christian Africans (descendants of those recruited into the Indische army since 1831) were classified as European equivalents. Non-Christian Africans (also called "the Black Dutch") were classified as native. See William Edward van Mastenbroek, *De historische ontwikkeling van de staatsrechtejlijke indeeling der bevolking van Nederlandsch-Indië*, Ph.D. Diss., University of Amsterdam (Veenman: Wageningen, 1934), 61–81.

restricted and impoverished category of "pauper" made up as much as 18 percent of the European population.[51]

These are striking figures. But more impressive is how easily they were dismissed and how quickly the commission insisted that the percentages should prompt no "needless" alarm.[52] Interpretative labor tamed the numbers. Cultural assessments of race redrew the proportions of those who were needy, as they likewise refigured racial lines. But it was the distribution of income and its correlation to marital status that, not surprisingly, attracted the commission's attention. For it was the prevalence of concubinage and its effects that the commission had intended to document in the first place. Ranking the needy by monthly income, only 35 percent were married, and it was these persons, as opposed to those living in concubinage, who were better off. No conclusions were drawn about the 35 percent of the respondents not included in the statistics because they refused to discuss their income.[53]

Those counted were people employed in nearly every low-end job and just about every middling occupation for Europeans in the Indies: former soldiers; railway and tramworkers, clerks in commercial offices and legal bureaus; supervisors and scribes on the agricultural estates; craftsmen; innkeepers; blacksmiths; waiters; watchmakers; photographers; barbers; tailors; bookbinders; storefront lawyers; shoemakers; coolie recruiters; roadside shopkeepers; and shop attendants—all jobs that were increasingly being filled by Javanese and Chinese women and men and that just twenty years later would be largely taken over by them. Other occupations of "dubious repute" included private tutors who had set themselves as teachers for "Native, Chinese, and needy Europeans," for whom they also wrote petitions and letters. In the central Javanese cities of Soerakarta and Jogjakarta thirty-three of those classified as needy Europeans served native royalty as coachmen, orderlies, and trumpeters. Others lived off their families and charities, off native villagers and their European neighbors.

But if one-third of those scheduled to be counted and questioned did not comply with the survey, this did not get in the way of the local reports. Officials who could not fill in the numbers could still, as they did in Batavia, do the political arithmetic that allowed them to fill in the interpretive slots. When statistics were absent, local officials were encouraged to impart their "impressions." Some refrained. Others did so with relish, and with rehearsed phrases of what "everyone knew" characterized Indos and the causes of their demise: lack of "will power," "energy," "initiative," "perseverance," "parental love" made up the ritualized litany from one district to another.

---

[51] *Rapport der Pauperisme Commissie* (Batavia: Landsdrukkerij,1903), 8.
[52] Ibid., 7.
[53] *Uitkomsten der Pauperisme-Enquête. Algemeen Verslag, 9.*

But there were also remarks and notations that had no fixed association with a particular social group. Adjectives slipped from poor white to mixed blood, confusing the commission's efforts to distinguish among them. Much of the confusion rested on the issue of "choice": how to account for a young woman who had converted to Islam, or a "European" family living in a native quarter in ways that indicated not distress but a willing departure from the European milieu? How to make sense of European ex-soldiers whose domestic lives were more stable and less precarious precisely because they cohabited with native companions, while their unattached comrades were described as wallowing in drink and sloth? Nor was the moral landscape of choice clear. Was an Indo widow forced to beg for food from her better-off neighbors at a higher moral standard than an educated young Indo woman who chose to live with a Javanese man and their children in a native *kampong*?

Contesting Pauperism, Miscalculating Race

If statistics help "determine the character of social facts," as Hacking contends, it is commissions that provide their interpretive, historical, and epistemic frames.[54] Despite the figures—in some areas as many as 18 percent of the European population were living in poverty—many local reports argued that pauperism was less a problem than the commission had originally thought. Some local committees refused to acknowledge a problem at all. As the Assistent Resident of Tegal told the commission:

> It is my personal feeling . . . that in this district, for the overall European population, the situation is satisfactory . . . it is a known fact that most of [the needy] children are European only in name; as a rule, they were not well raised and grew up as natives. That such people would feel themselves much happier as native and would more easily make their livelihoods as natives, certainly needs no demonstration. One could . . . stipulate that only those [children] could be [legally] recognized who have typical characteristics of a European origin, namely . . . white, brown or light eyes, brown or blonde hair and more or less white skin.[55]

Statistics were suspect because claims to neediness were doubted across the board. Some district officers were convinced that earnings were underestimated by those unwilling to divulge illegal activities.[56] Others insisted

---

[54] Ian Hacking, "How Should We Do the History of Statistics?" in *The Foucault Effect: Studies in Governmentality*, ed. Graham Burchell, Colin Gordon, Peter Miller (Chicago: University of Chicago Press, 1991), 181.

[55] *Uitkomsten der Pauperisme-Enquête. Gewestelijke Verslagen* I, Dekalongan, 14.

[56] *Uitkomsten der Pauperisme-Enquête. Gewestelijke Verslagen*, Semarang, 1.

that if concubinage was ended and discharged soldiers were sent back to Europe, the problem would all but disappear. Vignettes rather than figures made the point that real need was rare: someone seeking financial help to repair his house, a "spendthrift" who hoped to get out of debt by feigning need. One of the "poorest families" in Djombang was reported to have a storeroom stocked with rice and a gamelan set worth several hundred guilders. Several local reports noted that servants were retained even in the poorest households.

Comparison is always both a strategic and a political act. Comparisons to the hardships of the destitute in the Netherlands were invoked to argue that life in the tropics made pauperism less of a hardship: "poor clothing" mattered less in the heat; bamboo huts need not keep out the cold; food was adequate if simple, in accordance with "the [native] custom." But such refusals to acknowledge neediness sometimes flew in the face of those very statements. In Semarang the committee was appalled by Europeans living in shabby one-room hovels "that could barely fit a bed"; by windowless, dank, one-room huts with dirt floors; by a man who possessed only a raised bamboo mat (*kepang*) and rickety table for furniture; by an uneducated, seventeen-year-old Indo boy who "dressed as a native selling rice wine" in the local markets; by a boy of twenty-one, abandoned by his father, who worked for an Indo welfare association for twenty cents per day.

Compassion was selective, and often came with a distorted twist. For what was always left unsaid in these vignettes was the starkest fact of all: that these conditions of life, with people perched precariously at the edges of need, were the common conditions in which a majority of land-poor Javanese lived in rural areas and in urban slums. As later studies of *kampong* conditions in Batavia and Semarang attest, these were conditions that continued through to the end of the colonial period and well after.[57]

If many of the reports read as scripted, some officials seemed unsure about which script to follow. In those latter cases individual circumstances were seen as "exceptions," such that real neediness was again suspect. There was the pauper recluse who "didn't read, didn't hunt, talked to no one," and refused to leave his house. There were those with no "moral fiber"—gamblers, troublemakers, drunks, "the inveterate indolent," womanizers—who contributed to their own demise. There were misguided young women encouraged to live in concubinage by their

---

[57] On the conditions of *kampong* life in colonial Semarang, see James L. Cobban, "Kampungs and Conflict in Colonial Semarang," *Journal of Southeast Asian Studies* 19 (2) (September 1988): 266–91, esp. 278–79. Cobban distinguishes between the native and European quarters but makes no mention of the large population of European and mixed poor living in Semarang's poor quarters.

greedy parents. The Assistent Resident of Djombang was struck by "how easily young women of eighteen to twenty-five years old go from one man to another, and though not prostitutes, gladly do so."[58] Djepara authorities offered the example of a "neither really bad nor backward person" whose penchant for women prompted him to organize a puppet group "to nourish his erotic tendencies." Others who were assumed to be "demoralized" by living with native women had become "wholly indifferent" and were only "quasi" seeking work.[59] In Djoewana, the Assistent Resident described a traveling comedy troupe of young Indo women and men "living loose and indecent lives."[60] "Nor did it escape the committee," as the Soerabaja commission wrote, that some young Indo men married native women "merely to satisfy their sensual desires for sex,"—not to set up a "domestic life."[61]

The commission encouraged what it referred to as these "general impressions of a specific nature." Such impressions replaced responses by the needy themselves and thickened reports when statistics could not be gathered. Nor were the assessments of a civil servant cadet, newly arrived in the Indies (and perhaps newly posted in the region, since promotions entailed transfers every few years), ever subject to question. For this was credible knowledge that circulated widely and was already implicitly shared. Claims to know the moral dispositions and desires of the disadvantaged and the distributions of their affective states were expressions of an epistemology of race. Such sanctioned knowledge constituted the psychic and material privilege and violence of empire and the inequities that it so guarded and nurtured. These were the grounds on which the allocation of new resources was rendered unnecessary and unwarranted, as was the state's responsibility for social welfare. And thus the commission's final report in 1903 could state: "The solution to the pauperism question is not, *as so many think*, merely a question of money and, even less, exclusively a question of a good practical will on the part of the government.[62]

As Knaap had predicted, and as Henri H. van Kol, outspoken socialist member of the Dutch States-General was to write in 1911 in criticism of Minister of the Colonies Fock's official rejection of the commission's findings, no matter what the evidence, state authorities still concluded that "there was no pauperism" in the Indies, that "poverty does not exist

[58] *Uitkomsten der Pauperisme-Enquête. Gewestelijke Verslagen*, Soerabaja, 7.

[59] Ibid.

[60] *Uitkomsten der Pauperisme-Enquête. Gewestelijke Verslagen* 2, 6. The fact that actors in the widely acclaimed itinerant comedy troupes, the *komedie stamboel*, which played to full houses across Java, were clustered as part of the colonial underclass suggests again how poorly some local officials distinguished among the Indo population.

[61] *Uitkomsten der Pauperisme-Enquête. Gewestelijke Verslagen* 2, Soerabaja, 8.

[62] *Rapport van de Pauperisme Commissie* (1903), 5

among the Indo-European," and that there was more poverty in Amsterdam than in the Indies.[63]

PAUPERISM POLITICS

The term "pauperism" in the Indies was never applied to the native population. But the fact that it was inflected as "white," "Dutch," and "European," and also included their mixed Indo descendants, created categorical confusions from the start. For the Indies' European population had never been "pure" anything, not in 1900 or centuries earlier. In 1815 there were some 4,000 Europeans, among whom were prominent senior officials married to illegitimate "mestizas" or living in concubinage.[64] By the time of the 1901 commission, the number of Europeans throughout the entire archipelago was put at 75,000. In 1930, there were over 300,000 Europeans born in the Indies.

Distinguishing among those messy categories of who were "nativized" Europeans and those conferred European-"equivalent" status and between those Europeans who were Indies-bred but Europe-born shaped the commission's findings and constrained its license to initiate reform. Two solutions were seen as possible. One was to simply eliminate "the distinctions between nationalities" and to allow the lower class of Europeans "to dissolve into the [native] whole." As many were struggling to maintain a European standard, this was understood as something many of the Indo population "would prefer." But this dangerous option was seen as one that could easily give rise to an independent state, a concern that had emerged a half-century earlier. The second solution, considered in the "better interest of Motherland and the Indies itself, and not least the Native population," was to adhere to the existing policy and to maintain the hierarchical relations of privilege that distinguished Natives from Europeans. This, as the commission noted, remained the "ideal" but depended on three prerequisites: (1) removal from the Indies of those who could not "live without financial worries" in a European manner; (2) assurance that children of mixed marriages would be assigned the legal status of their (native) mothers and not that of their European fathers; and 3) more strictly enforced regulations for recognition of illegitimate children (within 5–10 days of birth with possession of a birth certificate and the presence of two witnesses who could attest to parentage). Not least, such

---

[63] H. van Kol, *Nederlandsch-Indië in de Staten-Generaal van 1897 tot 1909* ('s-Gravenhage: Martinus Nijhoff, 1911), 173.

[64] On the enormously "mixed" colonial culture of Java in the eighteenth and early nineteenth centuries, see J. Taylor, 95.

measures were to guarantee that which in practice, if not principle, "everyone" already knew: that European pauperism was a misnomer, a category error, a misapprehension. Those paupers of "mixed" descent who had reverted to their roots in the native world were, in fact, where they really belonged.

The term "pauperism" had wide currency in Europe: first in England, in France after 1815, and in the Netherlands a few decades later. Historians concerned with the pauper class in Holland hold that there the term connoted a "covert danger" and a social plague, an ambivalent sense of compassion and disgust for those impoverished. Used in the Netherlands to emphasize "the social responsibilities and financial burdens associated with the presence of enormous numbers of poor people in their midst," in the Indies it signaled the reverse.[65] If the lexicon was shared, as we have seen, the solutions were not.[66]

The European Pauperism Commission in the Indies gained moral authority by demonstrating its conscientious and disinterested restraint, its willingness to reflect on the colonial administration's own mishaps, to seek the truth "at whatever cost." But its power rested on more than its calculation of the moral pulse of the present and its prescriptions for the future. The commission justified its license to expend funds, time, and personnel in part by redirecting the vectors of accountability and blame. Race, as one commissioner upheld, was no way to distinguish need in a modern world. But the virulent effects of racialized policy were present and effective. Race thrived as a vital political concept and accrued power in its updated form. It conceptually set apart the cultural coordinates of those with the capacity to participate in the intimate and public practices of European privilege, even as it disenfranchised those who could not claim *echte* (real), *zuivere* (pure) full-blooded membership.

In the end the commission set aside many of the very statistics it had so sought to collect, in part because the terms by which race was assessed were better proved by what people in power already knew. Twelve years after the 1901 commission, the case would easily be made again that their "lack of initiative and a lack of driving force and power [*stuwkracht*]" kept the Indos dispossessed and where they were.[67] In 1922 their condition was still

[65] See Frances Gouda's excellent history of poverty and social welfare, *Poverty and Political Culture: The Rhetoric of Social Welfare in the Netherlands and France*, 1814–1854 (Lanham, Md.: Rowman and Littlefield, 1995). On the social etymology of paupers, see Gouda, 35–39. See also Ali de Regt, *Arbeidersgezinnen en beschavingsarbeid* (Boom: Amsterdam, 1984), 171.

[66] Piet de Rooy, "Armenzorg in Nederland," in Kruithof, Noordman, and De Rooy, 96–104.

[67] Mr. J. H. Carpentier, "Indische Europeanen," *Indologenblad* 5 (1913–14): 66–71, 67.

but the predictable result of their "character," their absence of "a sense of duty," a "sense of responsibility," and "self-respect."[68]

Histories bury themselves deep in words. So do causal narratives. In 1947 when the death rate of Indos in Japanese internment camps was found to be much greater than that of full-blooded Europeans, it was again attributed to the Indos' "weaker moral fibre."[69] But if everyone could claim to know something about the interior, mental lives of the Indo poor, they still knew next to nothing about how they lived. In 1922 a contributor to *Onze Stem*, a newspaper of one of the earliest Indo-European organizations, could write about the "very particular mentality" of the "*kampong*-Indos" and then acknowledge that a major obstacle to improved conditions was lack of knowledge about them.[70]

In 1847 Governor-General Rochussen wrote to Minister of Colonies Baud that although he was no "lover of mixed bloods" (*philoliplap*), it was his job to ensure they did not become a danger. He also promised that he would never—in present or future—appoint a "colored" to command natives who despised "the colored" and Europeans who disdained them even more.[71] Pauperism commissions were key tools of that social imaginary that productively fed off racial common sense while reproducing its resilient and refreshed modern forms. It was neither somatics nor essentialism that gave racialized knowledge its epistemic force. Racial essences, like those honed in the Indies, rested not "on immovable parts but on the strategic inclusion of different attributes, a changing constellation of features, and a changing weighing of them."[72]

The "Indo problem" did not go away, nor did fears of a communist and socialist movement that might captivate the disenfranchised and fuel their resentments. But the force field of the colonial archive that defined "the problem," who was a "problem," and who would write about it, realigned and dramatically changed. "Indos," many more than just Otto Knaap, were writing about themselves.[73] Newspapers, such as the *Blijvers-Bond*,

---

[68] S. Kalff, "Europeesch Pauperisme in Indië," *Koloniaal Tijdschrift* (1922): 573–85, 582.

[69] Charles Fischer, "The Eurasian Question in Indonesia," *International Affairs* 23 (1947): 522–30.

[70] H. Neuman, "Over kampongtoestanden en paupers," *Onze Stem* (1922): 489–91, 489.

[71] AR, Mr. 4566, 31 March 1847.

[72] Ann Laura Stoler, "Racial Histories and their Regimes of Truth," *Political Power and Social Theory* 11 (1997): 183–255. (This essay on racial epistemologies was largely motivated by the archival materials from this chapter.)

[73] *Blijvers-Bond* (Orgaan voor de Belangen der Indiërs) was published in Buitenzorg in 1901 under the editorship of G. A. Andriesse. For "voices" of Indos in the mainstream elite press, see, for example, J. De Gruyter, "Een Indo over Indo's," (part 1) *De Indische Gids* 35 (1913): 585–96.

whose declared purpose was to defend Indo interests, opened its first issue with these fighting words:[74] "If we want to show our pride in having the name Indo, so let us, from now on, lay aside our fatal meekness, submissiveness and docility. . . . Let us be considered not only as a minority for "tame rebellion" and such. Let us show who we are, show that we have *karakter* and are conscious of our spirit and our strength."[75] Novelists, too, captured the quotidian power of racial disparagement in details that played off the caricatures that appeared in the pauperism commission's often stylized vignettes. Most notable was the novelist Hans van de Wall, whose mother had been among the Indo poor. Writing under the pseudonym Victor Ido, his descriptions of racialized habits of heart and mind sliced through the myth of conviviality between "white and brown."[76]

Characterizations of people and things not only lodge in the tenacious hold of words: they burrow into bodies and then re-emerge as resurrected knowledge, upholding oppositional positions as they take on new political forms. Such was the tactic of the *Indischen Bond* in 1904 that took as its task representation of the Indo-European population with a platform based on acquiring land for them. The *Bond* prided itself on publishing a "meritorious study by a real Indo, by a real son of the Indies," who used the pseudonym Sinjo Frans.[77] It was an extraordinary piece of writing, if it did indeed come from "a son of the soil," for it was more contemptuous of impoverished Indos than anything that the more tempered commissioners could express themselves.

In Sinjo Fran's account the "quality" of Indos left "much to be desired," but they were not to be blamed for it. It was the abysmal lack of good child rearing that was at the root of all, fathers as well as mothers who knew neither the value of labor nor the importance of "*kontrole.*" In a narrative that drew on virtually every racialized cliché about Indos that now saturated the air of the colony, he did something else. He addressed the rich and well-off, their fear of revolt and demand for security from a state that had to take charge of the aimless and sullen Indo youth, if necessary "by force." The solution: to place the Indo youth in agricultural

---

[74] "*Blijvers*" referred literally to those Europeans who remained or "stayed on"—to those for whom the Indies was home, in contrast to the *Totok*, Dutch who came for work and returned to the Netherlands.

[75] *Blijvers-Bond*, 16 July 1901, l; italics in original.

[76] See, especially, *De Paria van Glodok*, which appeared in the *Java-Bode* in 1900, and *De Paupers*, which appeared in book form in 1915. See also Rob Nieuwenhuys's discussion of them in *Oost-Indische Spiegel* (*Mirror of the Indies*). The section on van de Wall does not appear in the English-language version of Nieuwenhuys's history of Dutch colonial literature.

[77] *Sinjo* was one of the terms used for Eurasian boys and young men. The use of psuedonyms for such writing was common. See Sinjo Frans, *Lotsverbetering van Indo-Europeanen* (Batavia: Albrecht and Company, 1905 [1904]).

training schools supported by the state and under its disciplined care. There is no parody in the account. The bid for Indo land rights, and the warning that the rich and the state would do well to grant them if they truly feared "anarchism," differed only slightly from the same argument made by the commission three years before and by those who proposed the rural penal colonies like Mettray sixty years earlier.

Others took different tacks. Even in the mainstream press it was quickly becoming a new journalistic fashion to feature an article by someone who called himself an "Indo." Between 1915 and 1935 dozens of novels, plays, and children's stories portrayed poor Indos in distress and the colonial full-blooded elite in visual and verbal caricature as hairy, bulging, sweaty, middle-aged men.[78] The emergence of Indo-European organizations and an active press animated a more vocal and contentious public debate. A sharply satiric edge, with starker political statements, was in evidence as Indonesian nationalism congealed in more organized forms.[79]

Accusations of racism and debates about discriminatory state practices increasingly exceeded official pronouncements and became less easily contained. Some of the new organizations remained loyal to Dutch rule as they spoke "on behalf" of the Indo poor (the *Indischen Bond* and the later *Indo-Europeesch Verbond*). Other associations took aim at other exclusions occluded in the public sphere but blatant in colonial law. Thus *Soeria Soemirat* boldly condemned the injustice of the new mixed-marriage regulations that sharply codified disenfranchisement of the next mixed generation from European status, no matter what the nationality of the father.[80] From those first decades in the 1900s through to the 1930s, new terms appeared—"racial hate" (*rassenhaat*); "racial difference" (*rasverschil*); racial feeling (rasgevoel). The singular term "*rassenwaan*" that so ambiguously references a "racial suspicion" or "racial phobia" was to appear in the early twentieth century and disappear less than two decades later. Such

---

[78] See Gerard Termorshuizen, "Les Eurasiens dans la littérature des Indes neerlandaises: Portrait d'une préjugé racial," in Denys Lombard, ed., *Rever l'Asie: Exotisme et littérature coloniale aux Indes, en Indochine et en Insulinde* (Paris: L'Ecole des hautes études en sciences sociales, 1993), 321–33. See also the list of forty novels provided in *Indische Nederlanders: Een onderzoek naar beeldvorming* (Den Haag: Moesson, 1984) and the more complete list of 1,503 entries for all kinds of sources, in *The Eurasians of Indonesia: A Political-Historical Bibliography*, comp. Paul W. van der Veur (Ithaca: Modern Indonesia Project, 1971).

[79] See, for example, the biting critique of Indos by "one of them" in "Het Indo-Vraagstuk," *Het Koloniaal Weekblad*, no. 3 (20 January 1910), published in The Hague. It admonished other Indos not to think of themselves as Europeans but as part of a "new race."

[80] *Soeria Soemirat* was an early and vocal opponent of this law. On this mixed-marriage law, see my "Sexual Affronts and Racial Frontiers," in Stoler (2002), 101–6.

terms occupied a different internationally charged force field with new referents, demands, and recriminations.[81] Perhaps it was "racial deception" after all, precisely the term with no residual dictionary trace that most captures the anxieties that "passing" left in its wake.

The debate was fierce and if the word "race" was not always invoked, its predicates were. As one author in a popular Batavian weekly wrote in 1916: "the descendants of Europeans who lived in purely native, and largely immoral surroundings" might not exhibit "savage anarchism or debauched bestiality as in Europe," but it was still the case that they formed *"in secret, hardly visibly . . .* a corrosive cancer gnawing at the sexual strength of our society."[82] Fabricated Europeans, too, remained a prevailing threat. No one could miss the dismissive irony of the same author or the targets of his scorn when he opined that some Dutch in the Indies had become so "enamored with the Javanese" that they would gladly make even them European.[83] For the Hans van de Walls of the colonial world in 1916, the empire could and should never allow native colonial subjects to be confused—legally or otherwise—with their masters.

The field changed once again on the cusp of the 1930s depression when drastic economizing measures were proposed for the civil service.[84] The same problem elicited the same question raised by the pauperism commissions of thirty and sixty years earlier: would the emergency wage reductions still allow the lower Indo rungs of the colonial bureaucracy to live at a level "that could still be called 'European' "? The doctor W. M. F. Mansvelt, who posed the question in his essay in the esteemed scholarly journal *Koloniale Studiën*, was sure they would not. He recited the failed efforts of the 1872 commission to have its proposals implemented and the "improved economic conditions" that made the recommendations of the 1901 commission superfluous. But his fear was the same: that a reduced standard of living would lead to stronger native connections, to a revival of Indo-European political parties of the turn of the century, and to a stronger collusion with the growing nationalist movement.

---

[81] See, for example, J. H. F. van de Wall, "Rassenhaat," *Jong Indië* 1 (1908): 120–22; J. H., "Het Indo-Vraagstuk en Rassenhaat," *De Indische Gids*, part 1, 34 (1912): 73–76; D. G. Stibbe, "Rasverschil," *Indië* 17 (25 July 1917): 259–61; T. K., "Rassenwaan en rassenbewustzijn," *De Taak* 18 (1 December 1917): 205–6.; D. M. G. Koch, "Rassenwaan," *Koloniale Studiën* 1 (1921): 399–410.

[82] J. H. F. van de Wall, "Het Indoisme: Een actueel vraagstuk," *De Reflector* 1, 39 (16 September 1916): 951–54, 953.

[83] Ibid.

[84] See, for example, the five-part essay of E. Moresco, "Het rassenvraagstuk," *Koloniaal Tijdschrift* (1928): 388–414, 628–52, and (1929): 24–41; W. M., "Het rassen-probleem in Nederlandsch-Indië, *Onze Stem* 10, 31 (August 1929): 886–88; Dr. W. M. F. Mansvelt, "De Positie der Indo-Europeanen," *Kolonial Studiën* 16 (1) (1932): 290–311.

As the expanse of the archive changed, the commissions of 1872 and 1901 remained authoritative reference points. Newspaper articles, scholarly papers, doctoral theses turned back to their "findings" to identify "the problem" again and again—not to document transformation, but rather to show how little had changed. In yet another essay in *Koloniale Studiën* in 1933, the respected lawyer W. F. Prins reminded his readers that "discontent with their lot" and "jealousy of full-blooded Europeans" (documented in the 1872 commission report and that had motivated the murder of a white, as he noted) was not unlike the "same mentality" that "only several years ago" had made a walk through the Indo-pauper quarters of the Kemajoran neighborhood of Batavia "a perilous undertaking."[85]

Such comparisons passed as scholarship because the force of race rendered these racialized assessments as equivalencies, as truth-claims with commensurability, untouched by time. The "house of glass" was more fragile than ever. If pass laws for natives were rescinded in 1914, and race (*rascriterium*) was abolished as a legal criterium in 1918, many of those who lived in the Indies in the 1930s would not have noticed.[86] Pramoedya had been right. It had become all the more pressing that there were Pangemannans who, both despised by the Dutch-born elite and contemptuous of poor Indos, remained loyal to the administration's project to wipe out the proliferation of Minke's ever more brazen nationalist descendants.

---

[85] Mr. W. F. Prins, "De bevolkingsgroepen in het Nederlandsch-Indische recht," *Koloniale Studiën* 17 (1933): 652–88, 672.

[86] On abolition of the race criterium, see William E. van Mastenboek, 97–101. *De historiche ontwikkeling van de staatsrechtelijke indeeling der bevolking van Nederlandsch-Indië* (Wageningen: H. Veeman and Sons, 1934). On the sentiment that with its abolition "not much would change," see Birnie, Dwidjosewojo, Stibbe, "Het rascriterium," *Volksraad* B3, nos. 1–2 (1918): 3.

PART 2

Watermarks in Colonial History

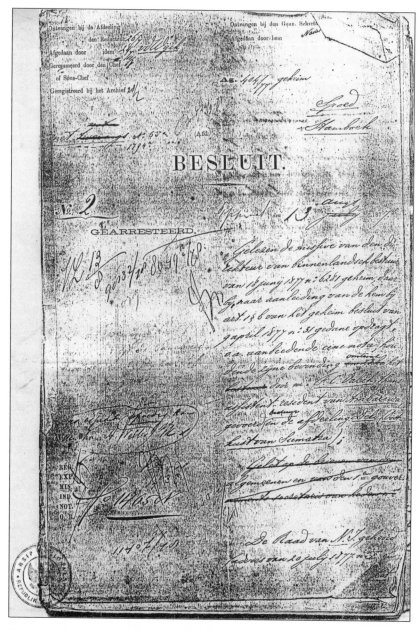

Figure 8. This report to the Minister of Colonies by the Governor-General concerning his decision on the fate of Resident Locker de Bruijne and Assistent Resident Frans Carl Valck was based on two very different assessments of events in Deli: one, the report by the head of the *Binnenlandsbestuur*, Henny, who counseled that Valck ought be dismissed; and two, the more sympathetic interpretation of Valck's behavior by the *Raad van Indië*, on which Valck's old schoolmate and uncle served. At this point, Valck is given a "second chance."

CHAPTER SIX

Hierarchies of Credibility

> Truths are illusions about which one has forgotten that this is
> what they are; metaphors which are worn out and without
> sensuous power.
>
> —Friedrich Nietzsche,
> "On Truth and Lie in an Non-Moral Sense"

SOME TWENTY YEARS AGO, on what I remember as one of Leiden's dark summer afternoons, in a desultory rummage for photographs of European colonial families who had lived in the Deli plantation belt of Sumatra, I experienced a jolt, what Roland Barthes once described in photography as a "floating flash"—the sort of "shock" of unexpected details that alters one's vision, "pricks" one's received understandings of what counts as a history and what makes up people's lives.[1] I had come across a thirty-page, handwritten letter, dated 28 October 1876, by a certain Frans Carl Valck, who was then Assistent Resident on Sumatra's East Coast.[2] It was written in the even, steady hand of one well accustomed to wielding a pen for long hours, remaining clear and legible to the end. Its salutation was vaguely familiar but respectful, to "My esteemed Levyssohn," with whom the writer evidently had an ongoing correspondence (Valck thanks him for his advice in a previous letter). Levyssohn might have been a family friend (greetings go to Valck's "sweetest wife") and influential enough that he might pass

---

[1] Roland Barthes, *Camera Lucida: Reflections on Photography* (New York: Hill and Wang, 1981), 53.

[2] Assistent Resident was a coveted post for a young man making his way up the ranks of the Dutch colonial Civil Service. Depending on the region, he might preside over the governance of a subregion and thus several districts within a single residency. In this case, because the Resident was stationed a long distance from Deli, and because the residency of the East Coast of Sumatra covered nearly ten thousand square kilometers, Valck was largely left on his own to manage Deli.

Valck's letter was originally filed in the Verbeek Collection, which had been given to the Royal Institute of Linguistics and Anthropology (KITLV) in the 1920s. Rogier D. M. Verbeek (1845–1926) was a prominent geologist in the investigation of the eruption of Krakatoa in 1883. In the early 1980s an archivist came across Valck's letter; having found that Verbeek had no experience or contacts in Deli, and that the letter made no reference to Verbeek, it was refiled in a separate dossier (KITLV, H 1122/Valck, as I refer to it here). No other correspondence with, or reference to, Valck had been found (Gerrit Genap, personal communication).

on troubling observations to the powers that be. Henry Norman Levyssohn, I learned much later, was a former law school classmate of Valck's in Leiden, recently promoted at the time of Valck's letter to the Governor-General's advisory council.[3]

It was a misplaced missive and a displaced document, removed from the archival shelter of adornments—annexes, commentary, prior documents, and cross-references—in which official exchanges would usually reside. Catalogued as a single, spare dossier in the personal documentation center of the Royal Institute of Linguistics and Anthropology in Leiden was a letter that stood alone, and was not addressed to the person in whose file it was placed. It struck me as a muffled shriek in the night, raw and exposed. I had spent a year and half in North Sumatra—"Deli" in Valck's time—tracing the colonial lineaments of the contemporary plantation industry and thought myself well versed in the French, Dutch, English, and Indonesian language histories of the region (there were not that many). None had mentioned his name.[4]

DISABLED FICTIONS

But the "prick" of the letter was less in its misplaced location than in its unusual content and desperate tone. It was written eleven days after what subsequent official and newspaper accounts were to refer to as one of the "most horrendous" multiple murders of Europeans in Deli's plantation history. The wife and two young children of the planter Luhmann had been knifed and dismembered by workers formerly employed on his estate.[5] Valck's letter was arresting precisely because it was *not* about the horror of these muti-

---

[3] *Stamboeken Indische Ambtenaren*, Part M-330, 523; *Album Studiosorum Lugdunum Batavorum*, folio 1362/1363. For these references and most of the documents cited here, I owe immeasurable thanks to Mr. M. G. H. A. de Graff, then archivist of the Second Section of the Algemeen Rijksarchief, for his assistance in helping me trace Valck's personal and professional trajectory and for tracking down the correspondence on the Luhmann family murders.

[4] Valck is never referred to by name, but the disruptive situation in Deli in 1876, in which he found himself overburdened and without sufficient police reinforcements, is referenced by Blink, Broersma, and Schadee, among others. As he was the most senior local government official in Deli (the Resident still being seated in Bengkalis, a week's travel to the south), all comments on inept management and backlogged judicial cases were, in fact, direct references to him. That Valck is not named would be less surprising if Deli's Resident had not been so far away and it had not been Valck who was charged with presiding over the European court, handling land concessions, and mediating government relations with the planters. The absence of his name probably has more to do with what he was considered to have bungled, what he knew, and what he did not do.

[5] Anonymous, *Deli-Batavia Maatschappij 1875–1925* (Amsterdam: Deli-Batavia Maatschappij, 1925), 12. See also W. Schadee, *Geschiedenis van Sumatra's Oostkust*, 2 Vols (Amsterdam: Oostkust van Sumatra Instituut, 1918–19), 16–17.

lations. Instead it indicted Luhmann as one in a "gang of Cartouche"—a reference to eighteenth-century Paris's most notoriously prosperous highway robber. It named names, giving detailed testimony to the atrocities perpetrated by those Valck indignantly called the "so-called pioneers of civilization." In tenor it was at once foreboding, tempered, and pleading. What he learned he knew would not be believed.

Valck's letter, as it turned out, was the stray in a dense corpus of correspondence and official missives about the Luhmann family murder that circulated in 1876 and 1877 between Valck, his immediate superior, Locker de Bruijne, military commanders, and high officials in Batavia and The Hague. It also represented one variation in a series of accounts he gave of the murder. Three were composed in late October, one in December 1876. In each he provided an altered sense of what he knew and how he could know about the outrageous conditions into which he was plunged. Read against one another, his accounts open to the mutable terms in which evidence was construed, to the kinds of stories that could be told about violence, the sorts of cultural knowledge on which those stories were based, and the "storeyed" levels[6] through which those accounts were written and could be read.[6] His narratives trace a compressed time of successive reassessment, in which his understanding rapidly shifted as Deli's subject population exploited European confusions about the attacks and what their violences meant.

Valck's letters disable colonial fictions at many registers. In place of an omniscient colonial apparatus, he makes us privy to a nascent, disjointed, and perplexed one. In place of an assured narrative of what violence meant, he recounted events peopled by agents whose imaginings propelled their actions, whose "evidence" derived from their fantasies, and whose anticipatory fears promoted the harsh measures they deemed appropriate to counter the threatening conditions they had produced.

Within a period of several months, Valck and other Dutch civil servants, military personnel, and European planters partook in hundreds of official exchanges, expressing their own versions of what was causing arson, robbery, and murder on Sumatra's East Coast. Their discrepant accounts stand in relief against their common sources. Was the Luhmann murder an isolated incident or, as Valck contended, part of a patterned response to European abuse? The identity of the assailants was far from clear. Were they ethnic Gayo woodcutters or Javanese estate workers, were they estate workers set on revenge against their employer or guerilla supporters of the ongoing Aceh War to the north? Was Luhmann the object of their wrath or the hapless victim of a random assault on planters or on Europeans?

---

[6] On writing a history of evidence, see James Chandler's response to Lorrain Daston, "Proving a History of Evidence," in *Questions of Evidence*, ed. James Chandler, Arnold Davidson, and Harry Harootunian (Chicago: University of Chicago Press, 1991), 275–81.

The confused space of Valck's readings of the situation challenge interpretive strategies, unsettling the comfort that they can be merely pragmatic
or benign. Hard questions are forced to the forefront, "contexts" are desta-
bilized, the outlines of "events" appear less clearly bound, commonsense
assumptions are on the line. How should narrative inconsistencies be read?
Would a dense agreement between versions be "proof" of shared cultural
assumptions and a common standard of reliability? Would that agreement
cancel out those accounts out of sync with them? How and how much can
we know about what Valck and other colonial agents really knew about
what was going on?

With his contrary letters in hand, I sought to find out how much his reconstructions were at odds with other official versions, how deeply his
renderings went along—or bristled against—their grain.[7] Genealogies of
the murder varied, as did the physical settings and psychological motiva-
tions in which different versions were cast. Some related the killings to
the Aceh War, some hundred miles to the north, that had begun three
years earlier. Other observers personalized its origins in a planter's abusive character. Narratives slipped between visual and verbal evidence, appealing to rumor to buttress one version or dismiss a counterclaim.

Paradoxically, what they held in common—a loosely standardized logic
of blame—only underscored what set them apart, as individual planters
and officials appropriated that logic differently to interpret what some
had never seen but thought or claimed they knew. A stylized convention
of dichotomies ordered their plots. Personal acts of revenge were set in
contrast to collective political acts, criminality was set off from subversion, the order of the plantations was contrasted to the disorder of the
hinterland, "war" proper in Aceh stood apart from Deli's so-called labor
disturbances. Not least, loyal subjects stood distinct from enemies of the
state. But these stories contested each other in their uneven adherence to
and suspicion of those very dichotomies on which they drew. Honed categories did not always serve them well. Some dichotomies crumbled in the
face of acts that were both personal *and* political. Some cut across the
ethnic distinctions Dutch authorities fostered and to which they so confidently prescribed—the imagining of primordial loyalties that in other
places and other moments had served them well.

Such compelling discrepancies undermine some obvious interpretive
options. To seek out the most appropriate social context in which to cast
"the event" would overwrite a critical feature of this moment: contextu-

---

[7] The "selectivity bias" here was of course in one, albeit changing, direction: cases that
came to the attention of the Governor-General and Ministry of Colonies were those deemed of
some special "political" attention. Attached to them are lower-level reports by district officers,
advices and evaluations by local colonial agents on which these higher decisions were based.
At issue are varied interpretations—and reassessments—of what constituted "the political."

alization itself was precisely in question and politically charged at the time. To smooth out incompatible versions would be to ignore the different frames in which events were understood, reported, and played out. To imagine a specific set of stories intentionally crafted to obscure "what really happened" would be to miss the frenzied scramble to know what happened and the conditions that sabotaged those efforts again and again. Finally, the assumption that if we as historians were only privy to the "crucial facts," the story would unfold, is to miss a key feature of colonial governance. Partial understandings, epistemic confusion, and undigested bits of cultural "information" made up the modus vivendi of high and low civil servants across the Indies—of those traipsing through Deli plantations, isolated in Bali outposts, cloistered in the bowels of the state's archives in Batavia, or even sheltered in its most iconic "house of glass," the Governor-General's palatial dwelling in Buitenzorg.[8] Here I start from another premise: that these discrepant stories provide ethnographic entry into the confused space in which people lived, to the fragmented knowledge on which they relied, and to the ill-informed and inept responses that knowledge engendered. Coherence is seductive for narrative form but disparities are, from an ethnographic perspective, more compelling. It is the latter that opens onto competing conventions of credibility about what and whose evidence could be trusted and those moments in which it could not.

Disparate reconstructions of the murder often drew on a shared vocabulary but not shared sources of knowledge. Each was filtered through distinct local channels for learning what was transpiring on Deli's estates. Valck's knowledge was limited in multiple ways: by the fact that he had only just arrived, by the planters' hostility to what he proudly referred to as his "clean-up" task, and not least by different groups within Sumatra's subject population who themselves played European fears and rumors of revenge back on their authors. In the fractious social and political environment that characterized Deli's mythic "pioneering" years, rumor carried uneven weight—sometimes dismissed as everything the "facts" were not, at other moments the best sources of them. Workers, in turn, further amplified European stories of native violence, interrupting official efforts to identify its sources and perpetrators.[9]

---

[8] On "coherence" as the ultimate criteria for a convincing historical narrative see, Lloyd Kramer's, "Literature, Criticism, and Historical Imagination," in *The New Cultural History*, ed. Lynn Hunt (Berkeley: University of California Press, 1989), 97–128.

[9] For two compelling treatments of rumor as "truth," see Edgar Morin, *La rumeur d'Orléans* (Paris: Seuil, 1969), and Luise White, *Speaking with Vampires: Rumor and History in Colonial Africa* (Berkeley: University of California Press, 2000). On rumor and colonial insurgence, see Ranajit Guha, *Elementary Aspects of Peasant Insurgency in Colonial India* (Delhi: Oxford University Press, 1983), 220–77, and Shadid Amin, "Gandhi as Mahatma,"

As importantly, European knowledge was shaped by Gayo, Javanese, Malay, and Chinese assailants, who, in writing their own acts in such ambiguous ways, *assured that those acts rarely could be easily and neatly read.* Subalterns "speak" throughout the European accounts only in muted voices clipped words, distorted speech. But such ventriloquisms have a power of their own. The uncertain meanings of their seemingly straightforward deeds of theft and arson repeatedly cut through official reason with forms of subversion that reflectively called upon rumor to stoke fears of impending violence. James Scott persuasively argues that subalterns use the "official transcript" of elites while maintaining hidden ones for themselves. But in Deli subalterns tapped into the uncertainties, fears, and fantasies of European hidden scripts by playing them back to planters and officials for their own political purposes.[10]

The confused and incomplete knowledge of Valck and his comrades in the civil service did not deter them from telling their stories. Rather, it enhanced the formulaic quality of their accounts, their dependence on shared refrains and on what they presumed to know. Gaps in their knowledge were filled with culturally reasonable conjectures that made their reports persuasive, relevant, and racially plausible to immediate superiors and high officials, whom they knew or imagined would be their readers in Batavia and The Hague. Plantation "unrest" had a hydraulic lexicon of its own: "coolie outbursts" were "instinctual responses" of revenge or orchestrated actions by "outside agitators" imposed on a duped and otherwise passive population. As such, not all accounts made their way to the top. Some dropped out as reports were consolidated, summarized, and pared down. Others were embellished with detail as they were cribbed and sifted as they made their way up the administrative ladder. It was this "cribbing" process that determined which readings of events became part of the evidential package.

Not least important to the credibility of these accounts were shared beliefs about the psychological and physical vulnerabilities of whites in the tropics. These were beliefs that called more on Lamarckian notions of acquired character than on the biological surety of race. Europeans were susceptible to cultural and moral contamination by those degraded whites within their midst and by those they were there to manage and rule. Such explanations were selectively used to different political ends. Thus, when the performance of Valck's superior, the Resident Locker de Bruijne, was criticized by the Director of the Civil Service (in whose good favor De

---

in *Selected Subaltern Studies,* ed. Ranajit Guha and Gayatri Chakravorty Spivak (New York: Oxford University Press, 1988), 288–350.

[10] See James Scott, *Domination and the Arts of Resistance* (New Haven: Yale University Press, 1990).

Bruijne stood), his transgressions were forgiven on the argument that his lapses were due to his lengthy tenure in the Siak region and to "his association solely with native heads [from whom] he has taken over some of their inertia."[11] What worked to protect Valck's superior was not to work for Valck.

This chapter wrestles with both the reading strategies we bring to such texts and the rhetorical strategies of these sources. To stay within the allusive, muddy register of what colonial agents thought they knew is to retain and remain with their incoherencies—not to overwrite them with a neater story that might read more smoothly and work more persuasively in the telling. Sorting through multiple motives and effects is an opening of sorts: to the dim clarity of conditions in which events were investigated, recorded, and constituted as evidence. These were the "historiographic operations" that set the terms for new repressions, subsequent violences, and renewed commitment to retaliating against what were perceived as counterinsurgent acts. Here, rumor is a key form of cultural knowledge. In Deli, it shaped what people thought they knew, blurring the boundaries between events that could be claimed to have been "witnessed" and those envisioned, between performed brutality and the potential for it.

VALCK'S READING AND READING VALCK

> When I was appointed . . . Assistent Resident of Deli, I knew very well that I would not land in a "bed of roses"; but that I would find such an Augean stable as I did here, I could never have imagined.
> —Frans Carl Valck, Letter to Henry Norman Levyssohn

With this dramatic opening to Levyssohn, Valck prepares his reader for the Herculean task with which he is faced and the heroic stance he must assume for that effort.[12] His tone is urgent with indignation and moral disgust. He directly charges Deli's planters with maltreatment, murder, and torture of Asian workers. His argument is stylized, at once self-conscious, tentative, and bold, with carefully chosen examples and a cautious effort to avoid the sensational. The narrative is one of inversions: colonizers rather than the colonized are condemned for their violence; "delinquents" are not

---

[11] AR, Mr. 6281, 18 June 1877, urgent, confidential, Director of the *Binnenlandsbestuur* to the Governor-General.

[12] All subsequent quotations from Valck in this section are from his correspondence with Henry Norman Levyssohn (KITLV, H 1122) unless otherwise noted.

recalcitrant workers—as they are for the planters—but Europeans instead. Standards of "barbarism" are turned on their head. In Valck's hands, rumor is a viable source, representing reasonable conjecture, a legitimate, if still dubious, measure of the publicly denied and unspeakable "facts" of life and labor on Sumatra's East Coast. Explaining the severe labor shortage on the estates, in his letter to Levyssohn he offers an abbreviated, relentless description of violences: "It would be a miracle indeed, if respectable Chinese coolies would be attracted to a place where coolies are beaten to death or at least so mistreated that the thrashings leave permanent scars, where manhunts are the order of the day." But it is the gratuitous nature of the torture on which he insists, on the non-exceptional forms of violence perpetrated, on the nonchalance of a planter who never thought to deny the torture, only his own confusion about who had carried it out. The name of Luhmann, whose wife and children were murdered, emerges midstream in his list, one of many who fed the banal terror of the everyday:

> Just recently I heard a rumor about a certain European who prided himself on having hung a Chinese only having cut him down after the coolie had turned entirely blue (people say that it was probably a bluff, but this sort of bluff is the same as committing the act). The brave one who is thought to have done this was Heer Luhmann: I mentioned this sample of humanitarianism to a planter who responded: "no, I heard this about someone else." Who this other one is I don't know, but I do know, that such unheard of things occur or at least have occurred.

He says he will not even bother to recount the most disgracefully inhumane case of all as he proceeds to describe it, leaving his reader with the sense of how many more atrocities he has not conveyed, heightening the grotesque that remains unsaid: "I won't even mention the case of the cutoff ear kept in alcohol as a curiosity by a down and out tanner from Batavia. . . . But I mean inhumaneness that brings the greatest disgrace upon humankind."

Valck charges the planters with more than brutality. He accuses them of participation in a conspiracy of silence, deceit, and terror in which their reports "contain some truth but more often are filled with unashamed lies." His accusations are not only aimed at subordinate European "no goods," as he puts it. They are aimed higher and more dangerously at what he derisively calls the "gentlemen" (with their "blood-stained hands") of the most established plantation companies. On his investigation of the fatal beating of a Chinese coolie by the planter Nederveen Pieterse, he writes:

> [The Pieterse affair] has taught us a noteworthy lesson. The gentlemen of the Deli Company and the most important planters have gone so low as to hold back witnesses and to assure they disappear. One of them

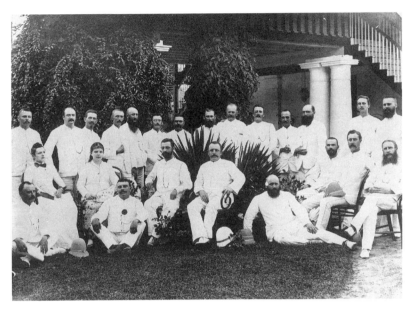

Figure 9. A group of Dutch Planters in Deli, c. 1870.

admitted this to me personally, and another said, "All of us have been guilty of things such as those that occurred at Rudolphsburg [Pieterse's estate]." All of these men have been accomplices in the offenses committed by Pieterse; by assisting him they have shown themselves to be a tightly grouped gang of Cartouche. It is anything but an enviable task to have to fight against them. If only you knew all that has happened here; if only you could hear what the planters themselves have to tell, *even though that of course can never be proved*; you would be deeply saddened. Heaven knows how many Chinese have been killed and tortured by the so-called pioneers of civilization!

Valck is shocked by what the planters willingly admit, but more so by the lengths they will go to conceal their actions:

Be assured my friend, that there are several among them who would not consider it a heinous wrong to do away with a government official who would dare to reveal their crimes! But I better leave it at this, for you might start to accuse me of exaggeration, and that I don't want. "To go beyond the point is to miss it," as the song so rightfully says.

Valck's personal letter and official reports confirm what some historians have surmised from other sources; that sustained violence and a complicity

Figure 10. Some of the same planters, perhaps the worse for wear, c. 1870–1872.

of silence marked colonial capitalism in one of the most lucrative and rapidly expanding plantation regions of the Netherlands Indies, and did so from its formative period through its later expansion.[13] Jan Breman has estimated that at least one-fourth of the coolie population (then still primarily Chinese) must have been killed or died on Deli's estates at the turn of the century.[14] By Valck's account of twenty-five years earlier, workers died in derelict and overcrowded prisons, barracks, and hospitals, where the sickly were often discharged and left on roadsides to die of disease and hunger, or to scavenge in the forests on their own. Valck gives no figures, but after five months in Deli, he writes of his outrage at "heaven knows how many

[13] See Ann Laura Stoler, "Perceptions of Protest: Defining the Dangerous in Colonial Sumatra," *American Ethnologist* 12 (4) (1985): 642–58, and *Capitalism and Confrontation in Sumatra's Plantation Belt, 1870–1979* (Ann Arbor: University of Michigan Press, 1995); Jan Breman, *Taming the Coolie Beast: Plantation Society and the Colonial Order in Southeast Asia* (Delhi: Oxford University Press, 1989). Breman's critics have charged him with overplaying the role of white planters (as opposed to Asian overseers) in Deli's violence; see in this regard Vincent Houben, "History and Morality: East Sumatran Incidents as Described by Jan Breman," *Itinerario* 12 (2) (1998): 97–100. Valck's letter, however, supports Breman's interpretation. Virtually all the cases of maltreatment reported between 1876 and 1877 directly implicate European planters and their European subordinates.

[14] Breman, 59.

Chinese . . . murdered." As he aptly put it: "People make such a great to do over the enormous development of this region, but [it] is as thin as cat-ice."

What explains that silence around those labor conditions is less clear. Breman contends that government officials systematically covered up what they knew about the Deli situation, and there is more than ample correspondence between high officials in Batavia and those in Sumatra to suggest that he is right.[15] But the planters also saw themselves pitted against state authorities, secreting what they construed as their "private" affairs from public scrutiny to keep disciplinary measures in their own hands.[16] Valck's letter alludes to a rarely noted twist in the story, more ominous still: that planter violence and acts of murder could turn the planters against government agents themselves. Neither Breman's account nor my initial work on Deli captures what colonial agents knew and how they knew it, what they talked about and with whom, which stories were discredited as rumor and suppressed, or which rumors were inscribed as evidence and "fact." Neither addresses an everyday reality in which violence was experienced as both ordinary and outrageous, silent and ever present in the stories people listened to—what they chose to repeat, and what they refused to say about what they knew. Nor did the planters not speak the unspeakable. Valck's letter to Norman Levyssohn, and even his official reports, refer to the rumors passed on by "reliable" sources, to "what planters themselves have to tell," to the stories planters told to one another, and to those stories selectively tailored for Valck.

What was happening on Sumatra's East Coast in 1876? Framings makes sense of events, but what constituted "context" varied by observer. What Valck was cognizant of during his brief assignment in Deli was not the "context" that military officials offered in subsequent reports based on later reconnoiters in the villages and forests abutting the estates. Nor was it the same context offered by Major Demmemi, the region's military commander, whose focus and fears were riveted on the spread of insurgence from the Aceh War. Different perspectives yield different stories and causal arguments. In so doing they redefine the very breadth of "context" and the parameters of the "event."

Deli's plantation belt had been "opened" for just over ten years on Sumatra's northeastern coastal plain when Valck arrived in mid-July 1876. It was not his first post. He was not new to the Indies, or to life in the Indies outside of the Javanese heartland. He had spent the four preceding years in relative isolation, first as a Controleur (the administrative position just below that of Assistent Resident) in Bali and then, for two years, as an Assistent Resident in the opium entrepot of a Dutch outpost on Bali's still loosely

[15] Ibid.
[16] Stoler (1985), 647–48.

Figure 11. Postcard drawing of a street in Laboehan Deli, where Valck resided, c. 1876. *Source*: Royal Tropical Institute, no. 60013544.

subjugated northwest coast. Nor was he new to the fact of corruption between local rulers and Dutch officials. Early in his career he had helped expose just such collusion and was rewarded with a promotion for his initiative.[17] What was new to him in Deli were the vociferous tactics of the planters and the extremes they would go to protect their profits.

The civil service apparatus in Java was firmly in place in the 1870s. That was not the case in Sumatra, where it was minimally manned and badly

---

[17] Then but a lowly Controleur, he had sided against the current Resident and Assistent Resident, who had allegedly discovered a range of abuses perpetrated by the local Balinese Regent. An 1873 investigation concluded that the Regent had been set up by the Dutch Resident and Assistent Resident, who were more to blame for corruption. Both were dismissed and Valck was promoted to Assistent Resident, despite the report's being denounced by many Europeans in Batavia. According to Henk Schulte Nordholt, Valck's correspondence from 1873 already suggests that he feared the gossip among certain factions in "white Batavia" about his promotion. Whether he was sent to Deli in a routine transfer is unclear. The author of the Bali report who Valck supported was the father-in-law of the same Norman Levyssohn who was to defend him five years later. See Henk Schulte Nordholt, "Dekker, Havelaar en Bali," *Indische Letteren* 2 (4): 149–60.

I thank Henk Schulte Nordholt for bringing this Bali incident to my attention when I first presented a portion of this account in Amsterdam in October 1990. Valck's double-edged persona, as honorable and dishonorable whistle-blower, might have made the Bali affair too confused to be usefully invoked for Valck's prosecution or defense. In any case, no mention of his Bali years was made in evaluation of his poor performance in Sumatra.

short of officers. Deli's first Assistent Resident, Hallewijn, had just been installed three years earlier. By the time Valck arrived "to clean things up," as he thought, forty plantations were already in operation with just over 7,500 coolies employed (excluding those imprisoned and deserters).[18] The expansion was swift and the colonial bureaucracy could barely keep up. It was no surprise that the state apparatus was barely functional: Valck's young predecessor had deferred to the planters, turning a blind eye turned toward their methods of control, excesses of punishment, and corrupt financial arrangements with local rulers.

Valck's position as Assistent Resident, usually an easy stepping stone to higher office, hid an administrative nightmare in disguise—and a virtually impossible range of tasks. With the Resident stationed a week's trip to the south at Bengkalis, Valck was charged with overseeing the prison and a barebones local police force. He also presided over a rudimentary court. It was he who was responsible for negotiating land lease contracts with local Malay rulers and for providing reliable reports—firsthand accounts if necessary—concerning breaches of justice against "non-natives" (overseas Chinese employed as coolies), providing protection for planters, and dealing with security problems on the estates. To make matters worse, the Governor-General's mandate to bring "order" to Deli and its planters was to be carried out while he was largely dependent for lodging, estate surveillance, discipline of the tobacco workers, comradeship, and information on the very planters whose excesses he was charged to check.

His reception must have been lukewarm at best. With close connections to authorities in Batavia among the largest plantation holders, there is little doubt they knew why his predecessor had been replaced and why Valck was now there. His unfamiliarity with the region, the land lease arrangements, the system of labor recruitment, and those over whom he was supposed to exercise authority was not uncommon in the colonial civil service. What he did not know was how much those in Batavia who had sent him already knew about the situation. Matters were made worse by the planters' suspicion. Expressly excluded from their confidences, he turned to the reliability of rumor about what they were claimed to have done and said.

The European planters, for their part, saw an extraordinary opportunity for profit in the 1870s, stymied by a lack of labor to do the work. The local population made up of Malay fishermen and farmers under local sultanates, shifting swidden cultivators of ethnic Batak origin, could neither be coerced nor cajoled to work as coolies for the estates. Some did

---

[18] Breman, 24–29. The 1877 Government Almanac lists 176 Europeans in the Residency of the East Coast of Sumatra, 60,545 Chinese, and 250 "others." Among government agents were counted 13 Europeans. *Regeringsalmanak 1877*, 214. From just under 2,000 workers in 1873, by 1881 the numbers reached nearly 26,000. Ibid, 138.

Figure 12. Chinese "contract coolies" in the tobacco-sorting shed, c. 1888. *Source*: Royal Tropical Institute no. 60010553.

work but under job-specific agreements and in other capacities. Batak and Malay farmers, for their part, were confronted with a sudden invasion of money-hungry foreigners promising high wages for short-term contract work (for road building, forest clearing, and construction of tobacco sheds). Sometimes those promises were honored: more often planters did not make good on what they originally agreed to pay. On the plantations themselves, recruitment, discipline, and retention of labor was ad hoc and still unregulated by the state. The first tobacco workers, Chinese lured through "coolie brokers" in Penang, Singapore, and southern China, were slowly supplemented with recruitment from Java. With the opening of rubber estates after the turn of the century and later expansion into palm oil, Javanese eventually replaced Chinese labor.

The year Valck arrived, Deli's unregulated recruitment practices were already infamous across the Straits; so much so that so that British and Chinese authorities from China and Penang had threatened to prohibit shipments of workers from their ports.[19] A specifically heated issue upon

[19] See Schadee, 32, and R. Broersma, *Oostkust van Sumatra: De ontluiking van Deli* (Batavia, 1919) and *Oostkust van Sumatra: De ontwikkeling van het gewest* (Deventer, 1921), 85.

Figure 13. Transport was by cart and horse, c. 1876. *Source*: Royal Tropical Institute, no. 60019110.

his arrival was the measures that so barely distinguished the terms of indenture under "contract" work from slavery: that is, the conditions under which a coolie could be compelled to remain at his place of work and the punishment that could be meted out for breach of contract.[20] Valck's predecessor, Hallewijn, had sided with the planters in arguing that Deli was an exceptional situation in the Indies and that the industry's viability demanded that strict punitive measures for recalcitrant, runaway coolies be enforced.

Some higher officials in Batavia were unconvinced. Contrary to planter opposition, an 1876 ruling forbade the *forced* return of workers to those estates upon breach of their contracts. Siding with the *Raad van Indië*'s

[20] This debate went on for years, produced several government investigations, and culminated in the landmark 1880 Coolie Ordinance, the first of many government regulations to harness workers for the development of the expanding mining and the estate industries. Ostensibly for the protection of indentured workers, the ordinance lengthened the contract period to three years, instituted an "antikidnapping" clause to protect planters from the "theft" of their workers by other estates, and in the end did little more than "legalize the coercive measures already in use." See Breman, 38–44.

Figure 14. Twenty-five years later, "The Dollar Land of Deli" emerged as the moniker of a region known for high-quality cigar tobacco (and later for rubber and palm oil) and one of the most lucrative capitalist ventures among the Euro-American colonial empires. Here, tobacco samples are being inspected in the Frascati auction-room, Amsterdam (1905). *Source*: Royal Tropical Institute, album 322/27a/neg: 911.20a.

ruling (and his Uncle Otto van Rees, Vice-Chairman of the *Raad* and his uncle by marriage to his first wife's aunt), Valck pitted himself openly against the major company heads from the outset. More to his detriment, he interpreted the ruling very differently than either the planters or state authorities had ever intended. By his reading, runaways were no longer legally bound to return to their estates and were thereby released from re-paying the three-month advances by which they were recruited.

As subsequent government reports made clear, Valck's interpretation was deemed impolitic, foolhardy, and too "generous." That workers could not be *forced* back to their estates was never to suggest that they should not be *brought* back by other means.[21] According to Valck's most severe critic, Director G. S. H. Henny of the Civil Service, Valck was incompetent and dangerous. It was his overly lenient reading of the law (and not the planters' abuses), Henny later argued, that had encouraged increased

[21] AR, Mr 518, 18 June 1877, Director of the Civil Service to the Governor-General.

vagabondage among the region's ex-coolies.[22] By allowing workers to choose twelve days in prison in lieu of repaying their advances or working the full duration of their contracts, Valck had (inadvertently?) undercut an unspoken principle of the indenture system that provided no easy way out or quick exit from the onerous contracts and debt peonage that kept workers on the estates.

But Valck's misinterpretation of the ruling does not explain why Deli was overrun with clandestine forest encampments or who was in them, or, for that matter, the fact that many of them had been there for years prior to his arrival. What was the relationship between the estate enclaves and the rural hinterland? Or is it anachronistic to speak of such a clear distinction at all? Why was there such a large roaming population of unemployed men?

Valck was caught in several lines of fire: the planters were intent on recruiting workers in increasing numbers while curtailing their mobility through their own coercive or state-endorsed measures. A growing population of migrant workers with weak ties to the estates and minimal possibilities for redress still refused to submit to the terms of the contract system. Moreover, the public secret was out: Indies authorities were forced to reckon with and reform a labor system that the Indies, Singapore, and European press insisted was blatantly abusive.

But that was not all. Those sharp divisions between ethnic groups so familiar in descriptions of late-colonial Indonesia—where Batak was pitted against Javanese, Gayo against Malay, Chinese against Javanese—were proving to be less clear-cut on the ground. When military agents "discovered" jungle encampments on the plantation peripheries, they found refuges that were not limited to ex-Chinese coolies in one place and Gayo resistance fighters in another. Instead they came upon encampments with material traces (utensils, clothing, letters) of hundreds of Gayos, Malays, Chinese, and Javanese hiding out together in makeshift shelters. To account for these, Valck had no ready categories on which he could draw. This "vagabond" population refused to work *for* the estates, but instead lived *off* them, carrying out night raids in search of food, weapons, clothing, and cash. "Vagabondage" was an administrative misnomer for an unrecognizable social space—one occupied by a diverse underclass made up of those rejected from the estates, who fled the estates, or who chose to maintain equivocal, temporary, or predatory ties to them.

The fact that there is no trace of these encampments in the colonial historiography of Sumatra's East Coast—or in more recent histories—merits reflection. Colonial historiography arguably followed the administrative maps that demarcated Aceh from Deli and that distinguished what was feared to be a belligerent "Islamic stronghold" from a region of intensive

---

[22] Ibid.

capitalist venture. But these distinctions made for purpose of governance were not maintained in practice. In working from this sharply differentiated administrative and cognitive map, Valck found certain kinds of relations among these groups at once logically inconsistent and inadmissible as he sought to piece together the events leading up to and subsequent to the Luhmann family murders.

Deli's "labor problem" was then but one context for these stories. The Aceh War was another. In 1873, after years of treaty negotiations between the British, Dutch, and Acehnese over the terms under which Aceh and the principalities to the south—the future plantation belt—would be made accessible to British trade while subject to Dutch sovereignty, Dutch authorities mounted a military campaign against Aceh that was to last for some thirty years and to be considered among the most destructive of colonial wars.[23] Southern Aceh, abutting the Langkat district in the northern plantation belt where Luhmann's plantation lay, was the corridor through which an increasing number of men moved south to seek estate work as more trading activities were cut off by Dutch blockades.[24] Among these were members of the Gayo, a highland tribal group that despite its long subjection to Acehnese influence, had remained neutral in the war.

By the mid 1870s, as Dutch troops moved closer to their homelands, more Gayo faced the choice of submitting to Acehnese authority, of surrendering to Dutch rule, or of fleeing into the forests from both.[25] Whether the Gayos who worked for the planter Luhmann were partisans of the war or pacifist refugees is unclear. Valck and his contemporaries appear to have had only the vaguest notions of where these Gayos came from and with whom they were allied, yet their felt presence was no weaker for it. In official missives the terms "Gayo" and "Acehnese" were distinguished in some accounts, but used interchangeably in others. How did Valck and his fellow reporters know how to tell a Gayo thief in the night from an Acehnese dissident? As we shall see, these terms often served to mark not ethnic identity but the degree of threat to this new colonial enterprise, those whose actions were to be classified as "common criminal" or "insurgent rebel."

---

[23] For a now-classic account, see Anthony Reid, *The Contest for North Sumatra: Acheh, the Netherlands and Britain, 1858–1898* (Kuala Lumpur: Oxford University Press, 1969). On the visual and verbal representations of the war in the European press, see *Atjeh: De verbeelding van een koloniale oorlog*, ed. Liesbeth Dolk (Amsterdam: Bakker, 2001).

[24] See John Bowen, *Sumatran Politics and Poetics: Gayo History 1900–1989* (New Haven: Yale University Press, 1991), 61. On the blockade's repercussions, see Reid, 71–118.

[25] Reid (1969), 153.

VALCK'S UNEASY READERS

Valck writes to Norman Levyssohn with frustration, despair, and indignation. But each of those sentiments are tempered by his ambivalence about how much he wants the "facts" about European atrocities communicated and to whom. Aware that his observations and actions would leave him open to criticism, he worries that his story would be deemed suspect and not believed. His assessment is not off the mark. He boldly contradicted the most cherished claim of the trading companies, plantation firms, and government authorities: that Deli was flourishing, that plantation profits were secure despite the Aceh War, and that both planters and coolies were "in hand." But it was his oblique if unmistakable reference to "leniency pursued for years towards the planters" that sealed his fate. Valck was accusing government officials—high and low—of looking away and condoning the planters' acts. Indeed, this was the major issue that would arise after what was officially registered as his "honorable" dismissal two years later when a Dutch parliamentarian questioned whether the Governor-General and the Minister of Colonies could really not have known, as they claimed, what European atrocities were taking place on the Deli estates.[26] As Valck wrote his friend: "If you think I paint a darker picture of the situation, that I exaggerate, I repeat that the situation is as bad as it can be and this is *due to a policy of leniency pursued for years toward the planters.* . . . Believe me, Levyssohn! I don't see the situation blacker than it is." And again, with reference to the Augean stables and his own distraught state: "Don't think that I write in a moment of agitation. I am totally calm but utterly indignant. Everyday I see more muck that needs to be cleaned up."

Colonial muckraking was still only a developing genre in the Netherlands, pale next to the antislavery campaigns in Britain and the United States. But Valck was of a generation familiar with one of its most widely acclaimed practitioners, Eduard Douwes Dekker, whose exposé-novel *Max Havelaar* (1860) put the Indies administration in the political limelight of scandal and Douwes Dekker on the international literary map.

As an assault on Dutch colonial policy, there was no equal. According to Van Hoëvell, *Max Havelaar*'s publication had sent "a tremor through the country."[27] In part based on his own quarrel as a newly stationed, mid-ranking civil servant struggling with his superiors over abuses of power by Javanese authorities in the Lebak district, no one mistook the novel for fiction. Like Valck, Douwes Dekker was a new Assistent Resident. Both

---

[26] Geen Planter (No Planter), *Open Brief aan den Heer H.A. Insinger over zijn aanvalen in de Tweede Kamer tegen de Indische "Planters"* (Amsterdam: M. M. Olivier, 1879).

[27] Quoted in Rob Nieuwenhuys, *Mirror of the Indies: A History of Dutch Colonial Literature* (Amherst: University of Massachusetts Press, 1982), 83.

men had condemned European corruption and policy based on their own experience. Both men were destined for very short Indies careers. On learning that he was about to dismissed, Douwes Dekker resigned three months after he was appointed; Valck was transferred out of Deli to the central Javanese district of Ambarawa within the year.

The similarities are striking, but the contrasts are as telling. *Max Havelaar* was, in D. H. Lawrence's words, a successful "tract-novel," considered a "Dutch classic" outside of Holland, with major impact on public opinion and government reform.[28] Douwes Dekker's attack was on the corrupt collusion of Dutch officials with native rulers, who together abused privilege and abetted the impoverishment of peasant Javanese. Valck's accusation targeted the "cold-blooded" barbarism of Europeans themselves. Douwes Dekker resigned and remained indignant; Valck was indignant and was dismissed. His charges against European conduct never received a public airing, nor were they really designed for it. His accusations were so thoroughly expunged from the official record that even his limited readership (his superior officer and *Raad van Indië* advisors to the Governor-General) excised his account of atrocities in their exchanges and never repeated his words. Valck was erased from colonial historiography, while Douwes Dekker became, posthumously, a revered antihero. Valck was intent on telling his (in)credible story but was equally concerned that the "real situation" be made accessible only to selective ears. Unlike Douwes Dekker, whose denunciation of Dutch colonial practice was written for, and received, an immediate popular response, Valck was more circumspect on the issue of public consumption. As he insisted, "It is hoped that such facts as I mention do not become public because our name might then be mentioned in the same breath with that of the Spanish in America."

It was one thing to condemn the practices of low-ranking civil servants. And at some rarefied level his loyalty to Dutch authority did remain intact. As he wrote Norman Levyssohn, he desired only that "his excellence the Governor-General and Van Rees [his uncle] should know the real situation here."[29] He was forthright in criticizing his predecessor Hallewijn for complicity in the planters' silence and "government people in Batavia [who] have painted the situation entirely the color of roses, however incorrectly." Convinced that he would be opposed for his actions by planters and government agents in their service, he placed faith in Governor-General van

---

[28] See D. H. Lawrence's introduction to the 1927 English-language translation of Mulatuli's *Max Havelaar* (Leyden: Sijthoff, 1967), 11–13.

[29] The relationship between Otto van Rees (1823–1892) and Valck was close: Van Rees was married to Johanna Henriette Lucassen, the half-sister of Valck's first wife, Susanna Antoinette Lucassen (1840–1864) (*Nederlands Patriciaat* 21e, 1933–1934, 255), and it was at "Oom van Rees's house" that Valck's daughter stayed on her first trip to Java as a married woman, when Van Rees was by then Governor-General of the Indies (1884–1888).

Lansberge, who he believed would commend him and not share in this condemnation. His declaration is righteous and sincere:

> The situation is untenable. Change must come and has started to come. It will take a great deal of my effort to bring this about. I will be thwarted, duped and slandered from all sides. But I will not move from the honorable post given me by the Governor-General. . . . It may be necessary, I consider it very necessary, that the real situation becomes better known by the highest placed people in the Netherlands Indies.

What happened to Valck and his letter? He was not destined for long in the civil service. Less than a year after his appointment in Deli, he was, as noted above, transferred (in February 1877) to Java, while an official investigation of his "serious misconduct" continued after his departure.[30] The following year he was honorably dismissed from the civil service with a meager pension and placed on the retired list at the relatively young age of forty-three. The Resident Locker de Bruijne, reprimanded for allocating too much responsibility to Valck and for blaming the latter for his own mistakes, emerged from the inquiry with his character, though not his position, intact.[31] What was wrong with Valck? Was he merely a bungling bureaucrat, as some investigators later contended, or the right person in the wrong place at the wrong time? Were the increased disturbances during his tenure of his own making, as Director Henny of the Civil Service charged, or the result of a situation inherited from his predecessor, as his friend Norman Levyssohn and his uncle van Rees were to assert on his behalf? Or was it, as Valck in his own defense continually claimed, "the result of a long-standing government policy of leniency towards the planters"?

What did Norman Levyssohn do with Valck's letter? None of the communications dealing with Valck's reprimand suggest that his concerns were passed on to the Governor-General, or that Levyssohn alerted his fellow advisors on the *Raad van Indië* to Valck's warnings about European excesses and the wide scope of the crimes. Instead, Norman Levyssohn drew selectively on Valck's letter to defend his friend's *person*—but not the validity of Valck's accusations of torture and corruption. When Henny

---

[30] The discussion of Valck's qualifications and the decision concerning his misconduct, transfer, and dismissal appear in the decision of the Governor-General of 13 August 1877, number 2. The Director of the Civil Service's report "On the capability of Resident Locker de Bruijne and other civil servants on the East Coast" (AN mr. 6281, 18 June 1877) mentioned in this decision is located at the Arsip Nasional in Jakarta. Norman Levyssohn's addendum to the advice of the Director of the Colonial Civil Service seems not to have been sent to the Minister of Colonies in The Hague and remained with the Governor-General's decision (Ag.404/77/geheim).

[31] AN, Mr. 628lx, 18 June 1877. Locker de Bruijne is also dismissed for his ineptitude in keeping tabs on Valck, for his actions and not his beliefs.

recommended Valck's immediate dismissal, Norman Levyssohn (along with Van Rees) refused to endorse it. Instead, he appended a separate defense of Valck's conduct, summarizing the "mitigating circumstances" that had to be taken into account.[32] He argued that Valck's loyalties were never in question. Unfairly overburdened, he inherited a neglected administrative situation, and received no guidance from his immediate superior, Locker de Bruijne. "His shortcomings" had to be "seen in light of a course of events which apparently made his mood oversensitive" (an "agitation" that, as has been noted, Valck denied). On 13 August 1877 the Governor-General accorded Valck "a second chance" based on an argument borrowed word for word from Levyssohn's addendum. Neither Norman Levyssohn nor Van Rees nor the Governor-General refer to what Valck deemed sadistic torture and inhumane conduct in the plantation belt, to the government cover-up, or to the conduct of Deli's Europeans.

ANATOMY OF A MURDER: REVENGE AND BLAME

On the night of 17 October 1876 Valck learned that several members of the Luhmann family were murdered. He immediately telegrammed the Consul General in Singapore, asking him to forward his message to the Governor-General in Buitenzorg, presumably the quickest way to get his communication to authorities in Java. He stated only the following: "[O]ffenders four Gayos though mostly *kampong* [Malay village] people. *Appears to be private retaliation* in the affair, Malayan kicked by Luhmann. Also issue about clearing forest. *As for political motive, there seems to be none.*"[33] His brief report of five days later to Resident Locker de Bruijne again stressed Luhmann's actions, promising more detailed information in his next mailing: "It appeared that by his own confession Mr. Luhmann had once kicked a Malay and was told the next day that this could have serious consequences for him."[34] Here too Valck notes that the attackers were mostly "from the neighboring villages and that only four Gayos and a few Bataks were among them." In all, he had thirty suspects arrested, "who were in possession of bloody weapons and clothing. Many of them were recognized by Mr. Luhmann's daughter and a few by [his brother-in-law] Mr. Revening."

With these synoptic statements Valck conveys several messages: (1) Luhmann was responsible for what happened to him; (2) more Malays were

---

[32] AR Ag. 404/77x, 13 August 1877, Letter of Vice-President van Rees and Norman Levyssohn, 20 July 1877.

[33] AR, Mr. 741, [date illegible] October 1876.

[34] AR, Mr. 837, 22 October 1876

involved in the attack, with some Gayos among the assailants; and (3) the assault was an act of "private revenge," not "political," and should be viewed neither as an assault instigated by anti-Dutch partisans of the Aceh War nor as a collective aggression on all Europeans. Valck was versed in the official vernacular of "unrest" but chose not to abide by its common and proper use. To classify an assault as a private matter was a well-honed convention for dismissing an assailant's broader claims. Thus, in the Deli Tobacco Company's 1925 commemorating volume, it could note that in the repeated assaults on Europeans of fifty years earlier, "people were constantly uncertain as to whether an assault should be considered as 'hostile' or indeed *only* as 'rapacious' and 'cut-throat' though in fact people lost goods and lives in both cases."[35] Valck, on the contrary, was unwilling to relegate the violence to "only" personal revenge. He saw a *pattern* to it and his subsequent report told a story of violent retaliation and resentments that extended far beyond the particulars of the Luhmann family murder alone.

But a week later, Valck's account of the murder took on a different cast.[36] Here, he provides a careful description of the attack, with the first blow inflicted by "a Gayo, thick-set, dark and with a mustache who was employed at the estate as a woodcutter." It is here that he provides details of the specific mutilations of each of the Luhmann family members as told to him by Luhmann's brother-in-law:

> Mr. Browne walked around the house and found his sister lying on the ground. She was slashed in her neck, head, chest, stomach and both legs. Having gathered some men he brought her home with them. It was a terrible sight. In the rather wide passage that formed some sort of indoor veranda, lay the body of the eldest child Johny [*sic*] about nine years of age. With one cut, the head had been severed from the body. Next to him lay the corpse of little Marthe, about five years of age. Her right arm had been severed almost completely from the body by a slash that had opened the chest. All kinds of objects and clothes were also spread on the floor, and in both front rooms of the house. In the one Mr. and Mrs. Luhmann use as a bedroom a wooden chest where the money was kept had been cut open and the money, about eight hundred dollars, was gone. The fifteen-month-old youngest child asleep there was left unharmed. The room next to it had also been ransacked, but the other backroom, where Mr. Browne lived, remained untouched, although a watch was on the table. This gentleman, after helping to bring his sister inside, went to get Mr. Revening, who was lying on the front

---

[35] Anonymous, *Deli-Batavia Maatschappij 1875–1925* (Amsterdam: Deli-Batavia Maatschappij, 1925), 11; my emphasis.

[36] AR, Mr. 920, Valck to Locker de Bruijne, 29 October 1876.

indoor veranda and whose wounds he bound up as well as possible. There were no less than fourteen, with one above both brows, one over the chest and one over the stomach seeming the most serious. The right hand was severed at the wrist. This man was in a complete bloodbath. Later, little Clara said that the criminals put her in a crate and hit her several times on her neck with the flat side of a weapon and threatened to kill her if she did not tell them immediately where the money was kept. As soon as she did the criminals forced the strongbox open and she ran away.[37]

His description is gruesome. The grim details provided by Luhmann's brother-in-law stand in contrast with the tone of his own commentary that directly followed: "One peculiarity was that a couple of little Manila dogs, that usually began barking at the slightest sound, had remained completely silent; and another thing, without anyone noticing, all around the Chinese barracks traps had been set to injure the feet of those who went outside when they heard the noise." Valck interrupts the narrative with those "flashes" of detail that carry new implications. Was the assault carefully planned but with the bulk of the coolie population uninvolved? Did these "pecularities" speak to the hidden powers of the assailants? Was this a carefully arranged theft or an ad hominem attack on Luhmann? Valck continues:

> According to Mr. Luhmann and Mr. Browne the attackers only injured the former in order to scare off he and his family so they would leave the house to allow [the assailants] free play in ransacking the house, *which seems to me rather unlikely.* According to them, Mr. Revening had been injured so terribly because he defended himself, while Mrs. Luhmann and Johny [*sic*] were killed because they knew many of the attackers, and they [the assailants] feared that later they would point them out as the offenders. (my emphasis)

Valck rejects this analysis outright and offers a more damning hypothesis, one to which he had alluded in his letter to Levyssohn:

> However, the question then arises, why little Marthe, who was only five years old, was killed and her three-year-old sister, who, as later became evident, knew almost all of the criminals, had been spared? I feel that once blood had flowed, the tiger-[like] temperament [*tijgernatuur*] of the Malay emerged and bloodthirstyness [*bloeddorst*] should be seen as the cause of the crime. By the manner in which it was committed, in a state of excitement, it is easier to excuse than the horrors [*gruwelen*] that are said to be done *in cold blood by so-called civilized Europeans* on their plantations to the helpless Chinese coolies, horrors that cannot

[37] Ibid.

be unknown to the Malay because they were committed over such a long period of time. (my emphasis)

Valck's account here is both ambiguous and contradictory. He frames a scene of premeditated action and sensible revenge but attributes the crime and its viciousness to the atavistic nature of uncivilized Malays. But why were the "bloodthirsty" Malays out for revenge when it was Chinese workers who were being victimized by the planters, here "helpless" and barred from leaving their dwellings with "traps" set by the assailants? Hot-blooded native rage contrasts with cold-blooded and calculated murder by Europeans. Native excesses are explicable and deemed excusable within a frame that *expects* natives to express quick bursts of passion, in contrast to the sustained, long-range reasoning on which he saw more insidious European violence to rest. Valck deploys this racial logic to turn the prevailing explanation of violence on its head and to get to his central point: that the killing "in cold blood" done by Europeans was the "the horror" that preceded all other violence—that allowed it and called it forth.

Valck's grisly report on the murders was not an end in itself. His graphic narrative prepares the reader for his bolder claim: the interpretations offered by Luhmann and his brother-in-law were incorrect. The assault could not be reduced to a bungled theft because "a watch on the table was untouched." It must have been directed at Luhmann because such excessive violence could only be a response to the abuses perpetrated by Luhmann himself. Or as he more tersely put it, "cruelty breeds cruelty."

Authority interrupts and takes over the page. In the margin of Valck's text—in angry and assertive script—bold black lines are slashed from top to bottom. An oversized question mark next to Valck's description of the "atrocities of Europeans" who acted "in cold blood" breaks the narrative and halts the reader. The query, most likely of the Governor-General to whom the report was sent—and who would have had the stature to scribble across the report in impatient rage—demands: "What is meant by this? This must be clarified."

Anticipating the query, Valck sets out to clarify the situation. Abruptly, he leaves off discussion of Luhmann and shifts to a diary-like chronicle of his own activities on the day in question, resituating the pertinent "context" for another story he is intent to tell:

The 17th, the day of the attack on the Soengei Diski estate, I had left for Padang Boelan in order to go to Soengei Sipoet the following morning to investigate the matter of retired artillery captain in the Indies Army, Mr. Nederveen Pieterse, who, among other things, was accused of flogging several Chinese to death, beating others with a ratan whip and using a copy press to elicit the truth when his estate had been burglarized.

Even in Dutch it is a long, breathless, run-on sentence. The copy press, that mainstay of archival production, was a preferred weapon of torture. By cranking the two metal surfaces of the press together, the victim's fingers were initially crushed and eventually broken. This is the same Nederveen Pieterse to whom Valck's letter to Norman Levyssohn had referred, whose maltreatment of workers had been covered up by the powerful clique of Deli Europeans. It is the same person to whom the Indies Army had awarded a distinguished military medal six years earlier.[38] It is also the same Nederveen Pieterse whose presence as a member of Deli's European judiciary had made Valck feel, as he wrote to Norman Levyssohn, that he could not convene a session without it being a "slap in the face of the court's dignity." There is no official correspondence that defends Nederveen Pieterse or ventures to describe his crimes. Only Valck's letter specifies the man's actions: if not seen as a substantiation of his larger story, the reference to this poorly regarded planter would seem inappropriate if not gratuitous. Nederveen Pieterse's behavior was condemned as exceptional by some officials, but it was Valck who was later admonished for having "lost perspective, [for having] judged all planters alike and having [wrongly] considered all equally as cruel as Mr. Nederveen Pieterse."[39]

It is probably Nederveen Pieterse to whom an "Open Letter" sent in 1879 to Insinger, a member of the Dutch Second Chamber in The Hague, referred when it assailed his indiscriminate "attack on the planters." Everyone knew there were one or two bad apples, but these were exceptions. Insinger's accusations were dismissed because he had based them on "unfounded rumor" (*onbestemd gerucht*). He refused to exonerate the planters by providing just one or two "exceptional" names.[40]

Nederveen Pieterse's appearance in Valck's narrative underscored his principal point that "cruelty breeds cruelty." It also relocated the story's context once again. While the military reports emphasized the Gayos' role in the attack, Valck placed the cause squarely on the plantations, as a response to resented work conditions of a longer durée. While investigating the Nederveen Pieterse case the prior month, he reports having received two communications: a telegram from the director of the powerful

---

[38] By 1877 George Samuel Nederveen Pieterse, then 44 years old, was already considered "notorious" in The Hague (AR, Vb 24 May 1877). This description was strangely at odds with his previous military career, for which he was awarded the military honor of Willem Orde in 1870 for distinguished service in the Ceram expedition of 1865–66 (AR, Mr. 920/1876).

[39] AR, Mr. 6281, 18 June 1877, Report of the Director of the Civil Service.

[40] Geen Planter, *Open Brief*, facetiously attacked the parliamentarian H. A. Insinger for his "highly original," though nevertheless totally unfounded, claim that the war in Aceh was intimately connected to the labor grievances in Deli.

Deli Plantation Company about the Luhmann assault, and a letter from Commander Demmemi, citing Gayos as the perpetrators. Valck reports that he immediately left for the Soengei Diski estate but was prevented by flooded roads and ill-repaired bridges from getting any further than the neighboring Kloempang plantation. This he presents as a fortuitous mishap that gave him the opportunity to learn from "Count van Benthem Tecklenburg Rheda several facts that later appeared to be of importance in tracking down the criminals."

Reference to the planter's titled, full family name may have served to give these "facts" additional authority. But it is the reliability of his own judgment Valck seeks to affirm, justifying his prudent decision not to leave directly for the crime scene, but to stay at Van Benthem's for an extra day.[41] Valck keeps his readers in suspense and refrains from divulging what he learned. Instead, he describes his arrival at Soengei Diski the next morning where, armed with these "facts," he confronts Luhmann. Interlacing his own account with the planter's narrative, he enhances his own credibility by exposing Luhmann's implausible explanation:

In connection with what I had already been told at Kloempang, I asked Mr. Luhmann what the reason could have been for the attack on his plantation and for the murders of his family. He answered that there could not have been any reason because he and his subordinates always treated his Chinese, Battaks, Gayo, and Malays with the utmost humanity [*de meeste menschlievendheid*]. The previous day he had even given money to some of them on the occasion of the end of the Mohammedan fast. Then I said to him that so far all the planters whose plantations had been attacked had given me the same assurance, except Mr. Droop who admitted having insulted a Gayo headman. There were rumors [*geruchten*], however, about things that had happened on each of those plantations that in the eyes of uncivilized people would motivate retaliation, that I had to rely on those statements [*verklaringen*] and had to take measures accordingly; that those measures might have been wrong because of false information, and that the misery that struck them might have been prevented if the other planters would have told the truth; that I also heard something about him, Mr. Luhmann, that could have caused the attack at his estate, because people had told me that he had kicked a Malay or hit him with a slipper, a fact that I had heard from a reliable person, who, in turn could point out the people who had told him.

Rumors here are transformed into "statements," actionable evidence by a sleight of hand. Valck underscores his argument by quoting his own words in conversation with Luhmann. He recounts how he reprimands

---

[41] His concerns are well founded; a year later he is criticized precisely for that delay.

Luhmann for withholding information, and with him all the planters. He blames them for forcing him to take these rumors as facts because the "facts" *they* report are clearly lies. And, while directing his accusations at Europeans, he invokes the "uncivilized" instincts motivating native retaliation—affirming the very racialized distinctions on which of Dutch (and his own) authority relied.

In response to Valck and in self-defense Luhmann recounts the following:

> that a certain Djamal from the Kloempang village who was labor crew leader of seven Battaks came to him on September 11th to talk about the job of cutting some wood. Djamal had already received an advance to hire woodcutters. When he came to talk about the matter, more people were with him as well as the Battaks. They too wanted a similar contract. Luhmann was willing to pay thirty dollars per square but Djamal wanted thirty-five although the wood was small and easy to handle. Mr. Luhmann refused to pay the extra sum but finally gave in; *then they refused to work at all*. Having paid the advance Mr. Luhmann got angry and said: "You think you can fool me? If you refuse to work I'll send you to jail." Then one of the Malays laughed at Mr. Luhmann, who then kicked him, but as he states, without hitting him. According to a Malay version . . . the Malay was kicked down the stairs. Angered, the man ran off, and Djamal said to Mr. Luhmann: "*kenapa toean bikin begitoe ini boekan toean poenja orang, kalau dia bikin salah saja jang boleh poekoel*" [Why did you do that, sir, he's not yours to deal with (literally, he doesn't belong to you), if he did something wrong it's I who should hit him]. The next day Djamal returned to say that the man had complained to Mr. van Benthem under whose protection he put himself, and that Mr. Luhmann should expect trouble (*soesah*).

Luhmann's actions have everything of the ordinary and everyday about them. They seem not dissimilar to the pitiful motives of George Orwell's district officer in "Shooting an Elephant." Both feared to look the fool and responded with violence to defend their own tenuous standing and that of their European compatriots.[42] In Orwell's story that fear prompted the pointless shooting of an elephant; in Luhmann's case, his family members were the victims of his own violent deeds.

But in Valck's recounting, it is difficult to know where his story begins and Luhmann's ends. Valck never grants Luhmann a first-person voice. Instead, he tells Luhmann's story for him, referring throughout to "Mr. Luhmann," and "this gentleman." In contrast, Djamal, the Malay foreman, speaks in his own—albeit carefully excerpted—words. It is one of

---

[42] George Orwell, "Shooting an Elephant," in *Collected Essays* (London: Secker and Warburg, 1961), 154–62.

the few Malay-language entries in Valck's narrative (or for that matter in any other of the reports).[43]

Why does Luhmann report Djamal's words in Malay and why does Valck chose to repeat them? Perhaps both gestures supported their respective claims. Djamal's voice authenticates two principles of plantation protocol: (1) for Luhmann, that the beating of coolies was acceptable and carried out by Asian overseers, thereby justifying his own nonexceptional behavior; and (2) for Valck, that Luhmann transgressed a basic prescription for labor control, one codified in handbooks for new estate supervisors decades later: that estate managers should neither reprimand nor *directly* give orders to native workers, for, if they did so, they would surely pay.

Valck's narrative continues with his day of enquiry, taking up first Van Benthem's story and then returning to Luhmann's account:

> Later Mr. van Benthem told me that indeed some Malays did come complaining that Mr. Luhmann had kicked one of them and that he advised them to go to Laboean, to the district officer, and that he could be sure that if that gentleman was wrong he would be punished, *even if he (the Malay) would not be aware of it.* A few days later, he [Van Benthem] met one of the plaintiffs and asked whether the abused person had gone to Laboean, and was told that he first wanted to complain to the village head of Hamperan Perak. Among those who attacked the Luhmann plantation were only four Gayos. Those men were employed with him since August 22 and no fault was found with their behavior except that they worked slowly. Together with twelve Bataks and three Malays they belonged to the crew controlled by the foremen Deli and Saman, both from Kloempang. Finally Mr. Luhmann told me that a certain Datoe Gembang,[44] head of the nearby village of Sala Moeda, might have had a share in the attack on his estate.

The advice of Van Benthem was at best naive, and, given the planters' power and the rudimentary judicial system in Deli, at worst absurd. How could a laborer leave work and travel at least two days round trip to complain to a Dutch officer about a "kick"? Or does this exchange suggest that what was everyday fare for immigrant estate workers with nowhere to vent their grievances was *not* for those Malays from surrounding villages and with more tenuous ties to the estates?

---

[43] One of the only other Malay-language quotes appears in the Director of Civil Service's report on Resident Locker de Bruijne, where he explains the latter's lack of initiative by noting his too frequent association with native heads, who are always saying, "*nanti, saja maoe pikir lebih dhoeloe*" ("Later, I want to think about it for a while first.") Presumably, like Djamal's quote, such an utterance captures what Europeans thought was quintessentially "Malay."

[44] *Datoe* is the term for a Malay village head.

The names of the foremen, Saman and Deli, do not surface again for another month. Luhmann's story refocuses the causes of the murder around the disgruntled Datoe Gembang, to whom Luhmann twice refused to extend a cash loan for harvesting tobacco that Datoe Gembang planted at his own expense. By Luhmann's account, after Datoe Gembang made unsuccessful efforts to sell his tobacco at several other estates, he disappeared to Langkat for sometime. Within a few days of his return, the attack took place. Whether Valck is quoting Luhmann is again difficult to tell, signaled only by a temporal shift as the narrative returns to the day of his enquiry and his own story:

> In the late afternoon [of 18 October 1876] the Radja Moeda of Deli arrived with a few Chinese guards from the Sultan. Datoe Gembang was sent for immediately and came, with seven followers armed with swords. He declared that he knew nothing of the affair (as he told Major Demmemi the previous day) and very much regretted that it happened. He had nothing whatsoever to say in answer to our questions. While we were still questioning him, one of my men noticed a small bloodstain on the sword scabbard of one of Datoe Gembang's followers and took it from him. After close inspection all the weapons or clothes of Datoe Gembang's seven followers appeared to have traces of blood and they were thus arrested. Having a clue it was easier to track down other persons, especially after the arrival of Deli's sheriff Lucas and a few policemen. From Kloempang he brought a certain Djamal whom he strongly suspected of having taken part in the attack. All those who had been employed by Mr. Luhmann and who lived nearby were arrested and on most of them traces of blood were found on their weapons and clothing. *It was curious that nobody seemed to have bothered to cover up the traces of the murder.* (my emphasis)

This "curiosity" could be read as the punch line in Valck's story. No one covered up the murder because they did not *want* to. They intended for some people to know (other workers, other villagers, other planters?) who did it and why. Or perhaps it framed another plot. There was no cover up because there was no *need* for one. The assailants were strong in number and well backed by a broader anti-planter sentiment. They simply had no fear of recrimination. Valck reads their blood-stained weapons one way. Other district officers, military personnel, and some planters were to read it another.

Valck's earlier account seemed to convincingly capture a plausible story: Luhmann deserved what he got, and that revenge, not "political" motivation, was at issue, and Luhmann was hiding the "facts." But as Valck's narrative develops, the introduction of new actors makes the casting of blame more problematic. What connected the Chinese coolies working on the estate (said to have played no part in this assault), Datoe Gembang from the village of Salah [Sialang] Moeda, those assailants allegedly from Kloempang, and the four Gayos? Were there nineteen assailants from Kloempang, as Van Benthem's informant counted, only seven from Sialang Moeda, or more than thirty, the number Valck arrested? How did so many men of such diverse origins, residences, and estate engagement come together and under whom, and then dare *not* to hide their crime? Valck concludes with the "well-founded remark" of the Malay man with whom he spoke,

> it could not have been the assailants' intention to rob, because if so, it would have been much easier for them to attack and overpower one of the convoys transporting money for the estates and traveling under small escort than to first do hard labor for sometime and only then attack the estate. Therefore, I still feel that revenge [*wraak*] was the cause of every one of the committed crimes.

Several categories begin to collide. Unlike the accounts of the planters, Valck's schema stages robbery as retribution for justified grievance. His effort to flesh out the context of retaliation shapes both the chronology and logic of his argument. His adherence to the prevailing understanding of the "political"—actions of direct threat to government authority—remains largely unchanged. Still, his belief in a collective threat to European security, based on *patterned* revenge, falls somewhere between the personal and political, anticipating his failed challenge to the categories themselves.

A Genealogy of the Murder: Patterns of Protest

Valck's interpretation of the Luhmann family murder was in keeping with his more general thesis: the planters were attributing estate assaults to external Aceh influence to deflect attention from internal tensions in their own affairs. He first articulated this position a month earlier, in September, when other government, military, and estate personnel were blaming a series of attacks on the Van Sluijs, Peyer, and Baay estates on Gayo gangs in league with Acehnese fighting the imposition of Dutch rule.

On 6 September 1876 Valck reported that Droop, the administrator of the Van Sluijs estate on the Babalan river, was physically assaulted by Gayos and much of the estate property was destroyed. Droop had recently hired a certain Panglima Laoet who, with his twenty-seven men, had come to seek work.[45] Droop engaged them and paid an advance to build a road.

---

[45] John Bowen has suggested to me that the "Petambiang" cited in this report might have been the Raja Petiam[b]ang, one of the Gayo *kejurun*, which would "fit" with what Valck reports; in this regard, see Bowen, 62.

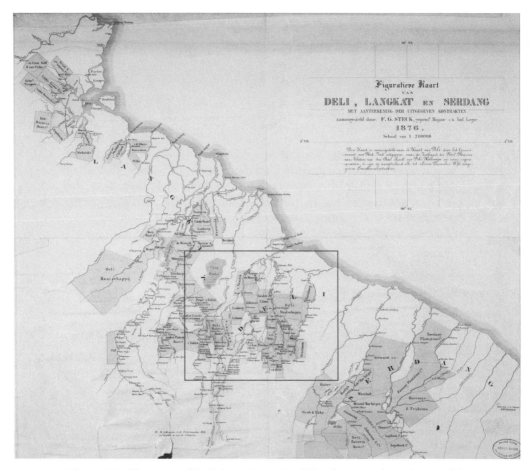

Figure 15a. This map of Deli from December 1876 shows the boundaries of the privately owned plantations. It was drawn up by Major F. G. Steck of the Netherlands Indies army with the help of Assistent Resident Hallewijn, Frans Carl Valck's predecessor. *Source*: KIT.

Several days later another fourteen Gayos led by a certain Radjah Petambiang were also engaged under similar terms. "The trouble began" when Panglima Laoet asked for a personal loan of several dollars. Hearing about this, Radjah Petambiang demanded that Droop give the same to every Gayo. The planter explained that it was a personal loan, refused the request, and turned back to his house. When Radjah Petambiang attempted to follow, Droop turned around, calling him a *"Radja Mawas"* (monkey prince). Valck implies that the insult was not taken lightly.

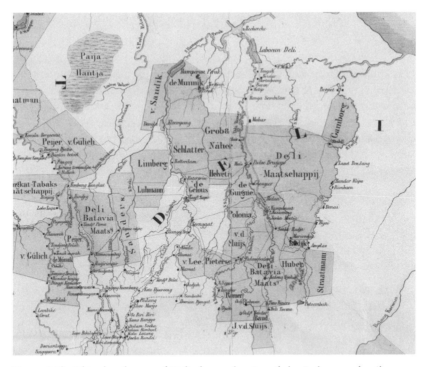

Figure 15b. This detail map of Deli shows the site of the Luhmann family murders and the plantations surrounding it.

Droop was warned by an Acehnese living on the estate to beware of the Gayos and not to go out unarmed because Petambiang was out to kill him. The following day when Petambiang returned to tell Droop that the work had been completed and he now expected his pay, Droop did not agree but decided to consider the work finished as long as they returned his tools. Again he was warned that the Gayos would attack his estate and murder him that night. Droop only prepared his weapons and, not trusting his subordinates with his four guns, kept them in the house. Valck wrote:

> The Gayos appeared that night and began cutting through the plaited roofing when Droop fired his pistol at them four times. Several Gayo were wounded and he was cut by a sabre across the hand. When the assailants withdrew to get a torch to set the house on fire, he escaped. *According to Droop the Gayos attacked him while calling "Labilloellah," the common Muslim war-cry and it was clear from this that they were in contact with the Acehnese and had come with the purpose of murdering him, a European. This last part seemed strange to me right*

away, because if this was their intent it certainly would not have been necessary to first work for many days in a row; they could have just killed him.

This final sentence offers the same reasoning expressed in the "well-founded remark" by the Malay informant, quoted by Valck with regard to the Luhmann murder. In both cases Valck used it to confirm the soundness of his own reasoning. But the question remains, why did these Gayos utter a "Muslim war-cry"? Was this a deft play on the planters' fears of an Acehnese assault or was something else transpiring in Deli that Valck's fixation on the planters' abuses could not allow him to see? Or was Valck resistant to the possibility of a broader assault on Dutch authorities because it would weaken his own case that the planters, and not the assailants, were the real culprits who were responsible for the increasingly threatening situation?

In the meantime, Resident Locker de Bruijne, *without* Valck's report in hand, sent the following communiqué to the Governor-General:

From private information, but *from a very reliable source*, I was informed that on one of the Langkat plantations, disturbances took place during which a European administrator was wounded and some damage was done to personal property. According to my informant, the offenders were some of the Gayos working on the estates, who because of injudicious action by the administrator took bitter revenge on him and who afterwards disappeared to their own region without creating further disturbances. It seems to me, therefore, that *this fact has no political significance whatsoever . . . I have not yet received a report from the Assistent Resident of Deli [Valck].*[46] (my emphasis)

Locker de Bruijne pretends to a knowledge that barely masks his unfamiliarity with the circumstances of the assault. He unambiguously blames Valck for not filing a report sooner, although Valck's preliminary report is actually written four days before Locker de Bruijne's. Valck's second lengthy report on the Droop assault—only five days before he reports the Luhmann story, and four days before he writes Norman Levyssohn—makes his case against the planters again. He categorically dismisses the report by the military commander, Vogel, who both "suspects instigation from Acehnese quarters" and argues that the assaults on the Baay estate included "four Acehnese [who] took employ with the purpose of sedition."[47] Vogel notes that he had heard from "various quarters" that Heer Peyer badly treated his workers, whereas Heer Baay did not, further

[46] AR, Mr. 741, 10 September 1876.
[47] AR, Mr. 844, 21 September 1876, Report of the Commander of the expeditionary column in Langkat.

"proof" that political instigation and not personal revenge was the common denominator that explained the events.[48] Major Demmemi makes a similar, if somewhat more equivocal, case. In a communiqué of 28 October with the Commander-in-Chief, eleven days after the Luhmann murder, he claims to present only "the facts and rumors because there are such discrepant interpretations of the events."[49]

Both Demmemi's and Valck's accounts make a curious omission. Both fail to note that the planters' fears are *not* fueled by the assaults per se, but by the numerous "friendly natives" who repeatedly warn them of possible dangers. Demmemi reports that the planter J. Cremer is "warned twice that he should not leave his estate because of the danger outside." The planter August is "advised by a Batak not to go out at night without a bayonet"; and Droop "is warned by an Acehnese living on the estate to beware of the Gayos." Demmeni attributes these fears to "exaggeration in all this news" and calls a meeting with Malay authorities, who counsel him that the Salah Moeda and Kloempang villages "are not to be trusted." But when he asks who was leading the "unruliness," they answer, "No one from Deli; the influences come from outside."[50] Fears here are mobile and in active motion, but who is playing off whose violence and whose trepidations goes unaddressed. Demmemi clearly does not know when he questions whether the assaults should be seen as part of a larger conspiratorial effort or as the work of "common thieves as occurs elsewhere." Though unsure, based on rumors of possible insurgence, he requests 128 reinforcements be sent to Deli to strengthen the troop of 90 armed soldiers already stationed there to protect the planters.

Valck still resists casting the assaults as expressions of subversion. Instead he argues for what he takes to be the more plausible parallels to be drawn between the attacks:

> I feel I should mention the connection I notice between the events at the Droop [Van Sluijs], Peyer, and Baay plantations. As I informed Your Honor in my letter of 6 September, no. 520, Mr. Droop had insulted the head of the Gayos who worked for him. . . . His plantation was ransacked, the empty strongbox was removed from the house by the Gayos and he was attacked and injured while the house was set afire. . . . As far as I am informed at this moment, the Gayos employed at the Perseverance estate were dissatisfied with the wages Mr. Peyer had given them and they were all allegedly beaten by Mr. Buck. Those Gayos, as well as those working for Mr. Droop, not knowing where to

[48] Ibid.
[49] AR, Mr. 916, 28 October 1876, Confidential report of Commander of the East Coast of Sumatra Demmemi to Chief of Staff, Department of War.
[50] Ibid.

demand justice, probably took the law into their own hands and took revenge by killing Mr. Buck. . . . Mr. Sijthoff allegedly had beaten the Gayos too. They also took revenge on him. It is curious that they did not attack the estates of [. . .] and Shaw, situated on the road in front of the Baay estate, nor the Ayer Ham estate or that of Mr. Menzies, in whose vicinity they remained for about a day. They also remained for days near the plantations of the gentlemen O'Flaherty, de Munnick, and Hirschman without doing them any harm. Their attacks occurred so unexpectedly that if they had intended to attack, no one would have been safe.[51]

Valck represents the Gayos as avengers, not thieves. Specific Europeans are targeted for assault, while others are informed in advance that they will go unharmed: "Mr Thompson [of the Ayer Ham estate] later told me repeatedly that an *inlander* not belonging on his estate had told him that same day that he had nothing to fear since nobody had anything against him." Here again, Valck insists that the attacks were strategically directed and planned. He makes no comment, however, on a more unsettling implication: that many more people from Sumatra's subject populations knew in advance about the assaults than those who actively participated in them.

By now, Valck is more exasperated with the invocation of Aceh influence and reiterates his own conclusion in no uncertain terms:

I feel that no one with a trace of common sense, after being informed of the above, will believe that Aceh influence is behind those attacks and that everyone must agree that they have resulted from personal feuds. Only the interested parties at the attacked plantations feel differently, unpleasant as it must be to find the blame put back on themselves or their subordinates. The truth of the matter later will become evident.

Valck's "common sense" is not that of others. His interpretation of "personal feuds" implicates and jeopardizes Deli's European community at large. The danger is real, he asserts, but not because of the Aceh War:

After all of the above, it need not be said that when it comes to retaliation no one is safe, even if one were surrounded by a complete battalion. . . . We only agreed to leave a detachment with planters in the Langkat lowlands who were most afraid. This was merely done to calm the feelings of these gentlemen. No government, no matter how well organized, no police force, no matter how diligent, no troops, no matter how numerous, are capable of securing the planters from attacks like those which have taken place. Fairness and justice toward their subordinates will always be the best weapons against them.

[51] AR, Mr. 864, 24 October 1876.

The Luhmann family murder stood out from other similar attacks because the victims were considered "innocents," a woman and children, but this is not Valck's primary concern. Focused on Luhmann's guilt, his interpretation invokes the exigencies of a situation that went beyond what he learned from the acknowledged facts of that case alone.[52]

From accounts of preceding and subsequent assaults, two kinds of stories of white murder emerge, and both hold fast to stylized plots. Attacks were considered personal or political, criminal or subversive, with these conceived as mutually exclusive categories. Within this frame, the assaults could be understood in only one of these two ways: either as retaliations against an individual who *happened* to be European, or expressions of an orchestrated assault on Europeans tout court. Valck's accounts succumbed to neither. Instead, his cut across both categories with yet another scenario, one in which the personal could transform into the political and often did. Outrage at planter abuses—be they physical, financial, moral, or psychological—were differently experienced by Deli's ethnically distinct colonial subjects. At different moments they met the affronts of the estate economy by challenging its order both in consort and in their own ways.

The categories available to most colonial officials constrained what they could envision as a possible plot. Bracketing these dichotomies allows for the possibility that rumor, arson, murder, and theft made up a gradient of responses that subverted the simpler logic on which planter assumptions were based. These responses most often made little dent, nor was this necessarily their "real" intent. Suspending these dichotomies makes room for a more complex range of social and labor relations that better reflects how people were likely to have lived: not a world divided neatly between plantation and hinterland, personal and political acts, or between criminal and revolutionary motives. People who identified themselves as Gayo, Javanese, Malay, or Batak were alternately attracted and repelled by the plantations' demands for labor, land, and services. Drawn by this pull of power and opportunity, they enlisted in the plantation economy by varied means and exited with varying degrees of success.

Valck's account fits awkwardly within the then-prevalent colonial caricature of suppliant, dog-headed coolies who, in response to what they considered verbal or physical abuse, would vent their frustration by running amok.[53] On the contrary, in each case European planters were pitted against a sophisticated trade network controlled by the sultanates, as well

---

[52] Strikingly, no allusions or accusations of sexual assault were ever made against the assailants. For other moments in which violence was perceived as sexually charged, see Stoler (2002), 58–60.

[53] These tales of "coolie rows" pervade the planters' representations of protest as well as that of the government's labor inspectorate into the 1920s; see Stoler (1985), 47–92.

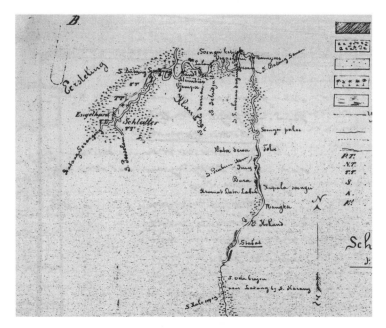

Figure 16. Commander of East Sumatra Demmemi's drawing of military placement and weapons available for protection of the estates, 1876. *Source*: AR, Mr. 880, Extract from Demmemi's journal, 6–19 October 1876.

as assertive Batak, Malay, and Gayo negotiators who were assured of what their proper payment should be, self-confident enough to make reasonable demands and even to press *additional* claims. Gayo and Batak woodcutters did more than defend their due for agreed-upon piecework. They *redefined* what their due was while the work was already in progress.

Deli planters in the late 1870s confronted a population with disparate investments in the colonial economy; but those disparities did not always divide along ethnic lines. Malay sultans buttressed—and profited from— the estate industry's incursions into their lands. By contrast, other non-landed members of the local and immigrant populations continued to contest the labor they sold, the services they performed, and the terms of those arrangements. Most violence was directed at Europeans, but Javanese, Malays, and Bataks were alternately the targets of those who saw them as pawns and participants in the redistribution of resources that came with the widening girth of European land concessions and the attractive wages the companies promised to pay.

Murder was in the air. Even before the Luhmann assault, a Javanese informant told Demmemi that "the Gayos plan to kill the Europeans as well

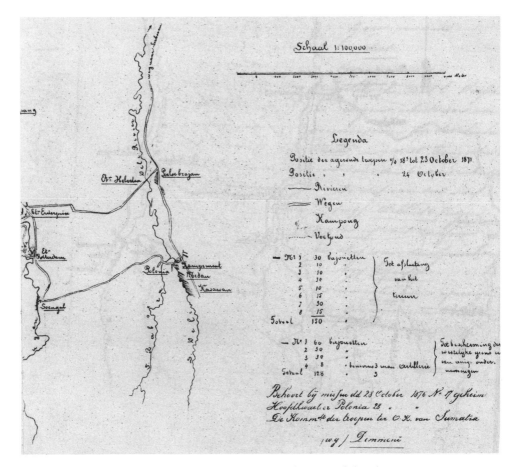

Figure 17. Commander of East Sumatra Demmemi's drawing of the plantations where assaults occurred, 1876. *Source*: AR, Mr. 880, Extract from Demmemi's journal, 6–19 October 1876.

as the Javanese in league with them."[54] But his Gayo informant, Ga, from Kampong Gala, insisted on the opposite: that the Gayo "had nothing against the Europeans, they were good; the Gayos only wanted to return to their own region with money in hand."[55]

[54] AR, Mr. 880, 8 October 1876, Commander of the East Coast of Sumatra Demmemi to Chief of Staff.

[55] AR, Mr. 880, 6–19 October 1876, Commander of the East Coast of Sumatra Demmemi's journal.

Rumors of Forest Encampments and Robber Bands

The Luhmann family murder was not over with the burial of its victims or with Valck's report. Over the next few weeks, official correspondence about the continuing assaults in Langkat invoked the name of Luhmann and suspected assailants of his family at every turn. But by mid-November (a month after the murder), Datoe Gembang and those of the other thirty suspects initially arrested by Valck were no longer central figures in these stories. Increased military patrols coupled with the recruitment of more native spies in the villages surrounding the estates turned up new kinds of evidence, and thus a new causal sequence of events. Native spies informed Demmemi that they "discovered" armed fortifications (*benting*) in the forest, occupied and lead by a certain Panglima Selan, "a Gayo, feared by the local Bataks." Resident Locker de Bruijne's 25 November letter to the Governor-General cites a "captured" coolie found in one of the forest hideouts who confirmed that Panglima Selan had raided the Baay and Peyer plantations, as well as Luhmann's and others.[56]

Valck's 11 November 1876 report on the discovery of the *benting* is troubled and perplexed. Forest hideouts do not fit his plot. He doubts their existence and takes a military convoy to Panglima Selan's encampment to see the *benting* for himself. He learns that two letters have been discovered there, addressed in German to Luhmann. When he questions the local Malay heads about the hideouts, he finds that they knew for at least six months about Panglima's activities but continued to report *rust* (peace) in their districts nonetheless.

Valck's confidence in his own analysis is shaken. He wonders whether the Malay chiefs are powerless to control the Gayos or, as he thinks more likely, that the chiefs are in complicity with them. When a Dutch military envoy is sent to destroy the fortifications, he reports that villagers professed great relief to be rid of Panglima and his gang, but Valck no longer knows what to believe. His spies confirm the existence of two encampments that seem to have been there for over a year. These, he learns, were occupied by Gayos, 50–60 in one alone, and an equal number of "runaway Chinese coolies," as well as Bataks and Malays, four of which were "under the foreman named Deli from Kloempang, who had played a major role in the Luhmann assault."[57] He becomes more concerned about the Malay leaders and orders that they be replaced "to make room for a different organization, the sooner the better." But now he is more alarmed about what he does not know and warns his superior about more serious danger if the Malay leaders are not immediately replaced. If they are not, he writes,

[56] AR, Mr. 964, 25 November 1876.
[57] AR, Mr. 53, 2 December 1876, Frans Carl Valck to Locker de Bruijne.

protection of the Europeans is out of the question. The investigation pointed to Panglima Selan as the main leader, if not the leader of those who attacked the plantations belonging to Peyer, Baay, and Luhmann. Those events were caused by rapacity mixed with rancor because of the insults suffered. *As I have always maintained, there were no politics involved.* Band leaders like Panglima Selan always will easily find followers in the Langkat area. Malcontents are quite plentiful here as long as there are planters who badly treat their coolies. There will always be enough deserters who are willing, if only out of desperation, to join a gang leader. To secure peace in this district, it must be made sure that the coolies are not being maltreated by their masters.

The Resident Locker de Bruijne's report to the Governor-General, based in large part on Valck's report, tells a very different story. He omits some parts and underscores others. He argues that the villagers' refusal to report Panglima Selan's presence—as well as the unexpected silence of the Malay village heads—was due to their fear of retribution. A Javanese informant conveys a more chilling tale. He reports that the followers of an important Gayo, killed by the police in the earlier assault on the Peyer estate, were set on avenging his death, first by attacking those villagers who had assisted the police, and then by mounting a full-scale rampage against the European planters "in general." He reports that "people say" [*men zegt*] as many as 500 Gayos were planning a mass assault on the estates for early December.[58] The administration of the Two Rivers estate reports to the military commander "rumors" (*geruchten*) of 800 Achenese in the Batak region to the north, and even some in a village just four hours from his plantation.[59]

Locker de Bruijne's report of ten days later is increasingly troubled by rumors, by the "agitated atmosphere in Deli, caused and fed by exaggerated representations of the situation given by some inhabitants."[60] Still, assured in a meeting with planters who "mentioned not one word about their concern for the safety and security of their estates," he concludes that "the recent rumors about the region's dangerous political situation should not be taken seriously." He makes no mention of maltreatment of workers or complicity on the part of the Malay heads. But if he was so convinced of his story of random theft and native rapacity—and believed the Governor-General would be, too—there would have been little reason to take the subsequent measures he did.

First, he rejects Valck's advice to dismiss the native district heads and instead seeks new ways to enlist their further support in eliminating both

[58] AR, Mr. 964, 25 November 1876.
[59] AR, Mr. 1005, 15 November 1876.
[60] AR, Mr. 973, 5 December 1876, Locker de Bruijne to Governor-General.

ex-coolies turned vagabonds and the robber bands. Two, he recommends that the increased number of government officials in Langkat be charged with "the task [of] *drilling our ideas of rule into the chief heads by means of gentle persuasion.*"[61] Three, he rejects the planters' proposal to establish a permanent military garrison in Deli, fearing that the local rulers will "feel dismissed of their responsibility for maintaining peace and order and will side with the Gayos" against the Dutch. Four, he requests authorization to send coolies back to their masters (contra the Procurer-General's edict) to curtail the presence of ex-coolies roaming outside the estates.[62] And finally, in the interests of "peace and order," he requests that the planters issue a curfew for workers, keep reliable guards in the coolie barracks all night, and enforce a pass system allowing only those with letters of permission to enter the plantation belt.[63]

This is not quite a state of emergency but it is coming close. Some of these measures could be construed as reasonable strategies to deal with "vagabonds" and "robber bands," if this is what they were. But the overall plan suggests that Locker de Bruijne took the rumors of popular revolt more seriously than his report admits. Each of the measures would effectively constrain and contain the movement of estate workers, intercept the lines of communication between Gayos, Malays, and Chinese estate coolies, and impose more stringent disciplinary measures. No enquiry was made to investigate the reasons for the "unrest" offered by Valck or the workers themselves. Like the first Coolie Ordinance three years later, Locker de Bruijne's strategy was to keep workers bound to their contracts, but, as importantly, to keep them confined, isolated, and in place.

In a modified version, this account becomes Deli's official history, first as it is written in the official Colonial Annual Report (*Koloniaal Verslag*) of 1887 and then in the authoritative and much-cited narrative of W. H. M. Schadee, published in 1919, derived verbatim (but without bothering to note his source) from that account provided in the *Verslag* where the government issued its annual summary of statistics, developments, and events. Schadee described the surge of unrest thus:

> In September [1876] there were assaults on the Tandem estate belonging to Mr. Peyer and Van Gulich in which a European supervisor was killed and several coolies were less seriously injured. The *thieves* [*roovers*] took all the available money with them. The same thing happened a day later on the Kwala Begoemit estate of Mr. Baud. In October the Soengei Diski estate was attacked, but this time not by Gayos alone, but also by Bataks and Malays from the neighboring village of

[61] AR, Mr. 53, 2 December 1876, Locker de Bruijne to Governor-General.
[62] AR, Mr. 170, 27 February 1877, Locker de Bruijne to Governor-General.
[63] AR, Mr. 70, 8 January 1877.

Sialang [Salah] Moeda. The wife of the planter Mr. J. Luhmann and his two children were murdered, while he and another house member were seriously wounded. The latter died from the wound a month later. Here too they were *plundered*. Measures were immediately taken to protect the estates. Thanks to the police, several perpetrators of these assaults were apprehended. Four Bataks and two Malays were sentenced to death, six others to forced labor, the village head of Sialang [Salah] Moeda was exiled for three months. The principal culprit, Radjal, died in prison. It appeared later that the three assaults mentioned above had occurred under the direction of a certain Panglima Selan, a Gayo very much feared by the Batak population, who previously had often made these districts unsafe and who now had gathered together a number of his compatriots after they had been dismissed from the Ajer Tawar estate. In November our military took without struggle a fortification they had erected at Si Oempih-Oempih. Selan seems to have fled but many of the goods stolen from Soengi Diski were found in his quarters.[64]

Schadee's story reduces the Luhmann family assailants to a gang of itinerant thieves. Torture is not at issue: European atrocities and labor grievances are not mentioned. Valck's condemnation of Luhmann's behavior and his suspicions about the close link between vagabondage and assaults are nowhere to be found. In faithful colonial format, Schadee celebrates the restoration of order, with the culprits identified and troubles overcome.

Anthony Reid has suggested that the aid Gayos and other inland tribes provided for Aceh's resistance to Dutch control "had nothing to do with the beginnings of an 'Indonesian consciousness,' but was simply an expression of their distrust of the foreign invaders."[65] He is undoubtedly right about some of these groups, but there was something distinctive about Gayo activities. Their assaults on the estates expressed more than "distrust." They were directed at planters and their property, and at specific persons. Nor were the Gayo encampments confined to Aceh exiles. They were peopled with Malays, Javanese, and Chinese ex-coolies, as well. While some workers might have been taken by force, as claimed by Locker de Bruijne, many more might have lived in these encampments by choice and for relatively long periods of time. During those stays they seem to have raided the estates for food when they could not get enough in the surrounding villages or could not gather enough in the forest.

Something more significant discredits Locker de Bruijne's account of pure plunder and rapacity by Gayo roving gangs—and thus the bowdlerized version of the situation adopted by Schadee. By any stretch of the

---

[64] Schadee, 16–17.

[65] Anthony Reid, *The Blood of the People* (Kuala Lumpur: Oxford University Press, 1979), 153.

imagination and evidence, the attacks were not random. Valck argued that they systematically occurred on estates where workers had experienced re- peated maltreatment while neighboring planters within "shooting dis- tance" of the estate attacked went unharmed. Valck's point was clear. There were more than enough angry and discontented estate workers for such types as Panglima Selan to enlist. Whether Panglima Selan was merely a clever thief who dovetailed his plundering with the desires of a coolie pop- ulation primed for retaliation is difficult to assess. But enough additional motivation for recurrent assaults points to intensities of violence that would be hard to reduce to theft alone.

Nor would the rumors on which Dutch authorities acted have made much sense. In November military commander Demmemi reported rumors of Gayos and Bataks preparing for a rampage to wipe out Europeans en masse. But no one knew if there were 80 Gayos lying in wait, or 800 Acehnese gathering in the Batak highlands four hours from the densest concentration of Deli estates.[66] Military officials were rattled by contradic- tory reports of their native spies but could not tell the difference between "news" and "rumors" and were unsure which of the informants were providing reliable information. Van Ende, a detachment commander, re- ported that none of the *kampong* heads had informed him about the *bent- ing*, although he was sure they knew that such fortifications existed. An- other of his spies sent to learn more about the forest encampments had been warned by villagers not to proceed further when he was still an hour's walk from the *benting* at Si Oempih-Oempih because people knew that he was working for the government.[67] The planter Peyer reports to Von Ende that his Batak spy, Si Oleh, came upon a *benting* of "forty meters' height" with another one close by. Other reports cited 500 men in Gayoland mak- ing feasts in preparation for a succession of assaults on the Langkat es- tates. Within less than a week the rumors were denied. With obvious pride, Demmemi reported that he had probably located its "source" in Laboehan Deli itself. He alleged the rumors to have been spread by family members of the Malays from Kloempang and Salah Moeda implicated in the Luhmann murder. As reported to him by troop commander Von Ende, the rumors were planted to impede the investigation, to cause confusion, and to "win time."[68]

But Demmemi's more tentative suggestion was more unsettling still: that the rumors might be true and that a full-scale assault on Langkat was being planned. In this scenario, rumors of Gayos in the southern planta- tion heartland were merely a distracting strategy. In either case the military

[66] AR, Mr. 1005, 15 November 1876.
[67] AR, Mr. 1005, 12 November 1876, No. 3 geheim, Detachment Commander von Ende.
[68] AR, Mr. 1005, 15 November 1876.

and political consequences were intense. "A reigning panic" engulfed Deli and Demmemi's officers were deluged with planters' requests for protection that the officers thought "unnecessary."[69]

On 13 November Mr. Thomson of the Entreprise estate had "news" (*bericht*) from "the Bataks of Tandjong Balek" of an armed *benting* nearby. Mr. Sanders of the Arendsburg estate asks for military protection of his house and his associates; the commander at Soengei Diski is dispatched to hear Sanders and carry out a "secret reconnoiter" at Tandjong Balek.[70] Demmemi's daily reports between 11 and 24 November waver. He maintains that *"roofzucht"* (rapacity) motivated the assaults on Peyer and Luhmann,[71] but then quotes a "very believable source," who reports on plans being made for full-scale rebellion in Deli two months later.[72]

During the *same week* that Resident Locker de Bruijne concluded that the exaggerated representation of disorder was unjustified, the Troop Commander of the East Coast of Sumatra provided the following extraordinary entry in his journal of 20 November 1876:

After the disturbing news concerning Deli of the 16th [November], the following news [*bericht*] was circulating among the planters:

—the plantation Grob en Nahr was entirely plundered;

—fortification was erected by Malays in Sialang [Salah] Moeda [the village of Luhmann's alleged assailants];

—Acehnese and Gayos were gathered at Laboean Deli;

—the estate of Thompson was plundered and he was murdered;

—Malays, Javanese, and Bataks in the next two months might come together and revolt (*oproer*), and would murder all Europeans along the way from Soengal to Laboean Deli;

—*the Assistant Resident of Deli was murdered on his trip to Si Oempih-Oempih.*[73]

Thompson was not killed; Assistant Resident Valck was, we know, not murdered in Si Oempih-Oempih, where the Gayo encampment was located. In fact, he complained of such exhaustion from the trip that he

---

[69] AR, Mr. 1005, 11–24 November 1876.

[70] AR, Mr. 2005, Letter 8, 13 November 1876.

[71] AR, Mr. 1005, 11–24 November 1876.

[72] AR, Mr. 929x, 10 November 1876, Telegram from Commander of the East Coast of Sumatra Demmemi to Chief of Staff.

[73] AR, Mr. 1005, 11–24 November 1876, Commander of the East Coast of Sumatra Demmemi's journal.

never even took part in the ambush. And the anticipated carnage of the Europeans never occurred. Major Demmemi was convinced that Panglima Selan was a common thief and in no way related to the Acehnese troops who might be preparing an attack in Langkat. But, then again, he was no longer sure, and neither was Locker de Bruijne nor Valck.

On Storytelling and Colonial Credibilities

Native assaults on European plantation personnel and property continued to be debated until the end of Dutch rule in similar terms: distinctions between personal and political and between criminals and insurgents were still being made right through the national revolution of 1945.[74] These were not residual categories of intelligibility, nor were they out of date. Indeed they had sustaining power and weight. In the 1930s they remained viable "modern" categories, relevant but wholly unreliable. In 1876, as Valck figured out, such distinctions were too wooden. The terror of a European slaughter was never realized in Deli nor, as far as any sources indicate, ever really attempted. But repeated sabotage of the plantations produced a scale of terror among Europeans, a scope of directed violence, and coordinated efforts among Sumatra's resident ethnic groups that was not to be repeated again until the mid-twentieth century. In other ways, it was a conjuncture of resentments that was one of a kind, animated by the intensification of Dutch incursions into the interior of Aceh and by unfettered intensification of physical abuse of workers on the estates. The forest *benting* had remained so long "unknowable" to the Dutch because they could not conceive of such a cross-section of concerted and collective guerilla actions against them.[75]

Despite the relative detail of these accounts, it is still not clear whether Valck was unusually inept or a would-be hero. Nor can we know how ordinary such challenges were. How many more Douwes Dekkers and Valcks were there, perhaps less well protected by high-placed connections, who dared to criticize the Indies administration and then were forced to make rapid and unfeted departures? There were probably many more than we know and many more than most colonial historiography allows us to imagine. Those who were most vocal and brazen in 1845 were not

---

[74] On the Dutch response to revolutionaries as "robber bands" as late as 1949, four years into the independence struggle, see my "Labor in the Revolution: The People's Militia in North Sumatra," *Journal of Asian Studies* 47 (2) (1988): 227–47.

[75] On the intensification of Dutch incursions into the "*dalam,*" the "interior" of Aceh, in 1875–1878, see Anthrony Reid's critical and alternative history of the Aceh War and a story that defies the later assessment of many historians, following Snouck Hurgronje, that the Acehnese were a "fanatical, anarchic and treacherous people." Reid (1969), 288.

those like Van Hoëvell whose names elicit recognition because they later rose, in other capacities, to prominence and national fame. In 1845 there were many more who suffered an official death, never to be heard from again. Douwes Dekker died in exile; Valck's name disappears from the state archives in 1880 without any further trace. Luhmann stays on, listed in the Indies business gazette as owner and operator of a good-sized rubber estate decades later.[76]

The evidence of Valck's bureaucratic carelessness was strong. When his successor, Faber, took over the job, he reported the prison ledgers to be in disarray, with much confusion and few dossiers treating the number of prisoners, the length of their sentences, and the nature of their crimes. Valck's predecessor, Hallewijn, might never have kept a register, but Valck never took it upon himself (or had the time) to start one. Among the few dossiers Faber did find was one of a prisoner given a four-month sentence but interned for over eleven months. On such negligence, Norman Levyssohn came to Valck's defense, arguing that his many tasks would have made it impossible, even for an efficient civil servant, to handle management of the court, prisons, concessions, and administration all at the same time. Considering the sheer quantity of reports that Valck filed in a matter of days (it will be remembered that the letter to Norman Levyssohn alone was thirty handwritten pages), it is difficult to imagine how he had time to travel to far-flung estates by horseback, do detailed interviews, write his lengthy reports, meet with military personnel, and still attend to prison ledgers, court proceedings, and the rest of his tasks on any given day.

The more serious charge against him made by Director Henny of the Civil Service—that he "totally misjudged his relationship to the Resident, either keeping him completely in the dark about the most important matters that occurred in his district or notifying him too late"—was more complicated in motive than Henny's condemnation professed. Valck's assessments of what was happening on Sumatra's East Coast did not conform to what his superior, Resident Locker de Bruijne, thought fitting to report. The latter's reputation rested on his ability to keep his residency in *"rust en orde"* whether he knew what was going on and whether he was present or not. Assaults caused by personal feuds or "outside" Acehnese agitation were disturbances that did not necessarily reflect badly on him. But Valck's accusation that the violence was selective, and

---

[76] Luhmann remained in Deli for another twenty-five years, running his Soengi Diski tobacco estate through the 1890s. In 1903 his name first appears in the Indies business directory as the owner and administrator of the Soengei Bloetoe rubber estate, which he ran at least through 1918 (*Handboek voor cultuur- en handelsondernemingen in Nederlands-Indië, 1892–1893,* 1918; *Nieuw adresboek van geheel Nederlands-Indië,* 1903).

that state complicity and leniency toward the planters was its cause, touched closer to issues about which Locker de Bruijne should have known and had in hand. Valck might not have "misjudged" his relationship to the Resident but, on the contrary, assessed accurately how much they were at loggerheads, and therefore how much evidence he had to muster to back his contrary claims.

Valck's family and personal history might have both prompted and discredited the kind of colonial story he chose to tell. The promising civil career of his father, one of the youngest civil servants to be promoted to Resident, ended with his dismissal as Resident of Jogjakarta in 1837, a fate his son was to share some forty years later. Frans Gerardus Valck (1799–1842) had been appointed Resident of several key districts in central Java during the formative years of the sugar industry. From 1823 to 1837 he held that position in the most prestigious posts in Java: at Krawang, Pasuruan, Kedoe, and finally in Jogjakarta, where Frans Carl was born.[77] While Resident in Jogjakarta, Governor-General De Eerens commissioned him to take over the Surabaya residency, where the Resident and Assistent Resident had just been dismissed on the recommendation of a commission charged to investigate their conduct. Frans Gerardus Valck, by his own report, was outraged by the fashion in which the dismissals had occurred. He argued to the Governor-General that their removal was engineered, that one of the Governor-General's own relatives had been implicated, and he proceeded to reinvestigate the commission itself. He was quickly withdrawn, suspended from the civil service for three months without salary and "only the memory of his good services" kept him from being dishonorably dismissed. Upon returning to the Netherlands on a two-year sick leave the following year, he filed a complaint against the Governor-General directly to the Minister of Colonies, brazenly bypassing the local Indies chain of authority all together. He died in the Netherlands in 1842 before his claims were ever reviewed. Seven-year-old Frans Carl would just have been starting boarding school.

The Valck family name was certainly a familiar one to Batavia's elite when Frans Carl took up his first post in 1862, eighteen years after his fa-

---

[77] Cees Fasseur mentions F. G. Valck in a passing footnote in his rich history of the Dutch colonial Civil Service, simply to note his extreme youth (twenty-fours years of age) when first appointed as Resident of Krawang. Fasseur, *Indologen: Ambtenaren voor de Oost, 1825–1950* (Amsterdam: Bert Bakker, 1993), 492. Neither father nor son makes it into H. W. van den Doel's equally comprehensive history of the European colonial Civil Service on Java. Van den Stoel, *De stille macht: Het Europese binnenlands bestuur op Java en Madoera, 1808–1942* (Amsterdam: Bert Bakker, 1994). On F. G. Valck's important relationships with various sultans and royal family members of Jogjakarta and Surakarta, as well as his "large-scale meddling" in Jogjakarta state affairs, see Vincent Houben, *Kraton and Kumpeni: Surakarta and Yogyakarta, 1830–1870* (Leiden: KITLV, 1994).

ther's death. Educated as a boy at the exclusive Noorthey boarding school outside of Haarlem, Frans Carl was schooled where many former and future heads of government and highly placed administrators in the colonial service went and to which they sent their young. Like many elite civil servants, he then enrolled in the Leiden law school at nineteen and was appointed to the Civil Service in 1861. His career was short and without luster. In 1866 he became a Controleur Second Class. Two years later he was reprimanded for challenging an Indies Army Captain to a duel when dueling was forbidden by law.[78] When his classmate Norman Levyssohn was already director of the colonial Civil Service, Valck was still only in a lowly Civil Service post as Controleur First Class.[79]

Evaluations of his conduct in Deli make no reference to Valck's personal life and earlier career, though both might well have colored his unofficial trial and the "crimes" with which he was charged.[80] Bad bookkeeping, backlogged cases, delayed reports, and inept management were among those misdeeds most prominent in the ledger. But the most serious accusation was directed at his indiscriminate and persistent harassment of the planters. For the latter, he was considered to have been guilty of three reprehensible acts. The first was to carry out his administrative and juridical duties in ways that consistently favored the coolies, "for ill-advisedly taking the Chinese coolies, the scum of Singapore and Penang, under his protection," when he should have been supporting the disciplinary actions of Europeans. The second was to neglect a key feature of his job: currying favor with the Deli sultanates whose cooperation and collaboration (in both annexing and policing the plantation belt) were critical to the region's security and the estate industry's growth. Finally, he had misinterpreted the letter of the law concerning breach of coolie contracts, releasing workers of the obligation to return to the plantations from which they fled. In this regard, the Director of the Civil Service charged him with misreading the Procurer-General's edict and with singlehandedly abetting the increase in number of vagrant ex-coolies and the roving bands they joined to plunder the estates.

RUMOR AND THE REAL

Valck's absence from the corpus of Deli histories contrasts sharply with the profusion of official and classified correspondence about him, by him,

---

[78] Brief reference to this incident appears in the *Stamboeken Indische Ambtenaren*, part O, 153.

[79] Ibid., part M-330, 523; *Album Studiosorum Lugdunum Batavorum*, folio 1362/1363.

[80] The cold reception Valck received for accusations against the Deli planters might have more to do with his own past whistle-blowing in the administrative scandal in North Bali (only four years prior to the Luhmann murder) than to the actions of his father.

and about the alternate states of calm and panic that reigned while he was there. His was not only a story of violence that could not be told, but one that confounded colonial common sense, the discrete domains of "rumor" (*gerucht*) and "news" (*bericht*), heresy and "facts." Valck's accounts revealed the extent to which rumor, rather than first-hand observation, shaped people's impressions and fears. Those fears, in turn, which passed along the borderlands of a multilingual region, underscored the clarity of some rumors, their ability to sustain the momentum of political critique, in contrast to the murky space of uncommon sense. New stories captured people's imaginations, shaping which versions spread across thousands of kilometers of forest and estate complex through the border villages, to return transformed back to the estates.

If gossip is based on rules of conduct, rumors must have plausible plots (even if an exaggerated relationship to what people believe is true about the world).[81] Rumors in Deli were cumulatively critical and creatively multivocal, the medium through which the unspeakable was spoken, with no one party on hand to blame.[82] Ironically, this never stopped the planters and colonial officials from trying to do so.[83] In Deli in 1876 rumors bore the cultural weight of social and political tensions, not the coziness of shared assumptions and shared knowledge.[84] When Deli's officials attempted to squash what they called "disquieting or disruptive" rumors of mass revolt or impending assaults, they did so by defining what constituted legitimate domains of inquiry and by ignoring others. They sought the *source* of the rumor, as if locating an individual and his or her willful intent of deceit was enough to negate the "disquieting" reality on which the rumors fed. Checking rumors obviously did nothing to curtail the labor abuses and the coercive conditions on which rage and resentments were based.

Rumors seemed to have moved up and down the east coast of Sumatra with enormous speed—far faster than official reports—suggesting that some kinds of knowledge traveled more deftly than others. And rumors voiced the possible. With the Aceh resistance still strong, and Gayos from the Aceh area involved in the Luhmann murder, it was not inconceivable, as several military personnel wrote, that there were 80 Gayos in waiting in the hills above the Deli estates, or was it, as one commander [mis]reported, 800?

---

[81] John Haviland similarly argues that participation in gossip entails a knowledge of cultural rules and presumably a cultural competence in applying them. Haviland, *Gossip, Reputation and Knowledge in Zinacantan* (Chicago: University of Chicago Press, 1977).

[82] On rumor as a critical tool of colonial history and perhaps a more accurate rendering of the realities in which people lived than other kinds of sources, no one makes the case more strongly and insistently than Luise White.

[83] See Guha (1983), 251–74.

[84] I owe this contrast between the "coziness" of gossip and the tension of rumor to Val Daniel.

Rumors resonated not only in the confines of local plantation culture, but in official missives that passed from Deli to Batavia, from Batavia to The Hague, and back again to the Deli estates. Rumors, directly and indirectly, placed army units on plantations, curfews in workers' barracks, watch guards at estate crossroads, and prompted labor contracts to be more strictly enforced. Rumors also prompted vague concerns over "peace and order" to translate into judicial action and military reconnoiters. This is not to suggest that rumor permeated the official discourse undigested and unchallenged. On the contrary, official reports self-consciously engaged the doubts of a readership that might suspect that these statements were based on hearsay alone. Thus Norman Levyssohn prefaced his defense of Valck with approval of Director Henny's report, using the sentence (repeated verbatim in the Governor-General's subsequent decision), "We are not dealing here with loose allegations but with carefully specified facts."

How often were central authorities dealing with "loose" local talk and how often did they know it? Facts were constituted out of rumor as often as the other way around. Rumor was a source of "what happened" in subtle if unmanaged ways. But then the archives themselves are, as Paul Veyne notes, "mutilated knowledge," sometimes no less so than rumors themselves.[85] Rumors registered what people believed could have happened in the past and what could happen in the future. Planters, sultans, coolies, and government agents played on the unpredictable power of rumor in gauging one another's perceptions of dangers and most visceral fears. The archive pulses erratically with affective and political excess that courses through this edgy space.

Ferreting out these cross-cutting rumors and competing agendas underscores how unevenly colonial capitalism joined the interests of plantation entrepreneurs and the state. For both, incomplete knowledge was the rule and not the exception. Tracing the tenuous filaments of these fragmented stories belies the fiction of an omniscient state, rather one ill-coordinated from top to bottom. The art of cribbing depended on knowing what would be considered speakable and plausible by one's superiors—a process that weeded out unthinkable plots. We might remember that Governor-General van Lansberge wrote his decision on Valck's fate borrowing the words of Norman Levyssohn, whose own opinion was based on a personal letter from Valck himself, whose outrage in turn derived in part from what was rumored about Gayo rebels and planter abuses on Sumatra's East Coast. Within that hierarchy of credibility, rumor controlled some people and terrorized others. It was damning and enabling. It could shore up Dutch authority and as quickly turn it into a vehicle of judgment and critique.

---

[85] Paul Veyne, *Essay on Epistmology* (Middletown, Conn.: Wesleyan University Press, 1984), 281.

In this quixotic and unquiet space, colonial authorities often found their policy statements unrealized in practice. Their efforts to maintain controlled mobility and sharp ethnic divides between captive workers and other subjects only had marginal success. The clandestine settlements of Gayos, Javanese, Bataks, Chinese, and Malays alert us to movements of other sorts, of large numbers of people in motion, moving in and out of the estate economy—some refusing as long as they could, some folding their fates into the enclosed enclaves for which Deli's estates were later so well known. A sorting system that placed people in the categories of "vengeful natives," "Aceh rebels," or "robber gangs" located violence where authorities knew it "belonged": that is, distant from those Europeans who were its architects, agents, and perpetrators. No wonder Valck's narratives were no good for the telling, were difficult to repeat or even hear. They repeatedly repositioned violence at the core of empire and in European hearts and minds.

Fiction in the Colonial Archives

These are not the luxuriant pardon tales of *Fiction in the Archives*, from which Natalie Davis so finely drew out the cultural nuances of sixteenth-century France.[86] They are drier, formulaic documents—administrative epistles, curt exchanges, and lengthy monthly reports. They are the product of a state in expansion and of bureaucrats eager to be viewed favorably by their superiors, on whose judgment their salaries, positions, and pensions would depend. They are careful to deflect attention from their own faults, add small flourishes that affirm their loyalties, and are quick to reiterate their investment in Dutch policy and its methods of rule. Unlike the pardon tales, these stories categorically deny the voices of those they feared. Thus, the Luhmann family's Gayo assailants could only be spoken for by what were imagined to be "trustworthy natives" whose allegiance to Dutch authority was thought to be secure. It is not the Gayo who are privileged in these accounts but a representation of them as geographically and cognitively caught between the Aceh War and the muggings in Deli, economically attracted to the estates but independent of them, politically labile and possibly dangerous.

These storied reports were fashioned cultural accounts *with political effects* that precluded some conclusions and encouraged others. Exploring what made some more credible, relevant, and reasonable to their authors and audience opens onto an ethnographic space of jumbled perceptions

---

[86] Natalie Zemon Davis, *Fiction in the Archives: Pardon Tales and their Tellers in Sixteenth-Century France* (Stanford: Stanford University Press, 1987).

and agentive forms that could not be contained and tempered by coherent colonial narratives. Communications that depended on flooded roads, forest bramble, tired horses, slow river rafts, small boats, great ships, and sparse telegraph connections produced a colonizing world that moved and responded with an uneven and ever varying pace.

The disorder of these stories and the reworking of their contexts challenge historiographic convention. Students of colonialisms are adept at challenging colonial representations of authority by pinning their inventions, authenticities, and mannerisms onto a specific time and place. Our stance is often ironic, knowing, and removed from the racial categories to which our subjects were bound, to the sentiments they expressed, to the racial fears upon which they acted and to which they reacted. Our readings presume more than we should about the schooled dispositions that their positions encouraged. Valck alone challenges us to think harder about ethical distance, about torture that is blamed on the bottom man rather than those at the top, and how much the history of what counts as credible is also a history of affective states. The official mannerisms and maneuvers around the Luhmann murder should make it no surprise how unevenly the conventions of categories were reworked on the ground. Sometimes political grammars constrained what colonial agents thought, sometimes those grammars delimited the political idioms in which people talked, indicating not what they thought but only what they said.

Anthropologists and their kin have long produced exemplary readings of ethnography as text. These "storeyed" narratives come layered with thick reflection about ways of knowing, about how anxieties and uncertainties figured in the epistemics of rule. What matters are the details of ethnography: who spoke to whom, who heard and repeated what or chose not to; who imagined what, when, and where. The accent is on the immediate and its juxtaposition with a colonial apparatus that was spare in Deli and was still far away from an administrative hub. The clues, as Michel Foucault, Michel de Certeau, and Carlo Ginzburg would insist, are in the objects of the everyday: the Manila dog that does not howl, letters written in German that find their way to a forest encampment where they cannot be read, a watch that remains untouched on a dresser while a child is slain.

Then there are the words of Valck, buried and emergent between the reported accounts of others, pleading and plaintive despite a genre of official writing that professes to militate for reason, and indeed against more impassioned states. It is a genre that leaves room for small mistakes, that lets slip desperation but refuses to provide witness to the pathos of excess, remorse, blatant outrage, ethical wavering, divided allegiances, and the expressed entreaty that one has been wrongly dishonored, intentionally silenced, and blamed. It is these moments that prick the seal of colonial convention as they dislodge standards of protocol. It is these suspensions from common sense that make room for displaced inflections in stories retold in disquieted European voices, tangled by multiple meanings that fold awkwardly into the order of things. Then—as now—they could not be easily read.

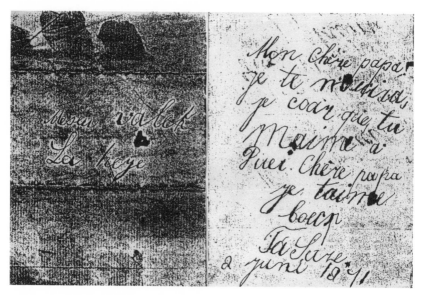

Figure 18. The first letter—or at least the first that has been preserved—that Susanna Valck probably sent to her father, Frans Carl Valck, at age seven.
On the front page: *Meseu Valck La heye [La Haye, The Hague] / Mon chère (sic) papa: Je [si] te m'ecrira je coas [sais] que tu m'aime a xxxx. / Chère papa je taime boecp [beaucoup] Ta Suze juni 1871. Source: CBG, FA.*

CHAPTER SEVEN

Imperial Dispositions of Disregard

> One never wholly believes what one believes.
> —Jean-Paul Sartre, *Being and Nothingness*

> One may certainly admire man, a mighty genius of construction,
> who succeeds in piling up an infinitely complicated dome of
> concepts upon an unstable foundation, and, as it were, on
> running water. His construction must be like one constructed of
> spiders' webs; delicate enough to be carried along by the waves,
> strong enough not to be blown apart by every wind.
> —Friedrich Nietzsche,
> "On Truth and Lie in a Non-Moral Sense"

THIS CHAPTER IS ABOUT THE LOGOS and pathos of empire, the durabilities of imperial dispositions steeped in matter and mind. In different guises, it wrestles with those habits of heart and comportment recruited to the service of colonial governance but not wholly subsumed by it. It seeks to broach the cast that imperial formations imposed over people's intimate social ecologies—both the intensities and the diminished qualities of their affective lives. European colonial communities built their interior frontiers on social distinctions that were schooled as well as those that could "go without saying" because they were, in C. S. Peirce's phrasing, "hidebound with habit" and had already been learned.[1] Colonial actors discerned those distinctions with care: colonial agents wrote anxiously about them. Students of colonialism, more geared to what was pressed on those persons colonized, for long did not attend to the analytic purchase such minor nuance could afford. Evidence of disdain, desire, and disaffection for thoughts and things native were basic to the colonial order of things. In recluse and repose, attachments were put to the test. In these taut and tender ties, relations of power were knotted and tightened, tangled and undone. As I have long held, these ties were not the soft undertissue of empire, but its marrow.

This chapter works closely through the life of a family whose lives moved in and out of colonial Indonesia in the late-nineteenth century to ask what sorts of personhoods imperial formations called forth and upon.

---

[1] C. S. Peirce, *Collected Papers*, vol. 6 (Cambridge, Mass.: Belknap, 1963).

At its core is a rejection of the premise that we who study the colonial know both what imperial rule looks like and the dispositions of those it empowers. It responds to the *flat interiorities* commonly attributed to those with whom we do *not* sympathize, politically or otherwise. Its aim is directed at the smug sense that colonial sensibilities are a given and we can now quickly move on to the complexities and more subtle, troubled dispositions of the postcolonial present.

ANOTHER ARCHIVE, ANOTHER LIFE: TWO STORIES FOR FRANS CARL VALCK

The following pages are trained upon a key and familiar figure, the same Frans Carl Valck whose "discoveries" of European atrocities and whose demise as Assistent Resident during his truncated stay in Deli was the subject of the preceding chapter. It is the same Frans Carl Valck who vanishes so abruptly in 1881 (with his meager pension by then allotted) from the official archival record and from the colonial histories written on its censored edges. Luhmann, the name of the planter whose family was murdered and who remained in Deli through the 1890s, merits passing mention in East Sumatra's historiography. Valck himself disappears, only signaled in passing by his title, caught up in a fraught and violent moment when the Resident was still stationed in Bengkalis far to the south. Valck is never again named.

I sought for some eighteen years to find what became of him since first reading his arresting letter to his friend Norman Levyssohn, along with his explicit official reports of European barbarisms on the Deli estates, which cost him his job. But enjoying neither success nor fame, Valck's scent was faint, his imprint gone, his account of torture excised if not erased. What can be located, however, is a family connection to one of the most successful and innovative entrepreneurs in the development of Java's mid-nineteenth-century agricultural industry—Theodore Lucassen, whose father in 1840 gained renown for first adapting French sugar beet refining techniques to large-scale sugar cane processing in the Indies.

His son, also called Theodore, was to inherit and further expand one of the most vast family-run sugar complexes in Java, an initiative that supplanted Caribbean sugar production on the world market.[2] It was in his affinal connection, as husband to one of Lucassen's sisters, as uncle and

---

[2] On the rise of the Lucassen family and their sugar enterprises in Tegal, see Margaret Leidelmeijer, *Van suikermolen tot grootbedrijf: technische vernieuwing in de Java-suikerindustrie in de negentiende eeuw* (Amsterdam: NEHA, 1997), and Roger Knight, *Colonial Production in Provincial Java* (Amsterdam: VU University Press, 1993), both of whom track the "financial fortunes" of the family through a "set of interlinked state officials, sugar contractors, factory administrators, merchants involved in the commodity trade and their family and commercial associates" (Knight, 8).

Figure 19. Frans Carl Valck's portrait, probably made at the time of his marriage when he was twenty-seven, and before he was sent to Bali and Sumatra. *Source*: IB No. 96200.

then father-in-law to one of his sons, and as grandfather to one pivotal member of the Netherland's Central Bureau of Genealogy that Frans Carl Valck was to emerge at his writing desk again.

Here, in the Bureau of Genealogy, was Valck, in both a familiar and un-expected guise, as one not-particularly-fêted member of a family whose thousands of letters—written to and from cousins, uncles, in-laws, children,

Figure 20. This portrait of Susanna Antoinette Lucassen was probably made when she was twenty-two years old, in 1862, at the time of her marriage to Frans Carl Valck. She was to die two years later, one year after the birth of her only daughter, Susanna Augusta Theodora. *Source*: IB No. 96201.

parents, lovers, and future husbands; to and from governesses, grandparents, and family friends—filled more than forty crammed boxes of a multi-generational family archive. Its location calls up the serendipities of archival holdings, their invisibilities blinding when right in one's face. For this family archive of three meters is housed one flight up the stairwell in the same grey building I had visited for nearly two decades, the same building that stores the colonial administrative archives in The Hague. The proximity and distance between these two pieces of Valck's life are the traces I follow.

The distance between the two archives is one "storey"; the distance in epistolary form and writerly genre not unexpectedly remote. In content, the filaments and phrases that join them are strong yet elusive. Sometimes phrases slip from official to personal letters like a double negative superimposed. Elsewhere the distance is exaggerated and delicately guarded to ensure no contact, not a hint that these worlds could possibly touch. There is no cross-referencing in the respective catalogues, nor mutual recognition of what is above and what below.[3] One is coded for the confidentialities of a bureaucracy, one for the confidences of cousins, sons-in-law, mothers, and daughters about cold remedies, parties attended, acquaintances met, travel plans, reliable dressmakers in Paris—the innocuous minutiae that could be read aloud and shared with other family members as "an entirely social affair."[4] More exceptional are those intended for the recipient alone. Their "appendices," too, are of a different kind. The latter are full of small objects designed to awaken longings and stir memory; tenderly preserved are pieces of ribbon, a pencil drawing, newspaper clippings, or, folded within translucent paper, a pressed flower, a child's drawing, a wisp of hair.

In this swirl of wealth, accomplishment, and family ties to military generals, Indies' governors, and the elite circles of Dutch colonial society, Valck's brief and minor career was eclipsed, barely marked as a haunting trace. His time in Deli is dim next to the luminous careers and movements

[3] In 1985, when I first inquired about Frans Carl Valck at the Algemeen Rijksarchief, Ms. F. van Anrooij had informed me that after 1880 Valck's name was not mentioned again in the state archives. I was first to learn about the Valck family archive fourteen years later in spring 1999 when working on this book. I wrote to Ms. F. van Anrooij again about my sense that Valck had been well connected to other elite colonial families and asked whether there might be somewhere else to look. She suggested I write to then-Director of the Central Bureau of Genealogy, Mr. Peter A. Christiaans, who might be able to help me. Neither she nor I knew of the Bureau of Genealogy's archive of the Valck-Lucassen family, with extensive materials on Frans Carl and his father. I thank both of them for their generous aid.

[4] Rebecca Earle, ed., *Epistolary Selves: Letters and Letter-Writers, 1600–1945* (Aldershot: Algate, 1999), 7, notes that "letter-writers indicated those unusual passages which should *not* be circulated, rather than the reverse."

of his kith and the wealthy Lucassen family, into which both he and his daughter married. By name and genealogy, Valck had much to offer: his ancestors were among the patrician Dutch regent class, hereditary members of the ruling bodies of towns and provinces, whose wealth came from those offices.[5] It was Valck's grandson, Theodore Reynirus Valck Lucassen, who eventually merged the Valck and Lucassen families into one prestigious hyphenated name and into one elaborate coat-of-arms. But the broader arch that conjoined and disjointed his life—as the father of an only child, as a husband with a succession of three wives, and as colonial official in his short-lived career—is richly preserved in measured language, as was the personhood he shaped with such deliberate care.

Here, Frans Carl Valck appears as just one affinal member (for it is the Lucassens who are fully present) of a family whose broad clan spent generations moving between Europe and the Indies, whose births, engagements, deaths, and dishonor family and friends chronicle in a steady stream of missives that made their way across the Netherlands on canal barges, across Europe by train, and most often by ship from Marseille to Singapore and then Java. These are letters carefully folded, their envelopes still intact, timed to make the next barge departing for the Dutch provinces, or sometimes hurried to make the next boat leaving from Marseille.

In this chapter I broach only a small portion of this compendium of the correspondence of kith and kin temporarily residing in, visiting, or traveling between Bali, outposts in East Sumatra, sugar factories in central Java, French country estates, Swiss spas, and stolid, brick family houses that still line the prestigious avenues overlooking the canals that run through The Hague. The generational rhythms of these lettered careers and lettered lives register the social habits and political sensibilities of those who dwelled in colonial worlds and on their political margins. Names unconnected in official archives are joined in these missives by birthday celebrations, by greetings sent to those close to the person addressed, by news of leaves, and by announcements of births, promotions, marriages, and deaths. Tracking Frans Carl's relationships through them opens a grid of power, honor, and constraint that eludes official chartings.

Those on which I focus are between Valck and his daughter, written over some thirty years in the late-nineteenth century, traversing the heyday of Dutch colonial empire, the opening of the Suez Canal, colonial expositions in Europe's capitals, riots in East Java, labor violence in

---

[5] On the power of regents in Dutch state-formation and imperial history, see the luminous study, which appears in abbreviated form, in Julia Adams, "The Familial State: Elite Family Practices and State-Making in the Early modern Netherlands," *Theory and Society* 23 (4) (August 1994): 505–39.

Deli, and the personal aloneness of colonial posts that were sometimes embraced as relished retreats, at other times experienced as exile.[6] These are letters that were regularly sent, sometimes impassioned, and often relentless in their efforts to connect on the part of the absent father, Frans Carl Valck, who served for some sixteen years in the Netherlands Indies, with his daughter, Susanna, with whom he maintained constant epistolary contact and in estranged physical proximity for most of their lives.

Between 1869, seven years after Valck took up his first post in Java, when his daughter in the Netherlands could not yet read and had just turned six, and 1892, when he died in The Hague and she was by then Susanna Antoinette Valck Lucassen—married to her deceased mother's nephew, mother of three, and daughter-in-law in residence on the Ke-manglen estate—he wrote to her monthly and she, as a young woman, bimonthly to him. Father and daughter moved back and forth between the Indies and Europe, in counter current on the mail boats that took him out to Singapore and Bali in 1871, and her along the same route sixteen years later, and then brought him back to Europe in 1878. She was to return to the Netherlands in 1893 upon the loss of her husband and a year after her father's death.

Their letters took a good month to arrive, hence two long months to receive a response. His were on thick, embossed stationery, adorned with the family coat-of-arms, and hers on transparent paper, often written twice over, cross-hatched at right angles, perhaps to command his attention, or, as she claimed, to save postage. Both were carefully stored with letters spanning different years. It was Valck's grandson who found them "disarranged in a wooden chest." These letters, endearingly addressed to the young "Suze," begin when Vlack was on leave in France in June 1869 and before he took up his second post in coastal Bali in January 1872, as Controleur of Djembrana. Hers he kept in their original envelopes, with just two remaining in the uneven scrawl of a child's unsteady hand. The bulk of hers only began in earnest when she was twenty, upon engagement to her Lucassen cousin and then throughout the conflict with her father prior to the marriage. It was a union of which Valck adamantly disapproved, in part because she had not secured his permission properly "in writing," in part because he found their engagement unduly rushed.

---

[6] Edward Said was critically right to distinguish the "discontinuous state of being" of those who suffer the indignities of exile from those whose choices of dislocation are their own. Valck and those who *chose* colonial service had no claims to the state of exile in these terms. Still, despite their privilege, they shared in what Said called a "jealous state," an "exaggerated sense of group solidarity" and the pathos of "loss of contact" that their racialized worlds so viscerally bestowed. See Edward Said, *Reflections on Exile and Other Essays* (Cambridge, Mass.: Harvard University Press, 2002), 178–79.

Figure 21. This portrait of Susanna Augusta Theodora Valck was probably made when she was nineteen years old, at the time of her marriage to Theodore (Theodoor) Lucassen, in 1883. *Source*: IB No. 96203.

The young Theodore Lucassen was still finishing his degree and had not yet completed his thesis. As Valck wrote, with palpable annoyance at Suze's precipitous decision, Theodore was still without a "calling." During this tense period of half a year, Valck refused to open a single one of her letters. When reconciled (despite her strong reproach of him and defense of her choice) they were to write regularly for the last nine years of his life.

Franciscus Carolus Valck, Ex Insula Java

Valck was seen as an unexceptional man, as the most common phrase applied to him put it, "a not-incompetent" one, ensconced at the apex of a Dutch colonial elite, but only partially protected by it. The official correspondence about him, some of which he participated in, but much of which he did not—his personal letters to his wives-to-be as well as to his sweet child turned a sullen grown daughter, to friends to whom he bitterly complained about his treatment and with whom he pleaded to defend his honor—provide narratives that might seem to fall easily into ready categories: the public and official versus the private, hidden, and authentic; the professional persona versus the caring father. I see them as something else: as *the plaintive notes of a history in a "minor key,"* an entry point into the "imperfect interval" between personal and public sensibilities, a rendering of distressed and elated physical and psychic condition that constituted estrangements from the self in disjointed lives.[7] Valck's premature fattening and balding were ostensibly "personal matters," about which he incessantly wrote to his child. But how he wrote about them are not.

In August 1873 he had been abruptly called back from Bali to deal with the eruption of what he calls a revolution in Eastern Java. He writes to her that the *"rebels gave me so little to do that I have gained weight in the most incredible manner. I absolutely look like a bulldog,"* an endearing self-portrait that conceals in its brushstrokes what has stressed his temperament and caused such strain. *"The Resident of Banjuwangi totally lost his head. . . . He just went mad. The scenes that passed during the revolt were grotesque. The Europeans showed themselves to be as cowardly and irresponsible as it is possible to be. I am still so ashamed."*[8]

Here is a man located dead center in the colonial enterprise, living in empire and off the colonies, loyal to a state, many of whose agents he does not trust. It is still five years before he will be called to Deli, when he will accuse planters and government authorities of stabbing him in the back. He does not yet despise his posts (he is indeed proud of his recent promotion). He is not yet wholly uninterested and bored by his surroundings (he describes to young Suze the exquisite views from his Bali

---

[7] This chapter draws on my book in progress, *History in a Minor Key: Love Letters in Colonial Exile.*

[8] CBG, FV, 16 June 1873, Frans Carl Valck to his daughter, Susanna Valck.

coast seafront desk). But it is a life of circular exile from the Netherlands and Java. As Albert Memmi so astutely noted, for many colonials there was no going home.[9]

Valck was not alone in his unmoored, peripatetic life. Other members of the colonial bureaucracy and agricultural industries also followed kin to family enterprises or were schooled for the Indies Civil Service because this is where opportunity lay, what their families expected, and where they imagined they could earn a step "toward an easier life."[10] Benedict Anderson's reference to the "tropical gothic" of this "bourgeois aristocracy" captures a slice of what he calls the "grimly amusing" quality of their starched sartorial trappings, the doily-filled interiors and class aspirations—the excessive comforts and arrogance that racism and the fruits of imperial profits bestowed.[11]

But wedged between those comforts was something else: the unruly nature of people's social imaginaries, discrepancies between the concerted and yearned for domestic "coziness" that empire induced and what emerges as its underside—estrangements from family, studied inattentiveness to the conditions around them, and to the local people whom they could not see and to whom they were beholden for their comforts and often for their survival. Valck looked away from them and away from himself. It is these spaces in between that offer a site for writing a "charmless" history—one whose rough analytic edges resist the tempered distance of a seamless narrative. It does not suffice to invoke a "social imaginary" in which "implicit and common understanding" and "normal expectations" (which Charles Taylor attributes so unproblematically to the term) were effortlessly and equally shared.[12] The "sense of how things usually go," what constituted "foul play," and "how things ought to go" was precisely what confronted Valck in Deli, in the belly of the beast, and on the northern Bali coast, on the outer reefs of empire. It is in the potent political and psychological registers in which he lived that his personhood was forged—and his possibilities ultimately foreclosed.[13]

---

[9] Albert Memmi, *The Colonizer and the Colonized* (Boston: Beacon, 1967), esp. 19–76.

[10] See Cees Fasseur, *De Indologen: Ambtenaren voor de Oost 1825–1950* (Amsterdam: Bert Bakker, 1993), for the best history of learned Indies experts and their participation in the Netherlands Indies administration. On changes in the colonial civil service structure and requirements, see H. W. van den Doel, *De stille macht: Het Europese binnenlands bestuur op Java en Madoera, 1808–1942* (Amsterdam: Bert Bakker, 1994).

[11] Benedict Anderson, *Imagined Communities* (New York: Verso, 1983), 137.

[12] Charles Taylor, *Modern Social Imaginaries* (Durham, N.C.: Duke University Press, 2004), 24–25.

[13] On "inner life processes" that "capture the violence and dynamism of everyday life," see the thoughtful introduction to *Subjectivity: Ethnographic Investigations*, ed. Joao Biehl, Bryon Good, and Arthur Kleinman (Berkeley: University of California Press, 2007), 5.

Beyond Ignorance and Bad Faith:
On Rendering a Colonial Life

Knowledge-production and its strategic absence—contrived ignorance—
are prevailing themes in the making of empire. Edward Said launched an
entire field of colonial studies on the basic Foucauldian principle that distorted forms of knowledge were fundamental features of empire and its
ruling technologies. In one of his last pieces, on the Iraq War, he characterized U.S. empire as one steeped in a deep "historical illiteracy," one
produced by a "cultivated ignorance" that celebrated a "sacrosanct altru-
ism" for what have been brutally calculated imperial interventions.[14] W.
E. B. Dubois captured that transposition much earlier in describing the
historical distortions of American empire as predicated on a "deliberately
educated ignorance" of the racist predicates of U.S. domestic and foreign
power.[15] For Gayatri Chakravorty Spivak, "sanctioned ignorance" is
what "every critic of imperialism must chart."[16]

Ignorance saturates efforts to understand the lived inequities of colonial
relations in more profound and prosaic ways. While marshaled to describe a cultivated condition among those at a safer metropolitan distance, it is as decisive in accounts of the hardened inerrability of those Europeans who made the colonies their permanent or temporary homes.
Writing of French North Africa in the 1950s, Albert Memmi contended
that there are really only two kinds of colonizers: those who accept or
those who refuse, those who turn their backs on what they know—who
"self-censure" and live a feigned ignorance—versus those who could not
bear the contradictions and righteously left.[17] For Pierre Bourdieu,
"learned ignorance" is a form of self-deception, when one is void of the
principles that comprise knowledge, what people hide from themselves.[18]

[14] Edward Said, "L'Autre Amerique," *Le Monde Diplomatique*, March 2001, and "The
Clash of Ignorance," *Nation*, Oct 22, 2001, 11–13.

[15] W. E. B. Du Bois, *Darkwater: Voices from within the Veil* (New York: Dover, 1999), 23.

[16] Gayatri Chakravorty Spivak, "Can the Subaltern Speak?" in *Marxism and the Interpretation of Culture*, ed. Cary Nelson and Lawrence Grossberg (Urbana: University of Illinois Press, 1988), 291. In a similar vein, Geoff Eley, in a scathing review of David Cannadine's *Ornamentalism*, puts ignorance upfront as part of the central question Cannadine
claims to address but does not—namely, how easily empire was "rather ignorantly taken for
granted" by those who enjoyed its profits and pleasures at its metropolitan center and in the
racial intimacies of its colonial margins. Geoff Eley, "Beneath the Skin: Or, How to Forget
About the Empire Without Really Trying," *Journal of Colonialism and Colonial History* 3
(1) (Spring 2002): 11.

[17] Memmi, 18.

[18] Bourdieu's account of "learned ignorance" is not explicitly about colonialism but it is
in a book in which the ethnographic site is Algeria under French rule. He writes, "The explanation agents may provide of their own practices . . . conceals, even from their own eyes,

In such accounts, the cultivation of "ignorance" and the vitality of empire go hand in hand. In this chapter I argue that these are accounts that elicit knowing approval but in the end they may be for us to question, if not reject. A standard critique of empire holds that imperial rule nourishes and feeds off the cultivation of ignorance, that empire is in the business of limiting, distorting, and obscuring knowledge and that with more of it, empires would be more vulnerable to critique; that critique should expose imperial pretenses, that knowledge pierces what obscures the workings of power, weakens its hold, and, with sustained exposure, could be made to crash. In this frame, moral conscience and increased knowledge are redemptive and, like ignorance and empire, thought to go hand in hand.

Several premises are questionable in this argument: one, that more knowledge necessarily leads to more power; two, that knowledge necessarily leads to ethical awareness; and three, that such awareness would produce the sort of active, ethical conscience that would lead people to reject imperial hypocrisies, or, at the very least, their basest acts. Fundamental to these accounts is the assumption that these unnuanced distinctions—knowledge versus ignorance, or acceptance versus refusal—adequately describe the inhabited space of empire for those in its service and those it empowered; that is, both the cognitive conditions and political choices of empire's European and American agents and actors.

But few of these premises are evinced in the historical particulars or borne out by the social facts. "Ignorance" versus "acceptance" fails to capture the more complex psychic space, tacit ambivalences and implicit ambiguities in which European agents and ancillaries to empire made their lives. Such categories represent not causes but effects. They are neither generative analytic sites nor starting points for analysis. "Ignorance" is an ongoing operation, a cumulative, *achieved*, and labored effect. Ignorance, then, is only symptomatic. At issue is *how* it is achieved and sustained, and what institutional, social, and psychic arrangements it responds to, produces, and requires. Both ignorance and acceptance, as labels, are too ready to fix the entangled middle ground that divides prescription from perception and both from practice. Such categories not only assume persons with far flatter, two-dimensional interior spaces than we would demand for treating our own fractious subjectivities. They

---

the true nature of their practical mastery, i.e., learned ignorance (*docta ignorantia*), a mode of practical knowledge not comprising knowledge of its own principles. It follows that this learned ignorance can only give rise to the misleading discourse of a speaker himself misled, ignorant of both the objective truth about his practical mastery (which is that it is ignorant of its own truth) and of the true principle of the knowledge his practical mastery contains." See Pierre Bourdieu, *Outline of a Theory of Practice* (Cambridge: Cambridge University Press, 1977), 19.

sever the imperial dilemmas of a finite "then" in the *passé composé* from a "now" of the decidedly present imperfect. Not least, they assiduously refuse recognition of comparisons, convergences, and accommodations that might compromise and implicate ourselves.

My starting point is elsewhere. Rather than assume that the worlds of empire's agents had clarity in ways ours today do not, I am drawn to the messier, unsettling space that spans knowing and not knowing, good and bad faith, refusal and acceptance, allegiance to and belief in. Such an inquiry might attend to the wide berth of colonial actors whose names historians of the period and region would barely recognize. They would be neither particularly malicious nor sympathetic figures, rather more like those that attracted Du Bois, "not the wicked, but calm, good [women and] men."[19] Nor would this be a matter of telling a tale of an unknown colonial everyman in any sense of the term. I think more of minor figures in major histories: not Van Hoëvell, who led the 1848 demonstration in Batavia described in chapter 3, but Ardesch, who turned against him; or Nauta, who joined the public assembly only to spy on its organizers; or Cantervisscher, who handed out petitions and was later exiled from Java,—or, as in the present chapter, of those expunged from the record like Valck. It might rather stay close to the sensibilities of the everyday—to what pressed on their bodies; what they chose to communicate differently to kin, colleague, and superior; what occupied their feelings; what slipped to the edges of their awareness, erupted, and then escaped their minds.

To do so, I turn to the social space of family and friendship, to the habits of heart and interest of several generations of this not remarkable colonial family of good standing and comfort, if not assured of station and wealth. These are not the Clives and Raffles of British colonial fame, not the Lyautey's, who forged new racist policy in Indochina, or the Van den Boschs, who make up the hagiographies of Dutch colonial good will, or the brunt of moral condemnation.

At *my* center is that rather mediocre member of the Dutch colonial administration, Frans Carl Valck. Born to the well-placed civil servant Frans Gerardus Valck (1799–1842), whose succession of prominent posts kept him in central Java, Frans Carl throughout his life rarely shared a continent, much less a home, with his mother or father. Frans Gerardus, whose own father died in Semarang when he was eight, would take leave of Frans Carl when the latter was but six. Born in the European quarter of Batavia, Frans Carl was sent to elite boarding schools in the Netherlands for most of the first two decades of his life. At twenty-six, he married Susanna Antoinette Lucassen, the twenty-one-year-old daughter of Theodore Lucassen. In 1863 she bore their only child, Susanna Augustus Theodora,

---

[19] W. E. B. Du Bois, *The Souls of Black Folk* (New York: Bantam, 1989), 155.

and died one year after the girl's birth. His second marriage ended abruptly and tragically when he "accidentally" shot his new wife on a hunting trip during their honeymoon. His third, more loveless marriage—to a thirty-nine-year-old woman of lesser social standing than his beloved first wife Susanna—lasted until his death.

It was in the Central Javanese sugar complex of Kemanglen that Theodore Lucassen's fortune was made, and in the Lucassens' extravagant mansion next to the factory that Frans Carl's wife, Susanna Antoinette Lucassen, was born, and in which she and her seven siblings had grown up. It was also where Valck's daughter Suze would return as wife of her cousin (Theodore Francois Lucassen) in 1887 with her first child, while pregnant with her second. She would bear two more while living at Kemanglen where one of her infant children died. This is a family whose extensive kinship ties were woven through the upper social sphere of high-government officials, merchants operating in the global market, and sugar manufacturers, who provided the economic backbone of the mid-nineteenth-century colonial economy.[20]

Still, to read their letters is to witness bodies and minds struggling to leapfrog over most of the population in their midst: landscapes are melancholy or luxuriant yet unpeopled as Javanese, Chinese, and Balinese are bracketed, only sporadically present, in their lettered lives. Far from a panoptic gaze, theirs was a strikingly selective one. Their concerns were fixed on an immediate and distant everyday, a guarded and sequestered cosmopolitan space that spanned the globe, ears perked to events in The Hague and Paris more than to those that one might imagine would command their senses and impinge on them in Java.

Valck's succession of posts spanned the Indies, as did those of many of his school cohort, from Java to Bali to Sumatra and back to Java, before ending in The Hague. It was during his very brief and troubled post as Assistent Resident in 1877–78 in East Sumatra's plantation district of East Sumatra that his career came to a crashing halt. Just months after his arrival, Valck, as we know, was confronted with a series of murders of European planters that he was convinced were the consequence of their own brutal labor policies and coercive tactics. Wholly unfamiliar with the local situation, he poorly judged what consequences would follow if he did not look away. Blocked by the steely silence of the planters, he at-

---

[20] See Roger Knight, "The Sugarmen's Women and the Tensions of Empire," in *Narratives of Colonialism: Sugar, Java, and the Dutch* (Huntington, N.Y.: Nova, 2000), 47–70, esp. 51–54 and his footnotes, where he traces out many of the marital and business links between these families. The Valcks' connections to the Lucassens are excluded from Knight's otherwise rich compilation, in part because the Valck father and son's careers were limited to the Civil Service, and in part because the Valck family did not really enjoy the fortune or renown of the Lucassen father and son.

tended to the rumors of tortured and murdered estate workers and reported what he understood those acts to be—not unreasoned retaliation against physical abuse and expressions of sensible rage.

His reports were unwelcome, inappropriate, and late. Quickly transferred out of Deli, he was dismissed shortly after. Much of the rest of his life was spent composing what seem to have been unsent letters to the Governor-General, by whom he felt betrayed, in a desperate effort to rewrite his moral contract with the colonial administration, to account for his actions, and restore his honor. If we can only give an account of ourselves, as Judith Butler's parse on Nietzsche suggests, when we "are rendered accountable by a system of justice and punishment," life in Deli was that for Valck.[21] Bear in mind, there is no evidence that these letters were ever sent. Nor do we know why he kept so many undated drafts of them. Perhaps they were all along really only meant for himself. If they were sent, Valck never indicates that any were ever answered.

Thinking toward a "Charmless" Colonial History

An arresting phrase appears in the second essay of Nietzsche's *Untimely Meditations*, on "The Uses and Disadvantages of History for Life," coincidentally written in the same year that Valck arrived in Bali. Chiding the feverish turn to history in his own age, Nietzsche urges his reader not to idle in the garden of history, to not shy as historical observers from our "rough and charmless needs and requirements." We must service history, he insists, "only to the extent that history serves life." Methodological insights are packed into those simple phrases. Together, they open to the "untimeliness" he advocates and the comfort zones he so abhors.[22]

Charmlessness was not a recurrent theme to which Nietzsche returned. It is never used again. Still, like so much of his phrasing, it stops the reader short, puts a break on smooth passage, prompts an uneasy recognition— or flat-out denial that the barbed accusation of dulling complacency might be aimed at us. He pierces one's most secure assumptions, most pointedly those that protectively seal stories too easy to tell. Derrida rightly called it a "spurring style" that perforates as it parries.[23]

---

[21] See Judith Butler, *Giving an Account of Oneself* (New York: Fordham University Press, 2005), 10–11, for her rendition of Nietzsche's position as outlined in a *Genealogy of Morals*.

[22] Friedrich Nietzsche, "On the Uses and Disadvantages of History for Life," in *Untimely Meditations*, trans. R. J. Hollingdale (Cambridge: Cambridge University Press, 1996 [1874]), 59.

[23] Jacques Derrida, *Spurs: Nietzsche's Styles* (Chicago: University of Chicago Press, 1979), 41.

Among students of the colonial, charmed accounts take many forms. Some are those with plots we know before they begin: they pit good against evil as easily as they solicit the "protection of white prestige" and a "politics of fear" to explain acts that may range from demonstrations of contemptuous disdain to hideous atrocities. Charmed accounts provide sluggish rubrics and too much slack. They coat complex commitments in generic ideologies and "shared" imaginaries as if people had to do little work with them. Charmed colonial accounts might turn the world upside down, making heroes of less vocal subalterns—or, alternately, redeem hidden heroes among empire's henchmen. Colonial critique provincializes European epistemologies to render them parochial rather than worldly, myopic rather than panoptic, local rather than universal—not common-sensical but strange. But if to charm is to comfort and seduce with almost "magical" grace, to show not a wisp of coercion, what sensibilities would a rough and charmless colonial history track—what would such a history look like now?

It might expose jagged analytic ridges, unsmooth at its bared edges. It might stay close to the out-of-sync, those minor events, the surplus that archives produce in spite of their voiced intent. It might linger over marginalia that neither fits nor coheres. It might dispense with heroes—subaltern or otherwise. As Orwell did so often in his stories, it might turn to the unheralded and unremarked, less to the lurid than to those Europeans confused by their own inappropriate desires and disdain. Evenhandedness would not be a requisite given or goal. Good and evil would be *historical* rather than *transcendent* categories. Such an account might attend to those neither endowed with enough wit, humor, or conscience to warrant a pause or moment to mark. At the risk of irritating an audience and alienating the ready reader, it might subject empire's actors and agents to a different sort of scrutiny that suspends judgment about who, why, and how people played out, in, and circumscribed their cultivated roles.

It is the elusive notion of "untimeliness" that provides some purchase on what Nietzsche might have considered it meant to be charmed. "Untimeliness" is at once a resolute, *critical stance* and a moving target—one no longer deemed critical once it is fixed. It is to look afresh at those analytic decorums of which our communities of interpretation are, as he put it, "rightly proud."[24] No methodological program is offered. Rather, Nietzsche proffers analytic tools for maintaining a distrusting posture. What he does is alert us to attend with suspicion to that which poses as most *timely* of all.[25] The assault is on the sheltering retreat to

[24] Nietzsche, 1996, 60.

[25] For Walter Kaufmann, "untimeliness" is to "go against the grain of one's age"; see Friedrich Nietzsche, *The Gay Science* (New York: Vintage, 1974), 21.

familiar plots.[26] In the case of empire, such an approach might question standard accounts and especially those to which we are most committed: that imperial pursuits can be measured by a relentless quest for knowledge in the pursuit of power—that empire produces its knowable subjects in predictable ways, that psychic space is impervious to or wholly requisitioned by the political regimes that people inhabit. Such honed "answers" that are already authorized may pre-empt harder, more impinging questions. We may instead pursue genealogies of empire in a more fulsome register that join structures of feeling to fields of force in histories of the present of a longer durée.

Knowledge-acquisition is only a piece of what makes empires work. It may abet allegiance or wither it. Blatantly coercive inculcation is not always the name of the imperial game. The force of rule lies in producing affiliations, loyalties, and allegiances among empire's own agents as much as the colonized. Rule by sustained pressure as much as overt violence makes "choices" and commitments—ones that subordinate family attachments to state mandates—difficult but ennobling ones. These were precisely what hundreds of Batavia's "city fathers" railed against when they took to the streets to protest educational policy, as we saw in chapter 3. Sometimes these sentiments depended on inchoate sensibilities, what Raymond Williams saw as beyond the semantic availability of their authors.[27] They shaped what people were *disposed to do*, were inclined to believe, thought they could intuit, or could choose to ignore. Imperial dispositions are composed of *trained habits of attention* channeled through principles of plausibility and rules of relevance. These are politicized cognitions and practices that distinguish sensory overloads from sensible acts.

I broach that disquieted space by asking what it took to live a colonial life, how those who lived off empire imagined themselves within it, what structured attachments heightened or dulled their sensory regimes, what interior space they inhabited, what distance might have existed between the "feel" of living off empire and what imperial states employed those in their service to do. Du Bois spells out the task mercilessly, urging "unusual points of vantage" to explore "souls undressed and from the back and side," and the "working of [white] entrails"—"white folk" "hung, bound by their own binding."[28]

---

[26] As Paul de Man put it, Nietzsche's critical historian refuses the "sheltering inwardness of history," as he performs "an act of critical judgment directed against himself." Paul de Man, *Blindness and Insight* (New York: Oxford University Press, 1971), 149.

[27] Raymond Williams, *Marxism and Literature* (Oxford: Oxford University Press, 1977), 134.

[28] W. E. B. Du Bois, "The Souls of White Folk," in *Darkwater: Voices from within the Veil* (Mineola, N.Y.: Dover, 1999 [1920]), 17; idem (1982), 29.

One might rightly argue that historical ethnography is unsuited to such a task. Such work is better left to those for whom interiorities are the grist of their work, to Marguerite Duras, who grew up in the French Empire and inhabited its seedy margins; to Nadine Gordimer and John M. Coetzee, who knew from the inside the beastly quality of empire and the fears of its white settlers.[29] There are the Dutch colonial women novelists like Madelon Székely-Lulofs, who spent her childhood in Aceh and who later, in the 1930s, as a rubber planter's wife in East Sumatra, so viscerally captured the confinements and constraints of a colonial life in petty anxieties and agitated boredoms of the everyday.[30] Or perhaps, it should just be left to their children, to the piercing fiction of someone like Hella Haasse, who was raised and played in the glare and shadows of empire, to those children who knew and did not know what they overheard, who unknowingly witnessed the shaky assurances that all was well, the whispered racial slurs, the empathies and disregards of their mothers and fathers.[31]

Such novels raise hard questions they do not purport to answer, ones that historical ethnography is obliged to address: How can we know when warped and despairing interiorities are empire's political effect? Are they arbitrary, tethered, or only loosely hinged to regimes of politics? Was Valck's daughter, Suze, crushed by too much awareness, or rendered stupid, as Avital Ronell might argue, by a cultural "lesson plan," in which her efforts were expended in concerted distractions that kept the Javanese world around her at bay?[32] Or could she really not see it all? How much do the conditions of empire produce stupefied serene states as well as racial anxieties, or something that uneasily combines both ways of not knowing and obliquely knowing at the same time?

---

[29] See especially Marguerite Duras, *Seawall* (New York: Harper and Row, 1952); Nadine Gordimer, *Something Out There* (London: Cape, 1984); and J. M. Coetzee, *Waiting for the Barbarians* (New York: Viking, 1980), and *Disgrace* (New York, Viking, 1999.)

[30] Among Székely-Lulof's many works, *De andere wereld* (Amsterdam: Elsevier, 1934) provides the rawest account, one of her few novels not translated into other languages.

[31] See Hella Haasse, *Heren van de thee* (Amsterdam: Querido, 1992), a much-acclaimed account of the real-life generations of a family enterprise, in which the protagonist appears as a man so obsessed with his colonial personal dream of success that he neglects to notice what is most dear around him—his children depart and his wife is slowly driven to despair and death. See also her *Sleuteloog* (Amsterdam: Querido, 2002), a disquieting account of a woman's colonial memories sealed in a family chest, to which she has lost the key and which, when finally opened, she finds empty. See Henk Maier, "Escape from the Green and Gloss of Java: Hella S. Haasse and Indies Literature," *Indonesia* 77 (April 2004): 79–107, for a thoughtful treatment of Haasse's disposition toward the colonial past. I thank him for sharing this latter book with me.

[32] On stupidity as an achieved condition, see Avital Ronell, *Stupidity* (Urbana and Chicago: University of Illinois Press, 2002), esp. 3–60, for a brilliant treatment of the subject.

As ethnographers and social historians, our attempts to describe that psychic and affective space often turn to caricature and invariably fall short. When David Cannadine purports to answer "how the British saw their empire," his stick figures are bereft of any interior space—theirs is a naturalized adherence to a class hierarchy brought with them.[33] Ronald Hyam's survey of "the British [sexual] experience" across "their empire" stays riveted on the sexual—affective dispositions are not broached further.[34] Johannes Fabian's subtle study of reason and unreason among European explorers of Central Africa comes closer when he argues that "bliss and despair, elation and depression often were close companions" that conditioned colonial knowledge-production as it engendered a "struggle for self-composure."[35] Fabian's actors are frontline explorers focused on the acquisition of scientific knowledge; it is what they were there to do. Many more of colonialism's agents were not.

On the Politics of Disregard

> A person can live in self-deception, which does not mean that he does not have *abrupt awakenings* to cynicism or to good faith, but which implies a constant and *particular style of life*.
> —Jean-Paul Sartre, *Being and Nothingness*

Imperial dispositions are at once ways of living in and responding to, ways of being and seeing oneself, ways of knowing that shape which sentiments are activated, and the affective states which circumscribe what one can know. Rather than the studied surveillance and panoptic gaze that have come to characterize the collective posture of empire's practitioners, I am drawn to something else: to "skittish seeing" and the adverted gaze, to acts of ignoring rather than ignorance, to inattention, to the shock of recognition, to Sartre's "abrupt awakenings" and the quick circumspections into which they fold.[36] Heidegger identified one register of "disclosure" as an "evasive turning-away."[37]

---

[33] David Cannadine, *Ornamentalism: How the British Saw Their Empire* (Oxford: Oxford University Press, 2001).

[34] Ronald Hyam, *Empire and Sexuality: The British Experience* (Manchester: Manchester University Press, 1990).

[35] Johannes Fabian, *Out of Our Minds: Reason and Madness in the Exploration of Central Africa* (Berkeley: University of California Press, 2000), 94–95.

[36] On "skittish seeing" and "irregular glances" that "throw the eyes into . . . confusion," see James Elkins, *The Object Stares Back: On the Nature of Seeing* (New York: Harcourt, 1996), esp. chap. 3, "Looking Away, and Seeing Too Much," 87.

[37] Martin Heidegger, *Being and Time* (New York: Harper and Row, 1962), 175.

Most importantly, imperial dispositions are marked by a negative space: *that from which those with privilege and standing could excuse themselves.* I call this ability to excuse oneself from wrought engagement, this refusal to witness and the almost legal legitimacy it confers, the *well-tended conditions of disregard.* One might consider the blinding near-sightedness of circumscribed community that sets out the proper *limits of care* and why it makes ethical sense for a community *not* to concern itself more broadly.[38] Ethics are not absent; rather they provide *exemptions* from what one need *not* do. To what extent this requires sanctioned igno-rance, self-deception, "cognitive dissonance," or the securely unflinching constraints of habit is not a transhistorical issue.[39] The conditions of dis-regard are located in the implicit meanings people assign and reassign to their own acts and agency. They manifest in how fully the macropolitics of a moment deepen or deflect the ethics of a self, train habits of atten-tion, and harness the affective strands and strains of a life.

Frans Carl Valck attended to some of the space in which he dwelled, but he did not always do so. His assessments of those Indies people that lived around him were subject to caricature more than insight, both at-tenuated attention and studied disregard. On the north Bali coast where he was posted for four years between 1872 and 1876, just prior to leav-ing for Sumatra, his final report as Assistent Resident of Boeleleng to his successor marks acute differences in attentiveness and analytic style. There is no temporal lag between how he sought to describe individual Balinese (on whose alliances he depended), and what he thought was rea-sonable to parse as a generic Balinese character. In treating the latter, he mocked their "semblances of sincerity," their untrustworthiness, their im-placable pleasure in boldfaced lies. As a subtext heading in the left mar-gin, he underlines the phrase: "Not to be trusted, is an unabashed liar" and notes in the text that that only "fear can make them control their pas-sions and desires."[40] Here Valck's "insights" prepared for his successor and his superiors rehearse clunky, scripted sterotypes and narratives.

But these scripts are not all he conveys. They are followed by incisive por-traits of persons who can be trusted; subtle familiarity with the hierarchy among the Balinese elite; awareness of the "transparent maneuvers" of Dutch officials who hide behind the native rulers; of native rulers who are maligned but are yet to be trusted; of individual Balinese of unsavory char-

---

[38] A good example is prescribed by Marvin Olasky, who coined the terms for George Bush's manifesto for "compassionate conservatism." See Marvin Olasky, *Compassionate Conservatism* (New York: Free Press, 2000).

[39] Leon Festinger, *A Theory of Cognitive Dissonance* (Stanford: Stanford University Press, 1957).

[40] CBG FA Valck-Lucassen, No. 415 (circa December 1875), Frans Carl Valck, "Nota voor mijnen opvolger: De Boelelenger."

acter. These are not just discrepant assessments; stylized social types remain resilient and unperturbed by what he otherwise seems (partially) to know.

In psychology, self-delusion and self-deception describe a temporal space of uncertainty, with the inference "that the person 'knows' and 'does not know' at the same time."[41] Self-deception, then, is an assessment about the self-knowledge of others. It is also an evaluation that may be made about one's own past actions but not made in situ, not in the active voice, about one's present self. Others describe it as "a suspension in the normal objective interest in reality," what one feels and believes "at the edge of awareness."[42] In this frame, self-deceptive constructions are "not judgments of reality" but actions done unknowingly to convince oneself.[43] Sartre rejects both the Freudian frame and the divided self on which it rests. We constantly believe and disbelieve the same propositions simultaneously, he argues. Rather than acting ignorantly, "We must know the truth very exactly, in order to conceal it" more carefully from ourselves.[44]

Psychology and philosophy treat self-deception as part of the human condition, as a mechanism that is activated in much the same way, regardless of time or place. Historians, on the other hand, might be expected to treat it as a way of acting in specific political situations. Historian Paul Veyne, for example, begins his *Did the Greeks Believe Their Myths?* with what he identifies as a basic human dilemma: "How is it possible to half-believe, or believe in contradictory things?" "What is going on in our minds" when we do so?[45] But Veyne's account is *in* history, not a rendering of historically and politically located half-beliefs. In the end, he

[41] Theodore Sarbin, "On Self Deception," in *The Clever Hans Phenomenon: Communication with Horses, Whales, Apes, and People*, ed. Thomas Seboek and Robert Rosenthal (New York: New York Academy of Sciences, 1981), 224.

[42] David Shapiro, "On the Psychology of Self-Deception," *Social Research* 63 (3) (Fall 1996): 792–93.

[43] Freudian understandings of repression often guide this analysis, posing self-deception as a state in which multiple subsystems of conscious and unconscious beliefs compete.

[44] Jean-Paul Sartre, "Self-Deception," in *Existentialism: From Dostoevsky to Sartre*, ed. Walter Kaufman (New York: Meridian, 1975), 302 . Sartre makes the point about simultaneity explicitly: "Nor is this a matter of two different moments of temporality which would permit us to reestablish the semblance of duality, but the unitary structure of one and the same project" (*Being and Nothingness*, trans. Hazel Barnes [New York: Citadel, 1966], 89). Akeel Bilgrami, *Self-Knowledge and Resentment* (Cambridge, Mass.: Harvard University Press, 2006), 278, makes a compelling distinction in understanding self-deception as discord between one's disposition "that leads to behavior" and one's sincerely avowed commitments (on the condition that one sees commitments as beliefs and desires).

[45] Paul Veyne, *Did the Greeks Believe in Their Myths? An Essay on the Constitutive Imagination* (Chicago: University of Chicago Press, 1983), xi, 2.

retreats: there are "only different programs of truth" (different "feelings" of truth), not bad faith (*mauvaise foi*).[46] For Veyne the demonstration of sincerity is the test that distinguishes good from bad faith.[47]

But as Sartre again argues, sincerity might not be opposed to self-deception but an active feature of it.[48] Men like Frans Carl Valck were not insincere in their belief in the principles of empire and in their condemnations of some of its personnel and practices. Sometimes the contradictions were harder to bear, particularly during those life moments when he at once believed in, lived by, and despised the principles themselves. Valck might better be seen as someone caught in the bind of being as Bakhtin remarked in another context, "a person [who] never coincides with himself."[49]

Historian Thomas Haskell works differently with "self-deception" to ask why abolitionists in the mid-nineteenth-century United States felt unobliged to go earlier to the aid of suffering slaves. Self-deception is not at issue, he argues, because they "did not need to hide anything from themselves." What they shared was an "ethical shelter afforded . . . by *our* society's conventions of moral responsibility," one that "allows *us* to confine our humane acts to a fraction of suffering humanity without feeling that we have thereby intended [to do so]."[50] Like Veyne, Haskell slips back and forth between subjects as well as between the verbal tenses of his argument: it is "us" and "our" society as much as the abolitionists that are at issue. The moral imagination is subject to the same constraints. The relationship between macropolity and moral disposition goes unaddressed.

The ability to know and not know, to believe yet not believe in, begs for a genealogy of its own. Hannah Arendt and Jacques Derrida both hint at an historical trajectory of dissimulation and self-deception on which

---

[46] Ibid., 21.

[47] Ibid. Veyne's call upon Foucault's regimes of truth may send him astray. As an analytic, "regimes of truth" is not easily mobilized to deal with the ambiguous space of sincerity and the "arduous work," as Lionel Trilling contended, that goes into it.

[48] As Sartre writes, "sincerity presents itself as *a demand* and consequently is not a state" ([1966], 313). Webb Keane casts the concept of sincerity as "interactive" and "inseparable from some kind of judgment." If sincerity entails "arduous effort" and "judgment," there can be no inner self to which it is true. Sincerity, like politeness and tolerance might rather be seen as that which is performed, as Keane sees it, or, as I would argue, labored on, a reining in of those sensibilities that it harnesses and subdues. See Lionel Trilling, *Sincerity and Authenticity* (Cambridge, Mass.: Harvard University Press, 1972), 6, and Webb Keane, "Sincerity, 'Modernity,' and the Protestants," *Cultural Anthropology* (2002): 75.

[49] Mikhail Bakhtin, *Problems of Dostoevsky's Poetics* (Minneapolis: University of Minnesota Press, 1987), 327.

[50] Thomas Haskell, "Capitalism and the Origins of Humanitarian Sensibility, Part I" *American Historical Review* 90 (2): 352.

modern polities increasingly depend.[51] For Arendt democratic conditions produce a "modern art of self-deception" in which "deception without self-deception is well-nigh impossible."[52] Arendt's attention to the modern raises a critical question. If the modern produces self-deception as one of its political requirements, and colonialism is the "underside of the modern," then are imperial dispositions the template for modern politics?[53] Or, as Sartre might have put it, do imperial formations *require* specific "procedures" of bad faith that cultivate scrutiny and disregard?[54]

Before returning to Valck, one final formulation strikes me as resonant for thinking across imperial contexts in Valck and Nietzsche's time and our imperial present today: this is Georg Simmel's understanding of the German expression "*Lebensluge.*"[55] In common usage, *Lebensluge* translates as "living a lie" or a "sham existence." But the more literal translation provides more analytic traction. *Lebensluge* is also translated as a "vital lie," enacted when a person is "in need of deceiving himself with regard to his capacities, even in regard to his feelings, and who cannot do

---

[51] See Hannah Arendt, "Truth and Politics," in *Between Past and Future: Eight Exercises in Political Thought* (New York: Viking, 1961), 227–64, and the discussion of Arendt in Jacques Derrida, "The History of the Lie: Prolegomena," in *Without Alibi* (Stanford: Stanford University Press, 2002), 28–70. See also Hannah Arendt, "Lying in Politics: Reflections on the Pentagon Papers," *New York Review of Books* 17 (8) (November 18, 1971). Hannah Arendt, *On Revolution* (New York, Penguin: 1990), esp. 94–109, provides a fuller treatment of hypocrisy: "The duplicity of the hypocrite is different from the duplicity of the liar and the cheat. The duplicity [of the hypocrite] boomerangs back upon himself, and he is no less a victim of his mendacity than those whom he set out to deceive. . . . The hypocrite is too ambitious; not only does he want to appear virtuous before others, he wants to convince himself" (99).

[52] Arendt (1961), 256.

[53] Enrique Dussel, *The Underside of Modernity: Apel, Ricoeur, Rorty, Taylor, and the Philosophy of Liberation*, ed. Eduardo Mendieta (Atlantic Highlands, N.J.: Humanities, 1996).

[54] If they do, they are not the only political formations that do so. Tvetzan Todorov argues that totalitarian states require those who live in them to adopt an Orwellian doublethink to get through the everyday. Doublethink, for Todorov, is *mauvaise foi* on a macropolitical scale: "To know and not to know, to be conscious of complete truthfulness while telling *carefully constructed lies*, to hold simultaneous two opinions which are canceled out, knowing them to be contradictory and believing both of them, to use logic against logic, to repudiate morality while laying claim to it . . ." For Todorov it is a conscious and intentional technique, a subterfuge that "allows you to dispense with the law of noncontradiction, *to pretend* there is coherence where incoherence reigns," that which "conditions reason not to notice." "Doublethink" lets the person off the hook. It is what insidious state projects do to people. Pretense underwrites his argument; knowing and not knowing is a conscious way of getting by, a weapon of the weak and a technology of the strong, not what "good and calm" people perform on themselves. See Todorov, "Dialogism and Schizophrenia," in *An Other Tongue*, ed. Alfred Artaega (Durham, N.C.: Duke University Press, 1994), 205.

[55] Georg Simmel, "Knowledge, Truth, and Falsehood in Human Relations," in *The Sociology of Georg Simmel* (New York: Free Press, 1950), 310.

without superstition about gods and men, in order to maintain his life and his potentialities."[56]

Might imperial dispositions indeed have at their core such a "vital lie"? This is not the colossal lie that Arendt describes for Eichmann and the political engineers of Nazi Germany.[57] Rather it is a "lie for life," not about religious gods but secular ones, about political myths, empire's "noble" projects, as Valck called them, and the do-good deeds of those who carried them out. Like conscience, it "tells us to whom we shall and shall not do what."[58] The latter is how Claudia Koonz defines Nazi conscience, that which sets the parameters of one's community of shared moral obligation. For Koonz conscience is derived from knowledge ("con" and "science"), joined to the institutional and conceptual structures of propaganda that prepare people to accept those categories. Her analysis stops short of accounting for the twisted lived psychic spaces of an ambiguous embrace like those of a Valck.

HISTORY IN A MINOR KEY

The phrase that followed Valck through the colonial archives and his unillustrious career was that he was "neither an incompetent man nor one without means." The double negative is telling. The assessment was deliberately circumspect, a product of the protection his connections afforded and the dishonor he and those close to him left discreetly unmentioned before and after his death.

Valck's letters make us privy to the ravages of a torn heart. But estrangement and dis-memberment were not his alone. Of good soul and good education, he was neither blind to the severities of Dutch rule nor squarely within its fold. In 1876 when newly posted as Assistent Resident in Deli, he proudly took his new assignment to be a "promotion," a vote of confidence from Governor-General van Lansberge, who had transferred him from the remote and, by then, less politically turbulent Bali coast.

But it was a set-up for failure from the start. Three of the most hotly contested issues in colonial governance of the time were being debated in Deli in precisely the year that Valck arrived: the creation of a "Coolie Ordinance" that would bind workers to three-year contracts and legalize indenture when slavery had just been abolished; the planters' stonewalling of a government investigation of severe maltreatment and high mortality

---

[56] Ibid., 310.

[57] Hannah Arendt, *Eichmann in Jerusalem: A Report on the Banality of Evil* (New York: Penguin, 1992).

[58] Claudia Koonz, *The Nazi Conscience* (Cambridge, Mass.: Harvard University Press, 2003), 1.

of workers on the estates; and the creation of long-lease, seventy-year contracts between local Malay sultans and the estate companies that gave the planters unparalleled license to take over what was deemed "vacant land."[59]

Each of these issues entailed theft (of land); cover-up (of tortured workers and bribed sultans); bribery (of local rulers); and deception (of Malay farmers). Coming from an outpost in Bali, Valck could have not possibly mastered the situation or known who was paying off whom, which Malay rulers he needed to ally and whose demands he could ignore. What his job demanded was submission to the planters' "state within a state," as had his obsequious, and perhaps more savvy, predecessor, Hallewijn. After ensuring that Valck was ousted, the leading estate owners created the Deli Planters' Association the following year, a powerful lobby that was to remain for another seventy-five years the de facto arbitrator of wages, with a monopoly on the tobacco trade and jurisdiction over and financing of basic services on the Sumatra's East Coast.

Valck stepped into what he later characterized as an untenable situation, what his superior described as a *"not difficult"* job, one that was *"neither unusual nor particularly demanding."*[60] Valck insisted on the opposite, that the conditions were extremely difficult, and that he was offered no help by the Resident who was formally in charge. He was sent to clean it up, he argued, precisely because there was nothing about Deli that was "normal" at all.[61]

In the grim confidences he conferred on his *"dearest friend Levyssohn,"* then General Secretary to the Governor-General (and on other *"high placed"* persons with whom he spoke), he described the abuses of European planters, named names, and accused them of killing "in cold blood." Begging his friend's intervention, he insisted on his own self-control, that he did not write *"in a moment of agitation,"* that he was *"totally calm but utterly indignant. Everyday I see more much that needs to be cleaned up."*[62] But in the letter he was to write and rewrite to the Governor-General after his dismissal, he had much more to say. He professed to have heard while still in Bali that the Chinese workers arriving in Deli were the *"dregs of that nation."* Still he saw no reason to *"believe*

---

[59] Each of these debates and resolutions has been well documented in Deli's historiography. See H. J. Bool, *De landbouwconcessies in de Residentie Oostkust van Sumatra* (Utrecht, 1903); In English, see Karl Pelzer, *Planter and Peasant: Colonial Policy and the Agrarian Struggle in East Sumatra, 1863–1947* (Leiden: KITLV, 1978); and Jan Breman, *Taming the Coolie Beast: Plantation Society and the Colonial Order in Southeast Asia* (Calcutta: Oxford University Press, 1989).

[60] AN, 18 June 1877, no. 6281x, Report of the Minister of the *Binnenlandsbestuur* to Governor-General van Lansberge.

[61] CBG FA, no. 420, Valck's draft of a letter to the Governor-General, n.d.

[62] KITLV, Collectie Westerse handschriften, H, 28 October 1876, F. C. Valck to Norman Levyssohn.

nearly everything the Europeans claimed, while the coolie went with no rights at all."[63] He argued that no one but he dared to apply the existing laws. He held that truthfulness had no place in Deli and that "*good faith was not kept in sight.*" Most insistently, he argued that he had been convicted without being heard, without recourse to defense. Appealing to his Excellency's "*sense of justice,*" he insisted that upon the knowledge Valck would provide, "*the verdict*" against him would be retracted. It was not.

What kind of critique is possible when you are positioned in the center of a system of power on which your livelihood, future, and family depend? How to imagine his position and portray his choices without lapsing into an apologia for them? In Valck's case the distinction at the moment was clear: between a good state and corrupt men, between a moral project and immoral people. But that too was to change. He knew he would be "*thwarted, duped, and slandered from all sides.*" Still, he trusted the Governor-General to back his efforts to expose "*the real situation to the highest placed people in the Indies.*"

But who was to be trusted? He did not want his condemnation to become public. It was only for certain ears, to protect "*our name.*" Selective reportage proved to be a poor option and Valck paid dearly for it. His dismissal was honorable, thanks only to the intervention of his well-placed friend Norman Levyssohn and his Uncle van Rees, both on the *Raad van Indië*. His uncle offered to help him get a post at the colonial depot in the Netherlands if he "*still felt so inclined.*"[64] He must not have been, for Valck was to spend the last thirteen years of a desultory life in a single labor: composing draft after draft, sometimes scribbled, sometimes excruciatingly neat, of that unsent letter accounting for his actions in the dim hope of redeeming his honor.

AN IMPERFECT INTERVAL

Let us turn back to 1872, to the letter written to his young daughter, Suze, on his way from Europe to take up his post in Bali. It conveys the promise of a different future, penned before the transfer to Sumatra that so abruptly ended his career. It was one of many he wrote regularly and without fail to this, his only offspring, then nine years old. He writes to her en route to the Indies, while she is to spend most of her youth in boarding schools and with her grandparents in the Dutch countryside and in The Hague. I have called him a distressed father because he writes knowing that the next time they meet, Suze will no longer be the girl-child

---

[63] CBG FA, no. 420, Valck's draft of a letter to the Governor-General, n.d.

[64] CBG FA, no. 379, 14 March 1879, Van Rees to F. C. Valck.

he left, for his post will keep him at least seven years in the Indies, 4,000 miles away. He knows and repeatedly tells her that he will have become an old man and she will have transformed into an unrecognizable young woman who he had known but briefly as his little girl. Such separation defined their early relationship and would continue to mark most of their lives. On a ship to Bali in February 1872 he writes in French:

> *My dear Suze, when we crossed the Suez Canal, I was very sad because it was as if I was so much further from you and from all that I love and that a door has been closed behind me. Ah! If I could remain in Europe how happy I would have been; but this is not possible and I console myself with the thought that you very much love me and that you will be so good and sweet that when I return I will find in you a young woman who will make me forget that I will have passed so many years far from her.*

But it is not really clear how much he actually missed that staid Dutch life. He loves that his thatched-roof house (that he tells her in at least three separate letters) lets in the breeze and fresh air so much better than tiles. He cannot hide his pleasure at having his servant, the "*loyal Ketjik,*" and the servant's wife, Mina, there to greet him and available at his beck and call. With delight he tells her of getting caught in a storm and having to wade through rivers, his hands blistered from helping to carrying his affairs, his pants hiked up and the trek along the shore in moonlight "*that was not disagreeable*" as his naked feet sunk in the cool, wet sand. But "*don't think for an instant that I did not think of you, my dear; several times I asked myself what you were doing at grandma's while I was here.*"[65]

In his earliest letters, he carefully leaves her world untouched by his. He creates a picture of his movements for her entertainment and pleasure, in the manner of a fairy tale, and seems to do so for both their sakes. In March, a month after settling on the Bali coast, he writes playfully "congratulating" her that she has become

> *princess of the country of which I am to be named king, or, as one says in this country, Radja. Now I would like to invite you as well as [Grand] Maman, Suzanne and all the household to come live in my palace and to admire its splendors; unfortunately, it is so old that it has been condemned but a new one will soon be built. Would you like to come when it is finished?*

But of course Valck is no king. He is a Controleur Second Class, a lowly civil servant stationed on the north Bali coast. He is there decades after three

---

[65] CBG, FA, 16 June 1872, F. C. Valck to Susanna Valck.

successive Dutch efforts to wrest control of the strategic port and to displace its charismatic leader, the Raja of Buleleng. It was in the 1846 expedition, the military assault ostensibly provoked by Balinese ransacking a wrecked cargo boat, that Dutch forces first bombed the royal palace. It was on that very Buleleng coast in 1840 where an earlier ship had been plundered—the ship that had carried the first sugar combines that Valck's father-in-law Theodore Lucassen's had converted for commercial production. More than two decades in shambles, this besieged structure is what Valck refers to as his palace, not in ruins because it was "*so old*" but because it had been destroyed by successive Dutch mortar attacks and was now condemned.[66]

Valck regales Suze with his importance, his "*new friendship*" with a Balinese princess who owes him a favor and who he will ask to weave a gold-threaded silk cloth for her new dress. In the first year, he appeals to what he hopes will interest a small girl, describes his house, his menagerie of chickens and rabbits, and his dear dog, Marie. He tells her to let grandma know that he is in superb health. Six months later, his fairy tale format fades with his long illness and his outlook is worn and worse:

> *To have the wings of a bird so I could escape my kingdom and come to embrace you just for a moment and to see all the family. Perhaps you wouldn't recognize me, since my illness I have become completely bald. But if you can wait a little until my hair grows back you won't be too shocked to see me. The only thing is I'm becoming so fat I barely could catch up to you running. Do you remember when we played hide and seek in the woods?*

He has never mentioned the prison but in a letter a year later he writes that it directly faces his house. He treats the prisoners well, he tells her, with enough to eat. There are no attempts at escape. Unlike his predecessor, he forbids smoking opium, which he claims his charges are wont to do all day. And then in the next paragraph, he reminds her to be good, that it is men and boys that rule in the world, that women and girls do not command but obey (an allusion to her fits of temper), reminding them both perhaps that one can accomplish as much through gentleness as violence, as did her sweet-souled, long-dead mother.

PATHOS AND POLITICS IN COLONIAL JAVA

For students of European bourgeois culture, the sedentary and sentient comforts that brick homes, stable, circumscribed family life, and privacy

---

[66] See Adrian Vickers, *Bali: A Paradise Created* (Sydney: Penguin, 1989), 28–32, on the intensity of the Balinese defense.

allowed is captured by Peter Gay in his many volumes on the bourgeois experience. It is most notably described in his book on Arthur Schnitzler that he calls not the biography of a man but "the biography of a class."[67] For Gay, Schnitzler is not a "representative" of bourgeois respectability and prosperity, but a participant-observer and witness to it. He is reliable in part because he writes about it (in his diary); participates in a privileged, domestic coziness (and requisite conflict with his father); enjoys a childhood of privacy; and remains content with limited movements from his beloved Vienna despite easily traversing a contained cosmopolitan world of European capitals. He is disdainful of (aristocratic) duels, self-reflective about distinctions and the entrapments of class.

Not least, as Gay underscores, Schnitzler was part of a class for which the "paradigm of domesticity" was achieved with an unprecedented intensity, "idealized as never before."[68] Some of these features are resonant with the sort of upper crust of Dutch colonial elite families, like those of the Lucassens and Valcks. In Dutch colonial history, too, domesticity and stability often have been viewed as highly valued in such families. Attainment of that rootedness and a sense of belonging were what they were thought to strive for, what their attentiveness to comportment, decorum, and dress were about.[69]

But a major difference sets off the Valcks and Lucassens and the thousands of families that followed similar itineraries of Gay's portrait: their participation in the life and labor of empire, what it did to the value they placed on domesticity, epistolary relations, and family connections. If "unsettledness" is a marker of modern sensibilities, as Marshall Berman tells us, then minor figures like Valck may have epitomized that sense of the world in the transient lives that imperial careers foisted upon them.[70]

The geopolitical transience of empire, (so removed from Gay's concerns) Gay, shaped the sentiments they harbored, the estrangements they weathered, and the ethics of their lives. Both confirming and contrasting that "paradigm of domesticity," the Valck and Lucassen family letters suggest something else: that nineteenth-century colonialisms thrived on constant movement and long-lapsed connections as they repeatedly reproduced

[67] Peter Gay, *Schnitzler's Century: The Making of Middle-Class Culture, 1815–1914* (New York: Norton, 2002), xix.

[68] Ibid., 43.

[69] For a slightly later period, see Frances Gouda, *Dutch Culture Overseas: Colonial Practice in the Netherlands Indies, 1900–1942* (Amsterdam: Amsterdam University Press, 1995); and my *Race and the Education of Desire: Foucault's History of Sexuality and the Colonial Order of Things* (Durham, N.C.: Duke University Press, 1995), esp. "Cultivating Bourgeois Bodies and Racial Selves," 95–136.

[70] Marshall Berman, *All That is Solid Melts into Air: The Experience of Modernity* (New York: Penguin, 1982).

fractured family relations, distorted sentimental structures, and estranged lives. These were not features aberrant to such bourgeois family relations, not exceptions to their otherwise firmly placed and in-place domestic arrangements, but constitutive elements. These were animated by the wider movements of capital investments, new requirements of a consolidating state apparatus, and new adaptations fitted to them.

The colonial permeates their lives. The letters course through colonial concerns, at times absentmindedly yet in vital ways. Still, *empire is the watermark of these relations*. Somehow they always return to an uncle just returned from Java, a niece marrying the son of a former colonial officer, an inadequate pension, a bolt of cloth lost in voyage, a tobacco or sugar stock that crashed, a squabble that endures continental divides. Not least, they offer a disquieting engagement and uncertain empathy. The closed-circuit social worlds of Suze and her cousins render it difficult for us to make the stretch. In fact, they instill an aversive distaste for their cosmopolitan leanings that so circumvented the people that hovered at their center and that they pushed to the margins.

Nor do these letters instill us with what Carlo Ginzburg celebrates as "the warmth of the narrator's intimate glance."[71] For so many of their missives only brush an interior space. Intimacies are styled and scripted as well. If the goal of self-deception is, as Sartre held, *to put oneself out of reach (from oneself)*, then Frans Carl and especially his daughter were well schooled in its arts. With their tightly constrained vision and muted interior space, theirs is a highly selective regard, both with respect to themselves and to the persons and places around them.

Honor and Shame

Suze's letters make up most of what Valck chose to preserve, along with his will, some correspondence with friends, a lengthy report on Bali, his account of his part in a duel for which he was reprimanded by the government. And folded within these uneven traces of a life, taking up the other bulk of his personal archive and obsession in retirement, were the several hundred pages of double folio foolscap paper containing three carefully scripted drafts—undated, crossed-out, and annotated—of an unsent letter to the Governor-General. In format, these are belabored, careful, and, at moments, full of rage. None note the place from which he wrote them (most likely from The Hague and Arnhem where he "retired"). None have a date. Nor we do we know whether it is to Governor-

---

[71] Carlo Ginzburg, John Tedeschi, Anne C. Tedeschi, "Micohistory: Two or Three Things I Know about It," *Critical Inquiry* 20 (1) (Autumn 1993): 10–35.

General van Lansberge to which he imagined they would be sent or to F. s'Jacobs, who assumed that position in 1881.

Frans Carl's letters were written to Suze, but were as much for himself and, when she was still a small girl, for those relatives that would share and read them aloud to her, and later, when she was grown, that she would pass on to them. His letters are hungry for her confidences (*"tell me the names of your favorite playmates"*), testimony to his father love (*"I only chide you because I love you so"*), and bear witness to his fatherly attention/surveillance (*"I note that your handwriting is less careful than usual"*). Others insist on evidence of his fatherly sacrifice (*"think of how much more I will earn for you and for us if I say just two more years"*) and thoughtful deeds (*"I sent you a bolt of raw silk and for your sweet cousin, too"*). In each of them he is watching himself as father, looking over the shoulder of those reading his letters to her, watching himself watched by his superiors and by those colonized subjects around him. In this multifocal gaze he watches his world brim with possibility and halt with failure.

If the "peculiar sensation" of an imposed "double-consciousness" is, as Du Bois held, the fate of those subject to a racialized identity, and is what Eduardo Glissant described those who endure a "schizoid self," it was also something that middling colonizers like Valck shared, as well.[72] Relations of power insure that this "double-consciousness" of ruler and ruled are not commensurate. But some features of doubling and dependence—as Hegel, Orwell, and Nadine Gordimer in her trenchant parody of "something out there" note—are resonant. Franz Carl's letters were self-conscious exercises that sometimes collapsed his bracketed worlds. In them he fashioned a "plausible" self: a promising and honorable civil servant; a cultivated man of knowledge; a dedicated, protective, and disciplining father.

Erupting between these selves—punctuated with apologies for too much emoting, what he calls an *"excess of sadness,"* and too much display (*"please forgive me Suze for my last letter in which I should have contained myself better"*)—were acerbic asides, attempts at humor, the inadvertent slip of a lonely, depressed and partly delusional man. He wrote from everywhere—ships, verandas, on his lap—of his sumptuous pleasure in receiving and reading whatever she wrote, describing in close detail his posture, attire, even the slippers he wore when he read them, as well as the color, shape, and compartments of his desk.

He wrote after what he called *"excruciatingly boring"* official visits to local Balinese royalty, after ceremonies he described as mere *"farces,"* in

[72] W. E. B. Du Bois (1982), 3; Eduardo Glissant, *Caribbean Discourse: Selected Essays* (Charlottesville: University of Virginia Press, 1989), x.

which he was obliged to play a part. Self-loathing and despair are always there. Dismayed at his increasing bulk, he recounts to her his need to order new horses from Makassar because the small ones in Bali could not bear his excessive weight. At other times he would write in stillness— when he seemed barely able to move from one room to the next, from his bed to his office, having not left his thatched residence for entire days. He wrote in anticipation of a fever, fending off depression, weighted down with a too-heavy evening meal. He wrote about his dogs but rarely about the people that he met. He wrote about the prison cook's young daughter who reminded him of her and who made sure that his fifteen dogs—these, along with his firearm, were kept for protection—did not get in the way of his veranda meals. Only the couple who work for him have names. And unlike the loveless stories in Dutch colonial novels of the time (that rarely missed an opportunity to hint at the secreted concubinary arrangements of European men and native women) in these heavily screened letters to his schoolgirl daughter there were—unsurprisingly—no hints of a housemaid/mistress at all.

And spliced between these spaces was always one just for, and about, Suze, triple declarations of his love and interest in her life. He asks about her dolls (*"tell me your favorites"*); her pets; schoolwork; and friends (*"do remind me of their names"*). Other times he wrote filled with tough love, disappointed at reports of her misbehavior, with presents promised if she worked harder and took more care with her sloppy prose. And to the daughter whose penmanship and grammar in French were strained, he would devise multilanguage games for them to *"play"*: he was to respond to her in English, she to him in French, and he to her in German or Dutch. She ignored them. He wrote to her of his love for her, her deceased mother, and his most adored Holland, with pride and self-mockery at his increasingly miserly ways (*"you can't imagine what an* avare [miser] *I have become"*). As his time in Bali wore less well on him (*"I don't feel very curious to travel here,"* he told her, *"[for] first of all I've voyaged enough in life but also the Indies' countryside is always the same"*).

And eventually, he wrote of his outrage at a colonial system into which he was born, for which he was groomed, from which he profited and was eventually condemned, banished to the Netherlands he had so sorely missed. From there he never left (though upon first returning he had dreamt of doing so). Instead, he quietly wrote, rewrote, and relived what had happened in those fateful months in Sumatra: of his loyalty to a colonial administration that no longer recognized his name. He in turn condemns state agents, people, but *not* the system in which his faith seems to remain.

These letters between a father and daughter are shaped by the exigencies of empire and estrangements of the everyday, by the common dislocations of careers that were the norm in tens of thousands of European colonial lives. They are love letters of a special sort. He declares his love more insistently as their distance increases (as he passes through the newly opened Suez Canal), affirms his hold on her as their ties become weaker ("*I know how boisterous you have been, Grandma Smits has told me*), and as he knows less (and cares to know less?) about whom she talks, what she reads, what makes up her days. These are love letters designed to instill attachment, to capture the taste of her childhood in which he takes no part, to create rather than affirm a closeness for the little girl who will grow into a young woman while he is away. What he tells her he most fears is that she will recognize neither his aged, stout physique nor his voice when they meet years later on the dock in Marseille.

Valck's letters are touching if pitiful; hers irritable and uninspired. His are as rich as hers are flat and mundane. If hers can assume his interest (even in the face of her cross-hatched prose), when she is little he works hard to create it. To get her attention he squeezes the affective from the immediacy of familiar objects and movements ("*I'm wearing slippers, my desk is black, the dogs scurry under my feet when I eat at midday*"). He implores her to believe that distance makes the heart grow fonder, but unsure himself, he tells stories to excite, elicit pity, or in someway touch: of seeing little Balinese girls "like" her, of his fat cow and geese, selective, censored images of his everyday. He tells her of his marvelous or ill health, of how much better he would be if he only had more time to move about and had fewer people coming "to complain of injustices done them"—demands that keep him "*as if glued to [his] desk.*"

These are the letters that replace a shared space—laments for a childhood he can only imagine. (When she is little he begs her to send the family names of her favorite schoolmates so that he might perhaps hear her name uttered by someone in his circle who might happen to be the parent of one of her friends.) He implores her, in each letter, to send yet another portrait, knowing it will never be recent enough to catch up with what he has missed and how she has changed. He asks her to measure her height so he can "*see her grow*" and tells her he will mark it on his office wall. He sends her his portrait (one not kept among her letters) that worries him before it arrives because he appears so old. He asks her to quickly "*touch up*" the blurred white spots so that he will look less gross and grey.

He presses for more and more evidence of their closeness as it seems to slip away—as his closings shift imperceptibly from "*Papa*" to "*Papa Valck*" and sometimes simply to "*Valck,*" signed in the florid hand he usually reserved for official letters. These closings become more removed, not so much with her growing up, but with his inadvertent forgetting of who she was and now is and how far he had drawn away from her. Unknowingly, the studied difference he so carefully had maintained between his writing to her and the official business that cluttered his office desk seems to collapse. But then a letter signed "*Valck*" might be followed by one of infantile intimacy, signed "*ton Pati-Pati*" ("*your Papa*"), as if grasping to reinvoke their closeness with the diminutive pet name she had given him as a small girl. Her letters, too, perhaps absentmindedly repeat that apartness a decade later when she is a young mother in Java and signs a letter to him with "*S. Lucassen*" rather than "*Suze.*" Intimacy over time and space was a labored state to maintain.

NOTHING BUT THE TRUTH

It was with the pet name "*ton Pati-Pati*" that he signed the most poignant and painful letter he would send to her, on 16 July 1878, written as he readied to leave his last post in Ambarawa for Batavia and the mail boat that would bring him back to Marseille. He writes on the joint occasion of her fifteenth birthday and on notification of his final dismissal from the Civil Service. He has just recently learned of a damning, "*highly unflattering*" report about his performance in Ambarawa written to the Governor-General by the Resident of Semarang. Valck is found wanting on multiple counts: in his treatment of tax arrears (he protests that one of his accountants was ill); detention of prisoners (he claims to have accounted for everyone); his handling of the outbreak of violence in a nearby village (that he claims to have handled judiciously and with the utmost care); and in his contradictory report on a local murder (he claims to have investigated further to find out the truth and two days later corrected his first erroneous report). His report to the Resident of Ambarawa protesting the slander and affirming his own virtue, honesty, and unfailing diligence falls on deaf ears. The Resident accuses him of continuing to treat important matters "*en bagatelle*" ("lightheartedly")—as he is said to have done in Deli.[73]

His letter to Suze, the week before, begins softly in French, telling her how pleased he is by her improved handwriting, still warning her not to press so hard with her pen because "*a scrawl is a fault not easily undone.*" Her congratulates her for her academic successes, and only then, on the point of seeing her for the first time after seven years (in each letter he has counted their years of separation in months and days), he tells her that she now has reached an age in which he can treat her as more than a daughter ("*there is no one that loves you more*"). She is now ready to become his most cherished confidant, to carry the burden of the financial and political knowledge of their situation—he calls her, heartbreakingly, "*his*

---

[73] CBG, FA, no. 420, *Beantwoording der nota voor den Assistent-Resident van Ambarawa*, F.C.Valck, 23 July 1878, sent from Semarang.

dearest friend"—wrenching from her the prospect of the daughter-father relationship for which he so yearned at the very moment that it and their physical proximity become possible.

In this longest letter he would ever write to her, he recounts for the first time the fierce backstabbing to which he has been subject and to which his career has succumbed. He explains why he was dismissed, how he was betrayed by those who knew the horrific situation in Deli and set him up (he even mentions the accusations against him in his final post in Ambarawa). After wishing her a happy birthday, he writes bitterly, in language that is only partly for her, repeating almost verbatim the argument he had made, and would make again, in his official reports, the very words he used to his friend Levyssohn two years earlier. He entreats her, as he did Levyssohn, not to imagine that he exaggerates, and pens the same phrases he would repeat in his unsent letter to the Governor-General written years later from The Hague:

> *You must then know, my friend, that I have always served the government with a devotion to which I have sacrificed more than many. I have usually served with pleasure until I was sent to Deli, a region for which I had little desire to go but where I had to fulfill a noble mission which was to protect those unfortunates who were treated in the most barbarous way. These were the Chinese, the Javanese, the Hindu coolies on whom the European planters, those one called the "civilizers," inflicted the whip and brutalized to the point of death. Don't think that I exaggerate, that I speak more than the truth. When I arrived in Deli, according to all reports it was a hell. Within eight months and by the time I left there was not a single European who would any longer dare to perform such atrocious acts as those that before had taken place everyday. You can imagine what enemies I made, enemies who were influential enough in the capital to ruin my reputation. But never was there a word that I was dishonest, this you must never forget. . . . The Governor-General chose me among more than 110 of my colleagues for Deli because he knew, as he told me, that I would act with complete impartiality, which is what I did. He told me that it was a distinction for me to be sent to Deli and promised to rescue and protect me. None of this was done. He abandoned me and left me to be reviled and insulted. No promise was kept, not even the chance to defend myself against the attacks made in a report of one of my superiors, a report with not an ounce of truth. And there is nothing more sacred than the right of one accused to self defense.*

His tone then switches from colonial politics to her everyday. He reminds her to keep the train receipts for her trip to meet him in Paris, to be sure not to spend the money carelessly because they can no longer afford to do so. Distinctions crumble as he calls on her, his *"dearest friend,"* to share his hardship and not to imagine him as someone who would ever lose courage. He scrambles to connect: warns her that money will be scarce, that his signature was just like hers at the same age, that he will always love his beloved daughter.

Should we have any doubt as to whether Suze was prepared for this new role, her schoolgirl letter responding to his a few months later from boarding school evinces that she was not, as she implores him to permit her to go with her classmates to the colonial exposition in Paris:

Dear dear Papa,

You will have certainly received [Grand] Maman's letter where she asked you to allow me to go to Paris, but I thought it kinder of me if I asked you myself. You know much I would love to go, oh I would so! It would be one such cruel deception for me [not to be allowed]! I have so hoped to go one time to Paris to the [colonial] exposition. Mademoiselle Jeanne has herself proposed it and you know that she will keep us well under guard so we won't get lost! There are a few girls who already have permission and it would be so hard for me to see them leave without me. I promise you and you can believe me, if you let me to do it, I will take far greater pains with my lessons and especially I won't feel the consequences of my escapades! And what's more I will see you! Oh, I want to so, so much! It would be the time when I would be going on vacation anyway. I implore you to not refuse me. Please allow me this pleasure! Don't refuse it, I implore you! If you permit me, please telegraph me immediately so I will not longer be in doubt. I'm sure now that I have asked you in such a way you can't refuse me. Just think, there are not expositions like that of the exposition of 1878 every year. Adieu dear Pati-Pati. I thank you already,

Your happy Suze . . . RSVP!!!

Whatever his expectation, it was neither confidant nor friend that Suze became. There are no letters from the months following his arrival in The Hague and she is still at school, none stored until after boarding school. Five years later, in spring 1882, she was to write in a steady, angry stream, long letters, still in French, over their heated conflict about her marriage plans to her cousin, Theodore. "Trust" is the word that each repeats again and again. She accuses him of distrusting Theodore and his father. He denies it and claims that he only wants Theodore to have a proper position before they marry. She tells him she loves him but it is to the man she intends to marry to whom she must be most loyal. Valck concedes after refusing to open her letters for several months. The marriage is a gilded affair and then they write again, she from France, in Abbeville, at the sugar beet factory where Theodore was learning his trade, and then on her way to the Kemanglen estate, the Lucassen family complex on Java.

She has bought a sumptuous red leather diary with a thin gold border especially, and hopefully, for her stay. The first entry, several days after her arrival, comes from her Uncle van Rees's (now Governor-General) official residence, where he is opulently installed in the palace in Buitenzorg, in the hills outside of Batavia. Her first entry hardly fills more than a page. In French she writes:

Buitenzorg, 29 April 1887

Arrived here at Uncle van Rees's charming Governor-General's reception. Slept very well in an enormous bed, breakfast this morning at seven thirty. After that the arrival of Uncle Daan and Aunt Suzette and Pieteke . . . to see Uncle Rees. With this delight of being in a palace like Buitenzorg, to be able to walk in a splendid park.

And the next day:

Buitenzorg, 30 April 1887

Had a very nice day. Did a tour in the pony carriage of Poppi, pulled by adorable little black horses. Saw Auguste Miesegars [?] who came to spend Sunday here. Did another tour in the carriage with Adrienne, Poppi, and Auguste. Life here still pleases me so much. The climate is ideal.

The next day's three-line entry is sullen, terse, and in Dutch:

Birthday of Mamie; little to note. Theo has been somewhat indisposed, cranky.

These are the first and last entries, a single page. My own marginalia escapes my efforts to temper judgment and remain observant, to not let my impatience get in the way:

My reaction is awful. Of course she couldn't keep to her diary, I think. She was too lazy and too dull to see, too bored (and too stupid/stupefied, Ronell might insist) to have anything worth writing or anything to say. But had she devotedly written, I would have derided her just the same, convinced that it was "proof" that she had nothing to care for but herself and her petty complaints and pleasures. How could she get by on knowing so little and emoting so much? How could she arrive in Java where she had not been since a year old when her mother died, and have nothing to say? How dare I assume I know her already? I think she is peevish and refuses to grow up. My reaction is worse when she is older. I know from her later letters she will spend them complaining, performing her duty as a fussy mother. But why no empathy? Wasn't her little girl to die at Ke-manglen as an infant? Who is this Suze I so disdain?

From Tegal her letters spiraled distractedly into a blinding immediacy—about her children's colds and molars. Peevishly, she wrote about her distaste for Java and everything else. In sporadic outpourings when "*ready to burst*," she wrote of resenting her life in a wing of the Lucassen great house, the surveillance of the Lucassen women, of no way of creating any "*coziness*," of nothing to call her own. She pines for a city, complains of her boredom living so far from one, and of her absent husband, who did nothing with her and nothing but work at the factory until late in the day.

It is not the story that Suze's husband, Theodore, chose to convey to his father-in-law several months after their arrival in Tegal. Born at the Ke-manglen family complex, he has not been back in ten years, since the age of nineteen. His memory, he says, is weak on the weather, he remembers it as having been much more unbearably hot ten years ago, when every night he would "*wring out*" his sweat-soaked pillow "*like a sponge.*" What stays vivid is how depressing he thought the countryside around Tegal then; he finds it "*less melancholic now.*" "*It really is a good country,*" he affirms, where he and Suze are living "*happily and contented*" and in good health. Still it is a "*monotonous landscape,*" nature so "*disappointing*" and so "*very untidy.*" Nostalgia for Europe is all that animates his prose as his letter drifts to the "*translucent lakes*" of Switzerland, and a walk along any Dutch canal, of "*ten times more aesthetic pleasure than the longest ride through an Indies landscape.*"[74] But nostalgias and yearnings sometimes pulled in other directions. The sheer exuberance of Frans Carl Valck's first letters to Suze when he arrives back in Bali in 1872 have nothing bored about them at all. On the contrary, nature was his favorite companion; it was from the Balinese he looked away.

For colonial civil servants and the women who accompanied them, such letters were lifelines of sorts—to civilities, sociality, and compassion—self-portraits for display. But they were awkward as well, as time lapsed and the comforts of the colony sometimes pulled them unknowingly further from European ways. Such purloined letters seem transparent, the sensibilities accessible and easy to convey. But are they? For they offer both predictable and contrary stories about how empire intruded on and escaped the everyday. If hagiographies are stuffed with personal letters, critical colonial histories are usually not—perhaps because of the sympathies they invoke, the shock of recognition, the disquiets they inspire. Or perhaps it is the "flitting glance" of embarrassed familiarity that turns us away.

[74] CBG, FA No. 374, 8 August 1877, Théodore Lucassen to F. C. Valck (occasionally the letters are signed and addressed to Theodore [French], while at other times to Theodoor [Dutch]).

The Ethics of Colonial Ethnography: On Walk-on Roles

As a window on what Valck felt, what deceptions he lived and how he was disposed, his narratives are wanting, full of holes. We know so many details and yet so little about him: not what books he read, how much he drank, what dreams he dreamt, whether he had a lover or frequented prostitutes during those seven years in the Indies—from which injustices he chose to disregard. His discrepant messages combine high morals and bold indifference, callousness and compassion, utter effectualness and power, depression and racialized distaste. They remind us that Valck's humanist indignations and disregard were both nourished by colonial politics, were lived through those politics and on its edges. His first promotion occurred on Bali's north coast, when he took a small part in blowing the whistle on the collusion of a Dutch official and a local regent. His demise followed his indictment of Deli's European planters and high-ranking colonial officials in Batavia who turned their backs on what they knew. But even within this do-good bent, the colonized appear with only walk-on roles. It is a sobering reminder of Salman Rushdie's warning that if colonial history has been written with the colonized as bit players, that gives no license for contemporary historians to do the same.[75]

By Rushdie's account, Valck's story—and Suze's still moreso—are not ones we should legitimately choose to tell. His life is predicated on the privileges of empire: for long periods embracing its pleasures, and at later moments involuntarily distanced from it. Hers transpires elsewhere, escapes into the ether of an obsessively tended, hothouse world. One is struck by what he refuses to write, what remains tacitly excised. Injustices sometimes matter. Others he notices but does not see. Still others he chooses not to convey. Injuries to his sense of self cut across both genres. If in Suze's personhood, Java only intrudes as bothersome, boring, or insufficiently picturesque, in his the colonized appear as blurred shadows in a sarong, at a prison door, as a generic Chinese coolie pinned down for a lashing—not persons with histories, and rarely those with reflective selves.

[75] Salman Rushdie, "Outside the Whale," in *Imaginary Homelands* (London: Penguin, 1992), 90. On Paul Scott's *Raj Quartet* he writes:

> Indians get walk-ons, but remain, for the part, bit-players in their own history. Once this form is set, it scarcely matters that individual fictional Brits get unsympathetic treatment from their author. The form insists that *they are the ones whose stories matter*, and this is so much less than the whole truth that it must be called a falsehood. It will not do to argue that Scott was attempting to portray the British in India, and that such was the nature of imperialist society that the Indians *would* only have had bit-parts. It is no defense to say that work adopts, in its structure, the very ethic which, in its content and tone, it pretends to dislike. It is, in fact, the case for the prosecution.

Nor are these letters "windows onto the soul," the truly private and intimate spaces of a personal self.[76] Sometimes they were proof of what empire conferred (service, spacious housing, and stature), sometimes evidence of tastes that, despite distance and discomfort, one retained. Frans Carl liked to joke about becoming *décivilisé*, of needing to visit friends and write in French so he would not lose touch. Suze rarely joked at all but prided herself on her children's "thank you's" in French rather than Malay. And in hushed whispers ("*please, Papa, don't dare tell anyone what I say, you know what rumors can do*"), she'd write of her unkempt kin, the Lucassen women who went barefoot, ate appalling (local) food, and disapprovingly, she wrote, policed what she would do or say. She in turn had contempt for their *Indische* ways. They were no longer oriented to Europe, kept inadequate distance from colonial customs, tastes, and dress, wore their sarongs out like bedclothes throughout the day.

Two years after her arrival at Kemanglen, she writes her father with expectant excitement. The arrival of more frequent French mailboats will allow them to finally "coordinate" their letters. Here is her response to his previous letter of a month earlier, arriving three days after hers had left.

> *I am busy sewing my household linen. Also kabaai must be made as I am planning to start wearing sarong and kabaai. Of course, only in the mornings, when I have to do the household chores. In the evening I will always keep dressing: I don't want to adopt that bad habit.*[77]

"*Of course*" marks off the world from which she distinguishes herself; of those "*who stay on*" (the *blijvers*) like the Lucassen women and what she vows she will never become. The daily accoutrements of Europe continue to hold her fast and she insists she must have them. In each letter she requests something more: an egg-rack from Sack's, "*a big jar of Dr. Aufeland's children's powder*," "*pastilles from Gerandel*."[78] It is in February 1889 that her own small house in the Kemanglen complex is finally being built and with exhausted excitement, awaiting the birth of her fourth child, she tells him of her longing to move in, of her relief at no longer having to live in a wing of the great house. She chides him for not understand-

---

[76] Most epistolary history dismissed that conceit long ago. As William Decker puts it, "Perhaps the most fundamental fiction of letter writing" is one that "assumes the existence of a certain confidentiality as its enabling condition," one belied by the social conventions of the letter-writing form. William Decker, *Epistolary Practices: Letter Writing in America before Telecommunications* (Chapel Hill: University of North Carolina Press, 1998), 5. On the "myth" of the "letter's status as a privileged marker of privacy," see Earle, 7.

[77] CBG, FA, 24 January 1889, Susanna Lucassen to F. C. Valck.

[78] CBG, FA, 6 February 1889, Susanna Lucassen to F.C. Valck.

ing how much she has suffered in waiting for it, how awful it was for two years to live *"with people so antipathetic to us, or especially to me."*[79]

> *I can see in your letters that you cannot imagine our position here and how unbearable it is. You can't imagine, dear Papa, how much the stay here has harmed me. Firstly I have gotten nervous; one could not tell by looking at me but I feel it all the more. When I feel so nervous, even my nails hurt. Also I have become ten years older indeed. I have become very resentful and finding fault, mon caractère c'est absolument aigri [my temperament is completely sour!].*[80]

Why have the Lucassen women become so hostile to her? Are they as disdainful of her clinging to European pretensions as she is of their *Indische* ways? When she returns to The Hague upon her husband's sudden death at Kemanglen (the day before she turns thirty years old) and upon her father's death the preceding year, her letters end. Her oldest son becomes the genealogist who deposits hers and her father's letters in the genealogical bureau in The Hague. Her second son becomes an entomologist. Her only daughter marries the French Marquis de Seilhac. No further generations are born in Java. No one returns to the Indies. Investments are transferred to African plantations. Before Indonesia's independence, the Kemanglen estates are already sold. The watermark of empire is scratched over and etched out of their lives. Descendants live in small apartments in the suburbs of The Hague with portraits of wealthier earlier generations on their walls. In 2002 the name of "Susanna Lucassen" appears on the program for an outdoor summer performance in the French Luberon for promising young ballet stars. I ask if her family ever lived in Java. "Oui," she smiles, "someone was in the Indies once," and she glides away. There is not an imperial trace. Or is there?

French historian Roger Chartier gives immense value to epistolarity *sans qualité*, not for the information conveyed but in the sense that Robert Musil uses the term in *The Man Without Qualities*, for entry into the affective and political expectations produced and the reciprocities they demanded and required.[81] Ordinary epistolarity provides what Chartier calls an act of "housebreaking" into private lives.[82] Mary Favret takes that violent trespass in another direction to suggest that such letters are less "windows into the intimate self" than a genre that introduces us into a

---

[79] CBG, FA, 6 March 1889, Susanna Lucassen to F.C. Valck.

[80] CBG, FA, 6 February, 1889, Susanna Lucassen to F.C. Valck.

[81] See Robert Musil, *The Man Without Qualities* (New York: Vintage, 1996).

[82] See Roger Chartier's introduction to *Ces bonnes lettres: une correspondance familiale au XIXe siècle*, ed. C. Dauphin, P. Lebrun-Pézerat, D. Poublan (Paris: Albin Michel, 1995), 17–25, 23.

world that "intrudes upon our own."[83] The letters between Valck and his daughter do something of both. We are privy to lives in which the politics of empire bleeds into the texture of the personal and then, as if too present, is carefully washed out.

"Information" is there—in abundance. It depends on what kinds of things we imagine such an archive could allow us to know. In this letter-writing trove of Frans Carl Valck, his daughter Susanna, and their acquaintances and family, no documents could offer thicker evidence of the veins of commitment, disregard, obligation, and investment that pulsed through their concerns and bound the life-force of personhoods and politics together. But clarity about what Valck "really felt" about living in empire and off its rewards is elusive at best. Family letters provide a personalized and ethnographic inflection in a minor key, not the crescendo of major chords, but the plaintive notes in which things may not be felt as they seem to be.

In tracking the molten relationship between bureaucratic missives and familial ones, sometimes these forms abruptly pull apart, elsewhere they merge registers of tone and mood, in which imperial dispositions were inhabited and remade. Rather than underscoring distinctions between the intimacies of empire and its public face, such letters address alternative senses of timing and distance, of expectation and exigency, of divided commitments that empire produced in its subjects and the elite hired help paid to manage them. Not least, our use of such letters demands hermeneutic humility, forcing longer reflection on what made up their common sense and how much imperial dispositions are sustained by the generative power of a "vital lie."

The noun "ignorance" and the verb "to ignore" share a social and legal etymology, where definition of the former, "want of knowledge," is predicated on the definition of the latter active, verbal form, "to refuse to take notice of." How these two are joined, what political measures and psychic processes produce subjectivities that instantiate both, is a condition of imperial histories we would do well not "to ignore." Both continue to haunt the logos and pathos of empire. Both inform what Mary Douglas called "those shadowed places" that states and more expansive procedures of governance protect. The epistemic incertitudes and ontological categories in which honor and white prestige, racial humiliations and critical refusals were inscribed may look different now. But they continue to bear on the residual effects of empire and, more importantly, on what people are "left with." The politics of disregard may cast longer shadows still, across the accounts we give of ourselves in the face of emergent predicaments of imperial formations in a contemporary world that is so visibly different and subjacently resonant today.

---

[83] Mary A. Favret, *Romantic Correspondence: Women, Politics and the Fiction of Letters* (Cambridge: Cambridge University press, 1993), 10.

APPENDIX 1

Colonial Chronologies

These chronologies are selective and intended to provide, for those less familiar with the history of colonial Indonesia, an overview of the major periods in which Indies colonial historiography is commonly divided (the VOC period, the Culture System, the Liberal Period, the Ethical Period, etc.). Entries in boldface to the right of dates are the common "events" that appear in colonial historiography of the Netherlands Indies. Entries in plain font are those of more direct relevance to issues mentioned in this book. Entries to the left of the dates are those in the life of F. C. Valck and his family. [Nb. Many of these dates are still debated among historians, none are "exact." The parameters of "events," as I argue throughout this book, depend on one's orienting frame and as should be evident in the preceding chapters, frames could and did change.

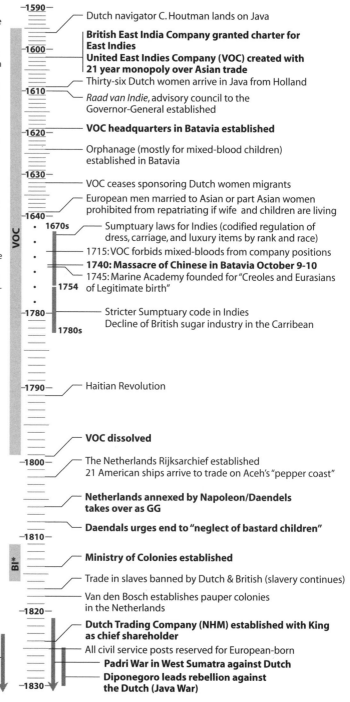

1590
Dutch navigator C. Houtman lands on Java

British East India Company granted charter for East Indies

1600
United East Indies Company (VOC) created with 21 year monopoly over Asian trade
Thirty-six Dutch women arrive in Java from Holland

1610
Raad van Indie, advisory council to the Governor-General established

1620
VOC headquarters in Batavia established

Orphanage (mostly for mixed-blood children) established in Batavia

1630
VOC ceases sponsoring Dutch women migrants

European men married to Asian or part Asian women prohibited from repatriating if wife and children are living

1640

1670s Sumptuary laws for Indies (codified regulation of dress, carriage, and luxury items by rank and race)

1715: VOC forbids mixed-bloods from company positions

1740: Massacre of Chinese in Batavia October 9-10

1745: Marine Academy founded for "Creoles and Eurasians

1754 of Legitimate birth"

1780
Stricter Sumptuary code in Indies
Decline of British sugar industry in the Carribean

1780s

1790
Haitian Revolution

VOC dissolved

1800
The Netherlands Rijksarchief established
21 American ships arrive to trade on Aceh's "pepper coast"

Netherlands annexed by Napoleon/Daendels takes over as GG

Daendels urges end to "neglect of bastard children"

1810

*British Interregnum

Ministry of Colonies established

Trade in slaves banned by Dutch & British (slavery continues)

Van den Bosch establishes pauper colonies in the Netherlands

1820
Dutch Trading Company (NHM) established with King as chief shareholder

All civil service posts reserved for European-born

Padri War in West Sumatra against Dutch

Valck's father Frans Gerardus is a Resident on Java

Diponegoro leads rebellion against the Dutch (Java War)

1830

VOC

BI*

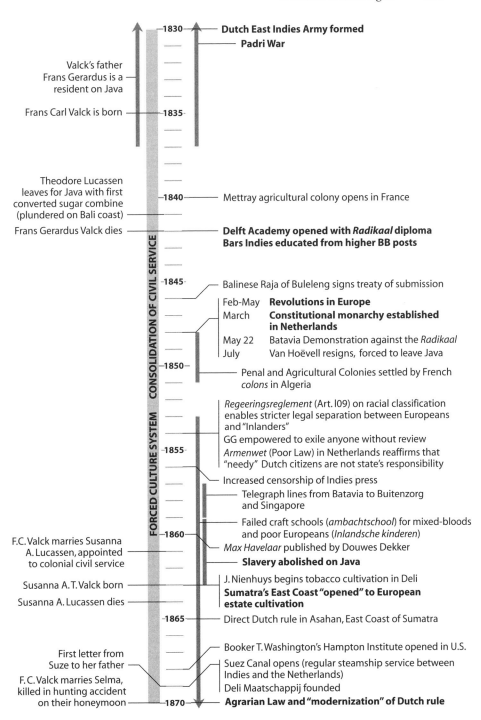

1830 — **Dutch East Indies Army formed**
Padri War

Valck's father
Frans Gerardus is a
resident on Java

Frans Carl Valck is born ——1835-

Theodore Lucassen
leaves for Java with first
converted sugar combine
(plundered on Bali coast)

1840 —— Mettray agricultural colony opens in France

Frans Gerardus Valck dies —— **Delft Academy opened with *Radikaal* diploma**
Bars Indies educated from higher BB posts

1845- —— Balinese Raja of Buleleng signs treaty of submission

Feb-May **Revolutions in Europe**
March **Constitutional monarchy established**
in Netherlands
May 22 Batavia Demonstration against the *Radikaal*
July Van Hoëvell resigns, forced to leave Java

1850— —— Penal and Agricultural Colonies settled by French
colons in Algeria

Regeeringsreglement (Art. l09) on racial classification
enables stricter legal separation between Europeans
and "Inlanders"
GG empowered to exile anyone without review

1855- *Armenwet* (Poor Law) in Netherlands reaffirms that
"needy" Dutch citizens are not state's responsibility

Increased censorship of Indies press
Telegraph lines from Batavia to Buitenzorg
and Singapore
Failed craft schools (*ambachtschool*) for mixed-bloods

1860— and poor Europeans (*Inlandsche kinderen*)

F.C. Valck marries Susanna *Max Havelaar* published by Douwes Dekker
A. Lucassen, appointed **Slavery abolished on Java**
to colonial civil service

Susanna A.T. Valck born —— J. Nienhuys begins tobacco cultivation in Deli
Sumatra's East Coast "opened" to European
Susanna A. Lucassen dies —— **estate cultivation**

1865— —— Direct Dutch rule in Asahan, East Coast of Sumatra

First letter from —— Booker T. Washington's Hampton Institute opened in U.S.
Suze to her father —— Suez Canal opens (regular steamship service between
Indies and the Netherlands)
F.C. Valck marries Selma, Deli Maatschappij founded
killed in hunting accident
on their honeymoon ——1870— **Agrarian Law and "modernization" of Dutch rule**

CONSOLIDATION OF CIVIL SERVICE

FORCED CULTURE SYSTEM

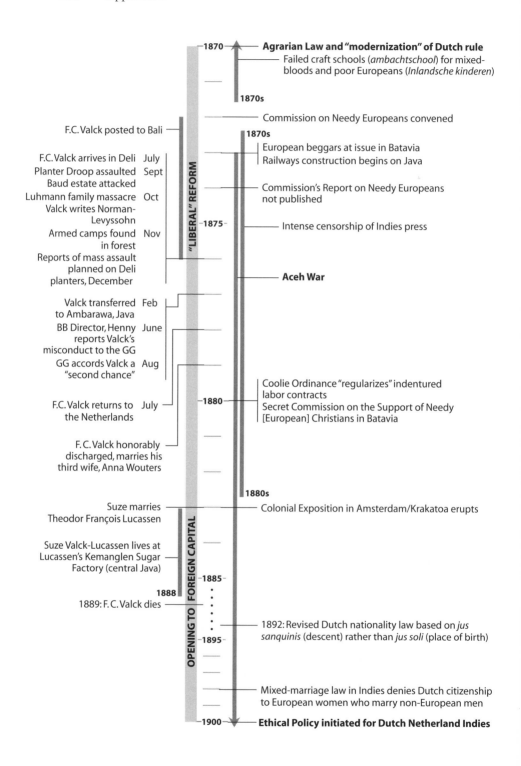

- 1870 — **Agrarian Law and "modernization" of Dutch rule**
  - Failed craft schools (*ambachtschool*) for mixed-bloods and poor Europeans (*Inlandsche kinderen*)

1870s

F.C. Valck posted to Bali — Commission on Needy Europeans convened

1870s

F.C. Valck arrives in Deli July — European beggars at issue in Batavia
Planter Droop assaulted Sept — Railways construction begins on Java
Baud estate attacked
Luhmann family massacre Oct — Commission's Report on Needy Europeans not published
Valck writes Norman-Levyssohn
Armed camps found Nov — -1875- — Intense censorship of Indies press
in forest
Reports of mass assault planned on Deli planters, December — **Aceh War**

"LIBERAL" REFORM

Valck transferred Feb
to Ambarawa, Java
BB Director, Henny June
reports Valck's
misconduct to the GG
GG accords Valck a Aug
"second chance" — Coolie Ordinance "regularizes" indentured labor contracts
F.C. Valck returns to July — -1880- — Secret Commission on the Support of Needy [European] Christians in Batavia
the Netherlands

F. C. Valck honorably discharged, marries his third wife, Anna Wouters

1880s

Suze marries — Colonial Exposition in Amsterdam/Krakatoa erupts
Theodor François Lucassen

OPENING TO FOREIGN CAPITAL

Suze Valck-Lucassen lives at
Lucassen's Kemanglen Sugar — -1885-
Factory (central Java)

1888
1889: F. C. Valck dies — 1892: Revised Dutch nationality law based on *jus sanquinis* (descent) rather than *jus soli* (place of birth)
-1895-

Mixed-marriage law in Indies denies Dutch citizenship to European women who marry non-European men

- 1900 — **Ethical Policy initiated for Dutch Netherland Indies**

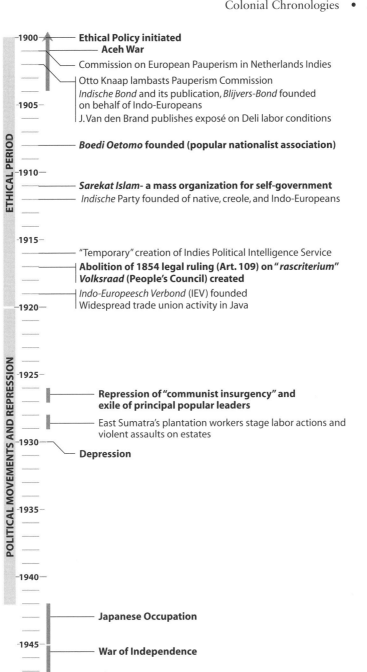

1900 Ethical Policy initiated
Aceh War

Commission on European Pauperism in Netherlands Indies

Otto Knaap lambasts Pauperism Commission
Indische Bond and its publication, *Blijvers-Bond* founded
on behalf of Indo-Europeans
1905 J. Van den Brand publishes exposé on Deli labor conditions

Boedi Oetomo founded (popular nationalist association)

1910

Sarekat Islam- a mass organization for self-government
Indische Party founded of native, creole, and Indo-Europeans

1915

"Temporary" creation of Indies Political Intelligence Service
Abolition of 1854 legal ruling (Art. 109) on "*rascriterium*"
Volksraad (People's Council) created
Indo-Europeesch Verbond (IEV) founded
1920 Widespread trade union activity in Java

1925

Repression of "communist insurgency" and
exile of principal popular leaders

East Sumatra's plantation workers stage labor actions and
violent assaults on estates
1930 Depression

1935

1940

Japanese Occupation

1945 War of Independence

"Police Actions" – attempt by Dutch to restore colonial rule
1950 Independence, renamed Indonesia

Governors-General of the Netherlands Indies, 1830–1930

1830–1834	Johannes van den Bosch (1780–1839)
1834–1836	Jean C. Baud (1789–1859)
1836–1840	Dominique J. de Eerens (1781–1840)
1841–1844	Pieter Merkus (1787–1844)
1845–1851	Jan J. Rochussen (1797–1871)
1851–1856	Albertus Duymaer van Twist (1809–1887)
1856–1861	Charles Pahud (1803–1873)
1861–1866	L. A. J. W. Baron Sloet van de Beele (1806–1890)
1866–1872	Pieter Mijer (1812–1881)
1872–1875	James Louden (1824–1884)
1875–1881	Johan Wilhelm van Lansberge (1830–1905)
1881–1884	Frederik's Jacob (1822–1901)
1884–1888	Otto van Rees (1823–1892)
1888–1893	Cornelis Pijnacker Hordijk (1847–1908)
1893–1899	Jhr Carel H. A. van der Wijck (1840–1914)
1899–1905	Willem Rooseboom (1843–1920)
1905–1909	Johannes van Heutsz (1851–1924)
1909–1916	Alexander Idenburg (1861–1935)
1916–1921	Jean Graaf van Limburg Stirum (1873–1948)
1921–1926	Dirk Fock (1858–1941)
1926–1931	Jhr Andries C. D. de Graeff (1871–1957)

BIBLIOGRAPHY

Abrams, Philip. "Notes on the Difficulty of Studying the State." *Journal of Historical Sociology* 1 (1) (March 1988 [1977]).

Adam, Ahmat B. *The Vernacular Press and the Emergence of the Modern Indonesian Consciousness, 1855–1913.* Ithaca: SEAP, 1995.

Adams, Julia. "The Familial State: Elite Family Practices and State-Making in the Early Modern Netherlands." *Theory and Society* 23 (4) (August 1994): 505–39.

Adas, Michael. *Machines as the Measure of Man.* Ithaca: Cornell University Press, 1989.

Alexander, Jennifer and Paul. "Shared Poverty as Ideology: Labor Relations in Rural Java." *Man* 17 (4) (1982): 597–619.

Amin, Shadid. "Gandhi as Mahatma." In *Selected Subaltern Studies*, ed. Ranajit Guha and Gayatri Chakravorty Spivak. New York: Oxford University Press, 1988, 288–350.

———. *Event, Metaphor, Memory: 1922–1992.* Berkeley: University of California Press, 1995.

Anderson, Benedict. *Imagined Communities.* New York: Verso, 1983.

Anonymous. *Deli-Batavia Maatschappij 1875–1925.* Amsterdam: Deli-Batavia Maatschappij, 1925.

Appadurai, Arjun. *Modernity at Large: Cultural Dimensions of Globalization.* Minneapolis: University of Minnesota, 1996.

———. "The Past as a Scarce Resource." *Man* 16 (1981): 201–19.

———. "Archive and Aspiration." In *Information Is Alive*, ed. Joke Brouwer and Arjen Mulder. Rotterdam: V2/NAI, 2002, 14–25.

Arendt, Hannah. *Eichmann in Jerusalem: A Report on the Banality of Evil.* New York: Penguin Books, 1992.

———. "Lying in Politics: Reflections on the Pentagon Papers," *New York Review of Books* 17 (8) (November 18, 1971).

———. *On Revolution.* New York: Viking, 1965.

———. "Truth and Politics." In *Between Past and Future: Eight Exercises in Political Thought.* New York: Viking, 1961.

Arnold, David. "White Colonization and Labour in Nineteenth Century India." *Journal of Imperial and Commonwealth History.* 11 (2) (1983): 133–58.

Arondekar, Anjai. "Without a Trace: Sexuality and the Colonial Archive." *Journal of the History of Sexuality* 14 (1–2) (January–April 2005): 10–27.

Ashforth, Andrew. *The Politics of Official Discourse in Twentieth-Century South Africa.* Oxford: Clarendon Press, 1990.

Axel, Brian. ed. *From the Margins: Historical Anthropology and Its Futures.* Durham, N.C.: Duke University Press, 2002.

Baier, Annette. *A Progress of Sentiments: Reflections on Hume's Treatise.* Cambridge, Mass.: Harvard University Press, 1991.

Bakhtin, Mikhail. *Problems of Dostoevsky's Poetics*. Trans. Caryl Emerson. Minneapolis: University of Minnesota Press, 1987.

Barker-Benfield, G. J. *The Culture of Sensibility: Sex and Society in Eighteenth-Century Britain*. Chicago: Chicago University Press, 1992.

Barth, Fredick. *Ritual and Knowledge among the Baktaman of New Guinea*. New Haven: Yale University Press, 1975.

Barthes, Roland. *Camera Lucida: Reflections on Photography*. New York: Hill and Wang, 1981.

———. *Image-Music-Text*. Trans. Stephen Heath. New York: Hill and Wang, 1977.

Bataviaasch Genootschap van Kunsten en Wetenschappen. *Oud Batavia:* Part I. Batavia, G. Kloff, 1922.

Bayly, Christopher. *Empire and Information: Intelligence Gathering and Social Communication in India, 1780–1870*. Cambridge: Cambridge University Press, 1996.

Beiser, Frederick C. *The Fate of Reason: German Philosophy from Kant to Fichte* Cambridge, Mass.: Harvard University Press, 1987.

Bell, Daniel. "The Debate on Alienation." In *Revisionism: Essays on the History of Marxist Ideas*, ed. Leopold Labedz. New York: Praeger, 1962, 195–211.

Belvaude, Catherine. *L'Algérie*. Paris: Karthala, 1991.

Berezin, Mabel. "Political Belonging: Emotion, Nation, and Identity in Fascist Italy." In *State/Culture: State Formation After the Cultural Turn*, ed. George Steinmetz. Ithaca: Cornell University Press, 1999, 355–77.

Berlant, Lauren. *The Anatomy of a Nationalist Fantasy: Hawthorne, Utopia, and Everyday Life*. Chicago: Chicago University Press, 1991.

Berman, Marshall. *All That is Solid Melts into Air: The Experience of Modernity*. New York: Penguin, 1982.

Berner, Richard. *Archival Theory and Practice in the United States: An Historical Analysis*. Seattle: University of Washington Press, 1983.

Bernstein, Richard. *The New Constellation: Ethical-Political Horizons of Modernity/Post-Modernity*. Cambridge, Mass.: The MIT Press, 1993.

Bhabha, Homi. *The Location of Culture*. New York: Routledge, 1994.

———. "Of Mimicry and Man: The Ambivalence of Colonial Discourse." *October* 28 (1984): 125–33.

Biehl, Joao, Bryon Good, Arthur Kleinman. "Introduction." In *Subjectivity: Ethnographic Investigations*, ed. Joao Biehl, Bryon Good, and Arthur Kleinman. Berkeley: University of California Press, 2007, 1–23.

Bilgrami, Akeel. *Self-Knowledge and Resentment*. Cambridge, Mass.: Harvard University Press, 2006.

Birnie, Dwidjosewojo, Stibbe, "Het rascriterium," *Volksraad* B3, nos. 1–2 (1918): 3

Block, Fred, and Margaret Somers. "In the Shadow of Speenhamland: Social Policy and the Old Poor Law." *Politics and Society* 31 (2) (2003): 1–41.

Blok, P. J. *Geschiedenis van het Nederlandsche volk*, 4. Leiden: Sijthoff, 1906.

Blouin, Francis X. Jr., and William G. Rosenberg, eds. *Archives, Documentation and Institutions of Social Memory: Essays from the Sawyer Seminar*. Ann Arbor: University of Michigan Press, 2006.

Blumberger, J. Th. Petrus. *De Indo-Europeesche beweging in Nederlansch-Indië*. Haarlem: Willink, 1939.

Boltanski, Luc. "The Politics of Pity." In *Distant Suffering: Morality, Media and Politics* New York: Cambridge University Press, 1999.

Boogman, J. C. "De politieke ontwikkeling in Nederland, 1840–1862." In *Geschiedenis van het Moderne Nederland*. Den Haag: De Haan, 1988.

Bool, H. J. *De landbouwconcessies in de Residentie Oostkust van Sumatra*. Utrecht, 1903.

Bosma, Ulbe. *Karel Zaalberg: journalist en strijder voor de Indo*. Leiden: KITLV, 1997.

Bourdieu, Pierre. *Pascalian Meditations*. Stanford: Stanford University Press, 1999.

———. *Outline of a Theory of Practice*. Cambridge: Cambridge University Press, 1977.

———. "Rethinking the State: Genesis and Structure of the Bureaucratic Field." In *State/Culture: State Formation After the Cultural Turn*, ed. George Steinmetz. Ithaca: Cornell, 1999, 53–75.

Bowen, John. *Sumatran Politics and Poetics: Gayo History 1900–1989* (New Haven: Yale University Press, 1991.

Breckenridge, Keith. "Verwoerd's Bureau of Proof: Total Information in the Making of Apartheid." *History Workshop Journal* 59 (2005): 83–108.

———. "From Hubris to Chaos: The Making of the Bewsyuro and the End of Documentary Government." Paper presented to Wits Institute for Social and Economic Research, Johannesburg, 20 May 2002.

———. "Flesh Made Words: Fingerprinting and the Archival Imperative in the Union of South Africa, 1900–1930." Paper presented at the History and African Studies Seminar, University of KwaZulu-Natal, Durban, South Africa, October 2, 2001.

———. "Confounding the Documentary State: Cape Workers' Letters on the Early Witwatersrand." Paper presented at the History and African Studies Seminar, University of KwaZulu-Natal, Durban, South Africa, 30 May 2000.

Breen, William J. "Foundations, Statistics, and State-Building." *Business History Review* 68 (1994): 451–82.

Breman, Jan. *Taming the Coolie Beast: Plantation Society and the Colonial Order in Southeast Asia*. Calcutta: Oxford University Press, 1989.

Broersma, R. *Oostkust van Sumatra: De ontluiking van Deli* (Batavia, 1919), *Oostkust van Sumatra: De ontwikkeling van het gewest*. 'S-Gravenhage: Deventer, 1921.

Brugmans, I. J. *De arbeidende klasse in Nederland in de 19e eeuw*. 'S-Gravenhage: Martinus Nijhoff, 1929.

Buck-Morss, Susan. "Hegel and Haiti." *Critical Inquiry* 6 (4) (Summer 2000): 821–65.

Bundy, Colin. "Vagabond Hollanders and Runaway Englishmen: White Poverty in the Cape before Poor Whiteism." In *Putting a Plough to the Ground: Accumulation and Dispossession in Rural South Africa, 1850–1930*. ed. William Beinart, Peter Delius and Stanley Trapido. Johannesburg. Raven, 1986, 101–28.

Burton, Antoinette, ed. *Archive Stories: Facts, Fictions and the Writing of History*. Durham, N.C.: Duke University Press, 2006.

———. *Dwelling in the Archive: Women Writing House, Home and History in Late Colonial India*. New York: Oxford, 2003.

Bury, J. P. T. *France 1814–1940*. London: Routledge, 1989.

Butler, Judith. *Giving an Account of Oneself*. New York: Fordham University Press, 2005.

Cannadine, David. *Ornamentalism: How the British Saw Their Empire*. Oxford: Oxford University Press, 2001.

Carpentier, J. H. "Indische Europeanen," *Indologenblad* 5 (1913–14): 66–71.

Cerutti, Mauro, Jean-Francois Fayet, and Michel Porret, eds. *Penser l'Archive: Histoire d'Archives-Archives d'Histoire*. Lausanne: Antipodes, 2006.

Césaire, Aimé. *Discourse on Colonialism*. New York: Monthly Review, 2000 [1955].

Chakrabarty, Dipesh. *Provincializing Europe*. Princeton: Princeton University Press, 2000.

Chandler, James. "Proving a History of Evidence." In *Questions of Evidence*, ed. James Chandler, Arnold Davidson, and Harry Hartoonian. Chicago: University of Chicago Press, 1991, 275–81.

Chartier, Roger, Alain Boureau, and Cecile Dauphin, eds. *Correspondence: Models of Letter-writing from the Middle Ages to the Nineteenth-Century*. Princeton: Princeton University Press, 1997.

———. "Introduction." In *Ces bonnes lettres: une correspondance familiale au XIXe siècle*, ed. C. Dauphin, P. Lebrun-Pézerat, and D. Poublan. Paris: Albin Michel, 1995, 17–25.

Chassat, Sophie, Luc Forlievesi, Georges-Francois Pottier, eds. *Eduquer et Punir: La colonie agricole et penitentiare de Mettray, 1839–1937*. Rennes: Presses Universitaires de Rennes, 2005.

Chatterjee, Partha. *The Nation and Its Fragments: Colonial and Postcolonial Histories*. Princeton: Princeton University Press, 1993.

———.*Nationalist Thought and the Colonial World: A Derivative Discourse*. Minneapolis: University of Minnesota Press, 1986.

Cheah, Pheng. *Spectral Nationality: Passages of Freedom from Kant to Postcolonial Literatures of Liberation*. New York: Columbia University Press, 2003.

Cobban, Allan. "Kampungs and Conflict in Colonial Semarang." *Journal of Southeast Asian Studies* 19 (2) (1988): 266–91.

Coetzee, J. M. *Disgrace*. New York: Viking, 1999.

———. *Waiting for the Barbarians*. New York: Viking, 1980.

Cohen, David William. *The Combing of History*. Chicago: University of Chicago Press, 1994.

———. *Burying SM: The Politics of Knowledge and the Sociology of Power in Africa*. Portsmouth, N.H.: Heineman, 1992.

Cohen, Matthew Isaac. *The Komedie Stamboel: Popular Theater in Colonial Indonesia, 1891–1903*. Athens: Ohio University Press, 2006.

Cohn, Bernard. *Colonialism and Its Forms of Knowledge: The British in India*. Princeton: Princeton University Press, 1996.

Colonna, Fanny. "Educating Conformity in French Colonial Algeria." In *Tensions of Empire: Colonial Cultures in a Bourgeois World*, ed., Frederick Cooper and Ann Laura Stoler. Berkeley: University of California Press, 1997, 346–70.

Comaroff, Jean and John Comaroff. *Ethnography and the Historical Imagination*. Boulder, Colo.: Westview, 1992.

Combe, Sonia. *Archives Interdites: Les peurs françaises face à l'histoire contemporaine*. Paris: Albin Michel, 1994.

Connolly, William. *Why I Am Not a Secularist*. Minneapolis: University of Minnesota Press, 1999.

Cook, Terry. "Electronic Records, Paper Minds: The Revolution in Information Management and Archives in the Post-Custodial and Post-Modernist Era." *Archives and Manuscripts*. 22 (2) (1994): 300–329.

———. "Mind over Matter: Towards a New theory of Archival Appraisal." In *The Archival Imagination: Essays in Honour of Hugh A. Taylor*. Ottawa: Association of Canadian Archivists, 1992, 38–69.

Cooper, Frederick. "The Dialectics of Decolonization." In *Tensions of Empire: Colonial Cultures in a Bourgeois World*, ed. Frederick Cooper and Ann Laura Stoler. Berkeley: University of California Press, 1997, 406–35.

———, and Ann Laura Stoler, eds. *Tensions of Empire: Colonial Cultures in a Bourgeois World*. Berkeley: University of California Press, 1997.

Corrigan, Phillip, and Derek Sayer. *The Great Arch: English State Formation as Cultural Revolution*. Oxford: Blackwell, 1985.

Couperus, Louis. *The Hidden Force (De stille kracht)*. Amherst: University of Massachusetts Press, 1985 [1900].

Crapanzano,Vincent. "Réflexions sur une anthropologie des émotions." *Terrain* 22 (March 1994) : 109–17.

Crossley, Ceri. "Using and Transforming the French Countryside: The 'Colonies Agricoles' (1820–1850)." *French Studies*. 44 (1) (1991): 36–54.

Darnton, Robert. *The Great Cat Massacre and Other Episodes in French Cultural History*. New York: Vintage, 1984.

Darwall, Stephen. *The British Moralist and the Internal "Ought," 1640–1740*. Cambridge: Cambridge University Press, 1995.

Das, Veena. *Critical Events: An Anthropological Perspective on Contemporary India*. Delhi: Oxford University Press, 1995.

Daston, Lorraine. *Biographies of Scientific Objects*. Chicago: University of Chicago Press, 2000.

———.*Classical Probability in the Enlightenment*. Princeton: Princeton University Press, 1995.

———, with Peter Galison. *Objectivity*. New York: Zone, 2007.

Davin, Anna. "Imperialism and Motherhood." In *Tensions of Empire: Colonial Cultures in a Bourgeois World*. ed. Frederick Cooper and Ann Laura Stoler. Berkeley: University of California Press, 1997, 87–151.

Davis, Natalie. *Fiction in the Archives: Pardon Tales and their Tellers in Sixteenth-Century France*. Stanford: Stanford University Press, 1987.

De Certeau, Michel. *The Writing of History*. Trans. Tom Conley. New York: Columbia University Press, 1988.

———. *Heterologies: Discourse on the Other*. Trans. Brian Massumi. Minneapolis: University of Minnesota Press, 1986.

Decker, William. *Epistolary Practices: Letter Writing in America before Telecommunications*. Chapel Hill: University of North Carolina Press, 1998.

De Gruyter, J. "Een Indo over Indo's." *De Indische Gids* 35 (1913): 585–96.

Dekker, Jeroen. "Transforming the Nation and the Child: Philanthropy in the Netherlands, Belgium, France and England." In *Charity, Philanthropy and Reform: From the 1690s to 1850*, ed. Hugh Cunningham and Joanna Innes. New York: St. Martin's, 1998, 130–47.

———. *Straffen, redden en opvoeden: Het onstaan en de ontwikkeling van de residentiële heropvoeding in West Europa, 1814–1914, met bijzondere aandacht voor "Nederlandsch Mettray."* Assen: Van Gorcum, 1985.

Deleuze, Gilles. *Foucault*. Trans. and ed. Sean Hand. Minneapolis: University of Minnesota Press, 1992.

———, and Felix Guattari, *Kafka: Toward a Minor Literature*. Minneapolis: University of Minnesota Press, 1986.

De Man, Paul. *Blindness and Insight*. New York: Oxford University Press, 1971.

De Medelsheim, Alphone Cerfberr, and J. H. Detrimont. *Projet de colonisation d'une partie de l'Algérie par les condamnés libérés, les pauvres and les orphelins*. Paris: Plon, 1846.

Dening, Greg. *The Death of William Gooch: A History's Anthropology*. Honolulu: University of Hawaii Press, 1995.

De Regt, Ali. *Arbeidersgezinnen en beschavingsarbeid*. Amsterdam: Boom, 1984.

De Rooy, Piet. "Armenzorg in Nederland." In *Geschiedenis van Opvoeding en Onderwijs*, ed. Noordman Kruithof and Piet De Rooy. Nijmegen: SUN, 1982, 96–104.

Derrida, Jacques. "The History of the Lie," In Derrida, *Without Alibi*. Stanford: Stanford University Press, 2002.

———. *Archive Fever: A Freudian Impression*. Chicago: University of Chicago Press, 1995.

———. *Spurs: Nietzsche's Styles*. Chicago: University of Chicago Press, 1979.

Desrosières, Alain. *The Politics of Large Numbers: A History of Statistical Reasoning*. Cambridge, Mass.: Harvard University Press, 1998.

Dick, H. W. "Nineteenth-Century Industrialization: A Missed Opportunity?" In *New Challenges in the Modern Economic History of Indonesia*, ed. J. Th. Lindlbad. Leiden: PRIS, 1993, 123–49.

Die Armblanke-Vraagstuk in Suid-Afrika. Verslag van die Carnegie-Kommissie Stellenbosch: Pro Ecclesia-Drukkerij, 1932.

Dirks, Nicholas. "Annals of the Archive: Ethnographic Notes on the Sources of History." In *From the Margins: Historical Anthropology and Its Futures*, ed. Brian Axel. Durham, N.C.: Duke University Press, 2002, 47–65.

———. "Colonial History and Native Informants: Biography of an Archive." In *Orientalism and the Postcolonial Predicament: Perspectives on South Asia*. ed. Carol Breckenridge and Peter van der Veer. Philadelphia: University of Pennsylvania Press, 1993, 279–313.

Dolk, Liesbeth, ed. *Atjeh: De verbeelding van een koloniale oorlog*. Amsterdam: Bert Bakker, 2001

Douglas, Mary. *How Institutions Think*. Syracuse: Syracuse University Press, 1986.

———. *Implicit Meanings: Essays in Anthropology*. London, 1975.

Driver, Felix. *Power and Pauperism: The Workhouse System, 1834–1884*. Cambridge: Cambridge University Press, 1993.

Drooglever, P. J. *De Vaderlandse Club, 1929–1942*. Franeker: Wever, 1980.

Du Bois, W. E. B. *Darkwater: Voices from within the Veil*. New York: Dover, 1999.

———. *The Souls of Black Folk*. New York: Penguin, 1982.

Duchein, Michel. "The History of European Archives and the Development of the Archival Profession in Europe." *American Archivist* 55 (1992): 14–25.

Dunlop, Francis. *The Education of Feeling and Emotion*. Boston: Allen and Unwin, 1984.

Duras, Marguerite. *Seawall*. New York: Harper and Row, 1952.

Dussel, Enrique. *The Underside of Modernity: Apel, Ricoeur, Rorty, Taylor, and the Philosophy of Liberation*. Ed. and trans. Eduardo Mendieta. Atlantic Highlands, N.J.: Humanities, 1996.

Earle, Rebecca, ed. *Epistolary Selves: Letters and Letter-Writers, 1600–1945*. Aldershot: Algate, 1999.

Eley, Geoff. "Beneath the Skin, or: How to Forget about the Empire without Really Trying." *Journal of Colonialism and Colonial History* 3 (1) (Spring 2002), available online at http://muse.jhu.edu/journals/journal_of_colonialism_and_colonial_history/v003/3.1eley.html.

Elias, Norbert. *The Civilizing Process*. New York: Pantheon, 1982.

Elkins, James. *The Object Stares Back: On the Nature of Seeing*. New York: Harcourt, 1996.

Ellison, Julie. *Cato's Tears and the Making of Anglo-American Emotion*. Chicago: University of Chicago Press, 1999.

Elster, Jon. *Alchemies of Mind: Rationality and the Emotions*. Cambridge: Cambridge University Press, 1999.

Encyclopaedie van Nederlandsch-Indië. 'S-Gravenhage: Martinus Nijhoff, 1917.

Evans-Pritchard, E. E. *Social Anthropology and Other Essays*. New York: Free Press, 1962.

———. "Social Anthropology: Past and Present: The Marett Lecture, 1950." in Evans-Pritchard, *Social Anthropology and Others Essays*. New York: Free Press, 1962.

Fabian, Johannes. *Out of Our Minds: Reason and Madness in the Exploration of Central Africa*. Berkeley: University of California Press, 2000.

Falk-Moore, Sally. *Moralizing States and the Ethnography of the Present*, Washington, D.C.: American Anthropological Association, 1993.

———. "Explaining the Present: Theoretical Dilemmas in Processual Ethnography." AES Distinguished Lecture, *American Ethnologist* 14 (4) (1987): 727–36.

Fanon, Frantz. *The Wretched of the Earth*. New York: Grove, 1979 [1961].

Farge, Arlette. *Le Gout de l'Archive*. Paris: Seuil, 1989.

Fasseur, Cees. *De Indologen: Ambtenaren voor de Oost, 1825–1950*. Amsterdam: Bert Bakker, 1993.

Fasseur, Cornelis. *The Politics of Colonial Exploitation: Java, The Dutch and the Cultivation System*. Ithaca: SEAP, 1992.

Fassin, Didier. "Compassion and Repression: The Moral Economy of Immigration Policies in France." *Cultural Anthropology* 20 (3) (August 2005): 389–405.

Favret, Mary A. *Romantic Correspondence: Women, Politics and the Fiction of Letters*. Cambridge: Cambridge University Press, 2005.

Feldman, Ilana. *Governing Gaza: Bureaucracy, Authority, and the Work of Rule (1917–1967)*. Durham, N.C.: Duke University Press, 2008.

Feuer, Lewis. "What Is Alienation? The Career of a Concept." In *Sociology on Trial*, ed. Maurice Stein and Arthur Vidich. Englewood Cliffs, N.J.: Prentice Hall, 1963, 127–47.

Fisher, Charles. "The Eurasian Question in Indonesia." *International Affairs* 23 (4) (October 1947): 522–30.

Foote, Kenneth E. "To Remember and Forget: Archives, Memory, and Culture." *American Archivist* 53 (3) (1990): 378–93.

Foucault, Michel. "Nietzsche, Genealogy, History." In *The Foucault Reader*, ed. Paul Rabinow. New York: Pantheon, 1984.

———. "Omnes et Singulatim." In *The Tanner Lectures on Human Values, 1979*, ed. Sterling M. McMurrin. Cambridge: Cambridge University Press, 1981, 225–54.

———. "Truth and Power." In Foucault, *Power/Knowledge*. Ed. and trans. Colin Gordon. New York: Pantheon, 1980.

———. "Two Lectures." In Foucault, *Power/Knowledge*. Ed. and trans. Colin Gordon. New York: Pantheon, 1980, 78–108.

———. *Naissance de la biopolitique: Cours au Collège de France, 1978–1979*. Paris: Gallimard, 2004.

———. *The History of Sexuality: Volume I*. New York: Vintage, 1978.

———. *Discipline and Punish*. Trans. A. M. Sheridan. New York: Vintage, 1977.

———. *Archaeology of Knowledge*. Trans. A. M. Sheridan. New York: Harper and Row, 1972.

Frankel, Oz. *States of Inquiry: Social Investigation and Print Culture in Nineteenth-Century Britain and the United States*. Baltimore: The Johns Hopkins University Press, 2006.

Frans, Sinjo. *Lotsverbetering van Indo-Europeanen*. Batavia: Albrecht, 1905 [1904].

Frederick, William. "Hidden Change in Late-Colonial Urban Society in Indonesia." *Journal of Southeast Asian Studies* 14 (2) (1983): 354–71.

Fuller, Steven. *Social Epistemology*. Bloomington: Indiana University Press, 2002.

Gay, Peter. *Schnitzler's Century: The Making of Middle-Class Culture, 1815–1914*. New York: W. W. Norton, 2002.

Geary, Patrick. *Phantoms of Remembrance: Memory and Oblivion at the End of the First Millennium*. Princeton: Princeton University Press, 1994.

Geen Planter. *Open brief aan den Heer H.A. Insinger over zijn aanvallen in de Tweede Kamer tegen de Indische "Planters."* Amsterdam: M. M. Olivier, 1879.

Geertz, Clifford. *Local Knowledge: Further Essays in Interpretive Anthropology*. New York: Basic, 1983.

———. *Agricultural Involution: The Process of Ecological Change in Indonesia*. Berkeley: University of California Press, 1963.

Ghosh, Durba. "Decoding the Nameless: Gender, Subjectivity and Historical Methodologies in Reading the Archives of Colonial India." In *A New Imperial*

History, ed. Kathleen Wilson. New York: Cambridge University Press, 2004, 297–316.

Gibbard, Allan. *Wise Choices, Apt Feelings: A Theory of Normative Judgment*. Cambridge, Mass.: Harvard University Press, 1990.

Gibbons, Luke. *Edmund Burke and Ireland: Aesthetics, Politics, and the Colonial Sublime*. Cambridge: Cambridge University Press, 2003.

Ginzburg, Carlo. "Microhistory: Two or Three Things I Know about It." *Critical Inquiry* 20 (1) (Autumn 1993): 10–35.

———. "Clues: Roots of an Evidential Paradigm." In *Clues, Myths and the Historical Method*. Baltimore: The Johns Hopkins University Press, 1989, 96–125.

———. *The Cheese and the Worms: The Cosmos of a Sixteenth-Century Miller*. Trans. John and Anne Tedeschi. New York: Penguin, 1982.

Glissant, Eduardo. *Caribbean Discourse: Selected Essays*. Charlottesville: University of Virginia Press, 1989.

GoGwitt, Chris. "Pramoedya's Fiction and History: An Interview with Indonesian Novelist Pramoedya Ananta Toer." *Yale Journal of Criticism* 9 (1) (1996): 147–64.

Gonzalez-Echevarria, Roberto. *Myth and Archive: A Theory of Latin American Narrative*. New York: Cambridge University Press, 1990.

Gordimer, Nadine. *Something Out There*. London: Cape, 1984.

Gouda, Frances. *Dutch Culture Overseas: Colonial Practice in the Netherlands Indies, 1900–1942*. Amsterdam: Amsterdam University Press, 1995.

———. *Poverty and Political Culture: The Rhetoric of Social Welfare in the Netherlands and France, 1814–1854*. Lanham, Md.: Rowman and Littlefield, 1995.

Gould, Roger V. *Insurgent Identities: Class, Community and Protest in Paris from 1848 to the Commune*. Chicago: University of Chicago Press, 1995.

Grafton, Anthony. *The Footnote: A Curious History*. Cambridge: Cambridge University Press, 1997.

Gramsci, Antonio. *Selections from Prison Notebooks*. London: Lawrence and Wishart, 1978.

Grossberg, Michael. *Governing the Hearth: Law and the Family in Nineteenth-Century America*. Chapel Hill: University of North Carolina Press, 1985.

Guha, Ranajit. *Dominance without Hegemony: History and Power in Colonial India*. Cambridge: Cambridge University Press, 1997.

———. "The Prose of Counter-insurgency." In *Culture, Power, History: A Reader in Contemporary Social Theory*, ed. Nicholas Dirks, Geoff Eley, and Sherry Ortner. Princeton: Princeton University Press, 1994, 336–71.

———. *Elementary Aspects of Peasant Insurgency in Colonial India*. Delhi: Oxford University Press, 1983.

Gupta, Akhil. "Blurred Boundaries: The Discourse of Corruption, the Culture of Politics and the Imagined State." *American Ethnologist* 22 (2) (1995): 375–402.

Hacking, Ian. *Historical Ontology*. Cambridge, Mass.: Harvard University Press, 2002.

———. "The Looping Effect of Human Kinds." In *Causal Cognition: An Interdisciplinary Approach*, ed. D. Sperber, D. Premack, and A. Premack. Oxford: Oxford University Press, 1996, 351–83.

————. "How Should We Do the History of Statistics?" In *The Foucault Effect: Studies in Governmentality*, ed. G. Burchell, C. Gordon, and P. Miller. Chicago: University of Chicago Press, 1991, 181–95.

————. *The Taming of Chance*. New York: Cambridge University Press, 1990.

————. "Two Kinds of 'New Historicism' for Philosophers." *New Literary History* 21 (2) (Winter 1990): 343–64.

Haasse, Hella. *Sleuteloog*. Amsterdam: Querido, 2002.

————. *Heeren van de thee*. Amsterdam: Querido, 1992.

Hamilton, Carolyn et al., eds. *Refiguring the Archive*. Cape Town: New African, 2002.

Handboek voor cultuur- en handelsondernemingen in Nederlands-Indië, 1892–93, 1918; Nieuw adresboek van geheel Nederlands-Indië, 1903.

Haskell, Thomas. "Capitalism and the Origins of Humanitarian Sensibility, Part 1." *American Historical Review* 90 (2) (1985): 339–61.

————. "Capitalism and the Origins of the Humanitarian Sensibility, Part 2" *American Historical Review* 90 (3) (1985): 547–66.

Haviland, John. *Gossip, Reputation and Knowledge in Zinacantan*. Chicago: University of Chicago Press, 1977.

Hawthorn, Geoffrey. *Plausible Worlds: Possibility and Understanding in History and the Social Sciences*. Cambridge: Cambridge University Press, 1991.

Heidegger, Martin. *Being and Time*. New York: Harper and Row, 1962.

Herzfeld, Michael. *Anthropology: Theoretical Practice in Culture and Society*. Malden, Mass.: Blackwell, 2001.

Herzog, Don. *Poisoning the Minds of the Lower Orders*. Princeton: Princeton University Press, 1998.

"Het Indo-Vraagstuk." *Het Koloniaal Weekblad* 3, 20 January 1910.

Hirschman, Albert. *The Passions and the Interests: Political Arguments for Capitalism before Its Triumph*. Princeton: Princeton University Press, 1977.

History of the Human Sciences. Two special Issues on "The Archive" 11 (4) (1998) and 12 (2) (1999).

Hodes, Martha. "Fractions and Fictions in the United States Census of 1890." In *Haunted by Empire*, ed. Ann Laura Stoler. Durham, N.C.: Duke University Press, 2006, 240–70.

Holmes, Douglas R., and George E. Marcus. "Fast Capitalism: Paraethnography and the Rise of the Symbolic Analyst." In *Frontiers of Capital: Ethnographic Perspectives on the New Economy*, ed. Melissa Fisher and Greg Downey. Durham, N.C.: Duke University Press, 2006, 33–58.

Horkheimer, Max. *The Eclipse of Reason*. New York: Seabury, 1974 [1947].

Houben, Vincent. "History and Morality: East Sumatran Incidents as Described by Jan Breman." *Itinerario* 12 (2) (1998): 97–100.

————. *Kraton and Kumpeni: Surakarta and Yogyakarta, 1830–1870*. Leiden: KITLV, 1994.

Hubert, Juin. *Victor Hugo: Choses Vues. Souvenirs, Journaux, Cahiers, 1830–1885*. Paris: Gallimard, 2002.

Hume, David. *A Treatise on Human Nature*. New York: Oxford, 2000 [1739].

Hunt, Lynn. *The Family Romance of the French Revolution*. Berkeley: University of California Press, 1992.

Husken, Frans. "Declining Welfare in Java: Government and Private Inquiries, 1903–1914." In *The Late Colonial State in Indonesia*, ed. Robert Cribb. Leiden: KITLV, 1994.

Hyam, Ronald. *Empire and Sexuality: The British Experience*. Manchester: Manchester University Press, 1990.

Indische Nederlanders: Een onderzoek naar beeldvorming. Den Haag: Moesson, 1984.

James, Susan. *Passion and Action: the Emotions in Seventeenth-Century Philosophy*. Oxford: Clarendon, 1997.

Jameson, Frederic. *The Political Unconscious: Narrative as a Socially Symbolic Act*. Ithaca: Cornell University Press, 1981.

Jay, Martin. *Force Fields: Between Intellectual History and Cultural Critique*. New York: Routledge, 1993.

Jenkins, Janis. "The State Construction of Affect: Political Ethos and Mental Health among Salvadoran Refugees." *Culture, Medicine, Psychiatry* 15 (1991): 139–65.

Joseph, Betty. *Reading the East India Company, 1720–1840: Colonial Currencies of Gender*. Chicago: University of Chicago Press, 2004.

Kalff, S. "Europeesch Pauperisme in Indië." *Koloniaal Tijdschrift* (1922): 573–85.

Kant, Immanuel. *Political Writings, Second Edition*, ed. Hans Reiss and trans. H. B. Nisbet. Cambridge: Cambridge University Press, 1970.

Walter Kaufmann. "Introduction." In Friedrich Nietzsche, *The Gay Science*, ed. and trans. Walter Kaufmann. New York: Vintage, 1974, 3–31.

Keane, Webb. "Sincerity, 'Modernity,' and the Protestants." In *Cultural Anthropology* 17 (1) (2002): 65–92.

Ketelaar, Eric. "Tacit Narratives: The Meanings of Archives." *Archival Science* 1 (2001): 131–41.

———. *The Archival Image: Critical Essays*. Hilversum: Verloren, 1997.

Kielstra, J.C. "The 'Indo-European' Problem in the Dutch East Indies." *Asiatic Review* (1929): 588–95.

Knaap, Otto. "Pauperisme onder de Indo-Europeanen." *De Amsterdammer*, 26 January 1902.

———. "Pauperisme onder de Indo-Europeanen," *De Indische Gids*, 27 March 1902.

Knight, Roger. "The Sugarmen's Women and the Tensions of Empire." In *Narratives of Colonialism: Sugar, Java, and the Dutch*, ed. Roger Knight. Huntington, N.Y.: Nova, 2000, 47–70.

———. *Colonial Production in Provincial Java*. Amsterdam: VU University Press, 1993.

Knorr-Cetina, K. *Epistemic Cultures: How the Sciences Make Knowledge*. Cambridge, Mass.: Harvard University Press, 1999.

———. "Epistemics in Society: On the Nesting of Knowledge Structures into Social Structures." In *Rural Reconstruction in a Market Economy*, ed. W. Hijman, H. Hetsen, and J. Frouws. Mansholt Studies 5.Wageningen: Wageningen University and Research Center Publications, 1996, 55–73.

Koloniaal Verslag. 1902–1903 ('S-Gravenhage).

Koonz, Claudia. *The Nazi Conscience*. Cambridge, Mass.: Harvard University Press, 2003.

Kramer, Lloyd. "Literature, Criticism, and Historical Imagination." In *The New Cultural History*, ed. Lynn Hunt. Berkeley: University of California Press, 1989, 97–128.

LaCapra, Dominick. "History, Language, and Reading: Waiting for Crillon." *American Historical Review* 100 (3) (June 1995): 799–828.

Lawrence, D. H. "Introduction" to Mulatuli, *Max Havelaar* (Leyden: Sijthoff, 1967 [1927]), 11–13.

Le Comte, A. De Toudonnet. *Essais sur l'éducation des enfants pauvres: des colonies agricoles d'éducation*, Volume 1. Paris: P. Brunet, 1862.

Leidelmeijer, Margaret. *Van suikermolen tot grootbedrijf: technische vernieuwing in de Java-suikerindustrie in de negentiende eeuw*. Amsterdam: NEHA, 1997.

Leger, Raoul. *La colonie agricole et penitentiare de Mettray*. Paris: Harmattan, 1997.

Lenders, Jan. *De burger en de volksschool*. Nijmegen: SUN, 1988.

Les Archives. From series *Que Sais-Je?* Paris: Presses Universitaires de France, 1959.

Lévi-Strauss, Claude. *The Savage Mind*. Chicago: University of Chicago Press, 1966.

———. *Structural Anthropology*. New York, Basic, 1958.

———. *Tristes Tropiques*. New York: Atheneum, 1955.

Loades, David. *"The Royal Commissions" in Power in Tudor England*. New York: St. Martin's, 1997.

Locher-Scholten, Elsbeth. "Dutch Expansion and the Imperialism Debate." *Journal of Southeast Asian Studies* 25 (1) (March 1994): 91–111.

———. *Ethiek in Fragmenten*. Utrecht: HES, 1981.

Lutz, Catherine, and Lila Abu-Lughod, eds. *Language and the Politics of Emotion*. New York: Cambridge University Press, 1990.

———. *Unnatural Emotions: Everyday Sentiments on a Micronesian Atoll and Their Challenge to Western Theory*. Chicago: University of Chicago Press, 1988.

MacCormack, Sabine. "The Heart Has Its Reasons: Predicaments of Missionary Christianity in Early Colonial Peru." *Hispanic American Historical Review* 65 (3) (1985): 443–66.

MacIntyre, Alisdair. *After Virtue: A Study in Moral Theory*. Notre Dame: Notre Dame University Press, 1981.

———. "Epistemological Crises, Dramatic Narrative and the Philosophy of Science." *Monist* 60 (4) (1977): 453–72.

Maier, Henk. "Escape from the Green and Gloss of Java: Hella S. Haasse and Indies Literature." *Indonesia* 77 (April 2004): 79–107.

Maitland, F. W. *Selected Essays*. Cambridge: Cambridge University Press, 1936.

Mandler, Peter, ed. *The Uses of Charity: The Poor on Relief in the Nineteenth-Century Metropolis*. Philadelphia: University of Pennsylvania Press, 1990.

Manoff, Marlene. "Theories of the Archive from Across the Disciplines." *Libraries and the Academy* 4 (1) (2004): 9–25.

Mastenboek, William Edward van. *De historiche ontwikkeling van de staatsrechtelijke indeeling der bevolking van Nederlandsch-Indië*. Wageningen: H. Veeman and Sons, 1934.

Mbembe, Achille. "The Power of the Archive and Its Limits." In *Refiguring the Archive*, ed. Carolyn Hamilton et al. Capetown: David Philip, 2002, 19–26.

McGranahan, Carole. "Truth, Fear, and Lies: Exile Politics and Arrested Histories of the Tibetan Resistance." *Cultural Anthropology* 25 (4) (November 2005): 570–600.

———. "Arrested Histories: Between Empire and Exile in Twentieth-Century Tibet." Ph.D. Diss., University of Michigan, 2001.

Mehta, Uday. "Liberal Strategies of Exclusion." In *Tensions of Empire: Colonial Cultures in a Bourgeois World*, ed. Frederick Cooper and Ann Laura Stoler. Berkeley: University of California Press, 1997, 59–86.

———. *The Anxiety of Freedom*. Ithaca: Cornell, 1992.

Memmi, Albert. *Portrait du Colonisé précedé du Portrait du Colonisateur*. Paris: Payot, 1973 [1957].

———. *The Colonizer and the Colonized*. Boston: Beacon, 1967.

Merwick, Donna. *Death of a Notary: Conquest and Change in Colonial New York*. Ithaca: Cornell University Press, 1999.

Miller, William Ian. *The Anatomy of Disgust*. Cambridge, Mass.: Harvard University Press, 1997.

Mitchell, Timothy. "The Limits of the State: Beyond Statist Approaches and Their Critics." *American Political Science Review* 85 (1) (1991): 77–96.

Mohanty, S. P. "Us and Them: On the Philosophical Bases of Political Criticism." *Yale Journal of Criticism* 2 (2) (1989): 1–31.

Mokyr, Joel. *Industrialization in the Low-Countries, 1795–1850*. New Haven: Yale University Press, 1976.

Morillo-Alicea, Javier. " 'Aquel laberinto de oficinas': Ways of Knowing Empire in Late Nineteenth-Century Spain." In *After Spanish Rule*, ed. Mark Thurner and Andres Guerrero. Durham, N.C.: Duke University Press, 2003, 111–40.

Morin, Edgar. *La Rumeur d'Orléans*. Paris: Seuil, 1969.

Morley, John David. "Warped by Empire." *New York Times Book Review*, 9 June 1996.

Mumford, Lewis. *The Story of Utopias*. New York: Boni and Liveright, 1922.

Neijndorff, Frank. *Nederlands-Indië: Een famliegeheim*. Den Haag: Nederlandse Dcoument Reproductie, 2001.

Neuman, H. "Over kampongtoestanden en paupers." *Onze Stem* (1922): 489–91.

Nietzsche, Friedrich. "On the Uses and Disadvantages of History for Life." In Nietzsche, *Untimely Meditations*, trans. R. J. Hollingdale. 57–124. Cambridge: Cambridge University Press, 1996.

———. "On Truth and Lie in a Non-Moral Sense." In *Philosophy and Truth: Selctions from Nietzsche's Notebooks of the Early 1870s*, ed. and trans. Daniel Breazeale. Atlantic Highlands, N.J.: Humanities, 1979, 79–91.

Nieuwenhuys, Rob. *Mirror of the Indies: A History of Dutch Colonial Literature*. Amherst: University of Massachusetts Press, 1982.

Nussbaum, Martha. *Upheavals of Thought: The Intelligence of Emotions*. New York: Cambridge University Press, 2001.

Nuttall, Sarah, and Carli Coetzee, eds. *Negotiating the Past: The Making of Memory in South Africa*. Cape Town: Oxford University Press, 1998.

O'Connor, Stephen. *Orphan Trains: The Story of Charles Loring Brace and the Children He Saved and Failed.* New York: Houghton Mifflin, 2001.

Olasky, Marvin. *Compassionate Conservatism.* New York: Free Press, 2000.

Orwell, George. "Shooting an Elephant." In Orwell, *Collected Essays.* London: Secker and Warburg, 1961.

Osborne, Thomas. "Bureaucracy as a Vocation: Governmentality and Administration in Nineteenth-Century Britain." *Journal of Historical Sociology* 7 (2) (1994): 289–313.

Oyono, Ferdinand. *Houseboy.* Trans John Reed. London: Heinemann, 1975 [1966].

O'Toole, James M. "On the Idea of Uniqueness." *American Archivist.* 57 (4) (1994): 632–59.

Papailias, Penelope. *Genres of Recollection: Archival Poetics and Modern Greece.* New York: Palgrave, 2005.

Pauperisme-enquête. Uitkomsten van de Pauperisme-Enquête. Algemeen verslag. Batavia: Landsdrukkerij, 1902.

Pauperisme-enquête. Uitkomsten van de Pauperisme-Enquête. Gewestelijke verslag I, Bantam, Batavia, Preanger-regentschappen, Cheribon, Pekalongan, Semarang en Rembang. Batavia: Landsdrukkerij, 1902.

Pauperisme-enquête. Uitkomsten van de Pauperisme-Enquête. Gewestelijke verslag I, Soerabaja, Madoera, Pasoeroean, Besoeki, Banjoemas, Kedoe, Soerakarta, Djokjakarta, Madioen en Kediri. Batavia: Landsdrukkerij, 1902.

[Het] Pauperisme onder de Europeanen in Nederlandsch-Indië. Armwezen en het pauperisme. Notas. door enkele Leden der Commissie, benoemd bij Artikel 2 van het Regeeringsbesluit van 29 Juni. Batavia: Landsdrukkerij, 1901.

[Het] Pauperisme onder de Europeanen in Nederlandsch-Indië, Bijlage, Behoorende bij het eerste gedeelte. Nota over het verleenen van landbouwcrediet van staatswege ten behoeve van den Europeeschen kleinen land of tuinbouw. Batavia: Landsdrukkerij, 1902.

[Het] Pauperisme onder de Europeanen in Nederlandsch-Indië. Derde gedeelte. Kleine Landbouw. Batavia: Landsdrukkerij, 1901.

[Het] Pauperisme onder de Europeanen in Nederlandsch-Indië. Eerste gedeelte. Algemeen overzicht. Batavia: Landsdrukkerij, 1901.

[Het] Pauperisme onder de Europeanen in Nederlandsch-Indië. Tweede gedeelte. 'S Landsdienst-werving-militaire pupillen-ambachtslieden-technische betrekkingen. Batavia: Landsdrukkerij, 1901.

[Het] Pauperisme onder de Europeanen in Nederlandsch-Indië, Vijfde gedeelte. Officiersrang-Onderwijzers-Militie-Erkenning-Mindere Militairen-pensioenen-Concubinaat-Vagbonden. Batavia: Landsdrukkerij, 1901.

Pauperisme. Rapport der Pauperisme-Commissie. Batavia: Landsdrukkerij, 1903.

Peirce, C. S. *Collected Papers,* vol. 6. Cambridge, Mass. Belknap, 1963.

Pels, Peter. "The Anthropology of Colonialism: Culture, History, and the Emergence of Western Governmentality." *Annual Review of Anthropology* 26 (1997): 163–83.

———. "The Politics of Aboriginality: Orientalism and the Emergence of an Ethnology of India, 1833–1869." 1994.

Pelzer, Karl. *Planter and Peasant: Colonial Policy and the Agrarian Struggle in East Sumatra, 1863–1947*. Leiden: KITLV, 1978.

Pinch, Adela. *Strange Fits of Passion: Epistemologies of Emotion, Hume to Austen*. Stanford: Stanford University Press, 1996.

Polanyi, Michael. *The Tacit Dimension*. Garden City, N.Y.: 1967.

Pollman, Tessel, and Ingrid Harms. *In Nederland door omstandigheden*. Den Haag: Novib, 1987.

Poovey, Mary. *A History of the Modern Fact: Problems of Knowledge in the Sciences of Wealth and Society*. Chicago: University of Chicago Press, 1998.

Posner, Ernst. "Some Aspects of Archival Development since the French Revolution" [1940]. In *A Modern Archives Reader*, ed. Maygene Daniels and Timothy Walch. Washington, D.C.: National Archives and Record Service, 3–21.

Praeadvies omtrent punten van den agenda van het Koloniaal Onderwijs-Congres. Leiden: Van Vollenhoven Instituut, 1916.

Prakash, Gyan. *Another Reason: Science and the Imagination of Modern India*. Princeton: Princeton University Press, 1999.

Pratt, Mary Louise. *Imperial Eyes: Travel Writing and Transculturation*. New York: Routledge, 1992.

Price, Richard. *The Convict and the Colonel*. Boston: Beacon, 1998.

Prins, W. F. "De bevolkingsgroepen in het Nederlandsch-Indische recht." *Koloniale Studiën* 17 (1933): 652–88.

Pyenson, Lewis. Empire of Reason: Exact Sciences in Indonesia, 1840–1940. Leiden: Brill, 1997.

Rabinow. Paul. *Anthropos Today: Reflections on Modern Equipment*. Princeton: Princeton University Press, 2003.

Rai, Amit S. *The Rule of Sympathy: Sentiment, Race and Power, 1750–1850*. New York: Palgrave, 2002.

Rama, Angel. *The Lettered City*, ed. and trans. John Charles Chasteen. Durham, N.C.: Duke University Press, 1996.

Rappaport, Joanne. *Cumbe Reborn: An Andean Ethnography of History*. Chicago: University of Chicago Press, 1994.

Reddy, William. *The Navigation of Feeling: A Framework for the History of Emotions*. New York: Cambridge University Press, 2001.

———. *The Invisible Code: Honor and Sentiment in Postrevolutionary France, 1814–1848*. Berkeley: University of California Press, 1997.

Reid, Anthony. *The Blood of the People*. Kuala Lumpur: Oxford University Press, 1979.

———. *The Contest for North Sumatra: Acheh, the Netherlands and Britain, 1858–1898*. Kuala Lumpur: Oxford, 1969.

Remmelink, Willem. *The Chinese War and the Collapse of the Javanese State, 1725–1743*. Leiden: KITLV, 1994.

Rheinberger, Hans-Jorg. *Toward a History of Epistemic Things: Synthesizing Proteins in the Test Tube*. Stanford: Stanford University Press, 1997.

Richards, Thomas. *The Imperial Archive: Knowledge and the Fantasy of Empire*. London and New York: Verso, 1993.

Ricoeur, Paul. *Time and Narrative, Volume 1*. Chicago: University of Chicago Press, 1984.

Riles, Annalies, ed. *Documents: Artifacts of Modern Knowledge*. Ann Arbor: University of Michigan Press, 2006.

Robijns, M. J. F. *Radicalen in Nederland (1840–1851)*. Leiden: Leiden Universitaire Pers, 1967.

Ronnell, Avital. *Stupidity*. Urbana: University of Illinois Press, 2002.

Rorty, Richard. *Philosophy and the Mirror of Nature*. Princeton: Princeton University Press, 1979.

Rosaldo, Michelle. "Toward an Anthropology of Self and Feeling." In *Culture Theory: Essays on Mind, Self and Emotion*, ed. Richard Shweder and Robert LeVine. Cambridge: Cambridge University Press, 1984, 137–57.

———. "The Shame of Headhunters and the Autonomy of Self." *Ethos* 11 (3) (1983): 135–51.

Rose, Jacqueline. *States of Fantasy*. Oxford: Clarendon, 1996.

Rose, Nikolas. *The Psychological Complex*. London: Routledge and Kegan Paul, 1985.

Runchiman, W. G., ed. *Weber: Selections in Translation*. Cambridge: Cambridge University Press, 1994.

Rushdie, Salman. "Outside the Whale." In *Imaginary Homelands*. London: Penguin, 1992, 87–101.

Said, Edward. *Reflections on Exile and Other Essays*. Cambridge, Mass.: Harvard University Press, 2002.

———. "L'Autre Amerique." *Le Monde Diplomatique*, March 2001.

———. "The Clash of Ignorance." *Nation*, 22 October 2001, 11–13.

———. *The World, the Text, and Critic*. Cambridge, Mass.: Harvard University Press, 1983.

Samuels, Shirley, ed. *The Culture of Sentiment: Race, Gender and Sentimentality in 19th-Century America*. New York: Oxford University Press, 1992.

Sarbin, Theodoor. "On Self Deception." *Clever Hans Phenomenon: Communication with Horses, Whales, Apes, and People*, ed. Thomas Seboek and Robert Rosenthal. New York: New York Academy of Sciences, 1981.

Sartre, Jean-Paul. *Existentialism: From Dostoyevsky to Sartre*, ed. Walter Kaufmann. New York: Meridian, 1975.

———. *Being and Nothingness*. Trans. Hazel Barnes. New York: Citadel, 1966.

Schadee, W. *Geschiedenis van Sumatra's Oostkust*, 2 vols. Amsterdam: Oostkust van Sumatra Instituut, 1918–19.

Schrauwers, Albert. "The 'Benevolent' Colonies of Johannes van den Bosch: Continuities in the Administration of Poverty in the Netherlands and Indonesia." *Comparative Studies in Society and History* 43 (2) (April 2001): 298–328.

Schulte Nordholt, Henk. "Dekker, Havelaar en Bali." In *Indische Letteren* 2 (4): 149–60.

Schwartz, Joan M., and Terry Cook. "Archives, Records, and Power." *Archival Science* 2 (1–2) (2002): 1–20.

Scott, David. *Refashioning Futures: Criticism after Postcoloniality*. Princeton: Princeton University Press, 1999.

Scott, James. *Domination and the Arts of Resistance*. New Haven: Yale University Press, 1990.

Seed, Patricia. *Ceremonies of Possession in Europe's Conquest of the New World, 1492–1640*. New York: Cambridge University Press, 1995.

Sekula, Allan. "The Body and the Archive." *October* 39 (Winter 1986): 3–64.

Sembene, Ousmane. *God's Bits of Wood*. Oxford: Heinemann, 1996 [1960].

[De] *Semi-officiële en particuliere briefwisseling tussen J. C. Baud en J. J. Rochussen, 1845–1851*. Assen: Van Gorcum, 1983.

Sewell, William. *Work and Revolution in France: The Language of Labor from the Old Regime to 1848*. New York: Cambridge University Press, 1980.

Shapin, Steven. *The Social History of Truth: Civility and Science in Seventeenth-Century England*. Chicago: University of Chicago Press, 1994.

Shapiro, David. "On the Psychology of Self-Deception." *Social Research* 63 (3) (1996): 785–800.

Shaw, George Bernard. *Major Barbara*. London: Penguin, 1982 [1907].

Shiraishi, Takahashi. *An Age in Motion: Popular Radicalism in Java, 1912–1926*. Ithaca: Cornell University Press, 1990.

Sica, Alan. *Weber, Irrationality and Social Order*. Berkeley: University of California Press, 1988.

Siep, Stuurman. *Wacht op onze daden: Het liberalisme en de vernieuwing van de Nederlandse staat*. Amsterdam: Bert Bakker, 1992.

Silverman, Kenneth. *A Cultural History of the American Revolution*. New York: Columbia University Press, 1987.

Simmel, George. "Knowledge, Truth, and Falsehood in Human Relations." In *The Sociology of Georg Simmel*. Ed. Kurt H. Wolff. New York: Free Press, 1950.

Simon, Jonathan. "Parrhesiastic Accountability: Investigatory Commissions and Executive Power in an Age of Terror." *Yale Law Journal* 114 (6) (April 2005): 1419–57.

Smelser, Neil. "The Rational and the Ambivalent." *American Sociological Review* 63 (1998): 1–16.

Smith, Bonnie G. "Gender and the Practices of Scientific History: The Seminar and Archival Research in the Nineteenth Century." *American Historical Review* 100 (4–5) (1995): 1150–76.

Solomon, Robert. "The Cross-Cultural Comparison of Emotion." In *Emotions in Asian Thought: A Dialogue in Comparative Philosophy*, ed. Joel Marks and Roger T. Ames. Binghamton: SUNY Press, 1995, 253–68.

———. "On Emotions as Judgments." *American Philosophical Quarterly* 45 (1988): 183–91.

———. *The Passions*. Garden City, N.Y.: Doubleday, 1976.

Somers, Margaret. "The Privatization of Citizenship: How to Unthink a Knowledge Culture." In *Beyond the Cultural Turn*, ed. Victoria E. Bonnell and Lynn Hunt. Berkeley: University of California Press, 1999, 121–64.

———. "Where is Sociology after the Historical Turn? Knowledge, Cultures, Narrativity, and Historical Epistemologies." In *The Historic Turn in the Human Sciences*, ed. T. McDonald. Ann Arbor: University of Michigan Press, 1996.

Sommer, Doris. *Foundational Fictions: The National Romances of Latin America*. Berkeley: University of California Press, 1991.

Spivak, Gayatri Chakravorty. "Can the Subaltern Speak?" In *Marxism and the Interpretation of Culture*, ed. Cary Nelson and Lawrence Grossberg. Urbana: University of Illinois Press, 1988, 271–313.

Stapelkamp, Herman. "De rol van Van Hoëvell in de Bataviase Mei-beweging van 1848," *Jambatan* 4 (3): 11–20.

Starr, Paul. "Social Categories and Claims in the Liberal State." In *How Classification Works: Nelson Goodman among the Social Sciences*, ed. Mary Douglas and David Hull. Edinburgh: Edinburgh University Press, 1992.

Stearns, Peter N. "Historical Analysis in the Study of Emotion," *Motivation and Emotion* 10 (2) (1986): 185–93.

———, with Carol Stearns. "Emotionology: Clarifying the History of Emotions and Emotional Standards." *American Historical Review* 90 (1985): 813–36.

Steedman, Carolyn. *Dust: The Archive and Cultural* History. New Brunswick, N.J.: Rutgers University Press, 2002.

Sterns, Steve. "Paradigms of Conquest: History, Historiography, and Politics." *Journal of Latin American Studies* 24 (1992): 1–34.

Stoler, Ann Laura, ed. *Haunted by Empire: Geographies of Intimacy in North American History*. Durham, N.C.: Duke University Press, 2006.

———.*Carnal Knowledge and Imperial Power: Race and the Intimate in Colonial Rule*. Berkeley: University of California Press, 2003.

———."Tense and Tender Ties: The Politics of Comparison in North American History and (Post) Colonial Studies." *Journal of American History* 88 (3) (2001): 829–65.

———"Racial Histories and Their Regimes of Truth." *Political Power and Social Theory* 11 (1997): 183–206.

———. *Race and the Education of Desire: Foucault's History of Sexuality and the Colonial Order of Things*. Durham, N.C.: Duke University Press, 1995.

———. "Perceptions of Protest: Defining the Dangerous in Colonial Sumatra." *American Ethnologist* 12 (4) (1985): 642–58.

———, and Carole McGranahan. "Refiguring Imperial Terrains." In *Imperial Formations*, ed. Ann Laura Stoler, Carole McGranahan, and Peter Perdue. Santa Fe: School of American Research, 2007.

Strassler, Karen. *Refracted Visions: Popular Photography in Postcolonial Java*. Durham, N.C.: Duke University Press, forthcoming.

Strathern, Marilyn. "The Ethnographic Effect." In *Property, Substance and Effect*. ed. Marilyn Strathern. London: Athlone, 1999.

Szekely-Lulof, Medelon. *De Andere Wereld*. Amsterdam: Elsevier, 1934.

Taylor, Charles. *Modern Social Imaginaries*. Durham, N.C.: Duke University Press, 2004.

Taylor, Jean. *The Social World of Batavia: European and Eurasian in Dutch Asia*. Madison: University of Wisconsin, 1983.

Termorshuizen, Gerard. *Journalisten en heethoofden: een geschiedenis van de Indische-Nederlandse dagbladpers, 1744–1905*. Leiden: KITLV, 2001.

———. "Les Eurasiens dans la littérature des Indes néerlandaises: Portrait d'une préjugé racial." In *Rever l'Asie: Exotisme et littérature coloniale aux Indes, en Indochine et en Insulinde*, ed. Denys Lombard. Paris: L'Ecole des Hautes Etudes en Sciences Sociales, 1993, 321–33.

Thorne, Susan. "Missionary Imperialism and the Language of Class in Early Industrial Britain." In *Tensions of Empire: Colonial Cultures in a Bourgeois World*, ed. Frederick Cooper and Ann Laura Stoler. Berkeley: University of California Press, 1997, 238–62.

Toer, Pramoedya Ananta. *House of Glass*. New York: William Morrow, 1992.

———. *Rumah Kaca*. Kuala Lumpur: Wira Karya, 1988.

Todorov, Tvetzan. "Dialogism and Schizoprenia." In *An Other Tongue*, ed. Alfred Artaega. Durham, N.C.: Duke University Press, 1994, 203–14.

Trilling, Lionel. *Sincerity and Authenticity*. Cambridge, Mass.: Harvard University Press, 1972.

Trouillot, Michel-Rolph. *Silencing the Past: Power and the Production of History*. Boston: Beacon, 1995.

Van den Doel, H. W. *De stille macht: Het Europese binnenlands bestuur op Java en Madoera, 1808–1942*. Amsterdam: Bert Bakker, 1994.

Van de Wall, J. H. F. "Rassenhaat." *Jong Indië* 1 (1908): 120–22.

Van der Put, Paul. *Het boek der Indo's: Kroniek*. Rotterdam: Indonet, 1997.

Van der Velde, Paul. *Een Indische Liefde: P. J. Veth, 1814–1895*. Leiden: Balans, 2000.

Van der Veur, Paul W. *The Eurasians of Indonesia: A Political-Historical Bibliography*. Ithaca: Modern Indonesia Project, 1971.

———. "The Eurasians of Indonesia: A Problem and Challenge in Colonial History." *Journal of Southeast Asian Studies*. 9, No. 2 (1968): 191–207.

———. *Introduction to a Socio-Political Study of the Eurasians of Indonesia*. Ann Arbor: UMI, 1955.

Van Hoëvell, W. R. "De ambachtschool te Soerabaja." *Tijdschrijft voor Nederlandsch-Indië* 1858 (1): 129–49.

———. *Beschuldiging en veroordeeling in Indië*. Zalt-Bommel: Joh. Noman en Zoon, 1850.

Van Kol, H. *Nederlandsch-Indië in de Staten-Generaal van 1897 tot 1909*. 'S-Gravenhage: Martinus Nijhoff, 1911.

Van Lente, Dirk. "The Crafts in Industrial Society: Ideals and Policy in the Netherlands, 1890–1930." *Economic and Social History in the Netherlands* 2: 99–119.

Van Marle, A. "De groep der Europeanen in Nederlands-Indië, iets over ontstaan en groei." *Indonesie* 5 (1951–52): 314–41.

Van 't Veer, P. *Geen Blad voor de Mond: Vijf Radicalen uit de negentiende eeuw*. Amsterdam: Arbeiderspers, 1958.

Ventresca, Marc. *When States Count: Institutional and Political Dynamics in Modern Census Establishment, 1800–1993*. Ph.D. Diss., Stanford University, 1996.

Verdes-Leroux, Jeanne. *Les Français d'Algérie*. Paris: Fayard, 2001.

Veth, P. J. *Bijdragen tot de kennis van den politieken toestand van Nederlandsch Indië*. Amsterdam: P. N. van Kampen, 1848.

Veyne, Paul. *Writing History: Essay on Epistemology*. Middletown, Conn.: Wesleyan University Press, 1984.

———. *Did the Greeks Believe in Their Myths? An Essay on the Constitutive Imagination*. Chicago: University of Chicago Press, 1983.

Vickers, Adrian. *Bali: A Paradise Created*. Sydney: Penguin, 1989.

Walraven, W. *Eendagsvliegen: Journalistieke getuigenissen uit kranten en tijdschriften*. Amsterdam: G. A. van Oorschot, 1971.

Weber, Max. *Economy and Society: An Outline of Interpretive Sociology*, ed. Guenther Roth and Claus Wittich. New York: Bedminister, 1968.

———. "Bureaucracy," in *Essays in Sociology*, ed. and trans. H. H. Gerth and C. Wright Mills. New York: Oxford University Press, 1946.

White, Benjamin. "Clifford Geertz: Paradoxcial Genius of Interpretive Anthropology," *Development and Change* (forthcoming).

———. "Agricultural Involution and Its Critics: Twenty Years Later." *Journal of Concerned Asian Scholars* 18 (1983): 18–31.

White, Hayden. *The Content of the Form*. Baltimore: The Johns Hopkins University Press, 1987.

White, Luise. *Speaking with Vampires: Rumor and History in Colonial Africa*. Berkeley: University of California Press, 2000.

Wilder, Gary. "The Politics of Failure: Historicizing Popular Front Colonial Policy in French West Africa." In *French Empire and the Popular Front*, ed. Tony Chafer and Amanda Sarkur. New York: Palgrave, 1999, 33–55.

Willems, Wim, ed. *Sporen van een Indisch verleden, 1600–1942*. Leiden: Centrum voor Onderzoek van Maatschappelijke Tegenstellingen, 1992.

———, ed. *Bronnen van kennis over Indische Nederlanders*. Leiden: Centrum voor Onderzoek van Maatschappelijke Tegenstellingen, 1991.

———. *Indische Nederlanders in de ogen van de wetenschap*. Leiden: Centrum voor Onderzoek van Maatschappelijke Tegenstellingen, 1990.

Williams, Raymond. *Marxism and Literature*. Oxford: Oxford University Press, 1977.

———. *George Orwell*. New York: Columbia University Press, 1971.

Winsemius, Johan. *Nieuw-Guinee als kolonisatie-gebied voor Europeanen en van Indo-Europeanen*. Ph.D. Diss., University of Amsterdam, 1936.

Woolard, Kathryn. "Simultaneity and Bivalency as Strategies in Bilingualism." *Journal of Linguistic Anthropology* 8 (1) (1999): 3–29.

Wright, Gwendolyn. *The Politics of Design in French Colonial Urbanism*. Chicago: University of Chicago Press, 1991.

Yazawa, Melvin. *From Colonies to Commonwealth: Familial Ideology and the Beginnings of the American Republic*. Baltimore: The Johns Hopkins University Press, 1985.

INDEX

Aceh, boundaries of, 197–98; war in, 183–84, 199; 216, 223

Acehnese, resistance to Dutch authority, 191, 197–98, 203, 211; role in Luhmann family murder, 212–14, 227, 232

Abrams, Philip, 26

affect, 33, 237, 277; attributions of, 43, 62, 65, 97, 119; dangers ascribed to, 13; economy of 94, 145, 171; in governance, 33, 41, 58, 60, 66, 69–71, 93, 98, 101, 106, 115, 255; labor and, 119, 126; in the archives, 106; in ethnography, 255; in relation to reason, 2, 63, 95; management of 59, 63–64, 98, 253; morality and, 68; surplus of 60, 101, 231; treatment in colonial studies 60–61. *See also* sentiment

affective knowledge, 18, 72, 98–99, 101, 278; portability of, 60

affective states, 3, 30, 40, 41, 53, 59, 95, 109, 139, 171, 255; history of, 233

Agrarian Law of 1870, 153

Algemeen Rijksarchief (Nationaal Archief), 9–10, 14

Algeria, colonialism in, 131–32, 281

Anderson, Benedict, 59, 70, 96, 246

Arabs, in Netherlands Indies, 81, 92; relations with European women, 159

archival practices, 3; annotation, 11–12, 34, 144, 205; appendices, 11–12, 241; cribbing, 20, 186, 231; details, 204; marginalia, 1, 41, 84, 101, 252; cross-referencing, 9, 156, 241. See *also* colonial archives

Ardesch, P. C., 75–77, 80–81, 83, 249

Arendt, Hannah, 66, 258–60

"arrested histories," 33. *See also* Carole McGranahan

anthropology, archival turn in, 44–45, 47; writing in, 1–3. *See also* ethnography; historiography

Ashforth, Andrew, 29

aspirations, shaping of, 64, 94, 21, 101, 115, 123, 126, 128, 133, 136, 246

attachments, affective, 2, 36, 40, 58, 62–63, 65, 143, 237; familial, 41, 58, 60, 63, 94, 99, 253, 269; national, 92–94, 99, 126. *See also* affect; sentiment; domestic arrangements

Australia, colonial governance in, 31, 112

Bacon, Francis, 71

Bakhtin, Mikhail, 258

Balinese, 105, 250, 264; ascribed characteristics of, 256, 267, 274. *See also* social categories; race

Barth, Frederick, 28

Barthes, Roland, 22, 181. *See also* "storeyed" narratives

Bataks, 105, 193–94, 197, 207, 218; involvement in Luhmann family Murder, 202, 215, 220–21, 222–25, 232. *See also* social categories

Baud, J. C. (Minister of Colonies), 10, 13, 56, 82, 85, 174, 222

Bayly, Christopher, 98

begging, 151–54; beggar letters (*bedelbriefen*), 154

Bentham, Jeremy, 142

Berman, Marshall, 265

Bhabha, Homi, 62, 116

Binnenlandsch Bestuur (Binnenlandsbestuur), 15, 180

Bosch, Dr. W., 80

Bourdieu, Pierre, 64, 247; habitus, 38–39

Breman, Jan, 190–91

Britain: antislavery campaigns in, 199; colonial policies of, 48, 65–66, 97–99, 111, 194, 255, 280; Poor Law Commission of 1834, 142; trade in Netherlands Indies, 198

bureaucracy, 26, 39–40, 57, 177, 193, 241. *See also* Max Weber

Bureau of Genealogy (Netherlands), xii, 14, 239

Butler, Judith, 251

Cannadine, David, 255

Cantervisscher, J. C., 75–76, 82–83, 249